A CULTURAL HISTORY OF RACE

VOLUME 1

A Cultural History of Race
General Editor: Marius Turda

Volume 1
A Cultural History of Race in Antiquity
Edited by Denise Eileen McCoskey

Volume 2
A Cultural History of Race in the Middle Ages
Edited by Thomas Hahn

Volume 3
A Cultural History of Race in the Renaissance and Early Modern Age
Edited by Kimberly Anne Coles and Dorothy Kim

Volume 4
A Cultural History of Race in the Reformation and Enlightenment
Edited by Nicholas Hudson

Volume 5
A Cultural History of Race in the Age of Empire and the Nation State
Edited by Marina B. Mogilner

Volume 6
A Cultural History of Race in the Modern and Genomic Age
Edited by Tanya Maria Golash-Boza

A CULTURAL HISTORY OF RACE

IN ANTIQUITY
VOLUME 1

Edited by Denise Eileen McCoskey

BLOOMSBURY ACADEMIC
LONDON • NEW YORK • OXFORD • NEW DELHI • SYDNEY

BLOOMSBURY ACADEMIC
Bloomsbury Publishing Plc
50 Bedford Square, London, WC1B 3DP, UK
1385 Broadway, New York, NY 10018, USA
29 Earlsfort Terrace, Dublin 2, Ireland

BLOOMSBURY, BLOOMSBURY ACADEMIC and the Diana logo
are trademarks of Bloomsbury Publishing Plc

First published in Great Britain 2022
Paperback edition published 2025

Copyright © Bloomsbury Publishing, 2022

Denise Eileen McCoskey has asserted her right under the Copyright,
Designs and Patents Act, 1988, to be identified as Editor of this work.

Series design by Raven Design Cover image: 1 May 1960 - Rome, Italy - Runner Abebe Bikila
sightseeing in Rome during the 1960 Olympic Games. (© KEYSTONE Pictures USA/ZUMAPRESS.com)

All rights reserved. No part of this publication may be reproduced or transmitted in any
form or by any means, electronic or mechanical, including photocopying, recording, or any information
storage or retrieval system, without prior permission in writing from the publishers.

Bloomsbury Publishing Plc does not have any control over, or responsibility for, any third-party
websites referred to or in this book. All internet addresses given in this book were correct at the
time of going to press. The editor and publisher regret any inconvenience caused if addresses have
changed or sites have ceased to exist, but can accept no responsibility for any such changes.

Every effort has been made to trace copyright holders and to obtain their permissions for the use
of copyright material. The publisher apologizes for any errors or omissions and would be grateful if
notified of any corrections that should be incorporated in future reprints or editions of this book.

A catalogue record for this book is available from the British Library.

Library of Congress Cataloging-in-Publication Data
Names: McCoskey, Denise Eileen, 1968- editor.
Title: A cultural history of race in antiquity / edited by Denise Eileen McCoskey.
Description: London, UK ; New York, NY : Bloomsbury Academic, 2021. | Series: Cultural histories
A cultural history of race ; volume 1 | Includes bibliographical references and index. |
Identifiers: LCCN 2021017367 | ISBN 9781350067424 (hardback)
Subjects: LCSH: Race–History–to 1500. | History, Ancient.
Classification: LCC HT1507 .C85 2021 | DDC 305.8009/01–dc23
LC record available at https://lccn.loc.gov/2021017367.

ISBN:	HB:	978-1-3500-6742-4
	HB Set:	978-1-3500-6757-8
	PB:	978-1-3505-1953-4
	PB Set:	978-1-3505-1969-5

Series: The Cultural Histories Series

Typeset by Integra Software Services Pvt. Ltd.
Printed and bound in Great Britain

To find out more about our authors and books visit www.bloomsbury.com
and sign up for our newsletters.

CONTENTS

LIST OF ILLUSTRATIONS — vi
PRAISE FOR *A CULTURAL HISTORY OF RACE* — ix
GENERAL EDITOR'S PREFACE
Marius Turda — xi

Introduction
Denise Eileen McCoskey — 1

1 Definitions and Representations of Race
  Sarah Derbew — 21

2 Race, Environment, Culture
  Joseph Skinner — 33

3 Race and Religion
  Denise Kimber Buell — 49

4 Race and Science
  David Kaufman — 67

5 Race and Politics
  Grant Parker — 83

6 Race and Ethnicity
  Naoíse Mac Sweeney — 103

7 Race and Gender
  Shelley P. Haley — 119

8 Race and Sexuality
  Jackie Murray — 137

9 Anti-Race
  Dan-el Padilla Peralta — 157

NOTES — 172
BIBLIOGRAPHY — 189
NOTES ON CONTRIBUTORS — 218
INDEX — 220

ILLUSTRATIONS

0.1	The empire of Alexander the Great	6
0.2	Racial chart from Nott and Gliddon's *Types of Mankind* (1854)	12
0.3	Cartoon depicting Uncle Sam putting quotas in place as dictated by the 1921 Act (19 May 1921)	14
0.4	Map from Madison Grant's *The Passing of the Great Race* (1916) showing the alleged distribution of European racial groups	15
0.5	Mildred and Richard Loving at a press conference following the Supreme Court's ruling in *Loving v. Virginia* (13 June 1967)	17
1.1	Cover of Benjamin Isaac's *The Invention of Racism in Classical Antiquity* (2004)	24
1.2	Black-figure water jar (hydria) of Hercules, sixth century BCE	25
1.3	Herodotus' map of the world	28
2.1	Terracotta rhyton depicting a crocodile devouring a Black youth, *c.* 350–300 BCE	40
2.2	Two views of a terracotta vase depicting the head of an African youth, first half of fourth century BCE	45
3.1	Amulet featuring Khepri the Scarab God, Egyptian, late Ptolemaic period	50
3.2	Mosaic featuring Roman Emperors Constantine and Justinian with the Virgin and Child, Hagia Sophia, Istanbul, Turkey, tenth century CE	55
3.3	Achaemenid earring featuring the deity Ahura Mazda, sixth–fourth century BCE	56
3.4	Grand Mosque, Diyarbakir, Turkey, converted from a Christian church in the mid-seventh century CE	59
3.5	Arch of Titus. Forum in Rome, late first century CE	64
3.6	Drawing based on a sixth-century CE equestrian statue of Justinian, sixteenth century CE	65
4.1	Pitcher (oinochoe) with a Greek warrior attacking a Persian archer, *c.* 450 BCE	69
4.2	The death of Orpheus at the hand of a Thracian woman, 450–440 BCE	71

ILLUSTRATIONS vii

4.3	The sage Aristotle and a pupil. *Kitab Na't al-hayawan* (*Book of the Characteristics of Animals*), thirteenth century	75
4.4	Illustration of a man with lion-like features in Giovanni Battista Della Porta's *On Human Physiognomy* (sixteenth century)	77
4.5	Hippocrates and Galen, fresco, early thirteenth century, in the Crypt of St Mary Cathedral, Anagni, Lazio	79
4.6	Polykleitos' Standard as represented in his Doryphoros (spear-bearer) statue, preserved in Roman copy	81
5.1	The Roman senate, interior (Curia Iulia), first century CE	84
5.2	Attic plate with a red-figure image of an archer in Scythian dress, fifth century BCE	87
5.3	Jacobus Elisa Johannes Capitein (1717–1747), illustration in his *Political-Theological Dissertation on the Compatibility of Slavery and Christian Freedom*	88
5.4	A young Tajik soldier from the Northern Alliance shows a vestige of the ancient Greek city of Ai Khanum	89
5.5	Freedom Charter memorial in Kliptown in Soweto, Johannesburg, South Africa, 2017	95
5.6	Statue of Lady Sennuwy. Egyptian, Middle Kingdom, Dynasty 12, reign of Senwosret I, 1971–1926 BCE. Found at Kerma in Nubia, Sudan	99
6.1	Shrine erected by the pharoah Tarharqa to Amun-Re at Kawa	106
6.2	View across Naqsh-e Rostam, showing the cruxiform tombs of Darius I (*right*) and Artaxerxes I (*left*). Also visible at the lower level are reliefs of later Sasanian kings (*right to left*): Bahram II; Shapur I; Shapur II; and Hormizd II	109
6.3	Sculptural relief above the tomb of Darius I at Naqsh-e Rostam	110
6.4	The Erechtheion (Temple of Erechtheus) on the Acropolis of Athens	112
6.5	The 'Dying Gaul', Roman marble statue based on a Hellenistic bronze original, commissioned at Pergamon	115
7.1	Amphora featuring the Ethiopian hero Memnon and his attendants, *c*. 530 BCE	124
7.2	Red-figure mixing vessel (calyx-krater) showing Medea in her chariot, *c*. 400 BCE	126
7.3	Mummy portrait of a bearded man, *c*. 150–70 CE	128
7.4	Fayum mummy portrait of a young woman	135
8.1	David Gyasi attends a preview screening of *Troy: Fall of a City* on 29 January 2018	138

8.2	Black-figure amphora by Exekias depicting Achilles and Penthesilea	139
8.3	Mummy portrait from Greco-Roman Egypt showing the ancient somatic norm for men	140
8.4	Detail of the blinding of the Cyclops, Roman copy of a Hellenistic statuary group	146
8.5	Brad Pitt at a photo call for *Troy* (2004) in Cannes	155
9.1	Frank Martin Snowden Jr, Professor of Classics at Howard University, with presidential press secretary James Hagerty	162
9.2	Frantz Omar Fanon (1925–61): psychiatrist, political philosopher, revolutionary	168
9.3	Cover of Claudia Rankine's *Citizen: An American Lyric*	171

PRAISE FOR
A CULTURAL HISTORY OF RACE

'The detailed, deep and comparative historicization of racial thinking is a very much needed and timely project: much writing about race is temporally and geographically focused and, in its wide-ranging ambitions, this Cultural History of Race represents a very welcome alternative. The use of a common chapter structure throughout the six volumes is a very valuable feature, which makes it easy for readers to follow particular themes, while the multidisciplinary approach is also highly attractive when dealing with a subject as mercurial as race.'
Peter Wade, Professor of Social Anthropology, University of Manchester, UK

'Learning from the past is a necessary act of cultural advancement and *A Cultural History of Race*, a project of sustained historical inquiry from Antiquity to the present, makes a much-needed and exquisitely timely contribution. It argues for rigor and depth of exploration through nine recurring categories of inquiry across the six volumes and challenges the notion of a restrictive timeline of the 'history of race' as the product of modernity. It transcends temporal and geographic limits while expanding our understanding of the variant and shifting terminologies of race. As a result, readers will appreciate the breadth of material and value highly the intellectual diversity of the project's multidisciplinary approach.'
Ian Smith, Richard and Joan Sell Professor of the Humanities, Lafayette College, USA

'Marius Turda, the eminent cultural historian of science and racialization is the general editor for this foundational six-volume study attuned to this 'moment of global reckoning' sparked by #BlackLivesMatter and Indigenous justice movements. This is an outstanding critical, nuanced, useful, anti-racist cartography from European 'Antiquity' through the 'Renaissance,' into colonial 'Empire' formations and state eugenics practices through the racially-coded high tech, big data 'Genomic Age.' Epic and often brilliant, we become painfully aware of how narrow nationalist and nation-bounded scholarship are so painfully limited in contrast to this masterful, satellite counter mapping. Yes, racism and contesting this degeneration of humans and the natural world is a deeply embedded history and of the moment, it's relational and intersectional, and it has infected all trans-regional cultural discourses. A must for all academic and public libraries - five stars!'
John Kuo Wei Tchen, Clement A. Price Professor of Public History & Humanities, Rutgers-Newark University, USA

'In a contemporary moment afflicted by concocted culture wars that are also proxy race wars, this important collection of essays does what is urgently needed - by explicating the concept of race in a historical frame. Between them, these volumes show how concepts of 'race' and 'an impressive racial edifice' emerged in the West over several centuries, and became such a powerful political, scientific and cultural force. An important contribution to the historical literacy that is needed if we are to challenge race and racism effectively.'
Priyamvada Gopal, Professor of Postcolonial Studies, University of Cambridge, UK

'*A Cultural History of Race* is an admirably ambitious survey of the cultural landscape of race and racism. Analysing the concept of race all the way from antiquity, and drawing in research from every relevant discipline, it paints a story of how difficult it has been for humans to grapple with the idea of human difference. Clarifying and comprehensive, it is sure to become necessary reading for every scholar who wants to understand what race means. It couldn't have more contemporary relevance either. Truly outstanding.'

Angela Saini, Author of Superior: The Return of Race Science *(2021)*

'*A Cultural History of Race* stands on a league of its own within the broad domain of race studies. This splendid, thoughtful array of essays by scholars in a truly diverse number of fields offers an unprecedented, kaleidoscopic panorama of the myriad permutations of race and racism in the West – from Greek and Roman antiquity all the way to the ages of the Genome and Black Lives Matter. The contributors to this collection exemplify just how fresh and engaging historical insight is when we as scholars remain fully engaged with the pressing issues of our own time. As a whole, this collection of essays forcefully delivers important lessons for a broad readership: first, race, racism and human rights advocacy itself are transhistorical phenomena reaching back to the foundational moments of Western civilization. Second, any truly critical history of race and racism requires an honest scrutiny of the manner in which our own fields of knowledge have been shaped by troubled legacies. And, most urgently, the identification of multiple forms of stigmatization, discrimination and persecution in our times – not to mention the quest for social justice – can hugely benefit from a rich reckoning of the multiplicity of *situated* forces that have shaped overt and systemic racism to this day. *A Cultural History of Race* will remain obligatory reference for generations of readers.'

Nicolás Wey Gómez, author of The Tropics of Empire: Why Columbus Sailed South to the Indies *(2008)*

'In this moment of global racial reckoning, there is a tectonic shift underway. As a more structural, systemic, and historical analysis of race and racialization is emerging, *A Cultural History of Race*, will be an important accelerant to this process. The pivot from a focus on identity towards one that more critically considers processes and patterns of identification is a process, one that takes time, sustained engagement and a nuanced understanding of the past and its relationship to the present. *A Cultural History of Race* is just such a text. Its recent completion will be a gift to scholars, activists, the human rights community, and others invested in a more just future, one that doesn't posit certain people or for that matter species as disposable; there is no such thing!

The time has come for us to embrace this reality and work towards a world in which this eliminationist ideology no longer governs our political, social, economic or philosophical spaces. A Cultural History of Race will prove to be a trusted companion and a useful tool for the long journey ahead and will certainly stake a claim to being a cornerstone text for the pivot that is underway.'

Milton Reynolds, Educator, Author, Diversity Equity Inclusion Practitioner, Critical Race Theorist

GENERAL EDITOR'S PREFACE

MARIUS TURDA

A Cultural History of Race documents the long history of the concept of race from antiquity to the present day. In the six volumes collected here, scholars from a range of academic disciplines engage not only with the historical, cultural and philosophical realities of race but also with its aesthetics, literary functions and representations. To capture the elasticity of race as a concept, one needs to travel widely, across historical periods and geographical locations, to examine texts and images, cutting through the multilayered fabric of culture, science and politics. Viewed on a broad timescale, the densely textured content of the history of race is approached intersectionally, with an understanding of race's complex relationship with other concepts such as gender, religion, class and nation.

Given these vast territories of knowledge, then, to harmonize so many different aspects of the history of race is not an easy task. Besides mediating between the localized traditions of race and their transnational framework, *A Cultural History of Race* highlights entanglements, disruptions and mutations. At the same time, various national traditions are examined from a global perspective, and, thus, their purported uniqueness is challenged. It is important to understand the long history of race, not only through references to past events but also through the prism of current systemic racism.

Engaging with the legacy of slavery, empire, colonialism and genocide, and not just with the overall historical trajectory of race, is another important aspect of this collective work. The concept of race cannot be decoupled from the very idioms that had been used throughout history to describe and classify humans, nor can it be expunged from projects of domination, subjugation and oppression. These projects were politically motivated, state sanctioned and often blessed by scholars and scientists. As adherence to a racial worldview became more explicit and formalized in culture, science and politics, however, its predatory ability widened. Scholars, politicians, artists, philosophers and poets were stirred by it. They created an impressive racial edifice that has, alas, endured until the twenty-first century.

A Cultural History of Race offers critical perspectives on the traditional paradigms of thinking about the concept. It reflects as much shifting methodologies in the scholarship as the need to engage publicly with the normative saliency of race in the production of various forms of knowledge. Yet this is not just another cultural history of race but a decidedly analytical attempt to dislodge race from the intellectual pre-eminence it had occupied for centuries, and to disclose racial conceptions, beliefs, values and practices that had been used throughout history to make distinctions among groups of peoples on the basis of the colour of their skin and/or their intellectual abilities. The concept of race manifested itself in different ways at different times, but it always had supporters as well as detractors. Acceptance of race was not always universal. It was often met with suspicion and occasionally rejected. Anti-race thinking occurred in numerous spheres, including but not limited to religion and science.

A considerable amount of literature exists on the history of race, particularly during the nineteenth and twentieth centuries. But race had infiltrated major traditions of cultural, religious and philosophical reflection about human diversity already in antiquity. Elements of this discussion survived in the medieval and early modern periods, and new ones were added, particularly as colonial and imperial projects began to emerge in Europe. During the Renaissance and Reformation, and then more forcefully during the Enlightenment, race became a powerful concept, used not just to describe physical features of peoples but also to explain cultural achievements and behavioural attitudes. The subjugation and exploitation of non-European peoples, alongside slavery and extermination of Indigenous populations, only enhanced the power of race in defining white Europeans and their global expansion and dominance.

During the nineteenth century and, especially, the twentieth, horrendous atrocities, most notably the Holocaust, discredited the concept of race and eroded its tentacular grip on social and political discourse and realities. Yet, race survived into the early twenty-first century, continuing to impact the lives of millions with reference to their biological attributes, cultural traditions and historical experiences. Although developments in human genetics, particularly in the second part of the twentieth century, completely dismantled any pretention of scientific respectability appropriated by racists, current debates in genomics reveal how race continues to impact our scientifically informed worldview. Incredibly, the completion of the Human Genome Project, for example, even spurred attempts to define a concept of race that is scientifically credible.

A Cultural History of Race is timely. It provides not only academic guidance but, equally important, a nuanced and innovative critique of race and racism as well. These six volumes are informed by research and academic reflection and, equally, by lived experience. This is a critical moment to review how myriad assumptions and attitudes rooted in the history of race and its toxic ideology continue to affect our world in ways both obvious and hidden. To understand the past and present of race in all its different representations is essential in order to name and remove its symbols of discrimination, injustice, abuse and violence against Black, Indigenous and other peoples of colour. Any work on the history of race must unambiguously expose the extraordinary damage caused by racist thinking and practice.

While not exhaustive, *A Cultural History of Race* nevertheless provides numerous historical examples and options of interpretation for anyone who wants to engage, in an accessible way, with problems of race and racism characterizing the world today. Both together and separately, these volumes reassess historical traditions, scientific paradigms and political agendas put forward in the name of race. Equally important, the volumes' insights and clarity are accompanied by incisiveness and commitment to anti-racist scholarship. The overall aim is to strike a balance between scholarly detachment, empathy and direct participation in the current conversations about decolonization, whiteness, anti-racism and Black Lives Matter. In the twenty-first century, the assumption is that race as a meaningful category of analysis has been de-ritualized and de-politicized. The truth is that race continues to lend itself to theories of social, cultural and political inequality. Combined with an aggressive rhetoric of national protectionism and ethnicity, race continues to frame regional, national and international issues around immigration, social justice and gender equality.

GENERAL EDITOR'S PREFACE

Wide in scope and detailed in analysis, *A Cultural History of Race* is therefore strongly embedded in current conversations about race and racism. We are in a moment of global reckoning. Presidents are banned from social media platforms, statues are being torn down, names of university buildings are being changed, museums are being decolonized and stolen artefacts are returned to their countries of origin. Continued scholarly engagement with anti-racist activism is critical, not just for understanding the decisions being made today but to help preserve the lessons learnt for future generations.

Introduction

DENISE EILEEN MCCOSKEY

In 1937, classical historian Aubrey Diller opened his work *Race Mixture Among the Greeks Before Alexander* by citing contemporary interest in 'the element of race in human history' (1937: 9), a trend he traced back to Joseph Arthur de Gobineau's *Essai sur l'inégalité des races humaines* (1853–5). Gobineau's influential work had played an important role in disseminating many of the tenets of scientific racism that were rapidly gaining steam in the nineteenth century, including the notion that human races were biologically distinct and that any crossing of bloodlines 'would lead to inferiority, weakness, and even increased mortality' (Sussman 2014: 39). Noting that racial theory of his day tended to focus on 'the comparative value of the races, and the effects of race mixture', Diller identified an important paradox, namely that although such discussions 'deal in terms of pure races', 'a superficial survey of history shows at once that races and peoples have moved and mixed from time immemorial' (1937: 9–10).

Diller's insistence on 'moving' and 'mixing' (today we would use terminology like 'migration' and 'hybridity') highlights well some of the dynamics that remain central to any account of race in past societies. Not only do such concepts upend the practice of treating historical populations as static and pure, but they also make visible the diverse networks of contact and mobility within which such groups operated and formed their conceptions of themselves and others. Yet even as Diller probed the assumptions underlying the racial theories of his day, he used those theories as his primary framework for evaluating race in ancient Greece. Such reliance on modern ideas has long characterized the study of race in antiquity, and any attempt to apprehend ancient racial identities and practices on their own terms demands explicit reckoning with what Roman historian Lloyd Thompson has called 'the tyranny of modern habits of mind' (1989: 9) – a theme that will recur throughout this volume.

Before commencing a cultural history of race in antiquity, it might be useful to define the scope of our inquiry, what we mean by antiquity itself. While the adjective 'ancient' can be applied loosely to anything pre-modern, 'antiquity' as a noun has tended to connote the ancient Mediterranean, a space inhabited by an array of societies and cultures, including the Assyrians, Persians, Egyptians, Scythians, Ethiopians, Phoenicians and Carthaginians (e.g. Andrade 2013 and Quinn 2017; the chronological limits of such a period are fluid, although 3000 BCE to 800 CE is one estimate). Despite such a diverse landscape, the ancient Greeks and Romans have long dominated the study of antiquity, a bias often signalled by the modifier 'classical', which marks the supreme value assigned to these two groups in hindsight.[1] Historians today are calling for a more inclusive approach to the ancient Mediterranean, and this volume aims to consider a wide range of peoples and places. Still, given the enduring popularity of the ancient Greeks and Romans, I want in this introduction to help reset our understanding of – and relationship to – classical antiquity by highlighting some of the ways the field of Classics itself has long been complicit in promoting misconceptions about race in the ancient world.

The elevated position accorded to classical antiquity in the West can be traced in large part back to its Renaissance 'rediscovery' (Weiss 1988), but it was only during the modern eighteenth and nineteenth centuries – a period that likewise saw the rise of modern 'scientific' approaches to race (Stepan 1982) – that the methods and contours of Classics as a professional academic enterprise became formalized. The convergence of these two phenomena would be profound, for just as race became a major preoccupation in the emerging fields of natural science, it became central to historiography, and early classical scholars – like other historians at the time – increasingly envisioned history in terms of 'the biographies of races', treating historical change as the product of 'the triumphs of strong and vital peoples over weak and feeble ones' (Bernal 1987: 32). Openly assessing the 'comparative value of the races', classicists sided firmly with Greece and Rome, often drawing on contemporary notions of 'progress' (Bowler 1989) in avowing their views. Thus, in 1900, Charles Eliot Norton, the founder and first president of the Archaeological Institute of America, would proclaim that 'Egypt and all the East are of comparatively little concern except as they prepared the way for Greece', later adding that '[i]t is to the study of this preeminent race [i.e. of the Greeks] that the archaeology of the elder world leads up, and through Greece to Rome, her complement and associate in the story of civilization' (1900: 13–14). Within such a climate, the long-standing affinity for classical culture in many Western nations had given way to more pointed claims of a shared racial heritage, and many European and American classical scholars not only professed deep admiration for the ancient Greeks and Romans, but also positioned themselves among their modern descendants – an affective bond between scholar and subject that all too often continues today, even as its racialized connotations have become more veiled.

Diller himself named some of the features he believed made the classical period unique, including its 'ideal completeness' and 'copiousness of ... records', as well as its 'high excellence and its proximity and similarity to our own age' (1937: 11). While subjective judgements about the 'high excellence' of classical antiquity are enshrined in the label 'classical', it should be noted that perceptions about the Greek and Roman historical record (rich as it is) can also become self-fulfilling, meaning the more resources devoted to recuperation, preservation and publication of that record, the more it dominates our vision. Nevertheless, the terms 'proximity' and 'similarity' demand perhaps our greatest attention since they convey the persistent ways classical antiquity has been treated as both a putative site of Western origin and also its mirror: a distant age that is somehow always relentlessly close at hand, evoked time and again to legitimize a range of modern causes and viewpoints.

Acknowledging the centrality of classical antiquity specifically to early twentieth-century debates about race, Diller noted that '[a]ll combatants in the field of race theory recognize Greece and Rome as their chief bone of contention', explaining that the 'rise, fruition, and decay' of various cultures 'and the participation of the various races' in such processes 'constitute the richest material for the speculation of race theorists' (1937: 11). As such observation suggests, even as 'scientific' discourses – and especially those tied to the body and its surface appearance – were central to race theorists of Diller's day, history remained crucial in providing them with alleged examples of the impact of race on past societies. The two fields thus collaborated closely with one another: while the work of historians was shaped by contemporary race theory, contemporary race theorists leaned on historians to confirm their views about the alleged superiority of certain races across time. Even more, convictions about what Diller called classical antiquity's 'ideal completeness' helped reinforce its privileged position as the premiere historical era from which such 'lessons' about race could be extracted and applied to the contemporary world. For social theorists and classical scholars believed not only that the precise beginning and end of antiquity could be pinpointed, but also that both 'moments' – that the lifespan of antiquity itself – could be accounted for via race and racial practices.

Such approaches positioned race as the main engine of human society, as the 'cause' of whether and how far civilizations 'advance' or, conversely, 'fail', and they have long haunted the field of classical studies. So although there are myriad ways to track the racial fallacies propagated by classical scholarship since its inception, I would like to focus here on some of the specific ways classical scholars of the nineteenth and early twentieth century applied contemporary racist ideologies to their interpretations of the beginning and end of antiquity, that is, to the alleged origin of Greek civilization and Rome's so-called 'fall'. The Second World War would eventually shock classical scholars, as the world at large, into a fundamental re-examination of prevailing racial theories, and so I turn in the final section to classical scholars' treatment of race since the 1950s.

Given the often-sordid history of classical scholarship, any argument today for the use of the word 'race' in the study of antiquity must be carefully situated. In asserting, as this volume does, that race mattered in antiquity, it is thus crucial to state outright that the assumptions and practices implicit in such a statement depart significantly from nineteenth-century claims that race can be used to 'explain' ancient history, including the alleged 'accomplishments' of various groups. At the same time, this volume also aims to go beyond a research focus that has tended to dominate in more recent decades – namely, what the ancient Greeks and Romans thought about 'other' people. While such a question has undeniably produced important work in the field of ancient ethnography,[2] it has too often left the Greeks and Romans themselves uninterrogated, while also reinforcing the primacy of their gaze. So before examining ways the field of Classics has deployed the concept of race, I want to suggest some initial frameworks for apprehending the meaning and operation of race in antiquity on its own terms, including the conditions under which the categories 'Greek' and 'Roman' themselves emerged and operated.

RACE IN ANTIQUITY

Race today is often viewed as a product of human biology, something we are by virtue of our physical appearance or genetic make-up. Despite such widespread belief, as Robert Wald Sussman notes, research over the past decades in fields such as biology, anthropology and genetics has demonstrated that 'biological races do not exist among modern humans today, and they have never existed in the past'. He clarifies that 'even though biological races do not exist, the concept of race obviously is still a reality', but it is a reality, he insists, that derives from culture rather than biology (2014: 8). Thus, as Audrey and Brian Smedley argue, 'it is necessary and essential to distinguish naturally occurring physical diversity in the human species from culturally based perceptions and interpretations of this diversity' (2012: 12) – meaning that race is not passively determined by the human body but actively formed in accordance with shifting *ideas* about how and why groups (and bodies) are different and what such differences mean. As critical race theory has demonstrated over the past decades, our methods for defining race – and the practices, often violent, that emanate from them – therefore come not from 'nature' but from mental, emotional and ideological systems that are connected to a specific time and place (on critical race theory, begin with Crenshaw et al. 1995); this is why race is now widely regarded as a social construction rather than biological fact (Coates 2013). Race is also invariably a *historical* construction and historians have shown that our current association of race with physiognomy and skin colour – key features of the scientific racism of the eighteenth, nineteenth and early twentieth centuries (Saini 2019) – emerged in specific response to 'European expansion and exploitation of non-European lands and peoples' (Smedley and Smedley 2012: 26).

Given that the meaning and operation of race is so closely tied to its context, we should not expect ancient and modern views of race, separated by thousands of years, to coincide seamlessly. And they do not. Perhaps most notably, although skin colour differences are represented in ancient art and literature, there is little indication that skin colour per se served as the primary means for defining ancient racial groups (Snowden 1970, 1983). It cannot be said often enough that the ancient Greeks and Romans did not identify collectively as 'white' (Dee 2003–4); indeed, the very notion of a 'white race' would have been completely unimaginable to them. Rather, as many chapters in this volume demonstrate, the role of the body in ancient racial thought was complex and its surface appearance was often only secondary to the performances undertaken by that body within racialized institutions such as religion, politics and the family.

While it is important to establish at the outset what race in antiquity did not entail, providing a concise summary of what it did can present serious challenges, since ideas about race differed across time and place and were also often in competition with one another. One prominent theory – often called the ancient environmental theory – was evoked by both Greek and Roman writers and it posited that geographic location and climate were responsible for producing the innate characteristics and capacities that ostensibly defined different groups.[3] More generally, there seems to have been conflicting opinions throughout antiquity about the putative source of human variation, including the degree to which fundamental human differences were based in 'essence' (e.g. one's ancestry or bloodline) versus 'practice' (e.g. the language one spoke or gods one worshipped). Although most of these views seem to have persisted in one form or another – one theory did not simply replace another – as Jonathan Hall has argued, the use of cultural performance nonetheless seems to have become more prominent over time in defining collective identity (2002: 189–220).

So, too, significant differences existed in the actual criteria employed by the Greeks versus Romans when setting racial boundaries, meaning there was important variation not only in the form of ancient racial identities but also their content. Greg Woolf argues that 'Greeks spoke Greek, worshipped the same gods, had certain customs and had a common descent that could be traced back to mythical times, but they were not characterized by a particular style. Romans, by contrast, valued common descent hardly at all, and regarded material culture and morality as much more central constituents of their sense of self' (1994: 130). Yet even the selection of these types of racial markers was not static but depended on circumstance, so I want to provide a short survey of some of the evolving historical contexts and political structures that circumscribed the formation of racial identities in first the Greek then Roman era.

RACE IN THE GREEK WORLD

By the eighth century BCE, when our written evidence becomes more robust, one's identity in the Greek-speaking world seems primarily defined by the local polis or city-state, for example by being 'Theban' or 'Corinthian' (J. Hall 2002: 35). Alongside this principal mode of identity formation, 'a range of broader, supraregional affiliations' also existed (35), including a sense of belonging to one of three major dialect or ethnic groups, Dorian, Ionian or Aeolian (J. Hall 1997: 34–40). In addition, a general feeling of connectedness was expressed throughout the Greek world not only through shared language use, but also shared religious sanctuaries and joint participation in Panhellenic institutions such as the Olympic Games (E. Hall 1989: 8).

It was only during the early fifth century, however, that a collective identification *as* 'Greeks' (or 'Hellenes' in ancient Greek) emerged, a concept that sought to unify members of the diverse and independent Greek city-states, many of whom had joined together to form the often tenuous military alliance that successfully repelled two separate invasions by the massive Persian Empire in 492–490 BCE and 480–479 BCE (E. Hall 1989: 1–2; J. Hall 2002: 175). While the main impetus for such a shared identity seems to have come from an external threat (i.e. the Persian Empire), the precise connotations of 'Hellenes' as a label depended greatly on the context of its mobilization; Jonathan Hall, for example, has suggested that deployment of the concept was originally a discursive strategy of the upper class (2002: 164) and its use of ideals associated with democratic citizenship, at least in the early stages, made the terminology especially appealing to the powerful city-state of Athens (186–9). More fundamentally, the racial contours of Greekness became articulated in relation to its presumed opposite: the barbarian (Thucydides, *History of the Peloponnesian War* 1.3.3; also E. Hall 1989: 5 and *passim*; and J. Hall 2002: 179); initially applied to the Persians, the term 'barbarian' soon connoted all outsiders or non-Greeks (E. Hall 1989: 10–11). The Greek/barbarian dichotomy served an important role within Greek society as well, especially when reinforcing the Greek practice of chattel slavery – namely the subjugation of peoples who, when labelled 'barbarians', could be cast as fundamentally different and, as expressed in the writings of Aristotle, slaves by their very nature (on Aristotle, see Kaufman in this volume; on Greek slavery, see also Skinner in this volume).

In an important and much-discussed passage, the Greek historian Herodotus suggests that by the latter half of the fifth century, Greek identity was determined by both bloodline and cultural practices such as language, religion and general way of life (*Histories* 8.144.2).[4] In the early part of the next century, however, the Athenian orator Isocrates (*c*. 380 BCE) professed that the label 'Greek' referred not to 'race' (*genos*) but 'mental attitude' and that people were called 'Greek' when they shared 'education' or 'culture' (*paideia*) rather than 'common birth' (*Panegyricus* 50). Such a claim intimates that, by the fourth century, Greekness was primarily linked not to blood or 'being' but rather to the acquisition and performance of select Greek cultural practices, to a process of 'becoming', which itself relied on access to certain key social institutions, such as Greek education. The operation of 'Greek' as an identity formed by public expression seemingly became even more widespread following the military campaigns of Alexander the Great (336–323 BCE), which introduced Greek language and culture across a vast territory in the east (Figure 0.1).[5] Following Alexander's death, most of the area he had conquered was broken into three so-called Hellenistic kingdoms, multicultural spaces in which the meanings of Greekness – as well as the contexts in which being Greek mattered – became even more diverse.

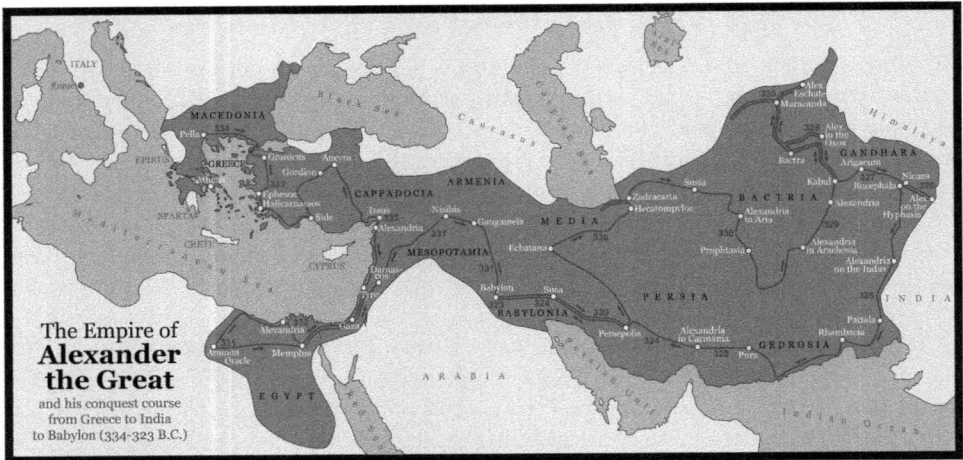

FIGURE 0.1 The empire of Alexander the Great. © Peter Hermes Furian/Alamy Stock Photo.

Documentary evidence from Egypt under the Greek Ptolemaic dynasty, for example, suggests that Greek identity conferred a distinct financial advantage there, even as it was tied closely to cultural activities. Assigning a tax break to 'Hellenes', the Greek Ptolemaic government thus granted exemptions specifically to those who promoted and practiced Greek culture, meaning 'schoolteachers, athletic coaches, (most probably) artists of Dionysus, and victors in the games of the various Alexandrian festivals' (Thompson 1997: 246–7). While the economic benefits of such tax policies were fairly modest, Dorothy Thompson has suggested they indicate the government's broader interest in transforming the racial identities of its subjects; or, as Thompson phrases it, such tax incentives seem designed to give 'dispensation to those prepared to "go Greek"' (248).

The Romans took possession of Egypt in 30 BCE following the death of Cleopatra VII, the last of the Ptolemies (and the most well-known Cleopatra for modern audiences), and from that point on racial boundaries became much more stringent there. The *Gnomon of the Idios Logos* (*BGU* V 1210) – a code of regulations produced for the 'Special Account' of Roman Egypt – notably lists a series of penalties specifically for those trying to 'pass' as Roman (Lewis 1999: 32–4). As with Greek identity, which would continue to have its own vicissitudes under the Romans,[6] it is important not to take the label 'Roman' for granted, however, but to consider some of the specific ways that identity intersected with racial ideology.

RACE IN THE ROMAN WORLD

Initially only minor players in the ancient Mediterranean, by the end of the first century BCE, the Romans controlled 'an empire which stretched from the English Channel to the Red Sea and from Algeria to the Black Sea' (Hopkins 1978: 102). Rome's political hegemony would last for centuries, weathering both systemic crises and shifting borders. In assessing the general dynamics that shaped Roman racial ideas and practices, the impact of population movement – Diller's 'moving' and 'mixing' – cannot be overemphasized. In addition to other forms of travel and migration, the increasing diversity of the Roman army itself meant that soldiers and veterans from a range of geographic origins were spread throughout the empire.⁷ Meanwhile, large cities such as Rome and Alexandria in Egypt housed especially diverse populations (Aelius Aristides, *To Rome* xi–xiii; Dio Chrysostom, *Discourses* 32.36–40).⁸ Reflecting on what it meant to leave one's homeland, the Roman author Seneca the Younger (b. 4 BCE–1 CE) proposed that Rome was scarcely able to house all the arriving immigrants and he credited them with a range of motivations for coming to a city 'not their own' (*On Consolation to Helvia* 6.2–4). The satirist Juvenal (b. 50–65 CE) complained bitterly that he could not tolerate the 'Greek city', pointedly targeting immigration from the east (a phenomenon that was picked up on by later classical scholars, as we shall see) and he charged that few of the Greeks in Rome actually originated in Greece, while even those who came as slaves held more prestige and power in the city than he did (*Satires* 3.60–1) – thus providing some indication of the city's diversity even if we read against Juvenal's strong nativist tone.

Roman citizenship was conferred on a wide range of individuals and groups, including some the Romans had conquered, and it played a major role in setting the boundary between Romans and non-Romans for centuries until the emperor Caracalla awarded it to all free-born residents of the empire in 212 CE. Still, Roman citizenship regularly operated alongside a nexus of other social attitudes and identities. For one, although enslaved persons could become Roman citizens when manumitted, a practice 'unique in the Graeco-Roman world', they were not uniformly treated as the equivalent of other citizens since 'social prejudice effectively excluded them and their sons from certain functions' (Sherwin-White 1973: 322 and 324). Nor was Romanness tied to citizenship alone; rather the term 'Roman' could be used to denote an identity that involved more than mere legal status. In his *Institutes of Oratory*, the Roman rhetorician Quintilian thus makes a pointed contrast between a Romanness attained by birth and one acquired only through citizenship (*donata civitate*) (8.1.3).

In structuring their racial imaginary, the Romans inherited the Greek concept of the barbarian, which they employed as a means for conveying the relative distance between their own cultural norms and those of other groups (Thompson 1989: 87).⁹ Even more, the Romans generally conceived of this gap as changeable, meaning that other groups could be 'brought closer' to Roman standards and practices – a premise that served at times as a mandate and could also set the parameters for Roman territorial ambition. Viewed through this lens, Julius Caesar's inclusion of descriptions of the contrasting customs and racial characteristics of the Germans and Gauls in his *Gallic Wars* can be read as 'justification at an ethnographic level, both for subjugating the three Gauls and for renouncing any conquest of the lands beyond the Rhine' (Ruggini 1987: 192). Such framing of Rome's manifest destiny vis-à-vis racial difference was so seductive that many early classical scholars openly cheered Roman conquest in their writings, firm in their convictions that the arrival of Rome had invariably improved the lives of those 'less-civilized'.¹⁰

Often treated as innately beneficial in its outcomes, Roman rule has likewise been characterized as surprisingly 'tolerant' in practice given the Romans' liberal extension of citizenship and the fact that they were generally disinclined to intervene forcibly in the cultural practices of those they had defeated; perhaps most notably, Greek remained the language of Roman administration in the eastern part of the empire, specifically in the territories previously controlled by the Greek Hellenistic kingdoms (on multilingualism and languages generally, see Mullen and James 2012). The emperor Claudius' speech urging the admission of certain Gauls into the Roman Senate in 48 CE is likewise often held up as proof of Roman broad-mindedness (Tacitus allegedly records the speech at

Annals 11.23–4; see also Griffin 1982 for discussion of its divergences from a tablet found at Lyon). But the Roman state certainly did not hesitate to single out and punish specific groups when it met their needs to do so.[11] In 215 CE, for example, the emperor Caracalla sought to expel native Egyptians from the city of Alexandria, an event that is especially notable because – in one of the few surviving Roman administrative documents to dictate precisely how members of a racial group can be identified – Caracalla explicitly instructs his officials that 'genuine' Egyptians can be recognized by appearance, speech and general lifestyle (*P. Giss.* 40 ii = *Select Papyri* 215; discussed at Lewis 1999: 201–3).

As targeted as such an order was, Caracalla nonetheless made a pointed exception, allowing those Egyptians who were undertaking occupations beneficial to the city's economy to remain. Such an exemption underlines the importance of taking into account both the workings of intersectionality (here, of race and economic status; for more on intersectionality, see Haley in this volume) and also Rome's own priorities when assessing 'tolerance' and the racial dimensions of Roman state power. Martin Goodman writes that

> [w]hat mattered to the Roman state, apart from the promotion of the image of the emperor, was the preservation in the provinces of peace, and the extraction of wealth, both for consumption in the city of Rome and for payment to the huge military force required to ensure the power of the emperor. Beyond such minimum requirements, the state could afford to be tolerant of social and cultural variety.
>
> (2004: 11)

As we have seen with the tax policy in Ptolemaic Egypt, the 'extraction of wealth' intersects in complicated ways with race, and the racial implications of various economic measures were even more palpable under the Romans, as might be implied by the demand that portions of the empire subsidize their own military occupation.

In addition, after the Jewish Wars (66–73 CE), the Romans imposed a tax specifically on Jews throughout the empire (the *fiscus Iudaicus*).[12] Meanwhile, in Roman Egypt, the burden of taxation became so oppressive that it led to a category of persons known as 'tax fugitives', and for a time Roman policy made the remaining community collectively responsible for the taxes of those who had fled, further crippling those areas (Lewis 1999: 161–5 and 172). Chastising his contemporaries who sought an environmental explanation for Egypt's economic collapse in the first century CE, specifically arguing that it had emanated from a 'natural' deterioration of the Egyptian soil, historian Michael Ivanovich Rostovtzeff forcefully countered that such devastation should be laid at the feet of the 'blind, ruthless financial policy of the government', that is, of Roman greed itself (1929: 363). Still, if we wanted to truly probe the intersections of race, empire and the 'extraction of wealth' during the Roman era, we would need to acknowledge first and foremost that the unprecedented accumulation of money and land in the hands of the Roman upper class during Rome's early period of expansion led to 'the most intensive development of agrarian slavery known in the ancient world' (Shaw 2001: 4).

It is impossible in this space to provide a comprehensive overview of all the conditions that produced racial categories and their attendant consequences in antiquity; the topic of ancient slavery alone would require considerable elaboration.[13] And, to be sure, any discussion of Rome's introduction of wide-scale systems of agrarian slavery would be woefully inadequate if not set alongside the three major slave revolts that took place between the years 140 and 70 BCE in response, including one led by the Thracian gladiator *cum* rebel Spartacus (Bradley 1998). So, too, I recognize that any attempt to highlight the racial work of labels such as 'Greek' and 'Roman' (including their collaborations with state power) leaves invisible the ways that the borders around such identities were challenged and crossed and not merely set and regulated – not to mention leaving silent the dissenting racial identifications that could be mobilized in, around and against such processes.[14] Still, I hoped here to suggest preliminary ways of recuperating some of the complexity of race in antiquity – including the dynamics that should keep the Greeks and Romans unfamiliar and far away rather than comfortable and close by. As this goal suggests, how we frame our reading of classical antiquity determines to a large degree the meaning we make of it. So, I would like to turn now to the history of classical scholarship and some of its long-standing interplay with race and racism.

RACE AND EARLY CLASSICAL STUDIES

The field of Classics was founded largely on philology – the in-depth study of linguistic structure and language development – and, throughout much of the nineteenth century, language served as a thinly veiled stand-in for identifying and tracking racial groups. Ancient Greek was subjected to especially close scrutiny; it had first been identified as an Indo-European language in the late eighteenth century after certain resemblances between Greek and Sanskrit, an ancient Indian language, were recognized (J. Hall 2002: 37–8). When, as Nell Irvin Painter observes, 'the nineteenth-century rage for races turned languages into peoples', the Indo-European language family became attached to a race, one called 'Aryan', a word taken from the Sanskrit '"*arya*," meaning "noble" or "spiritual"' (2010: 196). Nazi promotion of an 'Aryan race' would, of course, go on to have devastating consequences, but as J. P. Mallory points out, 'the implementation of Aryan supremacy by the Nazis was wholly inconsistent with Aryan as a linguistic term; Yiddish is as much an Indo-European language as any other German dialect' (1989: 269).

Such conflation of race and language pervaded much of early classical scholarship. Citing the view that 'language is really the surest of all known tests of race', Richard Wellington Husband, for example, maintained in a 1909 article that 'there was a racial difference between patricians and plebeians' in ancient Rome (1909: 63), like many at the time treating the boundaries of race and class as coterminous. Arguing that the 'patricians were composed of an amalgamation of Romani, Sabines, and Etruscans' and that the 'plebeians were in the main Ligurians' (63), Husband further sought to demonstrate that Ligurian was itself not an Indo-European language, a claim he believed was supported by, or 'in harmony' with, the supposed fact that 'Ligurian blood was not Indo-European' (81).[15] The geographic origin of Indo-European soon became a major preoccupation and although its 'arrival' in Greece was initially attributed to an invasion from central Asia, nineteenth-century scholars increasingly placed the putative homeland of Indo-European(s) in northern Europe itself (J. Hall 2002: 38; cf. Mallory 1989: 268), an impulse for defining the classical world in relation to contemporary Europe – rather than the ancient Mediterranean – that would only increase over time.

NORDIC GREEKS

While language study initially dominated Classics, the discipline of classical archaeology was emerging by the latter half of the nineteenth century, allowing scholars to grapple more fully with Greek history prior to the eighth century BCE, periods for which archaeological remains generally provided the strongest evidence – at least until the decipherment of Linear B, the earliest surviving form of ancient Greek, in the 1950s.[16] Like their counterparts in philology, classical archaeologists soon made the tracking of racial groups a primary concern; to them, as A. E. R. Boak phrased it, excavations at places such as Tiryns and Mycenae had 'raised the questions: "Who were the authors of this civilization?" and "If they were not Greeks, to what extent did the latter share in this culture?"' (1917: 25; cf. Ridgeway 1896). Classifying early groups via material culture, for example through differing architecture and pottery styles, archaeologists soon came up with a general chronology of early Greek history centred around two main populations: the Minoans, who had inhabited the island of Crete beginning around 3100 BCE, and the Mycenaeans, who had succeeded the Minoans by about 1600 BCE and whose civilization presumably consisted of a broad network of settlements especially on the Greek mainland.

Significantly, these early classical archaeologists also identified a precipitous break in the archaeological record around 1050 BCE, a break they associated with the fall of the Mycenaean civilization and one that allowed them to resolve a major conundrum presented by the Greek Bronze Age. For the more archaeologists learned about the Minoans and Mycenaeans, the less they seemed capable of initiating the later version of Greek culture that the public at large, not to mention classical scholars themselves, so revered. As one scholar opined: '[t]heir non-material survivals, institutions, etc. are so slight that the greatness of Greece is to be attributed not to the Minoan-Mycenaean civilization but to factors operating immediately afterward' (Robinson 1939: 185), and the ways these scholars filled in such 'factors' – most notably the proposal of a so-called 'Dorian invasion' (J. Hall 1997: 114–18) – has played an important role in racializing the origins of Greek civilization ever since.

According to this model, the Dorians – one of the major Greek ethnic groups – moved southwards from central and northwest Greece, 'conquering the Peloponnese, the southern Aegean islands and southwest Asia Minor' (J. Hall 1997: 11).[17] Eventually the Dorians would become linked by some to northern Europe itself, an alignment that reflected the conviction in nineteenth-century racial theory that the Nordic race – a group 'assumed to be the descendants of ancient Germanic tribes' (Sussman 2014: 37) – was superior to all other 'white' groups. It was only the Nordic race that was thought to possess the vigour and racial capacity necessary for dramatic cultural innovation, making it the ideal progenitor of the post-Bronze Age form of Greek culture that had become associated with classical Greece. While some classical scholars leaned figuratively on the association – the French scholar Georges Dumézil labelled the Dorians 'the most "nordic" of Greeks' (J. Hall 1997: 12) – others would openly place the origins of the Dorians in Germany itself (7). The impact of a Dorian narrative binding Germany and ancient Greece reached far beyond classical studies, and, as Jonathan Hall notes, classical scholars would later have cause 'to reflect soberly on the symbolism that the "Indogermanic" Dorians had provided for the Nazis' (13).

Classical historians today no longer believe that such an invasion took place,[18] although the theory continues to fester, including among white nationalist groups.[19] Indeed, it has become increasingly difficult to attribute the origins of Greek culture to a single founding event or even single population group, since we know that communities throughout the ancient Mediterranean were in contact from a very early period. Of the years specifically between 1500 and 1200 BCE, archaeologist Eric Cline has observed: 'the Mediterranean region played host to a complex international world in which Minoans, Mycenaeans,

Hittites, Assyrians, Babylonians, Mitannians, Canaanites, Cypriots, and Egyptians all interacted, creating a cosmopolitan and globalized world system such as has only rarely been seen before the current day' (2014: 171). Some classical scholars today go even further in arguing that any attempt to sort the early Mediterranean population into clear-cut groups is anachronistic and misleading.[20]

Debates about race and the alleged origins of Greek culture reignited in the 1980s following publication of volume 1 of Martin Bernal's *Black Athena: The Afroasiatic Roots of Classical Civilization* (1987). Arguing that racism and Eurocentric bias had distorted reconstructions of the roots and development of Greek civilization, Bernal specifically called out eighteenth- and nineteenth-century classical scholars for inventing what he called an 'Aryan Model' of Greek origin, one that sought to erase the influence of Egypt and the Near East on the development of Greek culture. Even more, Bernal insisted that the racist underpinnings of Classics as a discipline continued to shape contemporary study of the ancient world; as Bernal phrased it: 'what is claimed here is that modern archaeologists and ancient historians of this region are still working with models set up by men who were crudely positivist and racist' (1987: 9). Bernal's discussion of the ways early classical scholars had devalued Egyptian influence on Greece, in particular, received extensive press coverage globally with the presumed intersections of *Black Athena* and Afrocentrism, even resulting in a *Newsweek* cover story (23 September 1991).[21] Yet *Black Athena* also importantly charted the changing attitudes among classical historians towards the ancient Phoenicians, identifying a peak of anti-Semitism between the years 1920 and 1939 (1987: 387–8).

In later volumes, Bernal made the case for his own 'Revised Ancient Model', a model that asserted substantial 'Greek cultural borrowings from Egypt and the Levant' between the years 2100 and 1100 BCE (Bernal 1987: 17). 'Borrowings', however, proved to be something of a misnomer, and many classical scholars found the actual top-down mechanism of cultural influence proposed by Bernal – namely that of a 'long period of domination by Egypto-Semitic conquerors' (21) – curiously aligned with the very nineteenth-century models he was trying to topple.[22] Still, in his attempt to initiate a fundamental reimagining of Greek origin, Bernal sought, like Diller before, to challenge the long-standing practice of writing world history in terms of clearly defined population groups, groups whose relative 'achievements' could be quantified and ranked; as Bernal proclaimed: '[m]y enemy is not Europe, it's purity – the idea that purity ever exists, or that if it does exist, that it is somehow more culturally creative than mixture. I believe that the civilization of Greece is so attractive precisely because of those mixtures' (Vitello 2013).

Even as racial frameworks were being applied to the putative origins of Greek culture, racial theory was also being increasingly inscribed on the ancient Greek body itself during the nineteenth and early twentieth centuries. No longer just Nordic in spirit or cultural capacity, the ancient Greeks – in accordance with the rising use of biological criteria in defining race – were soon made to embody a Nordic physical type and, employing methods from contemporary physical anthropology, ancient crania were at times offered as 'proof' of such classifications.[23] Most notoriously, J. C. Nott and G. R. Gliddon in their widely read *Types of Mankind* (1854) placed the head of the statue of Apollo Belvedere atop a racial chart in illustration of the physique they associated with a Greek skull (Figure 0.2). Such a practice, adopted by many at the time, thus treated the idealized anatomy represented on Greek statuary – in this case, the representation of a literal Greek god – as historical record of 'real' Greeks and their supposedly superior 'Caucasian' body type

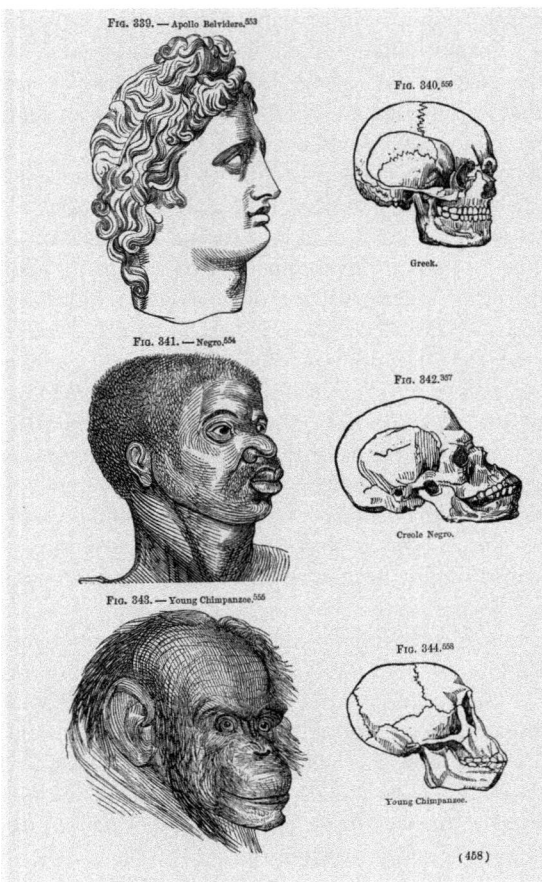

FIGURE 0.2 Racial chart from Nott and Gliddon's *Types of Mankind* (1854). © Science Photo Library.

(Challis 2010: 101–3). Even the alleged 'blondeness' of the heroes in Homer's epic poetry, a claim tenuous at best, would be brought into the fray.[24] Illustrating the combined allure of such ideas, Theodore Bedrick gushed in the 1949–50 *Classical Journal* that '[t]he roving Nordics who filtered down through Greece brought with them love of battle and joy in a hard-fought contest', adding that Homer himself presented 'an elaborate picture of the Achaean sports' undertaken by 'huge blond heroes' (1949–50: 136). As the terms of Bedrick's praise suggest, many observers singled out the ancient Greek athlete as a premiere symbol of Greek racial superiority during this period, a tendency only heightened by the modern Olympic movement (Challis 2011).

As the Second World War raged, Gilbert Highet, a Scottish-born classicist teaching in the United States, issued a scathing review of an Italian scholar whose work he considered part of an attempt 'to glorify Italy and … justify the policy of the Fascist party' (1942: 92). Highet went on to cast an even wider net, predicting that 'if millions of young Germans are taught … that the greatest figures in Greek and Roman history were demonstrably Nordic in blood and therefore German folk-comrades, then within two generations central Europe will have passed into a new Dark Age, full of all the particularism and obscurantism of the last' (104). Although Highet indicted Germany specifically, the myth of Nordic Greeks was clearly consumed and propagated by scholars in many Western countries. Yet, since the time of Edward Gibbon's *The History of the Decline and Fall of the Roman Empire* (1776–89), classical scholars have been obsessed by locating not just the beginnings of classical antiquity, but also its end,[25] and I want to turn now to American classicists' use of racial composition and 'race-mixing' in explaining Rome's so-called 'fall'.

'MIXED BLOOD' AT ROME[26]

At the dawn of the twentieth century, American classicists were still trying to define their role in a field that had long been dominated by Europe. Complicating the picture, many American classical scholars continued to gain at least part of their training in Germany, a practice that would be disrupted only by the outbreak of war in Europe in 1914. From its earliest periods, the American nation had forged a close bond with classical antiquity,[27] but as American classicists sought to establish their own methods for studying Classics in the early twentieth century, they were especially drawn to questions of how racially diverse populations conduct themselves, a theme that resonated strongly with their American context.

Drawing a direct parallel between Rome and the United States, Kirby Flower Smith proposed in 1910 that '[i]t is interesting to observe, especially for us Americans, that the Romans themselves were undoubtedly of mixed blood' (1910: 223). L. B. Mitchell later drew a more ominous lesson from the Roman analogy, however. Identifying a presumed decline in Rome wrought by the presence of slaves who brought with them their 'effete' Greek culture or 'vices' from their 'barbarous communities' in places such as Thrace and Gaul, Mitchell concluded that

> [t]he Roman melting pot had received into it more than it could melt and fuse together. This situation, no doubt, contributed largely to the collapse of the Roman Republic and gives pause to thoughtful Americans who have seen in the last four years that our melting pot ha[s] not fused its ingredients to the extent that had previously been imagined.
>
> (1922: 320)

Mitchell's phrase 'the last four years' hints at the public anxiety that had been growing in the United States throughout the early twentieth century over the waves of immigrants who, since the 1890s, had been coming not so much from northern Europe but from eastern and southern Europe instead, a group consisting primarily of poor and often unskilled or illiterate Catholics and Jews (Sussman 2014: 100). In response to this 'crisis', a temporary measure called the Emergency Quota Act of 1921 was enacted, drastically curtailing entry into the United States (Figure 0.3); a more permanent act, one whose provisions and quotas targeted Italians and Jews especially, would later be passed in 1924 and remain in force until 1965 (Painter 2010: 322–3).

Even as classical scholars made use of terminology such as the 'melting pot' to describe Roman social dynamics (a term that had come into general use in 1908 after a play by the same name), many social critics, in turn, called on the classical world in their diagnosis of modern ills. Thus, in *The Passing of the Great Race* (1916) – a book greatly

FIGURE 0.3 Cartoon depicting Uncle Sam putting quotas in place as dictated by the 1921 Act (19 May 1921). © MPI/Stringer/Getty Images.

admired by Hitler – Madison Grant, a lawyer heavily involved in the American eugenics movement, borrowed a Latin term *'cloaca gentium'* ('sewer of peoples'), first coined by H. S. Chamberlain, to encapsulate what he considered the disintegrating American urban landscape (1916: 81). Like other race theorists of his day, Grant divided the Caucasian race into three main groups: Alpine, Mediterranean and Nordic (Figure 0.4). Nordics, as we have seen, were considered 'the apex of development of the white race', while Mediterraneans (a group that included Jews) 'were inferior to both Nordics and Alpines in stamina but were superior in the arts' (Sussman 2014: 88). Unlike the fairly straightforward attribution of Nordic origin to the ancient Greeks, for many, the Romans

INTRODUCTION 15

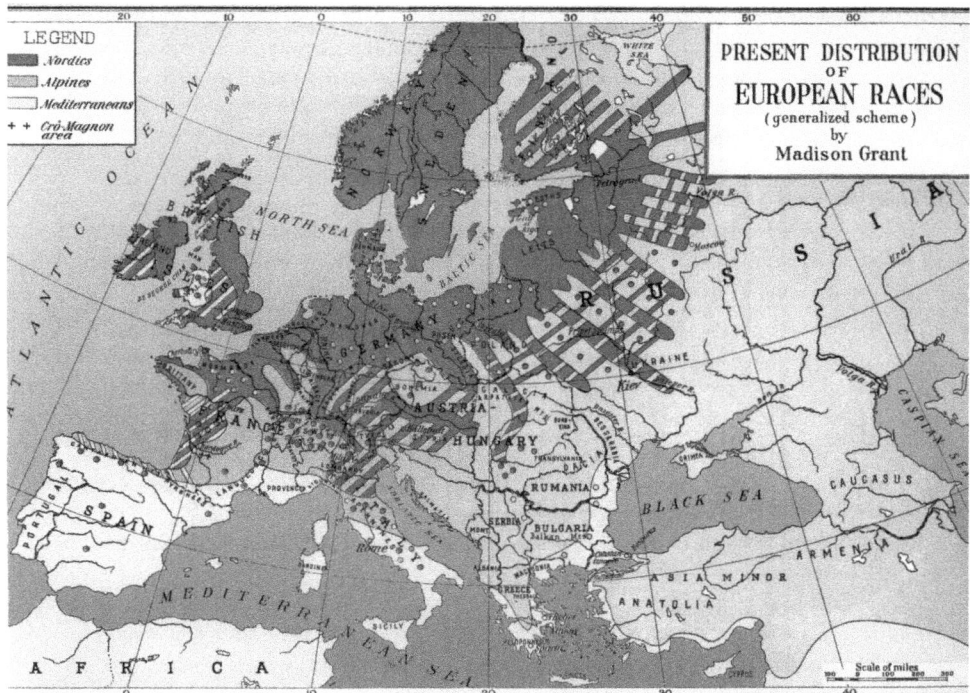

FIGURE 0.4 Map from Madison Grant's *The Passing of the Great Race* (1916) showing the alleged distribution of European racial groups. © Pictorial Press Ltd/Alamy Stock Photo.

demanded a more painstaking parsing of Nordic and Mediterranean, one influenced by the negative stereotypes attached to contemporary Italian immigrants. Grant himself sought to alleviate any tension by siding unconditionally with the Nordic, professing that 'the traditions of the Eternal City, its love of organization, of law and military efficiency, as well as the Roman ideals of family life, loyalty, and truth, point clearly to a Nordic rather than to a Mediterranean origin' (1916: 139). Not everyone would find the same answer.

In 1922, classical historian Frederick Shipley attempted to evaluate race mixture's 'effect upon the development of genius' (1922: 100) – a major preoccupation of contemporary race theorists – in four provinces that had allegedly witnessed a rise in literary culture following Roman conquest: North Italy, Spain, North Africa and Gaul. Asserting at the outset that 'all ethnologists' recognize '[t]hat the Roman race was itself a mixture' (101), Shipley proposed that the Roman upper class had once been Nordic (102) while 'the substratum of the population … was the Mediterranean race, a people short and slight of stature, long-skulled, dark haired and dark-eyed, and olive-skinned, of a distinctly artistic temperament' (101–2). By the third century BCE, however, Shipley professed that the Romans 'once a mixture of Nordic and Mediterranean elements' were now, as they began their expansion, a 'homogeneously blended race' (102). Given his overall view of Rome's mixed racial origins – and also his argument that the Romans who would have had most contact with natives were not patrician, but plebeian, namely traders or soldiers – Shipley concluded somewhat subversively for the time that the allegedly positive impact of Roman blood on literary creativity in the provinces did not 'fit well with theories of genius based upon the Nordic strains' (114). Nonetheless, Shipley raised the specter of a less harmonious 'blend' looming, one that would be tied to the very same group singled out by Mitchell: slaves, a group through whom 'the blood of every country about the basin of the Mediterranean Sea' would soon, according to Shipley, pour into Rome (102).

A few years earlier, Roman historian Tenney Frank had applied the concept of 'race mixture' to Roman history in a widely read article that would go on to have a long afterlife.[28] Proposing that 'the whole empire was a melting-pot and that the Oriental was always and everywhere a very large part of the ore' (1916: 702–3), Frank concluded that 'what lay behind and constantly reacted upon all such causes of Rome's disintegration was, after all, to a considerable extent, the fact that the people who built Rome had given way to a different race' (705). Although Frank placed particular emphasis on Roman 'mixture' with 'Orientals' arriving from the eastern part of the empire – meaning Greeks and Jews from places such as Syria and Asia Minor – he soon narrowed this group to 'ex-slaves and their offspring' (689), claiming that it was ultimately the 'liberal' practice of Roman manumission that had brought about the high rate of 'merg(ing)' between the 'servile classes' and 'civil population' (698).

While enslaved persons in classical antiquity were not defined by a single geographic origin (Harris 1999), arguments for the deleterious qualities of slave blood allowed classical scholars such as Frank to raise concerns not only about the east (and, by extension, Jewish immigrants) but also about an African American population finding its place in American society post-emancipation. In his Martin Classical Lectures published some sixteen years later, Frank made the connection between ancient and modern slavery more openly, proposing that 'the institution of slavery left consequences more serious to Roman society than to ours because there … lack of racial prejudice had permitted a more active absorption of indigestible foreign elements in the body politic' (1932: ix). In short, citing the *lack* of racial prejudice (and, in his earlier work, the 'liberal' practice of manumission itself) as the downfall of Roman society, Frank used 'mixed blood' and Roman 'decline' to argue for continuing segregation and discrimination in American life.

Of course, any attempt to separate out one strand of classical scholarship invariably oversimplifies the record, and not every American classicist of this era adhered to contemporary racist views. The Jewish classicist Moses Hadas, for one, argued in the early 1940s that a very different lesson be taken from the ancient world, namely what he considered its evolution from 'nationalism' to 'cosmopolitanism' (1943). Even more, the dire consequences of concepts such as 'race-mixing' would be laid bare by the Second World War, and '[t]he self-reflection which was required in the wake of the Holocaust left few intellectual disciplines unaffected' (J. Hall 1997: 13). Like many areas of study, Classics would radically alter its methods vis-à-vis race, albeit with sometimes questionable results.

RACE AND POST-SECOND WORLD WAR CLASSICAL SCHOLARSHIP

In 1947, the African American classicist Frank M. Snowden Jr openly challenged presumptions about the negative impact of 'race mixture' in the work of Frank and others, reminding his audience that '[n]o color bar existed in the Roman Empire and no laws prohibited unions of Blacks and Whites' (1947: 290). Such phrasing was unquestionably powerful at a time when laws banning marriage between white and non-white Americans were common in the United States; indeed, it would only be twenty years later, in 1967, that the Supreme Court deemed such laws unconstitutional in *Loving v. Virginia* (Sussman 2014: 74–5; Figure 0.5). Snowden eventually expanded his conclusion – that '[a]mong the Romans as among the Greeks, there was apparently no trace of "color prejudice"' (1947: 288) – into two book-length studies (1970, 1983), and his focus on Greek and Roman attitudes towards the group he labelled 'Blacks in antiquity' would set the agenda for research on race in antiquity for decades.

Significantly, even as he agreed with Snowden's conclusions about the lack of colour prejudice in the Roman world, Lloyd Thompson – who was born in Barbados and taught in Nigeria for forty years (Dominik 1997) – urged greater scrutiny of the premise behind such research, pointing out that it too often assumed from the outset that Black people functioned as a universally unique category (1989: 22). To the contrary, Thompson argued that it was necessary to position Roman attitudes towards black Africans within 'the context of Roman attitudes towards aliens in general' (5).[29] Thompson likewise challenged the now dominant (although, *pace* Snowden, increasingly unspoken) treatment of the Greeks and Romans as 'white'. Denying that the Romans, in particular, would 'link superiority to an ascending scale of whiteness', Thompson countered that the Roman worldview was based on the dominance of 'pale-brown Mediterraneans' (10–11).

FIGURE 0.5 Mildred and Richard Loving at a press conference following the Supreme Court's ruling in *Loving v. Virginia* (13 June 1967). © Francis Miller/The LIFE Picture Collection/Getty Images.

In the post-war context, classical scholarship had shifted markedly from the topic of 'race-mixing' to the more neutral-sounding 'race relations',[30] and it frequently focused, as in Snowden's work, on examining Greek and Roman attitudes towards other groups. Moreover, the precise labelling of such attitudes (especially when negative) remained a point of some contention. Responding to Benjamin Isaac's claims 'that early forms of racism' – which he called 'proto-racism' – 'were common in the Graeco-Roman world' (2004: 1), Erich Gruen conceded that '[t]he ancients were certainly not above prejudicial reflections on persons unlike themselves'; he nevertheless sought to draw a firm line, insisting that '[i]t is a very different matter, however, to tar them with a blanket characterization of xenophobia and ethnocentrism, let alone racism' (2011a: 3).[31]

As Gruen's phrasing – 'tar' and 'let alone' – might intimate, even as classical scholars often felt it necessary to defend the Greeks and Romans in such contexts, the terminology of race and racism was perceived as uniquely incendiary and over time a near-unanimous consensus that the concept of race was simply not applicable to the ancient world took hold. In rejecting race, most classical scholars credited Snowden's work with having proven not that the Greeks and Romans did not follow modern ideas about race, but rather that race itself did not exist in the ancient world; in this way – despite the advances being made since the 1990s by critical race theory – classical scholars continued for decades to treat skin colour as a transhistorical signifier of racial identity rather than merely its modern guise. Gruen articulated this general view, albeit in softened form, when he reflected that race 'may be an altogether misleading and erroneous category', explaining that '[t]here is little to suggest that the ancients ascribed moral, intellectual, or cultural deficiencies to persons on the basis of their color' (2011a: 197–8).

Consonant with the growing influence of 'cultural studies' (on this school of analysis, see Storey 1996), many classical scholars like Gruen enthusiastically employed 'culture' and 'cultural identity' instead when studying collective identity in antiquity[32] – a shift already evident in Adrian N. Sherwin-White's short study *Racial Prejudice in Imperial Rome* (1967). For although relying on the discursive power of 'race' in the title of his work, Sherwin-White dismissed its relevance almost immediately, declaring that '[i]t is commonplace to assert that the ancient world knew nothing of [the] colour bar and racial prejudice'. He then proposed that '[i]f there was no racial prejudice, there certainly was some culture prejudice. The question is, how much, how deep, and whether or why it became a problem in the Roman empire' (1967: 1). Sherwin-White's preference for the terminology of 'culture', moreover, persisted throughout his subsequent examination of Roman attitudes towards the Germans, Gauls, Greeks and Jews.

In addition to the oft-stated goal of shifting the discussion away from ancient skin colour, many classical scholars in the final decades of the twentieth century readily adopted terminology other than 'race' because they believed it would allow them to remain more 'neutral', meaning that, by eschewing the word, they thought they could avoid triggering the often unsettling modern connotations of the concept.[33] Yet mere avoidance of the term too often meant that it simply continued its work covertly. Arguing generally that 'culture has turned out to be a way of continuing rather than repudiating racial thought', Walter Benn Michaels explained that '[i]t is only the appeal to race that makes culture an object of affect and that gives notions like losing our culture, preserving it, stealing someone else's culture, restoring people's culture to them, and so on, their pathos' (1995: 61–2). This is especially true in the study of the ancient world, where the intersections of culture, race and questions about who 'owns' the past have been particularly fraught;

indeed, the controversies over *Black Athena* demonstrate well the tendency to muddy the line between race and culture given that responses to it focused on race whereas Bernal himself mainly used the language of ancient Greek culture and modern racism (skin colour and the Greeks' own views of race were actually quite peripheral to Bernal's project despite his provocative title; see McCoskey 2018b; also McCoskey 2012: 171–9).[34] So, too, any treatment of culture as innately more 'neutral' than race obscures the fact that, as we have seen, nineteenth-century race theorists openly attributed the very capacity for cultural achievement to race and racial composition.

Still, since the 1997 publication of Jonathan Hall's pioneering work *Ethnic Identity in Greek Antiquity*, 'ethnicity' has been the term used most prominently to fill the void left by race in classical studies.[35] Such preference was largely predicated on the view (widely shared in the post-war era) that ethnicity was a form of identity actively claimed through social performance, whereas race was an identity passively dictated by one's biological make-up (McCoskey 2012: 27–9). Such a simplistic distinction is now impossible to maintain and – given the growing recognition of race's foundation in social and historical processes rather than science – as Stuart Hall has remarked, the two terms increasingly seem to 'play hide-and-seek with each other' (Sollors 1996: xxxv; for ways of distinguishing the terms, see Mac Sweeney in this volume). Pondering whether ethnicity as a concept should now be discarded in classical studies, Jeremy McInerney recently echoed Michaels's concerns about the replacement of 'race' with 'culture', acknowledging '[i]f it [i.e. ethnicity] is nothing more than race repackaged, then that may not be such a bad idea' (2014a: 6).

Some years earlier, Jonathan Hall had similarly noted that the meaning of race 'is not so very different from that proposed for the ethnic group', continuing, 'though whether the term "race" has yet outgrown its troubled past sufficiently to re-enter current social-scientific discourse remains to be seen' (2002: 15). Race has clearly re-entered social science and also humanistic discourses, not to mention study of the classical world itself (e.g. Buell 2005; Haley 2009; Lape 2010; and McCoskey 2012). But given that the 'troubled past' of race intersects so strongly with the rise of Classics as a discipline, what should a cultural history of race in antiquity now entail?

CONCLUSION: TOWARDS A CULTURAL HISTORY OF RACE IN ANTIQUITY

In 1944, H. L. Tracy wryly asked, 'Is it ill-natured to suggest that the apologists for classics should make up their mind whether they are recommending study of ancient life because it is unlike ours, or because it is like ours?' (1944: 180). Over seventy years later, classical scholars are still struggling to answer that question, still struggling with how to appropriately set the ancient and modern world next to one another. As the cover image chosen for this volume insinuates, the two cannot and should not be easily reconciled; our experiences of modernity are invariably poised to disrupt even as they facilitate our engagement with – and expectations of – the ancient world. The point is never to take that process for granted. While Snowden, Thompson and others have long affirmed that skin colour did not hold the same racial meaning in classical antiquity that it does today, the task for authors in this volume and beyond is to determine how, where, when and why various groups in antiquity – and not merely the Greeks and Romans – formed *their* ideas about race, and what consequences those ideas and attendant practices had for themselves and those around them.

Yet it is also imperative that the field of Classics wrestles honestly with its own past, with both the racist methods and, now, the evasions that have had so much negative impact on our understanding of the ancient world (see also Padilla Peralta in this volume). In trying to explain why current scholars avoid the term 'race', McInerney posited that '[f]ew white academics wish to write about race'; he added of Classical Studies more specifically '[i]ronically, those who have suffered the most from the abuses masked by the term "race" have become those most likely to adopt it' (2014a: 1). While I struggle to find the latter critical practice in any way 'ironic', I am more concerned about the pernicious erasure the first claim makes – for, as we have seen, white scholars have written *a lot* about race when it comes to Greek and Roman antiquity over the centuries. Moreover, after centuries of eagerly wielding the term, for classicists to decide summarily that they are done with it is surely not just a 'wish' but a form of considerable privilege. So even as we revitalize the study of race in antiquity, such specious observations illustrate why we still need race in Classics so profoundly. We need race for as long as it remains a site of contest and struggle – not merely a space for expressing power but also for resisting and transforming it – and not just in the ancient world but also in terms of disciplinary practice itself. This volume takes on both.

CHAPTER ONE

Definitions and Representations of Race

In Ancient Greek Literature

SARAH DERBEW

It was Virgil's Aeneas who I loved
…
I who thought I could not love
both Virgil & Lumumba,
who secretly walked
with my flowers for them.

(Girmay 2016: 86)[1]

In her poem 'The Beauty of the World: Tenth Estrangement', Aracelis Girmay reveals her shared love for Vergil, the author of ancient Rome's foundational legend *The Aeneid*, and Patrice Lumumba, the first prime minister of an independent Democratic Republic of the Congo. Concurrent with Girmay's desire to embrace the two political masterminds, an insidious division has nestled itself into the world of the written text. Invisible yet palpable, the unspoken boulder of geography and time prevents Girmay from embracing both men together. Also lurking in the backdrop, a sloppy conflation between ancient Italians and contemporary Europeans potentially adds to the chasm with which Girmay contends. In particular, the imagined phenotype of White Virgil is juxtaposed with Lumumba's Black body.[2] By bringing these two figures together in a stanza, Girmay momentarily circumvents any prejudicial notions. Echoing Girmay's transhistorical scope, this chapter presents an expansive approach to representations of race in the field of Classics. Rather than project the current phenomenon of colour-based race into the past, this chapter opens up the definition of race in Greco-Roman antiquity to encompass a variety of visual and non-visual elements.[3] Careful contextualization of race will broaden modern perceptions of the past. Girmay will no longer have to walk in secret.

The distinction between definitions and representations complicates the landscape of race. Although the former implies objective truth and the latter hints at subjective descriptions, both warrant scrutiny. For, no current scholar can wholly inhabit the collective truths and thoughts of people who lived over two thousand years ago.

Furthermore, contemporary biases (particularly the troubling 'black = slaves in perpetuity' trope) have transported the colour-based category of modern race into the past. Seared into the world's collective consciousness, preconceived notions of Black people have conflated 'definitions' and 'representations' into an amorphous category in which damaging stereotypes run rampant. Lopsided interpretations of race in Greco-Roman antiquity frequently reflect the perspectives of academics rather than the actual subject material.[4] The seeping of these biases into classical scholarship poses striking implications for the academy at large. Unsubstantiated assumptions about the inferiority of black people muffle their plural representations in Greco-Roman antiquity. Greek writers describe black Egyptians, Aithiopians and Indians, but their skin colour is not always the most notable feature of their communities. In fact, any mention of their skin colour is sometimes omitted altogether (Herodotus, *Histories* 3.17–26).[5] A confrontation of these explosive dynamics helps to bolster the capaciousness of the ancient Greco-Roman world.[6]

Drawing inspiration from Ngũgĩ wa Thiong'o's (1986) dismantling of literary tiers, I am deeply invested in demolishing disciplinary hierarchies.[7] In an attempt to spur a horizontal model of knowledge production, this chapter pries apart the concept of race in classical scholarship. Since the disturbing manipulation of skin colour lurks behind any discourse on race, the complicity of Blackness, namely its inexorable relationship with power, and the historicization of black skin colour in ancient Greek literature are central to this discussion. Despite this collision, this chapter treats skin colour as only one site of racial difference in Greco-Roman antiquity. Chromatic distinctions appear in this chapter because they encourage readers to contextualize current distortions of skin colour. Therefore, after examining the chromatic nexus of black and white in classical scholarship, this chapter presents a capacious definition of race that speaks back to anachronistic renditions. An incorporation of visual and non-visual elements into the terminology of 'race' rejects the monolithic assessment of race in Greco-Roman antiquity as synonymous with skin colour.[8] My analysis of episodes from Herodotus' *Histories* (mid-fifth century BCE) and Heliodorus' *Aithiopika* (c. fourth century BCE) demonstrates the efficacy of this new definition in describing the Aithiopians' race. Overall, this exploration of race's contours provides readers with historically sensitive studies of the ancient Greco-Roman world. The reworked vocabulary and analyses in this chapter can benefit scholars who seek new methods for working through the valence of race in other ancient societies.

A brief caveat before this investigation begins: no one can speak with ultimate authority about Greco-Roman antiquity. A number of factors (time, geography, etc.) separate us from the ancient Greco-Roman world. Despite these inadequacies, a responsible study of antiquity is possible. Such a project requires critical self-reflection wherein people simultaneously reflect on and build upon their fraught positionality in the twenty-first century. As part of this reflexive undertaking, my vocabulary choices require close inspection before they can be applied to the past.

DEFINITIONS OF RACE

The prominence of skin colour as the leading determinant of race has a relatively contemporary history, fuelled by the desire of European slaveowners to buttress their myth of superiority during the transatlantic slave trade (K. Hall 1995).[9] This colour-tinged hierarchy continues to haunts the discourse of race in any time period.[10] Even though ancient Greek and Latin literature predate colonial racism, it is far too easy for classicists to overlook race's contentious history and perpetuate lopsided structures of power (Haley 2009). Without interrogating their own position as inheritors of a turbulent archive, they risk creating misinformed conflations of ancient and modern history.

One popular model of interpretation in classical scholarship treats race as a shorthand for skin colour. The landmark publications of Grace Hadley Beardsley (1929) and Frank Snowden Jr (1947, 1948, 1970, 1983) reify this perspective. Beardsley's consistently negative view and Snowden's uniformly positive perception of black skin colour mirror their modern perceptions of Black people.[11] Unlike Snowden's latent desire to upend stratification based on skin colour, Beardsley reinforces anachronistic and negative stereotypes. Throughout her discussion of the 'tribal dances' and 'grotesque depictions' of black people in Greco-Roman antiquity, she refrains from acknowledging the conflation of history present in her research (Beardsley 1929: 111–13).[12] Instead, her prejudicial views suffice as objective evidence to support her argument that Negroes,[13] her terminology for black people in Greco-Roman antiquity, occupied a servile position under Caucasians, her nomenclature for their Greek counterparts. Her projection of a Black–White binary into the past imposes the anachronistic category of Whiteness onto the ancient Greco-Roman world.[14] On the other hand, Snowden vehemently defends Greco-Roman antiquity from any claims of prejudice against black people. As a Black scholar in twentieth-century America, he recognizes the cultural importance denied to members of his community and implicitly strives to exonerate ancient representations of black people from the negative prejudices that contemporary Black people are forced to endure.

Taken together, Beardsley and Snowden both avoid a two-way investigation of blackness that probes the interference of Blackness as well as differential ways of understanding blackness in Greek antiquity. Unaddressed slippage between ancient representations of black people and modern views of Black people has also plagued historians. For instance, in a recent illustration of a sixth-century BCE black-figure Greek *hydria* (water jar) on the cover of Benjamin Isaac's *The Invention of Racism in Classical Antiquity* (2004), a dark-skinned figure violently strangles and tramples upon lighter-hued people who struggle to escape (Figures 1.1 and 1.2). Curiously enough, the original *hydria* on which this image is based depicts a dark-red central figure surrounded by black people. The darkening of the central figure on Isaac's cover perhaps reflects the worn state of the jar's surface or, more disturbingly, misguided assumptions about which contemporary bodies are inherent perpetrators of violence.[15] The artificial lightening of the people around the central figure contributes to this misframing of colour dynamics. In addition, the chromatic alteration suggests a link between non-blackness and victimhood which resonates eerily in the twenty-first century.

As the backbone of modern race, Whiteness exists in opposition to Blackness. The colour polarization falls apart in Greco-Roman antiquity because the valorization of Whiteness, and Whiteness itself, did not yet exist. The semantic distortion of light skin colour to represent an inherent right to power had no valence. Greeks and Romans did not assign power solely based on levels of melanin.[16] Furthermore, the impulse to present race in the ancient Greco-Roman world as a simple binary misrepresents the diverse portrayal of race in Greco-Roman antiquity. Lloyd Thompson's (1989) seminal monograph about the geographical connections between ancient Romans and black

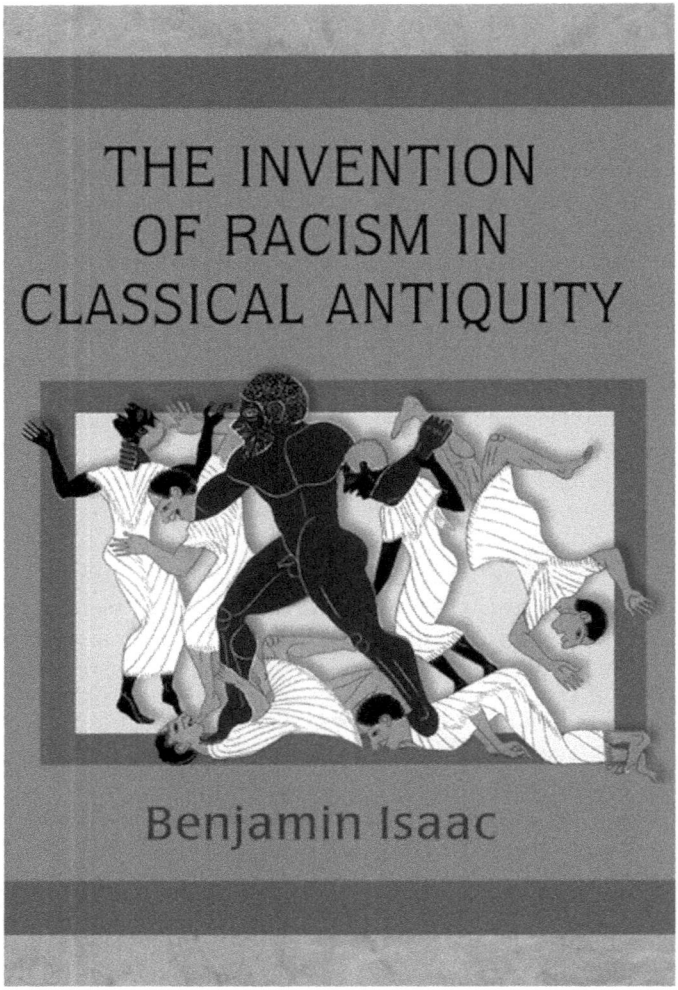

FIGURE 1.1 Cover of Benjamin Isaac's *The Invention of Racism in Classical Antiquity* (2004). © Princeton University Press, 2004.

people helpfully points out that the Romans disparaged many groups; the isolation of one group in order to emphasize particular biases is irresponsible.[17] After the publication of Thompson's *Romans and Blacks* (1989), the discipline of Classics seems to have absolved itself from explicit discourse on skin colour.[18] While a focus solely on skin colour avoids recognition that people had a wide range of opinions about race in Greco-Roman antiquity, complete avoidance of skin colour is also a questionable interpretative move (Kennedy, Roy and Goldman 2013: xiv). Colour was an unstable criterion, not an absent one. Therefore, there remains a need for articulations of race that are both grounded in Greco-Roman antiquity and mindful of modernity.[19] In what follows, my dismissal of a strictly chromatic frame of reference leads to a discussion of various ways that people distinguished each other in Greco-Roman literature.[20]

FIGURE 1.2 Black-figure water jar (hydria) of Hercules, sixth century BCE. © Kunsthistorisches Museum Wien.

(RE)DEFINING RACE

In response to the limited treatment of 'race' in Greco-Roman antiquity, the remainder of this chapter envisions race as a booming industry with a miscellaneous output. Theoretical frameworks are the tools that shape its raw products. Critical race theory helps to point out the unavoidable permutations of 'race' in our twenty-first-century context. Gaining momentum in the 1970s in the wake of the US civil rights movement, critical race theory builds on theories of critical legal studies and radical feminism. In its ability to function as a complex methodology that cuts across a wide range of identities, critical race theory has broken down crude polarizing boundaries. By demanding direct engagement with the present world, this framework fosters a transhistorical confrontation that benefits any study of the past.[21]

In this vein, Christina Sharpe's lexicon of 'anarranging' (arrange anew) informs my proposed definition of 'race' as it applies to Greco-Roman antiquity (2016: 75–7, looking back to Spillers 2003: 209; and Moten 2003: 1). Building on and beyond current notions of this term, I delineate 'race' as an outward-facing category that allows people to categorize and essentialize others. This category is entirely subject to the perceptions of others. In determining someone's race, people's preconceived notions sometimes collide with their perceptions. My rendition of race includes both visual elements, such as beauty and skin colour, and non-visual features, for instance longevity and language. The unusual pairing of seemingly fixed and variable features illustrates my fluid approach to race in Greco-Roman antiquity. This open-ended category generates radical groupings and theorizations of communities.

Conversely, 'identity' refers to people's self-ascribed definition of themselves. People dictate their own identities and therefore can change their identity at will. Outside forces can influence such changes, but people retain control of their identity. To put this in other words, 'race' denotes people's role within the public sphere while their self-articulated 'identity' offers more private insight. Taken apart, each of these terms enables me to toggle between outside perspectives, via race, and individual perspectives, via identity. Taken together, these indispensable constructs underscore the diverse outlooks at play in Greco-Roman antiquity. More capacious than our present vocabulary, these overlapping terms invite readers to delve into a world in which race and identity collide as characters struggle to equate their conception of themselves with others' views of them.

DEFINING RACISM

Etymologically linked to race, 'racism' warrants explicit attention. In the twenty-first century, race and racism are inextricably linked. Critical race theorists Karen E. Fields and Barbara J. Fields helpfully delineate race as a principal unit of racism. They define racism as a brutally convenient social practice of applying a double standard, 'the missing step between someone's physical appearance and an invidious outcome' (Fields and Fields [2012] 2014: 27). As they disentangle the logical hopscotch associated with these terms in different contexts, they wisely caution against conflating the two. Otherwise, the transformation of racism into race, deemed racecraft in Fields and Fields's terminology, exonerates perpetrators of racism and focuses attention solely on the racialized subject.[22]

Such careful demarcation of 'racism' has been muddled in classical scholarship. In his attempt to pinpoint the root of modern racism, Benjamin Isaac identifies its ancient referent as 'proto-racism', a loaded term of his own coining (2004).[23] Using copious quotations from a wide range of ancient sources, he asserts that present-day racism has its roots in the ancient Greco-Roman world. Isaac's passing remarks about black people in Greco-Roman antiquity further reflect the challenges of his terminology. Although 'proto-racism' has no colour bar, Isaac dismisses black people in Greco-Roman antiquity as fixedly inferior (2004: 49–50). This analysis reinforces history's dangerous manipulation of skin colour; it reeks of racecraft. That is, instead of focusing on the content of available source material, Isaac reproduces current assumptions about the perceived marginality of people based on skin colour. His blurred slippage between Black people in modernity and black people in Greco-Roman antiquity encourages an inaccurate timeline of oppression. Greco-Roman antiquity predates Whiteness, upon which racism is based, and therefore precludes the coexistence of Greco-Roman antiquity and racism. Especially in light of Isaac's chromatically polarizing book cover, a comprehensive approach to representations of black people in Greco-Roman antiquity would have provided important contextualization. Spanning from the fifth century BCE to the fourth century CE, writers describe black people who constantly unsettle rigid interpretations assigned to them. To name a few, Egyptians in Aeschylus' *Suppliant Women*, Indians in Herodotus' *Histories* (3.101) and Aithiopians in Strabo's *Geography* (17.1.54) all demand that their readers rethink preconceived notions about black people.

Isaac's repackaging of racism, a modern social practice, into an ancient product ('proto-racism') presumably allows his readers to escape the contentiousness of racism in the twenty-first century. But even as he pointedly avoids applying 'racism' to Greco-

Roman antiquity, he reinscribes problematic ideologies when he proposes that the antecedent of racism somehow sidestepped colour-based discrimination. Isaac insists that racism is based on discriminatory practices designed to perpetuate uneven hierarchies of power without addressing his oversight regarding skin colour (2004: 37). Moreover, his mapping of a prototype of 'racism' onto the past inadvertently lends temporal legitimacy to the violent acts that racist perpetrators committed against Black people from the fifteenth century onwards. Nonetheless, racism was built from violent archives of colour-based inequality; it cannot be repurposed to study the past.[24] That being said, Isaac's vocabulary presents a useful warning about the limitations of importing current vocabulary into studies of Greco-Roman antiquity. Therefore, this chapter treats the concept of racism as a phenomenon of reception, rather than a datum about ancient Greece and Rome.

Pushing back against the reduction of race and racism in the context of Greco-Roman antiquity, the next two sections apply my proposed definition of race to Herodotus' Aithiopian episode (3.17–26) and Heliodorus' birthmark episode (*Aethiopika* 10.12–16). Herodotus provides a five-pronged model of the Aithiopians' race that encompasses visual and non-visual elements: longevity, geography, food, physical attributes and language. Heliodorus' three-pronged paradigm of the Aithiopians' race incorporates parentage, external visual proofs and skin colour. Through these episodes, Herodotus and Heliodorus skillfully highlight the rich encounters that can occur when race and identity collide.

RACE IN GREEK ANTIQUITY: HERODOTUS

Herodotus' nine-book *Histories* relays information about the events that occur before and during the Greco-Persian Wars (492–449 BCE). Additionally, Herodotus recounts numerous digressions about people and places beyond his homeland of Ionia (Figure 1.3).[25] In one of his stories, he describes the Persian ruler Cambyses II's military expedition against the Carthaginians, Ammonians and Aithiopians.

At the outset of this Aithiopian episode (3.17–26), it becomes clear that the Aithiopians stand in a category of their own. Unlike the Carthaginians and Ammonians who lack descriptive adjectives, the Aithiopians are 'long-lived' people (3.17). Before Cambyses assembles a group of men to travel to Aithiopia, the Aithiopians' semi-divine status is an essentializing feature of their race.[26] Geography is another defining element of the Aithiopians' race: they live south of Libya near the Indian Ocean (3.17). Although Herodotus cannot pinpoint the Aithiopians' homeland, he geographically situates them to the best of his ability. Furthermore, his reiteration of the rumour that Aithiopians possess the Table of the Sun, a magical meadow with an endless supply of meat, contributes to the Aithiopians' race. That is, the presence of this meaty bounty enables outsiders to identify Aithiopians.[27] What is more, Herodotus offers brief visual access to the Aithiopians' race when he explains that the Aithiopians are said to be the strongest, most beautiful people (3.20). Previously privy only to the Aithiopians' location and food source, Herodotus' readers can now visualize this group of people. Together with longevity, geography and a perennial supply of meat, this visual element becomes part of the Aithiopians' race.

To satisfy his curiosity about the Aithiopians, Cambyses sends the Egyptian Fish-eaters to spy on the Aithiopians in his stead. The Fish-eaters travel from the Elephantine region of

The World According to Herodotus
H. G. Wells, The Outline of History (New York, NY: The Macmillan Company, 1921)
Downloaded from Maps ETC, on the web at http://etc.usf.edu/maps [map #03605]

FIGURE 1.3 Herodotus' map of the world. © University of South Florida.

Egypt to northern Egypt where Cambyses temporarily resides, then south to Aithiopia and finally back to northern Egypt (and presumably home to the Elephantine region after giving their report) with ease, while even one-third of this distance becomes an impassibly protracted trek for Cambyses as he prepares his under-equipped and ill-planned military expedition to Aithiopia. This lack of consistency reflects the instability of geography as an element of race. The Aithiopians' location is forever out of Cambyses' reach.[28] His linguistic limitation also complicates his mission in that he needs the Fish-eaters to communicate with the Aithiopians on his behalf.[29] The Fish-eaters' fluency in the Aithiopians' language marks another element of the Aithiopians' race: a specific linguistic register. A seemingly minor marker of race, language is crucial for interpersonal interactions. Without knowledge of the Aithiopians' language, Cambyses stands little chance of confirming whether his other predictions about the Aithiopians' race coincide with reality.

As the epitome of exchange between the two groups, the Aithiopian king learns more about the ways of the Persian people while the Fish-eaters double as ethnographers of Persia and eager inquirers of Aithiopian customs:

> The Aithiopian king asked what the king [of Persia] ate and what was the maximum age a Persian man lived. The Fish-eaters replied that the king ate bread, and they described how wheat was grown, and they said that eighty years is set as the maximum extent of a man's life …. When the Fish-eaters asked the Aithiopian king about his people's lives and diet, he replied that many of them lived to be 120 years old, with some even surpassing this age, and that they ate boiled meat and drank milk.
>
> (3.22–3)

In this passage, each group is eager to learn about the other. The reorientation of foreignness makes it difficult to disentangle which group is the norm against which all others are measured.[30] Four layers interact as an Ionian Greek writer describes a Persian ruler who sends Egyptians to speak with and learn about Aithiopians.[31] These gradations reshape the category of 'foreigner' in unpredictable ways; the information about the Aithiopians has passed through three hands, each presumably affecting the end result.[32] This new, four-layered model does not necessarily eliminate the idea of 'native' and 'foreigner'. This model instead highlights the intersubjective understanding of different groups in Herodotus' story.[33] The Aithiopians and Fish-eaters implicitly agree on a shared template for race with their reciprocal line of questioning. The Aithiopian king reduces the Persians' race to longevity and food, and the Fish-eaters apply the same metric to the Aithiopians' race.

Following Cambyses' deceitful orders, the Fish-eaters bring colourful gifts as tokens of friendship for the Aithiopian king. The Aithiopian king is underwhelmed when the Fish-eaters deliver a purple cloak, a gold necklace and bracelets, an alabaster of myrrh and deep red wine (3.20). The vivid colours of Cambyses' presents offer the only chromatic insight in this episode.[34] The absence of colour-based vocabulary in relation to the Aithiopians' appearance suggests that the skin colour of Aithiopians was so well known that it did not require repeating. The etymology of 'Aithiopia' provides the only clues about their chromatic appearance.[35] That being said, Herodotus' focus on a wide range of colours in this episode destabilizes any reductive reading of colour as the sole racial marker for a group of people. From Herodotus' perspective, traits other than skin colour determine the Aithiopians' race.[36]

Through the reports and actions of the Aithiopians, Herodotus reveals the uncanny slippage between the ways that Cambyses views the Aithiopians (i.e. their race) and the ways that the Aithiopians view themselves (their identity). Race's non-visual components (longevity, geography and language) and visual components (food, physical appearance) work in tandem. In addition, this intersubjective portrayal of two non-Greek communities, from whom Herodotus' readers learn about distant communities, refutes the salience of 'the foreigner' as a stable construct.

RACE IN GREEK ANTIQUITY: HELIODORUS

Heliodorus' *Aithiopika* offers another pivotal point from which to explore race in the ancient Greco-Roman world. In his ten-book novel, the *Aithiopika*, Heliodorus builds a full story around Herodotus' Aithiopians.[37] Writing at a time when Rome is the new superpower of the Mediterranean (fourth century CE), Heliodorus nonetheless underscores the resurgence of interest in fifth-century BCE Greek literature.[38] His readers follow the peripatetic journey of Charicleia, an Aithiopian princess exposed at birth because of the dissonance between her white skin and her parents' black skin. The source of her skin colour derives from a painting of a white Andromeda (the archetype for Aithiopian royalty) that her mother, Queen Persinna, viewed during conception.[39] This transmission of colour via sight suggests that colour is a weak signifier of identity. The depiction of Andromeda as white also disallows a direct correlation between black skin colour and the Aithiopian race. Despite the ease with which Charicleia's environment affects her skin colour, it holds insurmountable importance to her father, King Hydaspes. Persinna fears that Charicleia's skin colour will cause Hydaspes to question her fidelity because of his reliance on black skin as a defining characteristic of identity and race. Due to this precarious situation, Charicleia grows up with a host of fathers in Aithiopia, Greece and Egypt before finally returning home to her biological parents.

Heliodorus prevents Charicleia and his readers from learning about Charicleia's royal lineage until well into the novel (4.8–13). After suffering many trials and tribulations, Charicleia arrives in her homeland and faces a community who is still unaware of her parentage. In a desperate bid to prove her Aithiopian identity and thereby avoid becoming a sacrificial victim, she offers an array of external evidence to her father, including a ribbon onto which Persinna wrote about the heart-wrenching decision to expose her daughter and a royal ring that belonged to Hydaspes. Even after Hydaspes, the supreme arbiter of Charicleia's race, sees the portrait of white Andromeda, which Persinna looked at during conception, he stubbornly refuses to accept her race as Aithiopian (10.12–16). He still clings to colour as the sole determinant of Charicleia's race. In his eyes, white skin colour remains antithetical to the race of his fellow Aithiopians.

Hydaspes' assessment of Charicleia's race does not coincide with other characters' flexible evaluations in the *Aithiopika*. Namely, Sisimithres, the royal gymnosophist (wise man), believes Charicleia's claims. In his attempt to nuance Hydaspes' resolute conflation of skin colour and race, Sisimithres tells him that a wise man does not judge people by their appearance (10.10.4). Sisimithres recognizes that appearances can be misleading, a logical inference for a man who knew that Charicleia was Aithiopian even though her skin colour was different from her parents.[40] Through Sisimithres, the reader recognizes the instability of colour in this novel. That is, the convergence of Charicleia's race and identity need not depend on her skin colour.

Unlike those who have accepted that Charicleia's race transcends skin colour, Hydaspes relies heavily on her skin colour as an element of her race. Recognizing the inflexibility of Hydaspes' perception, Sisimithres delivers a final piece of evidence: a black birthmark on Charicleia's arm (10.15.2). After Charicleia bares her arm to show her father the mark that had been there since birth, he finally acknowledges that she is Aithiopian. From this revelation scene, Hydaspes treats blackness as the most powerful marker of race. Tokens of proof, such as the ribbon and ring, are insufficient. Even the painting of Andromeda whose central figure bears an uncanny resemblance to Charicleia does not convince him. His reticence suggests that black is the only colour he associates with Aithiopians. Once he sees Charicleia's black birthmark, he is able to draw a direct connection from his black body to his daughter's. This small mark wields great power, in that it enables Charicleia's race to coincide with Hydaspes' identity.

This novel, the earliest example in extant Greek literature of a plot in which black skin colour constitutes cultural privilege, yields competing treatments of race that eventually complement each other. Through his flexible characterization of Aithiopians, Heliodorus has revealed that colour is a negotiable marker of race. Colour has the potential to denote one's precise origins, but this is not a prerequisite for its presence.[41] Heliodorus' complex convergence of skin colour, visual proofs, race and identity provide a fluid site in which to unsettle boundaries and question perceptions. Here, readers can interrogate deep-set notions of what it means to identify and be identified as Aithiopian (Cioffi 2013: 2 and 173; for additional discussion of Charicleia's identity in Heliodorus, see Mac Sweeney and Haley in this volume).

CONCLUSION

In sum, Herodotus' and Heliodorus' Aithiopians undermine a unidimensional reading of their race. They force their distant neighbours to negotiate a shared space with them and reorient preconceived notions about them. More generally, Greek literature encourages readers to tease out and examine intercultural nuances (Doody 1997: 105). Both ancient and contemporary subjects are part of a dynamic literary landscape. Fresh perspectives that correct myopic generalizations and partial disavowals of skin colour enrich our understanding of the past. Such diverse assessments nudge the study of the ancient Greco-Roman world towards a deterritorialized and diasporic future.[42] This prospective reality requires constant confrontation of existing hierarchies within and outside of the ancient Greco-Roman world. Girmay has pointed us in the right direction; Vergil and Lumumba are excellent partners for this revolutionary project.

CHAPTER TWO

Race, Environment, Culture

JOSEPH SKINNER

'The word race ... forces us to confront our all-too frequent idealization of classical antiquity, and to view more critically a variety of Greek and Roman ideologies and practices, violent facets of the ancient world that can seem too sanitized when called something else' (McCoskey 2012: 31).

Before attempting to unpick the complicated alignments of race, environment and culture in antiquity we must first step back to consider not only the workings of culture more broadly but also the bases upon which it is now appropriate to speak of race or racism in a period prior to the nineteenth century. Although notoriously difficult to define, 'culture' is best understood as the shared conceptual maps which provide groups and individuals with common points of reference and a sense of the way these same points are connected, whether singly or as clusters of ideas or associations – take, for example, ideas about 'foreignness', 'barbarity' or 'the Orient'. These shared frameworks of intelligibility can display considerable variation whether at a community or even an individual level, whilst still providing the bases for meanings to be made. They are also subject to change – as opposed to remaining static, bounded entities – due to their undergoing a continual process of renegotiation and contestation. This makes them difficult to access and susceptible to distortion by later generations who cannot help but view them through lenses which reflect contemporary concerns or knowledge of events in the more recent past, be that the horrors of transatlantic slavery, the Holocaust or the history of racial violence and discrimination in countries such as the United States and South Africa.[1]

A particularly pertinent example of this phenomenon can be found in scholarly debate surrounding an early medical treatise on the relationship between human nature (and culture more broadly) and the environment. Lisl Walsh's analysis of the way modern stereotypes may have infiltrated W. H. S. Jones's Loeb translation of a passage from the Hippocratic *Airs, Waters, Places* (23.19–30) is intriguing both because it offers a sobering insight into the way linguistic nuances can be introduced to a text, whether subconsciously or not, and because her calling attention to the way racist attitudes and subconscious bias

---

I am greatly indebted to audiences in Glasgow, Newcastle and Buffalo for their insightful comments which have done much to improve the end result. Tom Harrison was kind enough to allow me access to unpublished materials long before they appeared in print as well as providing guidance and support at the drop of a hat. I have also benefited from conversations with Vicky Manolopoulou and the volume's editor, Denise McCoskey, whose unswerving patience has played a major role in insuring that this chapter made it into print.

have permeated scholarship, past and present, is itself rooted in historical experience, albeit a very different one (for more on *Airs, Waters, Places*, see Kaufman in this volume).²

Rather than addressing antiquity in its entirety this chapter focuses upon a single – albeit far from homogenous – group, namely the Greek-speaking communities scattered throughout the Mediterranean world. This decision might at first appear to run counter to the more globalized and pluralistic outlook that has become increasingly characteristic of ancient world studies³ were it not for the pivotal role which the Greek discourse surrounding the barbarian has played in shaping Western ideas surrounding identity and race. Indeed, scholarly discussion of Greek identity has too often perpetuated the Western discourse on and domination of the Oriental 'barbarian' – and other subaltern groups more generally – by aligning itself, whether consciously or otherwise, with the (highly privileged) views of the adult citizen male.⁴ It is only by relinquishing this top-down perspective that we can fully appreciate the way questions of race and identity were constantly unfolding in an ongoing play of power and knowledge.⁵ This is of course far easier to state than to put into practice not least because the results of such enquiries are often far less conclusive than we would like. It is surely better to attempt this rather more tentative and essentially open-ended approach, however, than risk doing the Greeks' representational work for them by simply accepting the monolithic opposition between Greek and barbarian, citizen and slave, as a fait accompli.⁶

Whilst it might not be possible to recapture what might collectively be referred to as subaltern voices per se, those marginalized and largely mute individuals who were systematically disenfranchised, coerced and exploited on a daily basis, we can still reframe the debate surrounding race and racism in such a way as to acknowledge the historical experiences of those on the receiving end of the countless acts of discrimination that underpinned relations of inequality which existed throughout Greek society, albeit with almost infinite variations depending on the period, place or context.⁷

'FINDING' RACE IN ANTIQUITY

When approaching the relationship between race, environment and culture in Greek thought and society more generally we need to find a way of taking this shifting and highly variegated backdrop into account in a manner that is sensitive to questions of power and agency. Creating an elaborate pastiche of all the ideas that can be ascribed to the 'Greeks' in general, regardless of the time or context, and then comparing these with modern notions as to what does or does not constitute racist stereotyping or racial thinking is inherently risky insofar as it places a disproportionate weight upon textual evidence, whether in the form of stray fragments or asides or material of a more broadly 'ethnographic' or 'scientific' nature such as Herodotus's *Histories* or *Airs, Waters, Places*.⁸ Comparisons between textual representations of non-Greek barbarians and the 'scientific' writings of modernity that used classificatory schemas to delineate physiological differences between supposedly superior and inferior races risk a degree of circularity when the latter are so reliant upon thought patterns that derive from antiquity (i.e. the work of Hippocrates, Aristotle and others).⁹ There are also potential drawbacks to our extrapolating from a dataset which is so heavily skewed towards particular regions or communities at the expense of others (e.g. Athens and, to a somewhat lesser extent, Ionia).

Our tendency to associate racial thinking with scientific theories surrounding genetic difference also merits careful consideration. The degree to which this association has become entrenched can arguably be attributed to knowledge of the manner in which such ideas would ultimately manifest themselves in National Socialist policies of racial hygiene. The horrifying consequences of the latter are seared onto our collective consciousness to such a degree that it has become extremely difficult to dissociate race or racism from 'science'. Whilst we are willing to acknowledge the existence of prejudice and bigotry in pretextual, non-scientific environments, all attempts to detect racism itself are either deemed entirely null or subject to substantial caveats due to the fact that 'science' itself is held to be absent. This is perhaps a mistake insofar as science itself was only ever a tool or marker of difference, as Stuart Hall has argued when discussing the cultural function of science within human cultural systems:

> The point I'm making is it is not science as such, but whatever is in the discourse of a culture, which grounds the truth about human diversity, which unlocks the secret of the relations between nature and culture. Which unties the puzzling fact of human difference, which matters. And what matters is not that they contain the scientific truth about difference, but that they function foundationally in the discourse of racial difference. They fix and secure what else otherwise cannot be fixed or secured. They warrant and guarantee the truth of differences, which they discursively construct.
>
> (Jhally 1997: 12–13)

The Greeks' discourse surrounding identity, culture and difference was for a long time thought to be grounded in the 'scientific' prose descriptions of foreign peoples which emerged during the late sixth to early fifth century BCE. Whilst the original impetus for these early accounts has been widely debated they were assumed to have made a significant contribution to the pool of knowledge and ideas into which the Attic tragedian Aeschylus would subsequently dip for inspiration when writing his *Persians*.[10] The assumption that ethnographic *prose* was a necessary precursor for the 'invention' of the barbarian stereotype and, by extension, Greek ideas of race and racism has since been qualified by research demonstrating that ethnographic discourse can in fact be traced back as far as our sources allow, transcending media or genre (Skinner 2012).[11] Whilst the emergence of prose accounts of foreign peoples might have caused a significant shift in register in terms of ongoing discourses surrounding culture and difference, it would be naive to assume that they were not preceded by other ways of marking difference that were equally authoritative and thus persuasive. In what follows I will argue that ideas surrounding environment and culture had a pivotal role to play in these processes from the outset, albeit on a rather more ad hoc basis, and that the 'truth' about difference could just as easily be grounded in epic and lyric poetry (notably Homer and Pindar).

It is now high time that I clarified what I mean by race and, by extension, racism and why the use of these terms is not just justifiable but also desirable in this context. Modern scholarship has typically defined racism as the use of an imagined construct, race, to rank groups hierarchically according to characteristics which are predetermined, whether due to environmental or hereditary factors (Isaac 2006: 32–48; see also Tuplin 1999, 2007a; Isaac 2004). In contrast, my working definitions of race/racism are framed rather more expansively in the light of Stuart Hall's argument that it is the discursive construction of difference which matters rather than the precise means by which human diversity is *explained* (i.e. science) (Jhally 1997: 12–13). If one is content to adopt this social constructionist approach then race can be construed relatively broadly as a way of thinking about human difference which is capable of generating the 'very potent social reality of racism, discrimination, [and] racial identities' when combined with one or more types of structural inequality (e.g. in a modern context, those of colonialism, class and gender; Wade 2002: 2). Although 'race' still consists of the arbitrary categorization of someone as 'other' based upon ascribed criteria – typically environment or culture-related – 'racism' can be construed in equally general terms to denote instances in which these ascribed characteristics form the basis for prejudicial attitudes or actions that perpetuate relations of inequality, whether directly or indirectly.[12] As such, an association with the institution of slavery becomes all but inevitable since servile status was by far the greatest bar upon self-determination or opportunity that antiquity had to offer.[13]

Whilst a recent study of the relationship between classical Greek ethnography and the slave trade has broken exciting new ground by suggesting that 'the institution of slavery was a major factor in fostering a discourse on the differences among foreign peoples' (Harrison 2019: 37) and that 'Greek ethnographic accounts were to a significant extent informed by, and mediated through, the experience of slavery' (43),[14] the analytical focus has primarily been on the ideas and stereotypes circulating amongst the slave-owning classes or those involved in their procurement such as the overall suitability of particular ethnic groups for specific roles as opposed to seeking to assess the day-to-day impact of any resulting acts of classification and whether these constituted racism per se.[15] What I am particularly concerned with in this context is the circumstances under which such discourses first gained traction together with the degree to which ideas of culture and environment might have fed into or otherwise shaped these processes.

Whilst discussions of why, when and how discourses of race and racial difference first came to converge with servile status typically focus upon external contact with people of a different outlook and culture – often resulting in the singling out of a particular historical moment as a catalyst for either wholesale ethnogenesis or the point at which hitherto nascent ideas of Hellenicity ('Greekness') crystallized into something far more concrete – the significance of socio-economic relations both within and between emerging urban communities still merits our attention despite the fact that scholarly opinion has since moved away from the idea, championed by Moses Finley, that the emergence of slave societies was inextricably linked to that of the free citizen (Finley 1959).[16]

One factor which these emerging city-state cultures shared in common was the fact that they were all variously predicated upon a distinction between members of a citizen community and its designated 'outsiders', those considered somehow marginal, foreign or alien (see Blok 2005). The emergence of these citizen communities as an (effectively) elite culture occurred by increments and with varying results throughout the Greek world, however, it has typically been associated with the rolling back of systems of debt-bondage and other forms of exploitation which had previously seen the rural and urban poor reduced to servile status or something pretty close to the same due to their having to work off debts upon their person (see e.g. Wrenhaven 2013: 2–3).

Although markedly Athenocentric in nature (insofar as it is wholly reliant upon what little we know regarding Solon's reforms) such changes were for a long time assumed to provide a credible explanation for the emergence of a slave society despite clear evidence for slave-taking and the fact that slave workers appear in sizeable numbers in Homeric epic (Lewis 2018: 107–17). It does not, however, detract from the fact that attempts to exploit the lower classes were increasingly resisted and eventually overturned during a period in which a sense of wider, Panhellenic identity was also emerging. It has long been argued that it was this awareness of a wider Hellenic community which created the at least notional bar on the enslavement of fellow Hellenes, although with some notable exceptions – there being numerous examples in which entire populations were marked out for exploitation by their immediate neighbours using mechanisms which endured for centuries (Lakonian and Messenian helots; Thessaly and Crete being the most celebrated and well-studied examples).[17] At the same time, the demand for cheap labour continued to rise making it increasingly likely that it would have to be imported whether in the form of itinerant wage labour or slaves. Eventually, the growing availability of slaves meant that even citizens of comparatively modest means could apparently afford to maintain an average of two to three slaves to assist them in activities ranging from craft production to agriculture or household tasks.[18]

Whilst the Athenocentric nature of this evidence should again be acknowledged, the fact that slaves were not entitled to the same rights and protections as members of the communities within which they were working was surely a universal since this would otherwise delegitimize their exploitation whether by the state or free citizens. In order for this to become the norm we have to envisage some sort of process whereby groups and individuals were increasingly conditioned to view outsiders and eventually all non-Greeks as somehow deserving of enslavement from the outset in contrast to their fellow citizens or Hellenes in general.

The classification of those outside the civic and wider Hellenic community as inferior or barbarian required a lot of cultural work in order to rationalize this shift in habitus. Being classified as an outsider (and therefore inferior) left an individual vulnerable to coercion and/or exploitation as a result of their being enslaved.[19] During the course of time, the blanket distinction between 'insider' and 'outsider' would come to be more or less synonymous with the (equally generic) distinction between Hellene and 'barbarian' (see Rosivach 1999).[20] As such, it provided a secure ideological basis for the stark inequalities of power, wealth and agency which underpinned social relations in many, if not all, of the communities which relied on a growing number of slaves to undertake a wide range of activities, even if slave labour was not the principle generator of wealth in all cases.

Although by no means solely responsible for the emergence of the Greek-Barbarian polarity, the day-to-day presence of slaves must have played a significant role in shaping the way foreigners were both represented and perceived more broadly insofar as it would have accounted for the vast majority of the daily contacts between the (free) inhabitants of Greek *poleis*, together with other social groupings, and those variously defined as 'foreign'.[21] The rationale for this asymmetrical relationship between the free and unfree had to be learnt and, to some greater or lesser degree, internalized by the groups and individuals whose lives we study.

Although rarely articulated explicitly in prose, or with such meticulous detail, the ideas we encounter in Aristotle's theorization of natural slavery[22] must have been widespread from a comparatively early stage in order for contemporaries to become habituated to the day-to-day presence of individuals stripped of their agency even if it was not immediately clear who occupied this category – as is perhaps implied by the frustrated grumblings of the author still referred to as the 'Old Oligarch':

> [I]f it were customary for a slave (or metic or freedman) to be struck by one who is free, you would often hit an Athenian citizen by mistake on the assumption that he was a slave. For the people there are no better dressed than the slaves and metics, nor are they any more handsome.
>
> ([Xen.], *Constitution of the Athenians* 1.10, trans. Loeb)[23]

Whilst the Athenian practice of applying the same label to all resident aliens makes it impossible to discern the relative proportion of Greeks to non-Greeks within the population, it has recently been suggested that metic status carried servile connotations by virtue of the fact that many of Athens' metics were freed slaves and that metics were particularly vulnerable to re-enslavement as a result of non-payment of fines (see Akrigg 2015).[24] Such an association may at least be inferred if we take Xenophon's comments to be representative of an elite and decidedly elitist perspective, namely the idea that asking all but the most wealthy metics to perform military service was undesirable on the grounds that it interfered with their ability to earn a livelihood and exposed young Athenian males to a variety of 'eastern' barbarians:

> For in them [resident aliens] we have one of the very best sources of revenue, in my opinion, inasmuch as they are self-supporting and, so far from receiving payment for the many services they render to states, they contribute by paying a special tax. I think that we should study their interests sufficiently, if we relieved them of the duties that seem to impose a certain measure of disability on the resident alien without conferring any benefit on the state, and also of the obligation to serve in the infantry along with the citizens. Apart from the personal risk, it is no small thing to leave their trades and their private affairs. The state itself too would gain if the citizens served in the ranks together, and no longer found themselves in the same company with Lydians, Phrygians, Syrians, and barbarians of all sorts, of whom a large part of our alien population consists.
>
> (Xenophon, *Ways and Means* 2.2–4, trans. Loeb)[25]

The degree to which this is representative of treatment meted out to resident aliens in other communities of course is open to question, it being implied by the Old Oligarch that Athens was more or less unique in this in terms of the 'equality' (ἰσηγορίαν ... ἐποιήσαμεν) it afforded metics and slaves – although the claim itself clearly reflects a top-down perspective ([Xen.], *Constitution of the Athenians* 1.12; cf. Thucydides 7.63.3 in relation to metics).

Xenophon's comments should also serve as a reminder both that opinion regarding the appropriate treatment of 'foreigners' and aliens would have been far from uniform even within individual communities and that precisely who counted as an outright barbarian (in contrast to the more acceptable form of alien) would have varied markedly depending upon geographical and temporal factors. Whereas the stereotypical elements of the 'Scythian' rider costume were either employed or invoked in a variety of different contexts in Athens, whether as a uniform for public slaves entrusted with upholding law and order, in vase-painting (symposia, warrior-arming, departure and combat scenes) or sculpture, a very different set of usages and associations appear to have been at play in Olbia in the North Pontic region, where individual citizens appear to have donned 'Scythian' costume as a matter of course whether during military operations (the Leoxos Stele) or whilst out riding in the hinterland (Dio Chrysostom, *Orations* 36.7).[26]

To study racism in antiquity is to examine the systems of representation that served to either justify or explain actions which reproduced social inequality within the city-state as much as interactions between these same communities and their non-Greek neighbours, real or imagined. Precisely how this worked in practice is far from clear, not least because we have no way of recapturing the verbal exchanges which made up the primary mode of day-to-day communication, whether in the hustle and bustle of public spaces, crowded workshops or the street,[27] or within the confines of the *oikos*. Our collective inability to access these unrecorded utterances leaves us grasping at straws in attempting to align disparate bodies of evidence in order to determine whether they expound a coherent set of theories surrounding race and racial difference. Like verbal communication, they both fed into and helped constitute wider systems for the circulation of meaning. Often they reference ideas relating to nature or the environment and culture for reasons that we will explore in due course, however, the relationship between these categories was never fixed in a single, overarching system.

There will of course be those who object to this refusal to distinguish between what is often referred to as chauvinism or xenophobia in the ancient world and modern ideas of race/racism on the grounds that this places excessive weight upon modern sensitives (e.g. political correctness, decolonizing or the Black Lives Matter movement) at the expense of analytical precision and is thus methodologically unsound.[28] It might equally be argued, however, that modern scholarship has allowed itself to become unduly preoccupied by the question as to whether the Greeks subscribed to a modern scientific understanding of race for far too long. Whilst it is widely accepted that the belief that the Greeks were in all cases superior to non-Greek barbarians legitimized the systematic exploitation of all foreigners as slaves,[29] scholarship on this topic has tended to assume that the Greeks need to have subscribed to a (single) racial ideology or to have both harboured and acted upon prejudices against those of different colour/appearance in a manner that was systematic in order for them to be considered racist.[30] The most forthright (but still noticeably guarded) is Benjamin Isaac's argument that we can identify signs of proto-racism in cases where groups are arranged hierarchically according to immutable criteria (as opposed, for example, to cultural or environmental factors which might be subject to change).[31]

To adopt such a narrow approach is arguably letting the Greeks as a whole off the hook as Tom Harrison has recently argued.[32] Although resolutely humane in outlook, modern scholarship has remained wedded to stock ideas as to what constitutes racism or racist behaviour for far too long (the author included). The bar is invariably set far too high as a result, making it impossible to envisage a situation in which racism or racist attitudes could be ascribed to the Greeks in general.[33] The contrast between our willingness to 'call out' racism in contemporary society (at least where other people's actions are concerned) and the sort of special pleading which takes place on behalf of the Greeks could not be starker.[34] The expectation that any racial ideology should be consistent or universal is a further case in point: if the Greeks were to be indicted as racists or harbouring racist views – as opposed to being chauvinists or xenophobes[35] – it would be on the strength of a preponderance of similar utterances/textual evidence and iconographic depictions of non-Greeks rather than isolated incidents.[36] This is arguably based on one or more flawed premises: that racism should perforce be systematic and rational (characteristics not typically exhibited by racists themselves) and that an overall paucity of surviving sources which might easily be described as racist is enough to *disprove* the existence of racism. Instead, a seemingly isolated derogatory comment on a Janus vase from Akanthos, 'I am the most beautiful Eronossa' and 'Timyllos is beautiful like this face', or rhyta depicting boys being devoured by Nile crocodiles, which were produced first in the Athenian workshop of Sotades before the design was taken up by south Italian potters, can be written off as either exceptional or rare as opposed to providing substance to the claim that the Greeks harboured racist or pejorative attitudes towards (in this case) those whom they called 'Ethiopians' (Figure 2.1).[37]

Finally, there is a widespread tendency to assume that historical sources represent an end result as opposed to being part of a process through which meaning itself was

FIGURE 2.1 Terracotta rhyton depicting a crocodile devouring a Black youth, *c.* 350–300 BCE. © Album/Alamy Stock Photo.

constructed. Take, for example, the way in which the Boeotian Apollonides was summarily denounced and expelled from the Greek camp for having advocated a point of view that was disagreeable to Xenophon and his fellow captains. In response to Apollonides' suggestion that the Greeks make overtures to Artaxerxes, Xenophon suggests that he be stripped of his rank and loaded with bags, it being implied that he is no better than a servant/slave (σκεύη ἀναθέντας ὡς τοιούτῳ χρῆσθαι). The deciding factor, noted by Agasias from Stymphalos, was that he had both his ears bored 'like a Lydian' (Xenophon, *Anabasis* 3.1.30–2; see Harman 2013; Vlassopoulos 2013b).[38] The practice of boring one's ears is a prime example of the way cultural traits could be cited to signal 'barbarity', however, this needed to be both identified and flagged as such first by Agasias (assuming the tale is indeed based in fact) and then by Xenophon when writing his *Anabasis*.

Both here and elsewhere we should be sensitive to the degree to which representation is inextricably linked to questions of power. Precisely who had the power to produce and circulate these meanings/representations can only be speculated in most cases. Agency would appear to reside overwhelmingly with the adult male citizen – there being only rare incidences in which traces of subaltern voices or the entirely voiceless are preserved, for example traditions ascribed to Aesop or the slave boy Lesis who wrote a letter to his parents pleading that they come and set him free from his abuser (Agora II, 1702, Side A).[39] Finally, and most poignantly, we have the unceremonial burial of a woman who died during childbirth before her baby had fully emerged from the womb. Both she and the dead infant were simply thrown into a pit in a necropolis in the Phaleron Delta (see Papadopoulou 2017: 163).[40] Whilst it cannot of course be ruled out that the woman in question was an impoverished citizen or metic, the casual disposal of both her and her child are more plausibly interpreted as an all too common occurrence at a time when lack of medical knowledge meant that the risks surrounding pregnancy and childbirth were extraordinarily high and the sexual availability of slaves (of both genders) to their masters was taken for granted.[41] When confronted by evidence of this nature we can only ask questions: What were the criteria upon which this individual was marked out as different or inferior? Was it the language she spoke, her mode of attire, the colour of her eyes or the pallor of her skin? By what means was she distinguished from a wife or daughter of freeborn status?

THE MARKING OF DIFFERENCE: CULTURE AND ENVIRONMENT

Having completed this (rather lengthy) preamble it is now time to address some of the ways in which race, environment and culture came to be aligned in an often arbitrary and non-systematic fashion. In the light of the earlier discussion it is important to emphasize that these alignments were often fleeting: the result of a process that was continually unfolding as opposed to remaining static or fixed, not because the distinctions were any less immutable but because this is how racism has been shown to work to begin with.[42] Whilst the presence of a wide variety of slaves of diverse origins, whether in the *oikos* or even in chance encounters in the street, would have necessitated an endless process of positioning and classification at different times and in different places, the experience of those subjected to these racist formations is likely to have been equally varied. Rather than contenting ourselves solely with analysing the elite or elitist perspective of figures such as the 'Old Oligarch' we should consider the effects on the recipient of this constant reaffirmation of the relations of dominance based on an individual's ethnic or cultural identity: the various degrees of denial, marginalization and social exclusion for which there was little (if any) form of redress.

The question as to how culture was conceived in an abstract sense can in part be answered through reference to Homeric epic in which both the accepted norms and their inversions were variously delineated.[43] We can also look to Herodotus' ethnographies to see a number of loosely divided categories which correspond to 'culture' (for seminal treatment, see Redfield 1985: 98–9). These include: *diaita* (which can be loosely construed as material culture, encompassing diet and costume, see for example 4.172 for the Nasamonean diet of dates and milk sprinkled with powdered locusts), *ēthea* which allow one to gauge the degree to which a people can be considered more or less civilized than their neighbours (e.g. the Egyptians in comparison to the Ethiopians, 2.30) and *nomos*, a term that refers to something more specific such as a particular law or custom: something with which one must comply and one whose absence is a hallmark of utter savagery (4.106). *Nomos* aside, it is entirely possible that the intricacies of these distinctions would in all likelihood be lost on Herodotus's non-specialist contemporaries who were far more likely to essentialize by boiling things down into stock epithets.[44]

When seeking to reconstruct elements of the shared conceptual maps which provided groups and individuals with common points of reference, together with a sense of the way these same points (or concepts) were connected, we need to pay close attention to the way in which these might have varied both geographically and across time. It has already been argued that scholarship on race and racism in antiquity has been hampered by the supposition that racism would have taken more or less the same form throughout the Greek world. We need to take account of how our chosen subject, the ancient Greeks, might have experienced diversity more broadly – not just in Athens but in urban and rural settings in mainland Greece and beyond. There appears to have been no shortage of stereotypes regarding either the physical appearance of various different types of Greeks, for example the strapping physique of Spartan women (Aristophanes, *Lysistrata* 77–84), being 'small-faced' like a Corinthian or a Leucadian (Pseudo-Aristotle, *Physiognomics* 808a, 30–3) or cultural practices that were thought to be specific to a particular group (e.g. acorn-eating Arcadians, Herodotus 1.66).[45] Such hints at diversity should discourage us from conceptualizing the Greeks as a whole as what a recent study of identity, multi-ethnicity and migration in ancient Greece termed 'red-figure vase people', that is to say a Caucasian race which epitomized all that was beautiful and good (see Bintliff 2012).[46] Whilst individual communities might have displayed a tendency towards a certain degree of physical homogeneity due to environmental factors and endogamous marriage practices, this would have been offset in part by intermarriage between elites (in periods where such practices were commonplace), widespread mobility and the presence of slaves.

Whilst modern discussions of race or racism have focused primarily on colour prejudice and/or reflected the assumption that the Greeks conceived themselves as an ethnically homogenous group, the overall importance attributed to such ideas appears to have varied depending on the time or context. Herodotus's pointed debunking of the notion that the leading citizens of Miletus enjoyed higher standing than their fellow townsmen due to the purity of their bloodlines indicates that this claim was 'in the air' at or around the time of writing (1.146). Instead, Herodotus informs us that the lack of any female settlers forced the Milesians to marry the wives and daughters of the non-Greek (Carian) population whose menfolk they had just slaughtered (1.146). The degree to which attitudes might change over time is illustrated by the fact that whilst Herodotus is quite content to acknowledge traditions concerning the Gerryhoi (descended from Cadmus) (5.57–9) or the Spartan kings (Egypt) (6.53), the fact that they were mentioned at all is a source of great antipathy to Plutarch who famously castigated Herodotus as *philobarbaros* for his slanderous misuse of history (*De Herod.* 12 and *passim*). Whatever one might think about Plutarch more broadly it is hard not to see these objections as being of a racist character. The pronouncements of the orator Polemon of Laodicea (88–145 CE) are equally notable both for their (to our eyes) overtly racist character (stress on racial purity and superiority of the Greeks) and their somewhat later date (M. Antonius Polemon, *De physiognomonia*; see Andre 1981; Isaac 2004: 156; see also Kaufman in this volume).

Since we are looking at a process, it becomes important to ask how far back we can trace the use of culture and environment to define the foreign or alien and the degree to which these meanings changed over time. Homeric epic had a hugely important role to play, both in terms of capturing ideas conveyed in earlier material, for example oral or catalogue poetry, which was then incorporated into the epic narrative like bees trapped in amber – and in the subtle inflections which accompanied its subsequent performance in response to changing historical circumstances. Compare, for example, the resonances generated by the tale of the Cyclopes which are born out in the apparent interest in depicting Polyphemus' blinding in early vase painting and the fact that Aristotle reaches for the classless, lawless, hearthless individual when illustrating what is alien to the polis and polis culture.[47] We also have variations in the depiction of Paris or the way audiences might have responded to passages describing Carians as dripping in gold (e.g. Homer, *Iliad* 2.867–75). Such material was arguably constitutive of the very fabric of Greek culture – by which I mean the shared conceptual maps which provided groups and individuals with common points of reference and a sense of the way these same points (or concepts) were connected.

Often environment and culture can be seen to overlap/intersect. The decision as to which should take precedence can seem somewhat arbitrary but was in all likelihood context-driven – like Agasias' invocation of Apollonides' earrings. The latter is important insofar as it implies that scrutiny of an individual in order to discern who they were, where they came from, or even whether they were slave or free was entirely commonplace. Whilst it is highly probable, as Christopher Tuplin has observed, that most Greeks would instinctively know a barbarian if they saw him (or presumably her), matters were often rather more complicated to the extent that further enquiries or proofs were required in order to pinpoint an individual's identity (Christopher Tuplin in personal conversation). We get a dramatically charged rendering of this in Aeschylus' *Suppliants* when the Argive king Pelasgos interrogates the Danaids in order to determine their origins:

> What you say, strangers, is unbelievable for me to hear, that this group of yours is of Argive descent. You bear more resemblance to the women of Libya—certainly not to those of this country. The Nile, too, might nurture such a crop; and a similar stamp is struck upon the dies of Cyprian womanhood by male artificers. I hear, too, that there are nomad women in India, near neighbours to the Ethiopians, who saddle their way across country on camels that run like horses; and then the man-shunning, meat-eating Amazons—if you were equipped with bows, I'd be very inclined to guess that you were them. If you explain to me, I may understand better how your birth and descent can be Argive.
>
> (Aeschylus, *Suppliant Women* 279–83; trans. Loeb)

What is notable about this passage is the messiness with which ideas about environment and culture are made to overlap: Pelasgos' initial comment on the Danaids' physical appearance as something that marks them out as foreign is further underlined by the subsequent reference to Cyprus and coin-production (see Skinner 2010, 2012: 136–9). Crops nurtured by the Nile are then referred to figuratively alongside bloodline and descent.[48] Whilst doubtless designed to captivate an audience's imagination with poetic references to far-flung populations the latter stands in contrast to the static grids which have been mapped out by scholars when analysing texts such as Herodotus' *Histories*. Whilst polarity undoubtedly played a pivotal role in ancient Greek thought we should be careful to distinguish between the elaborate displays of knowledge which we get from

Herodotus and others and the, in all likelihood, rather less sophisticated reasonings of individuals who made up their audiences.⁴⁹

It is important to stress that some of these ideas will have been in circulation in the form of exotica and travellers' tales long before they came to be associated with any nascent discourse surrounding race. What matters is the way in which they were progressively harnessed in order to legitimize the exploitation of certain peoples as opposed to others. Once the idea of enslaving non-Greeks achieved hegemony, it provided the impetus for myriad acts of positioning and classification. The fact that slaves varied in terms of their origins or ascribed identities necessitated a rather more fluid system capable of providing an effective rationale for the exploitation of groups or individuals, whatever this might entail, a process in which some slaves themselves may have been at least partially complicit – there being nothing to say that individuals should be rendered immune from these thought processes simply because they had experienced their effects first-hand.⁵⁰

One question which has yet to be addressed is the overall salience of skin colour in these racial combinations. The concluding section of this chapter will therefore attempt to do just that, focusing on a data set which has attracted relatively little discussion to date. The purpose of this case study is to experiment with new ways of thinking about this material not least by moving the debate away from its traditional epicentre, namely Athens. It is hoped that this will provide a template for future attempts to approach such topics in future, whether in research or in the classroom. In doing so we must remain sensitive to questions of power and agency, extending our analyses beyond the privileged realm of the adult male (i.e. citizen) audience to confront the structural inequalities which underpinned Greek society as a whole. We should also remain sensitive to the degree of variation which individual communities exhibited in the light of a burgeoning number of studies devoted to a particular region or polis: racism or racial formations are likely to have taken markedly different form depending on whether one found oneself in Naukratis in Egypt or Olbia in the North Pontic region.

In order to consider the question as to how skin pigmentation was perceived we shall now embark on a thought exercise which seeks to transcend the relatively narrow parameters of discussion concerning vase-painting/ideas regarding race and identity by placing the imagined viewing audience in a very different, specifically north Aegean, context, the better to explore what contemporary Greeks knew, or thought they knew, about the relationship between race, environment and culture.⁵¹

We cannot know precisely how or under what circumstances but at some point in the early fourth century BCE a number of Olynthus' more aspiring or well-to-do households acquired one or more African-head vases (Robinson 1931: nos. 405–8; 1933: nos. 400, 401, 403; 1952: nos. 413, 413A, 414–16, 429).⁵² These vessels were in all likelihood produced locally, whether in Olynthus itself or at some other location in the Chalkidike, as opposed to being imported from Athens. A number of the head vases are quite fragmentary, however, at least three different designs can be discerned, with multiple vessels being linked to the same moulds (for related discussion, see Tsigarida 2017: 80–2 and 456, no. 627).

The published findings of Robinson's excavations at Olynthus suggest that these objects would have been viewed as something of a novelty amongst the relatively wide array of designs on offer at the time, including veiled women, satyrs and old men. They must nevertheless have possessed broad societal appeal insofar as vessels identical to that depicted in Figure 2.2 have been recovered both in 'normal' town houses adjoining the city

FIGURE 2.2 Two views of a terracotta vase depicting the head of an African youth, first half of fourth century BCE. © Greek Archaeological Service, Ephorate of Antiquities of Chalkidike and Mount Athos.

wall on the western side of the North Hill and in the (considerably more opulent) 'Villa of Good Fortune' located outside the defensive circuit in the city's wealthy suburbs.[53] Although it is highly likely that Olynthians would have encountered various different groups and ethnicities in what was a famously cosmopolitan community they are perhaps more likely to have encountered marked somatic difference during travels abroad rather than on a daily basis in their home town. We are therefore faced with the question as to what these (presumably proud) customers saw when they gazed on their acquisitions and for what reasons? The same question, of course, applies to other members of the household, whether women, children or slaves, together with any guests or clients who might have had an opportunity to view the vessel either whilst in use during a symposium or when displayed on a prominent ledge or shelf.

We can only answer these questions in a very speculative fashion by pulling together the various fragments of information and ideas that we know to have been circulating by this time in order to get some sense of how such objects would have been viewed from their point of manufacture, whether by slaves, metics or citizen craftsmen, to the point of sale, before finally being transported to one of the bustling households or 'villas' which made up the town. An association with far-off foreign lands suggests that exoticism may have been a key driver in determining the purchase of such vessels. Beyond this we have a range of ideas which might be gleaned from epic and lyric poetry. An association with environmental conditions born of geographical location can therefore be inferred from very early on. Take, for example, vague references to a geographically distant population in Homer whose name is suggestive of their appearance (*Aithiopes* = 'Dark' or 'Burnt-faces').[54] One of the most popular types of head vase, an African youth crowned with ivy, undoubtedly has sympotic connotations (quite apart from the fact that the vessel was clearly designed to contain wine), however, poetic tales of interactions between the famously pious Ethiopians and Poseidon are unlikely to have been restricted to banqueting alone (Homer, *Odyssey* 1.22–6).[55] It is also possible that such depictions evoked memories of the Homeric hero Memnon, son of Eos, who led the Ethiopian contingent in *Iliad*[56] or the Ethiopian Macrobioi (either long-bowed or long-lived) whom we encounter in Herodotus' *Histories*, described as the most beautiful of all men due to their use of miraculous water – an association which may lie behind the appearance of 'Ethiopians' on perfume flasks as well as paraphernalia of the symposium (Herodotus 3.17–26; for more on Ethiopians in Herodotus, see Derbew in this volume).[57]

Perhaps the most pressing question of all, from the point of view of this chapter, is whether the purchase of such a vessel reflects a desire to dominate or possess the barbarian Other and whether the individual depicted was automatically interpreted as a servant or slave. This is another instance in which the perceptual filters of modernity may well have played a role. It has recently been argued that scholarly interpretation of Athenian head vases, whether Janus-types or those featuring a single head, display a marked predisposition towards interpreting black-skinned individuals as slaves despite there being only the slenderest of evidence to support this association (Derbew 2018).[58] The point is amply illustrated by Robinson's bald statement that 'Negroes were used as servants and bath attendants' citing, by way of evidence, a vase depicting a boy carrying stools on his head (Robinson 1931: 88).[59] Such assertions are more typically accompanied by a stray reference to Theophrastus, *Characters* 21.4 in which it is maintained that the man of petty ambition (*mikrophilotimia*) will make a point of having an Ethiopian as a servant. By this token it might be inferred that the wealthier households of Olynthus were doing the next best thing, namely replacing their Ethiopian attendant with a vessel that could serve as a proxy. Whilst it is entirely possible that the logic driving these interpretations reflects modern assumptions and prejudices as Derbew has maintained, it might equally be argued that the fact that these figures were visibly different insofar as they were associated with the outer, non-Hellenic world meant they were marked out for exploitation should the opportunity arise. On the other hand, we have material such as the gold phiale now on display in the National Archaeological Museum in Plovdiv, Bulgaria (phiale, AE, Plovdiv, National Archaeological Museum 3204), which features three concentric rows of Ethiopian heads on its exterior, separated by a band of acorns which increase progressively in size. Although exoticism may well be present, the latter seems far more likely to be an allusion to the Ethiopians' elevated piety and blessed good fortune (appropriate if the purpose of the vessel is the pouring of libations).

We might equally wonder whether these vessels might themselves have functioned foundationally in the discourse of racial difference by fixing and securing that which could not otherwise be fixed or secured, to use Stuart Hall's phrasing – a point of reference, for example, for the idea that it was the heat of the sun which caused the skin to darken (Herodotus 2.22). We should be open to the idea that encounters with such objects might have played a pivotal role in the actual formation of racial ideas rather than simply expressing them in the form of an 'outcome' or end result. They were thus very much part of the process of making-meaning discussed at the beginning of this chapter. Whilst markedly different from the racial formations from the nineteenth century onwards they were every bit as effective when it came to generating and then sustaining the potent social realities of racism, discrimination and racial identities, evidence of which we might detect in the fragment from Menander: 'If a man is of good character it doesn't matter if he is an Ethiopian' (Frag. 612) (for discussion, see Tuplin 1999: 59; Harrison 2020: 154). Our ability to detect these formations is contingent upon our willingness to confront such issues to begin with rather than taking refuge in the notion that for all their faults, the ancient Greeks were somehow immune from racial thinking.

CHAPTER THREE

Race and Religion

DENISE KIMBER BUELL

INTRODUCTION

The categories of race and religion, contested and variegated as they are, owe a debt to antiquity in two ways: modern people have shaped understandings of race and religion through the study of the ancient past, and ancient religious materials contain ways of knowing that anticipate and serve as building blocks for the modern racial imaginary.[1] Neither race nor religion has precise ancient correlates, but we cannot study the history of race (or religion) without grappling both with modern claims about these categories and with ancient claims about how human/non-human relations inform intra-human difference.

Reconstructions of the past are always acts of interpretation and translation. When modern readers either insist upon or refuse to discern race in ancient sources, that is an interpretive act. Ancient sources likewise perform interpretations of the complicated actions of everyday people. When the Roman orator Cicero insists (in the first century BCE) that Romans are superior to other peoples on the basis of their superior piety (see *de Haruspicum Responso* 19 and *On the Nature of the Gods* 2.2), that is an interpretive act declaring cultic practices as the way to differentiate one group of humans, 'Romans', from other kinds of humans.

Humans in Mediterranean antiquity lived as if their worlds were filled with invisible non-human forces (including deities but also spirits, daemons, djinns and planets). Accordingly, humans devised practices and objects to avoid, attract and safely manage non-human entities as well as other humans (Figure 3.1); sometimes, but not always, these practices were linked with institutions such as the popular cult of Isis or the Chalcedonian form of Christianity. When scholars study religion in antiquity, they consider both evidence for these practices and the meanings that ancient people attributed to them. A range of practices flourished between 500 BCE and 800 CE, including the emergence of orientations that are seen as continuous with forms of religion today, notably Zoroastrianism, Jainism and Buddhism (said to have begun in the fifth century BCE), as well as rabbinic Judaism and Christianity (said to have begun in the first century CE), Manicheism (said to have begun in the third century CE) and Islam (said to have begun in the seventh century CE). The period also includes orientations that have not survived, mostly encompassed by the shorthand of 'polytheism' as well as non-rabbinic forms of being a Jew, and many ways of being a Christian. Because this brief chapter cannot survey the full complexity of antiquity, it instead provides a conceptual framework to interpret materials that far exceed the examples explored below.

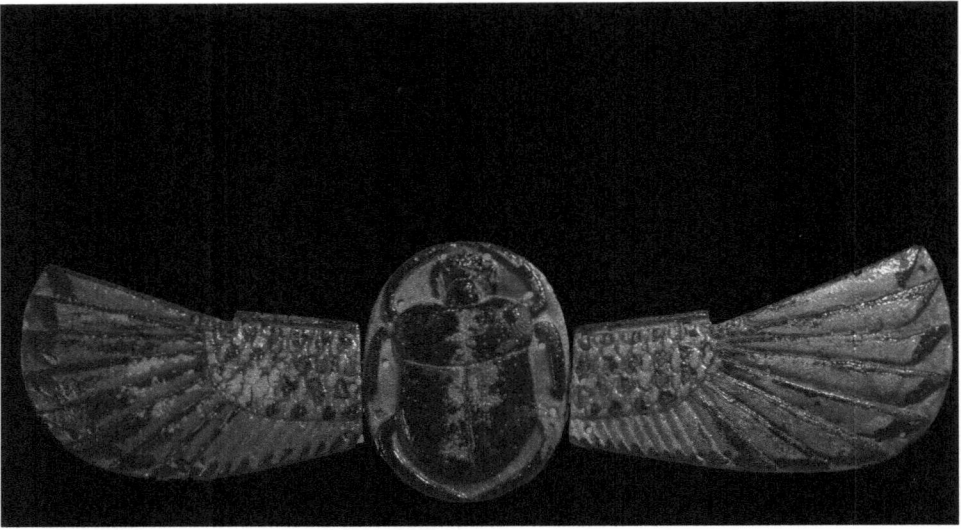

FIGURE 3.1 Amulet featuring Khepri the Scarab God, Egyptian, late Ptolemaic period. © Werner Forman/Getty Images.

The chapter proceeds in four main parts. The first section focuses on the modern study of race and religion in antiquity because our interpretive lenses and their histories shape how we perceive antiquity. The remaining three sections demonstrate ways that what we can study as ancient religion functioned partly as a structuring device for articulating and managing differences among humans,[2] including differences we might study as racial. Section two illustrates the salience of religion for conceptualizations of collective belonging, using the examples of the collective terms Greek, Roman, Ethiopian, Persian, Jew, Christian and Muslim. The third section presents an interpretive framework for these overlapping and co-constituting fields of identity making. The fourth and final section considers ancient arguments and practices that anticipate modern colonizing and imperial mindsets.

MODERN FRAMEWORKS FOR STUDYING RACE AND RELIGION

Today, most humans view religion and race as distinct from one another. But late nineteenth- and early twentieth-century scholars of antiquity frequently viewed them as linked. In explanations of the 'decline' of the Roman Empire, for example, some scholars of this period argued that 'oriental' immigrants were responsible for the alleged spiritual, cultural and political decadence of Rome, by bringing their religious traditions and outnumbering or intermarrying, and thus racially diluting, 'real' Romans through both cultural and reproductive shifts (e.g. Houston Stewart Chamberlain, Otto Seeck and Tenney Frank); others countered this view (e.g. Franz Cumont) by viewing 'oriental' religions as a source of spiritual improvement for Romans (Scheerlink, Praet and Rey 2016). Also in this period, a number of African Americans countered white supremacist historical scholarship by reconstructing alternative narratives of both human racial and religious development (e.g. Benjamin Tucker Tanner and Pauline Hopkins; see Tanner 1902; Wallinger 2005; Malamud 2016).

New Testament and early Christian studies of this period often turn on claims about race and religion by insisting that Jews constituted a race but early Christians did not; narratives of early Christian development chart a historical break of Christians from Jews and the formation of a multiracial or multi-ethnic 'universal' religion (see Heschel 1998; Buell 2005; Marchand 2009). The legacies of these views still reverberate in the world and the academy. A number of scholars have challenged this narrative by showing how Christianity was central to the formation of whiteness and incipient nationalisms in both Europe itself and European and American imperial undertakings in the Middle East, North Africa and beyond (e.g. Johnson 2004; Bahrani 2006; Kidd 2006; Moxnes 2012; Wimbush 2017). Others argue that 'modernity's racial imagination has its genesis in the theological problem of Christianity's quest to sever itself from its Jewish roots' (Carter 2008: 4; see also Johnson 2004; Buell 2005; Wimbush 2012, 2017). Nonetheless, the idea that race and religion are distinct remains widespread.

Two powerful late twentieth- and early twenty-first-century narratives contribute to the tendency to distinguish race from religion: one positions race as a concept that *used* to be viewed as biologically determined; the other positions race as a concept that replaces religion as the predominant way to explain intra-human difference. Both narratives obscure 'that race and religion are *contemporary*, indeed, coextensive and, moreover, co-concealing categories' in the nineteenth century (Anidjar 2008: 28; emphasis in the original).

From biological determinism to social construction

The narrative that race is a concept that *used* to be viewed as biologically determined and immutable is often paired with the position that now 'we' know better that race is a social construction (Stoler 1997; Scheerlink, Praet and Rey 2016: 220; Schuller 2018). If it is a biological definition of race that must be overcome, religion seems irrelevant to race, past and present. This narrative renders invisible recent and contemporary ways race and religion intersect, such as Nazi and white supremacist targeting of Jews, and anti-Muslim sentiments and actions that pervade US and western European contexts.

Biological determinism did become the dominant (never the only) way of defining race by the early twentieth century, but nineteenth-century works often use race to mean a 'people' more broadly, in ways that make the term functionally equivalent to current uses of ethnicity. They depict racial change not simply through reproduction but through the Lamarckian acquisition of characteristics that become heritable (through 'civilizing' projects such as education and religious conversion to Christianity; see Chidester 2014; Schuller 2018). Understandings of race as changeable over time function in double-edged ways: to envision non-racist future forms of humanity (e.g. Hooker 2017), but also to justify colonial and imperial rule over peoples classified as belonging to races deemed 'lower' than those of the colonizers.

A pernicious yet enduring modern form of racial classification, that of Aryans in contrast to Semites, comes out of the nineteenth-century study of ancient religious past, as well as archaeology and comparative linguistics (Olender 1992). 'Semites' are identified with Jews and Muslims (Anidjar 2008: 13–38) and associated also with 'oriental' religions of antiquity.³ 'Aryans' are identified as the ancestors of white Europeans and traced variously to groups ranging from ancient Romans to Jesus to 'high caste' Indians.

Joseph Arthur comte de Gobineau (1816–82), influential for articulating race as an explanatory lens, argues that 'both the rise and decline of civilizations [are] the result of race mixture between Aryans and other races' (Scheerlink, Praet and Rey 2016: 224), classifying Aryans as the superior race. He calls 'Semites' the racial type of peoples of the East or 'Orient'. Drawing on ancient Roman stereotypes about Persians, Egyptians, Phrygians and Syrians, he charts a historical progression in which 'Greeks' become 'semitized' by contact with Eastern peoples; later, Romans likewise become 'semitic' first by mixing with 'semitized' Greeks and Carthaginians ('Orientals' who had colonized the North African region of modern Tunis) and then with 'Oriental immigrants' who 'fundamentally changed the population of Italy and the culture of Rome', especially by introducing 'their cultural habits, including their gods', referring to the worship of Isis, Serapis, Astarte, Mithras and Elagabal (224). In other words, this racial classification was never solely about biology but always also about religious and cultural encounters and transformations, formulated and justified through interpretation of ancient texts.

One recent alternative to nineteenth-century theories of 'racial contamination' through religious mixing is the view that peoples had been travelling, trading, migrating, interacting across the Mediterranean basin for centuries before antiquity. Instead of presuming an original purity of any religion or racial group, a late twentieth-century interpretation of Roman religion suggests that:

> rather than seeing pure Roman traditions gradually polluted from the outside, Roman religion was an amalgam of different traditions from at least as far back as we can hope to go .... Roman religion was always already multicultural. Archaeological evidence from the sixth century BC, for example, has shown that in cultural and religious terms Rome was part of a civilization dominated by Etruscans and receptive to the influence of Greeks and possibly Carthaginians too.
>
> (Beard, North and Price 1998a: 12)

Even this approach needs to grapple with how ancient folks made meaning in ways that imposed differences or similarities upon the much messier, entangled relations of daily life and thereby produced categories such as 'Greek' vs 'barbarian' with wide ripple effects.

From religion to race

The narrative that race is a successor concept to religion is also widespread today: religion *used* to be fully intertwined with (if not the controlling factor in) all dimensions of human social life but was supplanted by race in a movement from religiosity to secularism. According to this view, race did not exist in pre-modern eras, but once 'Europeans' 'encountered' Indigenous peoples in other parts of the world, race emerged as a way to explain and classify human variation and to justify enslavement, colonization, exploitation, displacement or annihilation of groups of humans deemed inferior to Europeans. The Christian lenses through which Europeans view human difference and the ancient sources, including biblical ones, produce the vision for modern secular race and racism; doctrines of Christianity were challenged and displaced by secular ideologies, laws and polities that nonetheless continue to be indebted to Christianity (e.g. Perkinson 2004; Kidd 2006; Hickman 2010).

This narrative places a religion, Christianity, squarely at the origin of the European racial imaginary. It also installs a rupture between the 'early modern' period and prior histories of how humans structured intra-human difference *and* between race and religion as if they are 'apparently unrelated grids of difference' (Anidjar 2008: 27). The attempt to preserve a clear distinction between these categories by positing an evolution from one to another fails to account for temporal interdependencies among and between ancient and modern sources and conceptualizations of race and religion.

As a kind of corrective, an increasing body of scholarship examines how racial categories shaped and informed the study of ancient religion in the nineteenth and early twentieth centuries, exposing how racialized and racist structures helped to shape the disciplines of Classics, ancient history and biblical studies as they became professionalized, with legacies that haunt us today (e.g. Bernal 1987; Heschel 1998, 2008; Kelley 2002; Marchand 2009; Lin 2016). A complementary trend emphasizes how religion itself is a modern interpretive category (e.g. Nongbri 2015; Barton and Boyarin 2016).

In addition to pointing out the contested and changing meanings of race (past and present), scholars offering alternatives to these narratives emphasize the work race does in its multiple guises (Stoler 1997). As Geraldine Heng puts it: 'race is a structural relationship for the articulation and management of human difference, rather than a substantive content' (2018: 3, 19). This approach has been central for those who study pre-modern contexts (e.g. Buell 2005; McCoskey 2012; Heng 2018). We now turn to consider how ancient sources are implicated in the building and challenging of racializing lenses.

ANCIENT MAPPINGS OF RACE AND RELIGION

This section demonstrates the centrality of religion for speaking about intra-human difference by examining the collective terms Greek, Roman, Ethiopian, Persian, Jew, Christian and Muslim. Each term had (and has) multiple, shifting meanings; those who claimed and used the terms often disagreed over their meanings and who had the right to claim the terms. These terms exemplify the slippage and overlap between race and religion; Greek, Persian, Ethiopian and Roman are not just 'ethnic' or 'racial'; Jew, Christian and Muslim are not just 'religious'.

Being Greek

Who and what makes a Greek (or Hellene) has been contested and changeable: 'The question "Who is a Greek?" has been asked time and again during the past three millennia. With shifting emphases and inconsistent application, categories of blood kinship, language, religion, and way of life were employed in antiquity' (Malkin 2001a: 1). Herodotus (late fifth century BCE) describes Greekness as consisting of five features: 'common purpose (avenging the burning of temples by Persians), kinship (having the same blood, *homaimon*), shared language (*homoglōsson*), shared sanctuaries of the gods and sacrifices *(theōn hidrumata koina kai thusiai)*, and similar ways of life or customs *(ēthea homotropa)*' (8.144.2; cf. Malkin 2001a: 5–6).

Defining Greekness by way of an oppositional binary of Greek/barbarian also emerged in the fifth century BCE, a time of Greek conflicts with the Achaemenid ('Persian') Empire. Hellenes who had previously begun to articulate a translocal collective belonging that brought together multiple subgroupings such as Athenians, Dorians, Spartans, Ionians and the like, in an aggregative fashion (Hall 1997), now began to define being Greek also in contrast with outsiders called barbarians, including but not limited to the Persians. Religion remained among the measures of distinction between Greek and barbarian.

In later periods, different groups claimed to be Greek in an aggregative fashion, but also in contrast to putative others; for example, Jews and the Macedonian ruling family (descendants of Alexander the Great) negotiated their relationship to 'Egyptians' during the period of Ptolemaic rule of Egypt (third through first centuries BCE), each by claiming a share in 'Greekness' (Honigman 2013). During the fourth century CE, as Roman rulers began to patronize and support Christian practices, Hellene became repurposed as shorthand for a polytheist, in contrast to Jews and Christians. By the late sixth century CE, meanings shifted again: 'the heritage of Christian, "Roman" Byzantium continued into the Ottoman Empire, where Greeks were called (and called themselves) Rum or Rumeli ("Romans") and Greekness was almost exclusively defined in term[s] of religion', meaning Christian (Malkin 2001a: 1).

Being Roman

The content of being Roman also shifted over time, with religion playing a significant role. Sources reflecting on the founding of Rome highlight the importance of deities in establishing the city and link Rome's success to the cults within the boundary of its *pomerium*. The specific cults featured inside the city expanded over time, so being Roman was not linked with the veneration of any single deity. Romans incorporate cults from other places (e.g. the cult of Magna Mater [Cybele] from Asia Minor) while selectively invoking concern about 'foreign' gods and foreign ways of worshipping (e.g. the worship of Bacchus [Dionysus] and Manicheanism [associated with Persia]).

Being properly religious becomes a self-defining feature of Romanness, as this passage from a 56 BCE speech by the orator Cicero illustrates:

> it is not in numbers that we are superior to the Spaniards, nor in personal strength to the Gauls, nor in cunning to the Carthaginians, nor in arts to the Greeks, nor in the natural acuteness which seems to be implanted in the people of this land and country, to the Italian and Latin tribes; but it is in and by means of piety and religion, and this especial wisdom of perceiving that all things are governed and managed by the divine power of the immortal gods, that we have been and are superior to all other countries and nations.
>
> (*de Haruspicum Responso* 19)

In 212 CE, the emperor Caracalla radically expanded the meaning and applicability of being 'Roman' by extending citizenship to all free provincials, with corresponding expectations of participation in the piety appropriate for Roman citizens. In 251 CE, the emperor Decius decreed that Roman belonging ought to be measured and demonstrated by a common, unifying religious act (Rives 1999). This innovation built upon the idea that proper piety correlates with political cohesion and success; it did not imply that worshipping other gods was a problem, so long as one also participated in this shared orientation.

In 381 CE, emperor Theodosius I decreed Christianity the proper form of piety for all Romans, changing the content but not the principle of linking religious observance with Romanness. Ironically, the very cults that had been central to being Roman until this point were reframed as 'Greek' or 'pagan', the latter a pejorative term connoting uncivilized behaviour of those who lived outside cities. The Greek term '*Romanoi*' ('Romans') gained traction after 381 CE, equating being Roman with a form of religious orientation, Christian, previously viewed as contrary to being a proper Roman prior to 313 CE (Figure 3.2).

FIGURE 3.2 Mosaic featuring Roman Emperors Constantine and Justinian with the Virgin and Child, Hagia Sophia, Istanbul, Turkey, tenth century CE. © Chris Hellier/Getty Images.

Being Persian

Few written sources illuminate Persian self-conceptions in antiquity (Figure 3.3). Persians were not only a catalyst for the category of 'barbarian'; classical Greek and later sources also associated Persians with the worship led by priests who oversaw Zoroastrian rituals and with 'magical' and astrological practices (Pliny, *Natural History* 30.1–2, 13–14), and later with Manicheism.

Mani (*c.* 216–74 CE), born and raised in Persia, created Manicheism as a deliberate universalizing synthesis of Zoroastrianism (the imperially sponsored cult in the Persian Empire), Buddhism, Judaism and Christianity. Its practices and ideas quickly spread outside of the Persian Empire. A late-third- or early-fourth-century CE Roman imperial decree criminalized the religion. The imperial decree below first disparages Manicheism as new, alleging that it is in opposition to established religious practices and then, damningly, links its practitioners with the empire's significant rival to the east, the Sasanian (Persian) Empire:

> Of these Manichaeans … we have heard that they quite recently, like strange [and] unexpected monstrosities, have advanced or have arisen in this world from the Persian race, a race hostile to us …. And it is to be feared that … in the passage of time they should attempt [through] accursed customs and perverse laws of the Persians to inject people of a more innocent nature, namely the temperate and peaceful Roman race and our whole world, with (as it were) their malignant drugs.
>
> (Beard, North and Price 1998b: 281–2)

Manicheans are thus condemned as Persian and thus poisonous to Romans.

FIGURE 3.3 Achaemenid earring featuring the deity Ahura Mazda, sixth–fourth century BCE. © DEA PICTURE LIBRARY/Getty Images.

Being Ethiopian

More than the other terms considered here, Ethiopian carries the connotation of skin colour that overdetermines the modern racial imaginary; Christianity is the vector for a religiously loaded association with dark skin, both positive and negative (Byron 2002). Ethiopians (and Egyptians) 'have been used inconsistently as polemical devices when referring to the presence of "Blacks" in antiquity' (Bryon 2002: 4). Our written sources for the inhabitants of the African regions south of Egypt variously known as Kush, Nubia and Ethiopia are primarily external (Burstein 1998; for archaeology, see Welsby 1998). Ethiopians appear as exemplars of those who inhabited the extreme south of the known world from the perspective of Greeks and later Romans, epitomized by their dark skin colour, sometimes contrasted with the paleness of those inhabiting the extreme north (Scythians). In Greek and Roman literature, being Ethiopian is not stereotypically associated with specific cultic practices, as are Persians and Egyptians, but Ethiopians are sometimes compared with intermediary spiritual beings (*daimones*) (Byron 2002: 37–8). The kingdoms in this region played important roles in the shifting religious and political landscape of late antiquity even as the figure of the Ethiopian takes on a discursive function in Christian literature, both positive and negative (Byron 2002).

Being a Jew

Many ways of being a Jew flourished in antiquity. Jews lived throughout the Mediterranean and Near East, with large populations living under Persian, Ptolemaic, Seleucid and, later, Roman rule; Jews also led kingdoms in the eastern Mediterranean in the second century BCE to the first century CE and during the late fourth and early fifth centuries CE on the Arabian peninsula. Culturally and linguistically Jews shared much with their non-Jewish contemporaries wherever they lived; nonetheless, in contrast to themselves – who maintained the practices of those in covenant with the God of Israel – Jews regularly distinguished as 'the nations' or 'gentiles' those who worshiped other gods, which Jews deemed wrong or false gods (or idols) (Cohen 1999: 1; Wasserman 2017: 9).

Jews did not simply define themselves in contrast to gentiles but also in relation to other Jews. During the Second Temple period (fifth century BCE–70 CE), Jews debated about their cultic centre in Jerusalem and its purity (although there was also a temple in Leontopolis in Egypt and many Jews lived outside of Judaea and Palestine), the interpretation of scripture (largely circulating in Greek) and concerns about the problem of evil, including ways of responding to political rule by non-Jews (Schwartz 2001). After the destruction of the temple in Jerusalem in 70 CE, Jewish communities persisted around the Mediterranean, often centred around the diaspora institutions of synagogues. In Palestine, Syria and the Sassanian Persian Empire, synagogue leaders formed a mode of teaching and interpretation that culminated in the compilation of the two Talmuds, the hallmark texts of rabbinic Judaism.

Ancient Jewish texts variously situate being Jewish in relation to religion and race. To give two examples: the rhetoric of Ezra and Nehemiah seems to anticipate biological determinism, while the book of Judith defines being a Jew in a manner that anticipates the Lamarckian idea that traits can be acquired and then transmitted intergenerationally. The biblical books of Ezra and Nehemiah, written during the fifth century BCE (in the wake of the Persian ruler Cyrus I's conquest of Babylonian territories and his edict that sent *yehudim* who had been brought as war captives to Babylon back to their home territory), give a glimpse at intra-Jewish tensions concerning self-definition. These writings define returning exiles as Jews and call 'for the forced separation, if not subordination, *if not the death*, of all foreigners and especially enemies' (Smith-Christopher [1996] 2002: 120; emphasis in the original). By limiting Israel to those of 'holy seed' (see Ezra 9–10 and Nehemiah 13) their prescriptions appear structurally racist. These texts may express the views of a minoritized group returning from exile to encounter rival expressions of what it means to follow the God of Israel. In contrast, Judith yokes piety with peoplehood but positions belonging as changeable through religious conversion and transmissible to one's descendants, featuring a central gentile antagonist who converts to become a Jew (see Buell 2005: 44).

The question 'Who is a Jew?' has been asked over the centuries by Jews and their contemporaries. Narratives that chart a historical shift from an 'ethnic' to a 'religious' category are typical in studies of Jews in antiquity, even when scholars identify different historical moments for the 'same watershed phenomenon' (Baker 2017: 20).[4] Rendering this distinction and shift from tribal/ethnic/racial to religious reinscribes 'ancient Christian, dualistic hierarchies of particular/universal, birth/faith, flesh/spirit, and the like' (40). We thus need to attend to these early Christian views, some of which depict 'Judaism and its adherents, the Jews, as necessary (but obsolete) elements of Christian salvation history' (41) even as they also position Christians as members of a racial or ethnic group.

Being Christian

The groups that we study as early Christians emerged first in the Eastern Roman Empire as the empire was itself gaining traction; by the middle of the seventh century CE, the majority of inhabitants from Britain to the Euphrates were Christians of some variety (Maas 2000: 103). What it means to be a Christian has always been contested, usually turning on interpretation of scripture (especially the writings shared with Jews, which Christians eventually refer to as the 'Old Testament') and the significance of the first-century CE Jew Jesus of Nazareth. Christian is a term that scholars have almost systematically distinguished from concepts of race or ethnicity even though, as we have seen, by late antiquity religious orientations marked as Christian became central for defining what it meant to be Greek and Roman, as well as increasingly for other groups (e.g. Franks, Goths, Celts). Explanations for why Christian is a religious and not an ethnic or racial concept include that Christian worship was an innovation in antiquity not a traditional orientation linked to collective belonging, that Christians 'lacked the ethnic links of Judaism' (Beard, North and Price 1998a: 276) and that anyone could become a Christian, regardless of background.

None of these claims is compelling. The crafting of what become Christian orientations is no more innovative than the shifting understandings of what kinds of piety characterize a Roman, or the production of rabbinic forms of orientation towards what it means to be a Jew in late antiquity. Christians were legible to others as those who neglected or wrongly practiced 'ancestral customs', whether those of Jews, Greeks, Romans or some other group. At the same time, early Christians regularly defined themselves as members of a people, constituted by individuals from a range of backgrounds, who have acquired shared ancestors and religious orientations and practices. Universalizing claims and aspirations also are claimed by Romans, Second Temple period and rabbinic Jews (Baker 2009; Berkowitz 2013), and Manicheans.

Early Christians repeatedly defined themselves in relation to Israelite history, claiming to embody either the true Israel or its legitimate successor (e.g. Pseudo-Clementine, *Recognitions* 1.39.1–2; Justin Martyr, *Dialogue with Trypho* 11.5; 123.6–8; 125.5). The late-first-century CE text 1 Peter locates initiation into worship of the God of Israel by way of an interpretation of (Jewish) scriptures, defining initiates as joining a chosen, elect people made up of an aggregation of former gentiles who have rejected their ancestral customs in favour of belonging with and to the true God (1 Pet. 2:9–10; see Buell 2005, 2009). The second-century CE philosopher Celsus critiques Christians as renegade Jews (see Origen, *Against Celsus* 3.5) or troublemakers who have abandoned the appropriate customs of their people (*patria*) (not only Jews); Origen responds by asserting that Christians' relation to God is better than that of other Jews towards God and by acknowledging that Christians form a historically recent *ethnos* made of individuals from many different backgrounds who are now, as Christians, defined by their relation to the God of Israel (Buell 2005: 74–5).

Early Christian writers conceptualized orientation to their God as joining an ancestral lineage, becoming a member of a saved or chosen people. Clement of Alexandria writes: 'those from the Hellenic training and also from the law [referring to Mosaic law] who accept faith [in Christ] are gathered into the one *genos* of the saved people (*laos*)' (*Stromateis* 6.42.2). That is, Christians are the saved people formed out of those who have been oriented religiously as Greeks and Jews (Buell 2005: 139). Eusebius of

Caesarea, a Christian leader of the early fourth century CE, argues that Christianity is the universal form of belonging appropriate for the Roman Empire: 'the integration of peoples under Constantine's providentially arranged dominion brings to fulfillment the promise that God "will transform all races of humankind, both Greek and barbarian, from savagery and barbarism to gentleness and mildness"' (*Demonstration*, 3.2; cf. Meier 2011: 163).

Far from exceptional, Christian practices and institutions were forged with the resources and practices of other religious orientations and grammars. These kinds of 'ethnic reasoning' (Buell 2005) by early Christians position Christian belonging as legible in terms we have seen above for Greeks and Romans, as well as Jews (see also Lieu 2004).

Being Muslim

Those we study as early Muslims began to articulate their collective self-understanding and practices on the Arabian peninsula during the seventh century CE. As is the case for Christians, the orientations that become legible as Muslim are forged with the resources and practices of other religious orientations and grammars, including local polytheistic, Jewish and Christian ones (al-Azmeh 2014; Penn 2015; Bowersock 2017). Early Muslims defined themselves in relation to the revelations received by Muhammad (*c*. 570–623 CE), which constitute the central scripture of the Qu'ran and the leadership of Muhammad and a number of successors. Although not restricted to any geopolitical boundaries, by 750 CE, Muslims gained political control over the territories that had been controlled by the Persian Empire, as well as significant portions of the territories that the Roman Empire had controlled, including North Africa and the Arabian peninsula, Palestine and Syria (Figure 3.4).

FIGURE 3.4 Grand Mosque, Diyarbakir, Turkey, converted from a Christian church in the mid-seventh century CE. © Selimaksan/Getty Images.

The terminology used to describe the members of what became Islam was initially variable and shifting, linked with pre-existing collective formations. Islam has been closely associated with Arabs, and the first 'Believers' were indeed Arabs; the Arabic language is valued as the language of the Qu'ran (Donner 2010). The earliest surviving sources from the mid- and late seventh century attesting to the emergence of Islam come from Christians who classify in-group members as 'Arabs' who are 'Children of Ishmael' (e.g. *Apocalypse of Pseudo-Methodius* 11.3) or 'Hagarenes' (e.g. Jacob of Edessa) thus linking them to the biblical narrative about Abraham's son Ishmael with the slave woman Hagar (Genesis). This language – much as is the case for perceptions of early Christians as either renegade Jews, true Israel or disobedient heirs to traditional ancestral customs – suggests that those who constituted the earliest Believers not only came from local ancestral polytheistic, Jewish and Christian contexts but also that the distinctions among these communities only became clearer over time; for example, Syriac Christian sources, composed by Christians under Muslim political control by the middle of the seventh century, 'frequently denied Islam its alterity and depicted it as a derivative form of Christianity' (Penn 2015: 11).

The terms 'Moors' and 'Moorish' are also terms associated with Islam, and with dark skin. But they appear first to depict relative location, not religion or skin colour, and later a relationship to Roman rule and customs: 'Moorish' emerges out of the context of Phoenician colonization of the North African city of Carthage. Derived from a word meaning 'westerners', it refers to people identified also as Numidian and Mauretanian and is 'used of tribal Africans outside Carthaginian territory but not living as far south as the Sahara desert. ... Mauri – Moors – eventually came to mean all the non-romanized inhabitants' (Raven 1993: xxvi–xxvii). After the region came under the control of the Muslim Umayyid Caliphate, the 'entire population: of this region was divided into "Roms" and Moors' (xxvii). Only beginning in the early eighth century CE, as the peoples linked with Rom were associated with Christianity, did the 'Moors' become linked with Islam, specifically North African converts from this region.

HOW RELIGION INTERACTED WITH RACE IN ANTIQUITY

The previous section makes clear that ancient conceptualizations of religion were relevant for claims about collective belonging in ways that resemble or anticipate modern race. Some collective identity categories are open to individuals who also identify with other subgroups. Advocates for these collectives may portray them as superior to others; in some contexts, they become the form of orientation one must hold in order to gain full legal and political rights. This section offers readers a modern mapping, outlining four central roles that religion plays in relation to race: religion can index race; religion can be a mechanism for racial transformation, for better or for worse; religion can link two or more groups otherwise viewed as distinct; and religion can be used to make claims about intra-group difference (see Buell 2005: 36–51). Readers can use this mapping as a heuristic device to interpret the role of religion in collective identifications, locations and time periods not discussed in this chapter.

Religion as an index of race

The previous pages have offered many examples of religion being used as emblematic if not definitive of collective belonging. Romans, Jews, Christians and Muslims distinguish themselves from other groups by affirming their superiority in piety. In addition to self-definition, authors living under Roman rule stereotyped non-Roman peoples by religious traits: we have already seen how Romans stereotyped or even outlawed 'Persians' on the basis of religion (for magic or Manicheism); Egyptians were especially known for venerating deities imaged in the forms of non-human animals such as birds, cats and crocodiles (Cicero, *On the Nature of the Gods* 1.81–2); Gauls were linked with the Druids; and Jews were associated with following teachings attributed to Moses, and practices such as sabbath observance, circumcision and worship in their own temple in Jerusalem (Tacitus, *Histories* 5.4–5; Juvenal, *Satires* 14.96–106).

Worship of deities did not always index membership in a specific group. Although Isis was a deity venerated by Egyptians, the worship of Isis became extremely popular during the Ptolemaic kingdom's rule of Egypt and later throughout the Roman Empire; participation in her cult did not necessarily signify Egyptianness even as it deliberately invoked it. By the third century CE, someone who worshipped the God of Israel might understand themselves as a Jew or a Christian. Nevertheless, because the veneration of a particular deity or set of deities and/or specific religious practices were associated with collective belonging, it is not surprising that when someone adopted those practices or deity/ies, this act was sometimes framed as altering that person's place among human groups.

Religion as means of racial transformation

Becoming an initiate of Isis did not make one Egyptian, but extended contact with a religious cult viewed as 'foreign' could be portrayed as transformative: 'in the *Bakkhai* Pentheus is progressively "orientalized" through contact with the followers of the "eastern" god, Dionysos' (Hall 2002: 181). Here, religion becomes a vector of racial change for the worse. Karla Pollman has shown that the fourth-century CE Christian poet Prudentius offers a similar view in his work *Against Symmachus* (see 2.343–369), 'the more Rome extended her sway, the more alien gods entered her realms' (2011: 184). Modern architects of race-thinking such as Gobineau found such examples very useful to support claims that 'foreign' religions cause 'racial' degeneration.

Ancient sources may also depict transformation through the adoption of new religious orientations as desirable. In a number of Jewish and Christian texts, orienting oneself to a different deity and taking on new customs causes a racial change; religious conversion is simultaneously an ethnic or racial transformation. In the book of Judith, Israelites are framed as former Chaldeans, turned into a new *ethnos* by Abram/Abraham's change of religious orientation; the text's antagonist Achior (and his descendants) likewise is transformed from Ammonite to Israelite by swearing allegiance to the God of Israel and becoming circumcised (Judith 14:10; Buell 2005: 44). In his first-century CE letters Paul writes that gentiles, or 'Greeks', who receive God's spirit (*pneuma*) by becoming 'in Christ' through the ritual of baptism, gain a new ancestor and become descendants of Abraham (Gal. 3:6–9, 14, 26–9). This genealogical transformation provides a superstructure for aggregating 'Jew' and 'Greek' together into God's covenant (Johnson-Hodge 2007). Some later Christians interpreted this kind of argument to mean that a new people, Christians, descended directly from Jesus (e.g. Aristides, *Apology* 2.4; Justin Martyr, *Dialogue with Trypho* 119.3; Clement of Alexandria, *Paidagogos* 1.42.2). Other early Christians employed colour symbolism to describe conversion and transformation in ways that both trouble and anticipate modern usages (Byron 2002).

Religion as a link between two or more groups

Many origin stories about religious practices recount borrowing from or development out of other groups; in turn, these narratives directly state or imply a historical link between groups viewed as distinct. Such linkages could give credibility to a group by referencing another group associated with greater antiquity (Egyptians, for Greeks; Greeks, for Romans; Jews, for Christians). Herodotus, for example, credits Egyptians with the origins of some Greek religious customs and the names for some Greek deities (2.4.2, 49–50, 58, 64.1, 171.2–3); writing under Roman rule, Dionysius of Halicarnassus links Romans with Greeks also on the basis of religious practices (*Roman Antiquities* 7.70.1–5). Two of the staples of Roman religious practices, the diviners (*haruspices*) and the interpretation of the Sibylline Oracles (by the *quindecimviri*) were attributed to foreigners (see Cicero, *On the Nature of the Gods* 2.10–12; Dionysius of Halicarnassus, *Roman Antiquities* 4.62). Alternatively, the link between groups could be used to claim either the superiority of a more recent group (Romans, as more pious; Christians, as the true Israel) or to undermine claims to distinctiveness (Christians, as renegade Jews; Muslims, as Hagarenes).

Using religion to regulate intra-group differences

We have seen examples of the ways that religion plays a role in distinguishing among those who would otherwise be viewed as insiders. Ezra and Nehemiah call for those who were likely fellow Jews to be expelled as 'foreigners' because they were defined as not having/being the holy seed associated with returning exiles and their forms of worship; in Roman contexts, Romans who became Manichean, for example, were subject to death for adopting so-called 'Persian' monstrosities. Before 313 CE, intra-Christian disagreements and rivalries had no political weight behind them but were often articulated in terms that intermingle religion and race, aligning charges of improper religiosity with putative genealogies and ethnographies (Buell 2005; Berzon 2016). After 381 CE Christians who followed a different understanding or practice of Christianity than that embraced by the imperial family ('heretics') or who left Christianity after being a Christian ('apostates') were 'deprived of their rights to live according to Roman law (*iure Romano*) and they would live from then on outside of Roman law (*absque iure Romano*)' (Kahlos 2011: 272, 271). High status individuals who left Christianity to practice 'pagan' rites not only lost their status but were described as no longer human: 'For what could these have in common with humans – these who in their gruesome and beastly minds, hating the respect of the community, withdraw from the company of humans?' (*Codex Theodosianus* 16.7.5; cf. Kahlos 2011: 272).

These examples of how Christians with political power deployed legal codes to minoritize rival Christians or non-Christians bring us to how political expressions of power and law codes structure intra-human difference along lines simultaneously religious and racialized; these ancient examples anticipate modern colonial and imperial formations in sometimes uncanny ways.

RELIGION AND POWER

During the fifth and sixth centuries CE, polytheistic orientations, Judaism, Manicheism, Zoroastrianism and multiple ways of being Christian persisted. Christian sources increasingly recommend or praise conversion to Christianity, even under conditions of coercion (e.g. Severus of Minorca, *Letter on the Conversion of the Jews*; Gregory the Great's letters; John of Ephesus, *Ecclesiastical History*). Roman civil law imposes restrictions that create a structurally minoritized and second-class status for Jews, those following polytheistic religious orientations, and those who practice Christianity differently from the version officially sanctioned by the imperial family. Roman legal codes thus offer one way to observe the coextensive religious and racial structuring of intra-human difference in systems of power.

Roman law codes recognized Jews as a people with distinctive laws, able to bring lawsuits 'and have them judged according to Jewish law, and the verdicts ... to be enforced by [Roman] magistrates', the right to marry according to their laws,[5] redress for theft of their property by Christians, as well as protection of existing synagogues and exemption from payments being due on the Sabbath or religious holidays (Chitworth 2015: 91). But Roman laws also excluded Jews in a range of ways; they could not hold public office, marry Christians, own Christian slaves, circumcise Christian men, build new synagogues and were supposed to 'read their sacred texts in Greek, Latin or other predominant local languages' (91–2).

If these restrictions effectively minoritized Jews, also marginalized were those following traditional civic religion or non-imperial forms of Christianity. Those still oriented to gods of the household, city or region were reclassified as participating in *superstitio* and thus were legally positioned as alien to the Roman state (see *Codex Theodosianus* 16.5.63 and 16.10.12); they were also banned from military or political administrative offices or from being nominated as judges (*Codex Theodosianus* 16.10.21) and were widely described as barbarians and non-human animals, as well as by the term pagan (see Ambrose of Milan, *Epistula* 18.7; Prudentius, *Against Symmachus* 2.812–15, 816–19) (Kahlos 2011: 267–72). And we have seen above, Christians deemed 'heretics' or 'apostates' were legally sanctioned and decried as less than human.

Turning from legal codes to other expressions of political power, we find that political rule and authority are often expressed in religious terms, referencing descent from, as well as patronage and indebtedness to, specific gods; political leaders might themselves be viewed as representatives of divinity (or even divine themselves); political leaders might have roles as religious leaders or associate themselves with religious specialists of one or more particular cults. Iconography on sculptural reliefs (e.g. Persian royal tombs at Naqš-I Rustam and Persepolis; the Sebasteion in Aphrodisias) and coins indicate that representations of conquered peoples were one way to signal political might. Conquest could be portrayed in religious terms: the Arch of Titus in Rome features religious objects associated specifically with Jews, such as a menorah, to memorialize Roman success in suppressing the revolts in the province of Judea, culminating in the destruction of the central sanctuary of Jews, the Temple in Jerusalem, in 70 CE (Figure 3.5).

In the early fourth century CE, Christian writers reinterpreted Roman ideas linking 'military and political success and adherence to the right religion' to depict Christianity as the right religion for Roman imperial success (Pollman 2011: 180, 184). Prudentius gives Virgil's *Aeneid* a Christian gloss (see *Against Symmachus*), while Eusebius of Caesarea, a bishop and chronicler of the actions and significance of the Roman emperor Constantine, draws from the widespread imagery of imperial conquest, transposing it into a Christian key in which 'subjection is not measured by the imprint of an emperor's boot on a subdued people's back, but by the embrace of saving religion' (Meier 2011: 165).

The intertwining of religion and race appears multiple times in Eusebius' writings. In his *Oration in Praise of Constantine* Eusebius elevates Constantine as a leader who has, through the Christian god, defeated both visible and invisible barbarians by simultaneous

FIGURE 3.5 Arch of Titus. Forum in Rome, late first century CE. © Oleg Albinsky/Getty Images.

political and religious victory (7.13). Eusebius compares those denoted as 'visible barbarians' with not only non-human animals (who are 'no better than savage beasts' and 'ruthless wolves') but also other humans who purportedly lack appropriate social and political organization (they are like 'wild nomad tribes' and act contrary to 'civilized men') (7.2; Meier 2011: 157–8). Here, religious difference marks the barbarians and is correlated with being uncivilized and less than fully human; conversion to Christianity is part of a 'civilizing' mission, anticipating much later associations of Christian mission with European and American imperialisms.

The notion that a Christian Roman Empire constitutes an 'us' to be distinguished from political and religious threats deemed 'barbarian' persisted further into late antiquity. The Christian writer Procopius (c. 500–70 CE) writes about an equestrian statue of the Roman emperor Justinian (527–65 CE) in Constantinople (aka New Rome) (Figure 3.6):

> He gazes towards the rising sun, steering his course, I suppose, against the Persians. In his left hand he holds a globe, by which the sculptor has signified that the whole earth and sea were subject to him, yet he carries neither sword nor spear nor any other weapon, but a cross surmounts his globe, by virtue of which alone he has won the kingship and victory in war. Stretching forth his right hand towards the regions of the East and spreading out his fingers, he commands the barbarians that dwell there to remain at home and not to advance any further.
>
> (*On Buildings* 1.2.8–19)

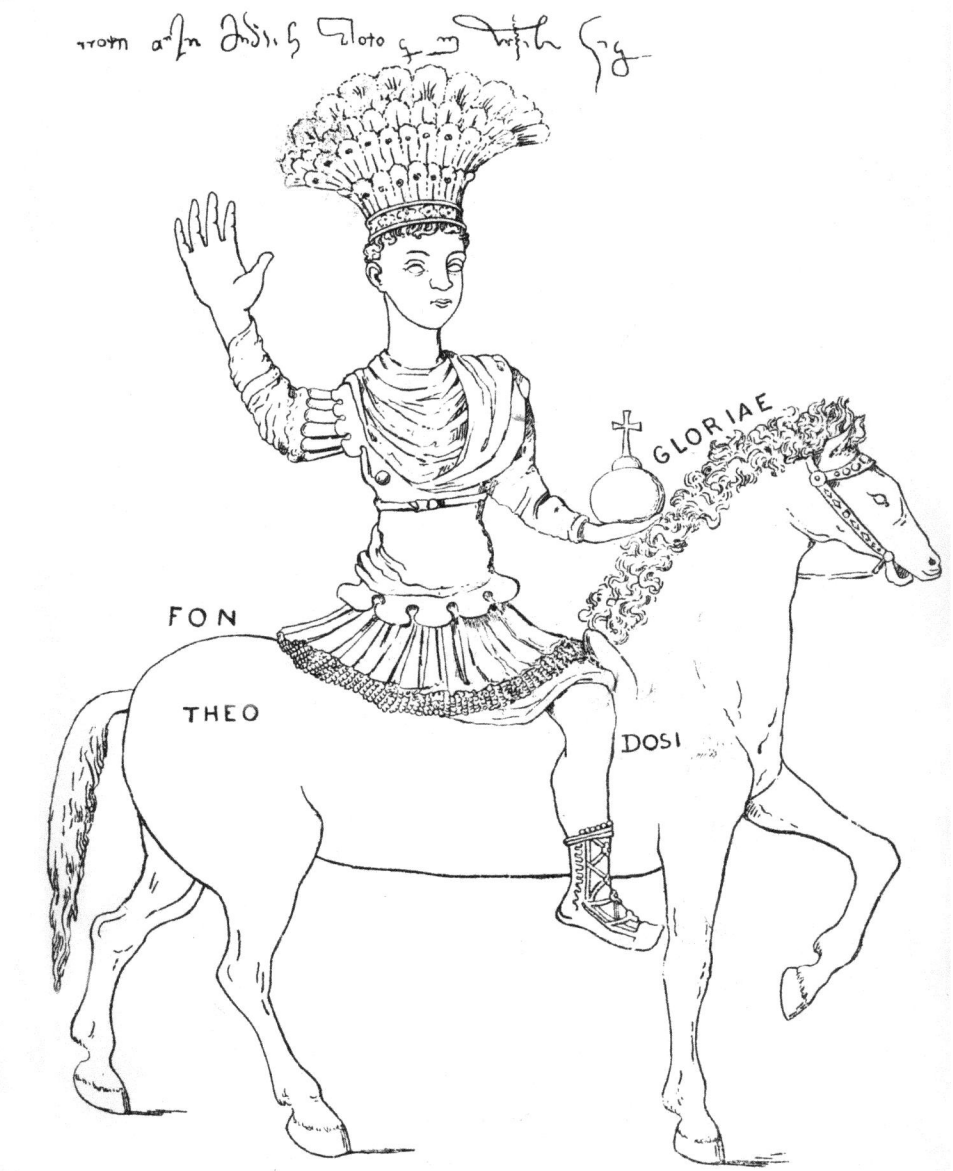

FIGURE 3.6 Drawing based on a sixth-century CE equestrian statue of Justinian, sixteenth century CE. © Photo 12/Getty Images.

Romans are here the 'us', and clearly aligned with being Christian; the Persians are the barbarians. Political success is credited to the key symbol of the Christian God, the cross, but also directly tied with what it means to be Roman. Insofar as being human, including ways of signifying differences among humans, is expressed in relation to non-human forces such as deities, religion is relevant for ancient conceptualizations of race.

CONCLUSION

In the last few decades there have been a number of interpretive 'turns' in the study of antiquity, ones that foreground persuasive speech in literary sources ('rhetoric' that tells us more about ideals than 'reality'), embodied lives and practices (attention to 'the body', to performativity), material evidence and objects (illuminating the diversity of embodied practices and the agency of non-human objects), and category criticism. These turns, not always neatly distinguishable in scholarly writings, have much to contribute to thinking about and complicating studies of race and religion. Analyses of the rhetoric of 'magic' and 'superstition' and 'heresy', for example – in conjunction with interpretation of evidence for spells of ritual power, amulets and handbooks for interpreting oracles – assist in reconstructing ancient lives as diverse, contested, changeable, improvisational and deeply interconnected with prior and concurrent practices associated rhetorically with both those framed as 'self' and 'others'. At the same time, while these turns call attention to the limits of collective categories such as 'Greek', 'Roman', 'Jew' and others, and to the vital importance of grappling with the material complexity of antiquity, they do not guarantee the undoing of racist inheritances in the interpretation of antiquity. Such undoings also require approaches that call attention to the histories of the *study* of antiquity alongside reconsiderations of ancient attempts to conceptualize the complexity of human lives. Our modern racial imaginary is not so easily contained by attempts to periodize and demarcate conceptual boundaries, including between race and religion.

CHAPTER FOUR

Race and Science

DAVID KAUFMAN

Although ethnic, gender and class prejudice, among others, were commonplace in the ancient Greek and Roman world, it is more controversial whether it makes sense to speak of racial prejudice in the period.[1] For one thing, the ancient Greeks and Romans did not recognize anything like contemporary racial categories. For example, while Greek and Roman sources discuss skin colour, they neither distinguish skin colour along the same lines, nor, in general, give skin colour anything like the same weight in distinguishing groups of people as is common in modern discussions of race.[2] Nevertheless, even if the ancient Greeks and Romans would not have recognized our racial distinctions, that does not mean that they did not draw racial distinctions of their own.

In this chapter, I focus especially on the construction of race in the Greco-Roman scientific and medical traditions. As we will see, there is strong evidence that the ancient medical and scientific traditions not only developed naturalistic theories reifying and reinforcing popular ethnic stereotypes, but also in some cases even proposed theories explicitly justifying the domination of 'barbarians' by Greeks and, later, Romans – theories that I believe come close to more contemporary notions of racial science.[3] This chapter provides an overview of several of the most important of these theories, beginning with the fifth-century BCE Hippocratic treatise *Airs, Waters, Places* and culminating in the innovative and influential work of the second-century CE medical author and philosopher Galen.

AIRS, WATERS, PLACES AND THE ENVIRONMENTAL THEORY OF RACE

Although there is evidence that human variation was a topic of investigation and debate already among earlier authors,[4] the best extant early evidence for a 'scientific' account discussing and endeavouring to explain perceived racial differences is found in the *Hippocratic Corpus*, which is by far our most extensive collection of early Greek scientific and philosophical texts. Despite its name, the *Hippocratic Corpus* consists of texts from a variety of authors, who propose quite different and, at times, even contradictory theories

---

My thanks to Jackie Murray and Mor Segev for their help with the chapter and, above all, to Denise McCoskey both for inviting me to be part of the volume and for all of her help with the chapter. The mistakes that remain are, of course, my own.

of health, physiology and medical ethics, but who share a broadly naturalistic approach to medicine.⁵ Although a more comprehensive study would focus on the construction of race in the *Hippocratic Corpus* as a whole, I focus here on a particularly detailed and influential text in the corpus: *Airs, Waters, Places*.

Airs, Waters, Places is presented to travelling physicians as a guide for effectively diagnosing and treating patients living in different communities. The text is divided into two main sections: the first half discusses how a city's exposure to certain winds and water sources affects its inhabitants' health, while the second half is a broad ethnographic survey, covering, in effect, the entire known world. According to the schema adopted in the text, the world is divided into two continents, Asia and Europe. It is worth noting right away that, as commonly in Greek and Roman geography, the text does not draw the boundaries of the continents in the same way that we would. For instance, it represents Asia as including not only the Persian Empire, but also Egypt and Libya, as well presumably as the rest of the known areas of Africa.⁶ The ethnographic section of the text focuses especially on the broad differences between the climates of Asia and Europe and on the ways in which the climate shapes the character of the inhabitants of each continent.

While the Asian climate is said to be largely temperate without great seasonal changes (*Aer.* 12.3), the European climate is described as far more variable and as including both greater extremes of heat and cold and also more significant seasonal alterations (*Aer.* 16.1–2).⁷ The text argues that these differences in climate deeply influence the animals, humans and even plants living in each continent. For instance, the plants, animals and humans of Asia are both larger and more beautiful than those of Europe on account of the temperate and well-balanced Asian climate (*Aer.* 12.2). Moreover, beyond its effects on their physique and stature, the text argues that the temperate Asian climate also has a significant effect on the character of the inhabitants in Asia, who are described as being 'gentler' and 'less warlike' than the inhabitants of Europe (*Aer.* 12.2 and 16.1). By contrast, the more inconstant and rougher European climate is said to produce more spirited and fiercer people (*Aer.* 16.2). The importance of this contrast in conduct at war is frequently highlighted by contemporary Greek art, which visually conveys the differences between Greek soldiers and Persian archers in terms of weapons and attire (Figure 4.1).

According to the model of environmental determinism developed in *Airs, Waters, Places*, the physical and ethical character of the inhabitants of an area is not simply shaped by their immediate environment, but even comes to resemble its key features. Thus, as we have seen, people living in the gentle climate of Asia are said to be gentle themselves, while those living in the rougher environment of Europe are rougher-edged, like their local environment. Indeed, the text applies this model even to more finely grained features of the environment. For instance, in Chapter Thirteen, after noting the close relationship of climate to landscape, the author argues that communities also tend to resemble their immediate landscapes. Thus, as the work describes, 'the nature of some people resembles well-wooded and watered mountains, others a thin and waterless soil, some grasslands and swamplands, and others a dry, bare earth' (*Aer.* 13.4). While it may seem rather mysterious to describe a person's nature as mountainous or swampy, the final chapter of the work develops this idea in greater detail, distinguishing seven different landscape-based typologies of character (*Aer.* 24.2). For instance, it describes mountainous people as tall, courageous and fierce, while people who live in low-lying lands with meadows are moderately sized, fleshy and have a more moderate temperament (*Aer.* 24.2–3). According to *Airs, Waters, Places*, there is, therefore, a natural tendency to *isomorphism* between the climate and landscape of a place and of the people inhabiting it.⁸

FIGURE 4.1 Pitcher (oinochoe) with a Greek warrior attacking a Persian archer, *c.* 450 BCE. Museum of Fine Arts, Boston; Bartlett Collection – Museum purchase with funds from the Francis Bartlett Donation of 1912; 13.196. © 2020 Museum of Fine Arts, Boston.

Nevertheless, if the local climate and landscape play a significant role in shaping the physique and character of the people living in it, *Airs, Waters, Places* is emphatic that the political organization of a community also plays an important and independent role in shaping the character of its members. For instance, the text argues that the inhabitants of Europe tend to be more courageous than those of Asia not only because the weather is harsher but also because they tend to be 'self-governing' (αὐτόνομοι), while those in Asia tend 'to live under absolute rulers' (δεσπόζονται, *Aer.* 16.4). As the text explains, people who live in self-governing communities are more courageous because when they go to war they fight for their own benefit rather than that of someone else. By contrast, when the subjects of absolute rulers go to war they risk their lives for the benefit of their rulers rather than themselves. There is, therefore, far more incentive to cultivate spiritedness and courage in self-governing than in monarchic societies (*Aer.* 16.5). As evidence that the form of government is an *independent* factor in determining the character of a community, the text appeals to cases where the character traits promoted by the form of government run against those promoted by the environment. In particular, the text focuses on the self-governing Greek and non-Greek communities of Asia, who are said to be 'the most warlike of all men' (μαχιμώτατοι πάντων) despite the unfavourably mild local climate (*Aer.* 16.7). According to *Airs, Waters, Places*, the local form of government and way of life thus play a crucial role in shaping the mental and ethical character of a community, over and beyond its particular climate.

According to the theory developed in *Airs, Waters, Places* the local landscape, climate and culture of a community thus deeply influence its physical and ethical character. In many ways, the text uses this model to provide a naturalistic explanation of contemporary Greek stereotypes of non-Greeks, stereotypes that are reflected throughout contemporary Greek art, including on a vase that portrays the killing of Orpheus by a Thracian woman (Figure 4.2), where gender difference is used to further heighten their conceptual distance from one another (for more on the intersections of gender and race in antiquity, see Haley in this volume).[9] Yet it is worth noting that, according to this account, the appearance, character and even the very nature of a community or individual are all quite mutable. For instance, as we have seen, the model predicts that if, say, the Persian Empire were to adopt a more democratic system of government, then its members would become progressively more spirited and warlike. Similarly, if the Athenians were to relocate to Scythia, there is every reason to expect that their physical and mental characteristics would become progressively more similar to their new surroundings. Thus, although the text seems to provide scientific backing to contemporary stereotypes about different Greek and non-Greek communities, it does not represent those differences as inalterable. Rather, it predicts that the character of a community would change radically if it were to relocate to a different climate or landscape or even simply to alter its form of government.

Along similar lines, despite dividing the world into rather simplistic ethnographic terms, *Airs, Waters, Places* gives little support to the idea that Greeks are superior to non-Greeks. While the one explicit mention of Greek people in the text praises the superlative military valour of the Ionian Greek community on the coast of Asia, who are not ruled by despots but are instead self-governing, the following line of the text emphasizes that such characteristics are shared *equally* by the self-governing non-Greek communities of Asia, belying any claim to Greek exceptionalism (*Aer.* 16.7). Accordingly, although there is good reason to think that the text's broad characterization of people living in Europe and Asia provides scientific backing for popular contemporary stereotypes, the model

FIGURE 4.2 The death of Orpheus at the hand of a Thracian woman, 450–440 BCE. © Erich Lessing/Art Resource, NY.

of environmental and cultural determinism it develops does not present non-Greeks as naturally inferior to Greeks, and even seems to make an effort to resist any such implication.[10] Matters are quite different with the next author we will consider, Aristotle, who influentially uses his own model of environmental determinism to argue for a radical version of Greek exceptionalism.

ARISTOTLE ON ETHNOGRAPHY, NATURAL SLAVERY AND ENVIRONMENTAL DETERMINISM

Although Aristotle does not give a great deal of attention in his extent works to ethnography, his ethnographic schema of the world and more general model of environmental determinism has significant implications for both his ethical and political theory. For one thing, it helps to explain his view argued in the *Politics* that the vast majority of people, including most notably women and non-Greeks, have natures that make it either very difficult or perhaps even simply impossible for them to become virtuous. Although there can be little doubt that Aristotle's views are deeply influenced by popular contemporary Greek racial and gender stereotypes, they also find support, as we will see, in his more detailed study of animal character and its physiological basis.

Aristotle describes his ethnographic views in the most detail in a well-known passage from Book Seven of the *Politics*, describing the qualities that a legislator should look for in potential citizens.

> Having spoken about the number of the citizens, let us now speak about what sort of nature they should have. One could almost grasp this by looking at the more celebrated cities of Greece and at the whole inhabited world, at how it has been divided into nations. For those who live in cold regions and in Europe are full of spirit, but are rather lacking in intelligence and technical skill; and therefore they live more freely but have no political organization and are incapable of ruling over their neighbors. Those who live in Asia, on the other hand, are intelligent and have technical skill, but are without spirit, and therefore they live in a state of subjection and slavery. The people of Greece, as they are located midway between them, so too they have a share of both, being both spirited and intelligent; and therefore they are both free and politically organized in the best possible way, and also, if they were to form a single political community, capable of ruling over everyone.
>
> (*Politics* 7.7.1327b18–39; trans. Jowett 1984, with modifications)

In this passage, Aristotle divides the inhabited world into three broad regions: Europe, Asia and Greece.[11] While the inhabitants of Europe, like those of colder climates more generally, are spirited but deficient in intelligence and technical skill, those of Asia are more intelligent and technically skilled but spiritless. These differences in character between the inhabitants of Asia and those of Europe are also said to explain their respective political structures. Thus, while the inhabitants of Asia live in a state of subjection and slavery owing to their lack of spirit, those of Europe enjoy a greater degree of freedom because of their spirited nature but are incapable of more complex forms of political organization because of their intellectual deficits. By contrast, Aristotle argues that the inhabitants of Greece, although they differ in similar ways amongst themselves, participate in the virtues of both the people of Asia and those of Europe because of their geographic position in-between the two continents and are, therefore, both intelligent and spirited. Accordingly, they are also politically organized in the best possible way and if they were to join together into a common political community, they would even be capable, in Aristotle's words, 'of ruling over everyone'.

Aristotle's emphasis here on the geographical position of Greece in-between Asia and Europe suggests that he takes its intermediate location and also, presumably, its more temperate, intermediate climate to be playing a key role in shaping the character of its inhabitants.[12] The importance of climate to Aristotle's account is also suggested by his claim in the passage above that the inhabitants of Europe share a common character with those living in cold climates more generally, which seems to imply that, in his view, it is the cooler European climate that is responsible for the character profile of the inhabitants of Europe. Thus, although he does not explicitly link Asia with a warmer climate in this passage, it seems attractive to see a similar climate-based model at play, according to which the character profile of the inhabitants of Asia is largely determined by the warmer Asian climate.

According to Aristotle, the inhabitants of Asia and Europe are thus, in effect, polar opposites both in character and political structure, while the inhabitants of Greece represent the virtuous mean between them. Like Aristotle's discussion of character virtue in his ethical works, where virtue is conceived of as a mean state between two extremes, the strong implication here is that Asians and Europeans each have defective or vicious natural characters, while Greeks are in the best possible or, in the normative sense of the term, the 'natural' condition.[13] Thus, although, in context, Aristotle introduces this ethnographic division of the world as a way of identifying the character traits that a lawgiver should select in potential citizens – namely, intelligence and spiritedness – the strong implication is that lawgivers would do well, given the opportunity, to select their citizens exclusively from among the Greek population.

While Aristotle's ethnographic account shares much in common with the ethnographic section of *Airs, Waters, Places* – for instance, both texts describe Europeans as warlike and spirited and Asians as comparatively spiritless – the differences between the two accounts are even more striking. First, while both texts distinguish the prevailing political systems in Asia and Europe along broadly similar lines, *Airs, Waters, Places* denies that the respective political systems in each continent are determined by their different environments but rather emphasizes that the lifestyle and form of government of a community shape the character of its inhabitants, *independently* of the local environment. By contrast, Aristotle argues that the environmentally determined character of the inhabitants of Europe and of Asia *explains* why Europeans tend to be self-governing, while people in Asia tend to live under despotic regimes.

Another important difference is that while the discussion in *Airs, Waters, Places* focuses particularly on the effects of the environment on the relative spiritedness of the inhabitants of Asia and those of Europe, Aristotle argues that the environment plays a significant role in determining *both* the spiritedness *and* the intelligence of communities. For example, according to him, Europeans are not only more spirited but also less intelligent than the inhabitants of Asia because of their environment. Aristotle's model of environmental determinism is, therefore, more encompassing than that of *Airs, Waters, Places*. Finally, while *Airs, Waters, Places* mentions the Greeks only in passing and gives no indication that Greeks are, in general, superior to non-Greeks, Aristotle's ethnographic sketch presents the Greeks as not only combining the best traits of the inhabitants of both Asia and Europe, but also as uniquely suited to rule over all other peoples.

In the broader context of the *Politics*, Aristotle's view that Greeks are naturally superior to non-Greeks and so too capable of ruling over them fits well with and further articulates his account of 'natural slavery' developed in Book One (1.4, 1254a13–1.7, 1255b39).[14] By natural slaves, Aristotle means people who suffer from a rational deficit such that they are incapable of directing their own lives but are rather better off living under the command of a more competent supervisor. As he explains, such people are not altogether irrational but have a share of reason only 'so far as to perceive it, but not to possess it' (1.5, 1254b22–3). Natural slaves are, therefore, capable of following directions and, as Malcolm Heath has persuasively argued, presumably even of carrying out complicated technical tasks, but lack the rational capacities required to rule themselves and others (2008: 244–53). Aristotle introduces the notion of natural slavery in response to the objection that slavery is simply a matter of brute force and so always unjust, as some of his contemporaries had argued (1.3, 1253b20–3, 1.6, 1255a4–11).[15] While Aristotle thinks that his opponents are right that some actual slaves are enslaved only by virtue of force and circumstance, and so are, in his terms, slaves by law rather than by nature, he is emphatic that many people are natural slaves, whether or not they are actually enslaved (1.5, 1254b16–23, 1.7, 1255b37–9).

In support of his distinction between natural and merely legal slavery, Aristotle appeals to contemporary Greek views about the natural superiority of Greeks to non-Greeks.

For instance, he supports his distinction between natural and merely legal slavery by appealing to the view of some of his contemporaries that the term 'slave' (δοῦλος) should be applied exclusively to non-Greeks, and again to the view that the term 'good birth' (εὐγένεια), if used strictly, applies only to Greeks (*Politics* 1.6, 1255a21–1255b1). As Aristotle explains, these views distinguish between a strict and a more colloquial use of terms such as 'slave' and 'good birth'. In their strict sense, he argues, such terms refer not to a person's current position in society but instead to their nature, whatever their position in society happens to be. For instance, according to Aristotle's analysis, when his contemporaries propose limiting the term 'slave' to non-Greeks, they implicitly commit themselves to the idea that while some people (namely, Greeks) are slaves nowhere, others (namely, at least some non-Greeks) are slaves everywhere (1.6, 1255a31–2). Aristotle also asserts the natural superiority of Greeks to non-Greeks elsewhere in the *Politics*. For instance, in a passage from Book Three, he explains why many non-Greeks live under legally established and ancestral monarchies by arguing that non-Greeks are naturally 'more slavish' than Greeks, and so 'endure despotic rule without any complaint' (3.14, 1285a18–22). There is therefore quite good evidence throughout the *Politics* that Aristotle both takes Greeks to be, on the whole, naturally superior to non-Greeks, and that he believes that, at least, many non-Greek men and women are natural slaves.

Aristotle's argument that Greeks are naturally superior to, and suited to rule over, non-Greeks presumably owes a great deal both to contemporary Greek stereotypes and to his contemporary political moment, which was dominated by the expansionist program of Philip II of Macedon and his son and Aristotle's pupil Alexander the Great. Yet, Aristotle's account in his biological works of what we might call the chemical basis of animal character also helps to provide a foundation for his radical distinction between the natural capacities of Greeks and non-Greeks, one based on his detailed account of the natural world.[16] In particular, in Book Two of *Parts of Animals* – a work that survives in part, like many of Aristotle's treatises, through its transmission in Arabic texts[17] – Aristotle argues that the particular quality of blood of an animal has significant implications for its relative spiritedness and intelligence, exactly the same two qualities that he focuses on in his ethnographic division of mankind (*Parts of Animals* 2.2 647b31–648a11 and 2.4 650b14–651a17) (Figure 4.3).

According to Aristotle's account, the blood of animals is differentiated in three ways: by its relative thinness or thickness, its relative purity or turbidity and its relative coolness or heat. In general, according to Aristotle's account, the hotter an animal's blood is, the more conducive it is to strength and spirit, while the purer and thinner it is, the more conducive it is to sensation and intelligence. In his discussion, Aristotle focuses especially on three broad character profiles among species of animals: some, such as deer, have blood that is cool, thin and pure and so are intelligent but timorous; others, such as bulls, have blood that is warm, thick and turbid and so are unintelligent but spirited; finally, the 'best' (ἄριστα) class of animals have blood that is *both* hot *and also* thin and pure and so are both spirited and intelligent (2.2, 648a9–11). By the best animals, Aristotle seems to have in mind particularly humans, whom he describes elsewhere as both the most intelligent of animals and also as having a particularly 'good-mixture' (εὐκρασία) of blood (*History of Animals* 3.19, 521a2–4; *Generation of Animals* 2.6, 744a26–31).[18]

Although Aristotle's account of the ethological implications of blood type is focused on explaining the differences in spiritedness and intelligence between different *species* of animals, the three animal character profiles he focuses on are strikingly similar to the character profiles of the *peoples* he distinguishes in his ethnographic account in the

FIGURE 4.3 The sage Aristotle and a pupil. *Kitab Na't al-hayawan* (*Book of the Characteristics of Animals*), thirteenth century. © Album/Alamy Stock Photo.

Politics. In particular, in both cases he distinguishes a character type that is courageous but stupid – Europeans and bulls; those who are intelligent but cowardly – Asians and deer; and those who are both intelligent and courageous – Greeks and humans.[19] While Aristotle does not explicitly bring his blood theory to bear on his account of human character, his account of the role of an animal's blood type in shaping its relative spiritedness and intelligence provides the materials for a detailed scientific explanation of the differences in natural character and intellectual capacity he identifies between Asians, Europeans and Greeks. Thus, following such a model, we might expect the inhabitants of Asia to have relatively thin, pure and cool blood, those of Europe to have hot, thick and turbid blood, and those from Greece to have hot, thin and pure blood.

While Aristotle does not explain why the inhabitants of hot climates such as Asia develop relatively cool and pure blood, but those of cold climates such as Europe develop relatively hot and thick blood, it is not too difficult to imagine several possible reasons he might have adduced. For instance, in considering the effects of climate on the local inhabitants, the later Peripatetic work *Problems* suggests (among other possible explanations) that people develop natures that *counteract* (ἐναντίως ἔχει) excesses in the surrounding environment (*Problems* 14.16 910a37–910b8).[20] Thus, the text explains, people who live in hot regions are able to survive the heat because they become cool and so too cowardly, while those who live in cold regions become hot and so too courageous. By contrast, according to such a model, people who live in a well-mixed and temperate climate, such as Greece, presumably have natures that remain in their natural, unaltered state, and so are better suited both for intelligence and courage.

While we cannot be certain that Aristotle would have developed his account along the lines suggested in *Problems*, we have seen that his biological theory provides, at the least, the materials for a detailed naturalistic explanation of the differences in character and intellectual capacity that he describes in his ethnographic account in the *Politics*. Aristotle thus not only argues for a particularly radical version of Greek exceptionalism, according to which Greeks are both superior to other peoples and ought also, if possible, to enslave and rule over them, but his work also provides at least the materials for a more comprehensive 'scientific' explanation both of the superiority of Greeks over non-Greeks and of his theory of natural slavery.

To a considerable degree, Aristotle's work, therefore, anticipates modern scientific racism, insofar as it both provides a naturalistic basis for contemporary racial stereotypes by linking the character and capacities that define different groups of people to the environment and its ostensible effects on human biology, and also uses these distinctions to justify and even to recommend the oppression of non-Greeks.[21] While it is unclear whether Aristotle's ethnographic views or theory of natural slavery had any effect on the treatment of non-Greeks in antiquity, his account of natural slavery proved quite influential in modern defences of slavery both in the Americas and later in the United States.[22] Nevertheless, although there are important affinities between Aristotle's account of Greek exceptionalism and more modern forms of scientific racism, there is an important difference between the two: while modern scientific racism often focuses a great deal on the appearance of different races, Aristotle's account gives relatively little attention to the appearance of Greeks and non-Greeks, but focuses instead on alleged differences in their ethical and intellectual capacities.[23] By contrast, in the next section, we will turn to the science of physiognomy, which developed a detailed account of how each aspect of a person's physical appearance offers insight into their character and intellectual ability.

GALEN AND THE PHYSIOGNOMISTS

Although a science of physiognomy seems to have been well established in Greece already in the classical period, our evidence for ancient physiognomy is almost exclusively post-classical.[24] In addition to the use of physiognomic theory in post-classical art, literature and rhetoric, we have several post-classical physiognomic handbooks that provide a detailed account of how to interpret the significance of each aspect of a person's appearance for their intellectual and ethical character and capacities. From a modern perspective, both the level of detail of the handbooks and the aspects of the body that the authors focus on are often quite surprising. For instance, roughly a third of the surviving material from the second-century CE sophist Polemon's influential physiognomic handbook *Physiognomics* focuses on the physiognomic significance of the features and movement of the eyes (Leiden Polemon A5–23).[25]

However, if Polemon's work focuses particularly on the eyes, he is emphatic that each part of the body has physiognomic significance. And indeed, his work includes chapters on the physiognomic significance of the area between the shoulders and the tops of the shoulders, and again, separate chapters on the knees and calves, as well as more likely areas for physiognomic scrutiny such as the face (B18, B7–8 and B23–9). It is worth noting that like most of the ancient handbooks on physiognomy, Polemon's work includes little by way of explanation of why certain features are correlated with a certain kind of character. Rather, his work simply provides a detailed list of which different physical features are correlated with different kinds of character without further explanation.

Perhaps the clearest account of the different sorts of methods that physiognomists might use in identifying and interpreting physiognomic signs is found in the post-classical Aristotelian treatise *Physiognomics*,[26] which distinguishes three particularly influential methods of drawing physiognomic inferences: first, by analogy to different species of animals – for example people with lion-like features are courageous (Figure 4.4); second, by analogy to different racial groups – for example people with Germanic features are courageous and unintelligent; and finally, by analogy to the facial expressions and physiological changes accompanying different emotional states, such as anger, fear or sadness – for example people whose standing expression resembles someone in a fit of rage are irascible (Pseudo-Aristotle, *Physiognomics* 805a20–31; cf. Anon. Lat. 9). Most relevant for my present purposes is the second method, which focuses on the characteristic appearance and character of different racial groups.

Despite its inclusion as one of the three basic methods of physiognomy, in practice the extant handbooks limit their use of race almost exclusively to discussion of skin colour and hair type.[27] While there is some variance both between and within the texts, the extant physiognomic handbooks largely agree on the physiognomic significance of different skin colours and hair type. According to our evidence, black skin is most often associated with cowardice and guile, while pale skin is associated either with weakness, by association with femininity, or with stupidity and aggressiveness.[28] The

FIGURE 4.4 Illustration of a man with lion-like features in Giovanni Battista Della Porta's *On Human Physiognomy* (sixteenth century). © ARCHIVIO GBB/Alamy Stock Photo.

physiognomic interpretation of hair is similar: people with curly hair are said to be cowardly and wily, while those with straight hair are wild and mindless. Hair colour is evaluated along the same lines: black hair is associated with cowardice and craftiness, while blond and pale hair indicates ignorance and wildness.[29] The physiognomic interpretation of skin colour, hair type and hair colour thus make use of the same stereotypes that we have seen already in Aristotle's ethnographic division of the world. For instance, as in Aristotle, people from the South, whom the physiognomic treatises describe as having dark skin and curly dark hair, are cowardly but intelligent, while those from the North, who are described as having pale skin and straight yellow hair, are hyper-spirited but unintelligent.

Several of the physiognomic handbooks also describe the appearance of the ideal Greek man. As Polemon describes him, the 'pure' Greek man – who is uncontaminated by foreign stock – has white-reddish skin and hair that is soft, red and moderately curled, and is also of medium stature both in height and girth and has medium palms and elbows, as well as a medium sized head and neck (B32; cf. Adamantius B32).[30] Beyond appealing to his aesthetic preference for median features, Polemon's more detailed account of each aspect of the ideal Greek type's appearance also contributes to his portrait of the ethical and intellectual character and capacities of the ideal man. For example, in his discussion of hair colour, Polemon distinguishes the pure Greek's moderate red hair colour from the extremes of the red/white hair of Slavs and Turks, and argues that moderate red hair indicates 'knowledge, experience, quietness, and magnanimity' (B37; cf. Adamantius B37).[31] Again, in his account of the physiognomic significance of skin colour, Polemon argues that the pure Greek's reddish white skin indicates 'boldness and great anger' (B33; cf. Adamantius B33). According to Polemon's account of skin and hair colour, the ideal Greek man is therefore both courageous and intelligent, once again closely fitting the racial stereotypes we find in Aristotle. Indeed, as Polemon describes him, the pure Greek man is composed of body parts each of which is in the mean state in its domain and that collectively indicate courage and intelligence, as well as the rest of the virtues.

Although the physiognomic handbooks give much more attention to the physical appearance of the different racial groups they describe than the ethnographic accounts we have discussed and, in particular, place a far greater emphasis on skin colour and hair type, it is worth noting that race-based signs play a quite limited role overall in the physiognomic handbooks.[32] In fact, Adamantius emphasizes that skin colour and hair colour are, at best, unreliable indications of character. For instance, before presenting his schema for skin colour and hair type, he cautions his reader that signs from skin colour and hair are 'not sufficient in themselves for the purposes of physiognomy' (B31).[33] For one thing, he explains, since different groups of people have mixed together, with Syrians living in Italy, Libyans in Thrace and others elsewhere, skin colour and hair type do not even serve as a reliable means of determining whether or not any given individual belongs to a certain racial group.

While Adamantius does not explain exactly why the immigration patterns he describes pose a challenge for physiognomic analysis, he presumably holds that in such cases a person's physical appearance or, at least, their skin colour and hair type simply do not provide a reliable indication of their character, perhaps because their skin colour and hair type have been altered by their current environment, while their character and intellectual capacities have remained more constant.[34] Adamantius' note of caution about the evidentiary value of skin colour and hair type also raises a more general difficulty for the physiognomic tradition. Because the ancient physiognomic tradition does not include a detailed causal account of *why* the physical features it focuses on indicate particular character traits and intellectual capacities, it is not well suited to disambiguating cases where the same physical feature might have different ethical and intellectual implications depending on its origin or aetiology. For example, even if we were to accept Polemon's claim that thin hips are often a sign of deceit, cunning and immorality (B9), we might doubt that thin hips have the same ethological significance whether someone has this trait from birth or acquires it only through the severe caloric restrictions of being stranded on a desert island.[35]

Like the authors of the physiognomic handbooks, the influential second-century CE Greek physician and philosopher Galen also argues that it is possible to learn a great deal about someone's character, intellectual capacities and their relative health by attending to detailed aspects of their physical features.[36] Moreover, as we will see, Galen also accepts the same basic ethnographic distinctions and stereotypes as the authors of the physiognomic handbooks. Nevertheless, if Galen agrees with the physiognomists that a person's detailed physical features may reveal a great deal about their physiological and psychological condition,[37] he explains their psychological significance in the context of his own detailed account of the fundamental constitution and structure of the body. In particular, he argues that such features indicate more fundamental underlying mixtures within the person's body, which, in turn, help to determine many of their physiological and psychological capacities and dispositions (Figure 4.5).

FIGURE 4.5 Hippocrates and Galen, fresco, early thirteenth century, in the Crypt of St Mary Cathedral, Anagni, Lazio. © DEA/A. DAGLI ORTI/Getty Images.

According to Galen, humans, like other animals, are composed of a particular mixture of four elemental qualities: hot, cold, dry and wet (*Mixtures* 1.1, 509–10 Kühn).[38] As he argues in his treatise *Mixtures*, a person's physical well-being, as well as their character and intellectual capacities, are deeply affected by the precise mixture of these qualities. While there are an indefinite number of proportions these elements might have, Galen distinguishes nine basic types of mixtures: eight 'bad-mixtures' (δυσκρασίαι), in which one or two elements are predominant – so (1) hot, (2) cold, (3) dry, (4) wet, (5) hot and dry, (6) hot and wet, (7) cold and dry, (8) cold and wet – and one 'good-mixture' (εὐκρασία) in which none of the elements is predominant (1.8, 1.559 Kühn). Galen illustrates his typology of bodily mixtures by considering which human being has the best mixture of all, whom he will use as a 'standard' (κανών) by which to judge whether other humans – and for that matter all other existent objects and animals – are hot, cold, dry or wet. As his model, Galen adopts a famous statue, the Standard (κανών) of Polykleitos, which he argues acquired this name because each of its parts are in a 'precise state of good balance' (ἀκριβὴς συμμετρία) with each other (1.9, 1.566 Kühn).[39] As he describes, a person resembling Polykleitos' Standard will be well-proportioned, his bodily parts will be well shaped, his body will be moderately firm and thick, and he will have an intermediate quantity of hair, which itself will be of an intermediate colour between white and black (Figure 4.6). Finally, and perhaps most importantly, he will also have skin that is perfectly calibrated to be well-suited both for accurate perception and grasping objects (1.9, 1.567–8 Kühn).[40] More generally, such a person is, in Galen's description, 'faultless in all his natural and psychological activities' (2.1, 1.577 Kühn).

Galen's image of the ideal human, each of whose features are in a mean condition between opposite excesses, is strikingly similar to the account of the 'pure Greek' type in the physiognomic treatises. It is worth noting, however, that while the physiognomic treatises contrast the ideal Greek with other 'defective' races, particularly people from Africa and northern Europe, Galen distinguishes the ideal human from humans with each of the eight different bad-mixtures described above. Thus, while Galen explicitly endorses the broad racial stereotypes of the physiognomic handbooks,[41] such stereotypes are far less important in his actual account of the physical and psychological implication of different physical features than his more detailed theory of elemental mixtures.[42] For instance, even in endeavouring to explain the popular physiognomic view that pale skin indicates spiritedness and boldness, Galen emphasizes that in his view 'it is not possible to clearly recognize the mixture of the internal parts from the condition of the skin', thereby cautioning his readers not to associate people with pale skin too hastily with stereotypical notions of northern Europeans as 'spirited and bold' (*Mixtures* 2.6, 1.627 Kühn). Moreover, in his account, Galen is also emphatic that a person's age, gender, diet, lifestyle and even the current season of the year all have a significant impact on their elemental constitution. Galen's mixture-based typology of human character is therefore not only far more complex but also allows for more mobility between the types he distinguishes than either the race-based accounts of the physiognomic treatises or Aristotle's ethnographic schema in the *Politics*. Thus, although Galen believes that we can learn a great deal about a person's physiological and psychological condition from their physical features and also explicitly endorses contemporary racial stereotypes, such stereotypes play a surprisingly limited role in his own articulated account of human physiology.

FIGURE 4.6 Polykleitos' Standard as represented in his Doryphoros (spear-bearer) statue, preserved in Roman copy. © DEA/G. Nimatallah/De Agostini/Getty Images.

CONCLUSION

This chapter has discussed several of the most influential ancient Greek and Roman scientific accounts of racial difference, beginning with the fifth-century BCE text *Airs, Waters, Places* and culminating in the sophisticated physiological theory developed by Galen in the second century CE. While the model of environmental determinism developed in *Airs, Waters, Places* proved extremely influential in the later Greek and Roman scientific tradition, the text's bipartite division of the world between the more gentle inhabitants of Asia and the more spirited and rougher inhabitants of Europe was dramatically altered by the later tradition. More influential in the development of a Greek model of scientific racism was Aristotle's Hellenocentric depiction of the Greeks as radically different from both the people of Asia and of Europe. As we have seen, by distinguishing the Greek environment and its inhabitants from those of Asia and Europe, Aristotle was able to use the scientific model of environmental determinism developed in *Airs, Waters, Places* to justify contemporary Hellenocentric views and even to encourage the domination and enslavement of, at least, most non-Greeks. Moreover, his work on the chemical basis of animal character shows the degree to which certain ideas about the biological roots of difference permeated his writings, bolstering his detailed account of the alleged differences in ethical and intellectual capacities of Greeks and non-Greeks.

The post-classical physiognomic tradition developed Aristotle's ethnographic schema along quite different lines. In particular, in its discussion of the characteristic appearance of different racial groups, it focused especially on differences in skin and hair colour and hair type, and argued that these differences in appearance have important implications for a person's ethical and intellectual character. The final section of the chapter turned to the second-century CE medical author and philosopher Galen of Pergamon and his idiosyncratic take on the physiognomic and ethnographic traditions. As we have seen, although Galen was sympathetic both to popular racial stereotypes and to the physiognomists' project of using detailed aspects of a person's appearance as indications of their ethical and intellectual character, he made little use of such stereotypes and rather divided humans along quite different lines in his own physiological theory. Thus, if Aristotle's model of environmental determinism and blood-based account of character difference pointed the way to racial science, Galen's scientific project seems to have led him away from the popular racial stereotypes promoted by Aristotle and the physiognomists in favour of a theory that categorized not by race but according to the individual's particular elemental mixture.

CHAPTER FIVE

Race and Politics

GRANT PARKER

In T. J. Haarhoff's *Stranger at the Gate: Aspects of Exclusiveness and Co-operation in Ancient Greece and Rome, with Some Reference to Modern Times* (1948), Julius Caesar plays a supporting but telling role. It was Caesar who introduced Gauls to the senate (Figure 5.1), for which he received strong criticism from the aristocracy. For his biographer Suetonius, this episode exemplifies both his liberality and the outrage he inflicted on senatorial sensibilities:

> When foreigners were admitted to the senate, the following placard was set up: 'Well done, those who refuse to show a new senator where the senate house is!' And the following verse was heard everywhere: 'Caesar led the Gauls in his triumph – and into the senate house; the Gauls put aside their trousers and put on the broad stripe.'
>
> (Suetonius, *Life of Julius Caesar* 80.2)

The prominence the senate receives in this anecdote is at odds with a very different Roman institution. By contrast, the triumph announced the military conquest of foreign peoples, framing it as metropolitan spectacle: its institution and structures have contributed to Rome's place in modern social memory (Beard 2007). In the passage quoted, the stereotyping detail of Gallic breeches serves to underline Caesar's tyrannical behaviour, contributing to Suetonius' effective explanation of the conspiracy that would be spearheaded by Cassius, Decimus Brutus and Marcus Brutus on 15 March 44 BCE. While the death of Caesar famously marks a major crisis in the Roman state, more significant here is the prevailing political order and the degree of its openness to the creation of new Romans.

It is easy to see this incident in a broader sweep of Roman history. In the most immediate sense, it looks forward to a speech made before the Roman senate in 48 CE, in which the emperor Claudius proposed the admission of landed Gauls into that body. The episode is famous because the speech survives in a bronze document known as the Lyon tablet, which appears to be an unembellished transcription (*Corpus Inscriptionum Latinarum* 13.1668), as well as Tacitus' tendentious literary version (*Annals* 11.23–4). The episode involving Caesar also looks forward to the Antonine Constitution of 212 CE, whereby the emperor Caracalla conferred citizenship on all the empire's free males. Such moments punctuate Haarhoff's broad historical sweep.

In so far as the passage articulates social differences between Gauls and Romans, as well as their political ramifications, it encourages a broader view of the dynamics of

FIGURE 5.1 The Roman senate, interior (Curia Iulia), first century CE. © Balage Balogh/archaeologyillustrated.com/akg-images.

inclusion and exclusion, which is the subject of the current chapter. Following some initial framing which questions what is at stake (in the first section), this chapter proceeds with a broad-brush sketch of ways in which race might be relevant to Greco-Roman history, with special attention to the Hellenistic period as well as Rome's late republican and early imperial periods (in the second and third sections). In making this choice I follow the lead of Haarhoff, to whom the focus turns thereafter. Significantly for our purposes, *Stranger at the Gate* connects this integrative view of Greco-Roman antiquity with Haarhoff's own country and world. Its theme seems prescient (Gladwell 2019). Haarhoff's insistence on tracing connections between ancient and modern racial histories is instructive in principle though compromised by its own implicit 'exclusiveness', something that emerges by comparison with his younger contemporary of different political stripe, Benjamin Kies (discussed in the fourth section). The South African Haarhoff's closer contemporary was Fritz Schachermeyr, an Austrian scholar and sometime Nazi Party member, whose scholarship also intersects with his politics (as examined in the fifth section): such connections frame the larger topic. A third and final case study (in the sixth section) takes us to the *Ancient Nubia Now* exhibit in Boston (2019–20), with attention to both its contents and its public interface. To conclude, in the final section, I take a broader approach to questions of continuities, elisions and identities, as well as the personal voice in scholarship which I present as key factors determining the supposed salience of race. This chapter thus has intertwined strands, ancient and modern. Its central claim is that the matter of race in antiquity crystalizes around diverging historical conceptions of cross-cultural interaction, which are necessarily framed by the assumptions and preoccupations of scholars in their own times. There is nothing new or surprising about this claim but its inflections and implications turn out to be considerable.

DOING RACE IN ANTIQUITY

Gauls entering the Roman senate are prima facie a case of racial identity for Haarhoff; yet the term race has been used in a wide range of senses. How then to deal with the terminological minefield? Certainly, the term race has been used in very different ways in modern times, and the more recent currency of the term ethnicity complicates the issue. In their overview, Moya and Markus insist that 'race is a doing – a dynamic set of historically derived and institutionalized ideas and practices that sorts people into ethnic group according to perceived physical and behavioral human characteristics … ; associates differential value, power, privilege with those characteristics; establishes hierarchy among the different groups, and confers opportunity accordingly' (2010: 21). In this they develop the idea, articulated by Michael Omi and Howard Winant in 1984, of 'racial formation', which emphasizes the socially constructed nature of race. For Moya and Markus, race 'emerges when groups are perceived to pose a threat … to each other's worldview or way of life; and/or to justify the denigration and exploitation … of other groups while exalting one's own group to claim an innate privilege' (21). The emphasis on doing is matched by the same authors' definition of ethnicity, which overlaps considerably, except in so far as ethnicity has emic as well etic elements, in other words contains a strong sense of self-definition: 'ethnicity … allows people to identify, or be identified, with a grouping of peoples on the basis of presumed, and usually claimed, commonalities, including several of the following: language, history, nation or region of origin, customs, religion, names, physical appearance and/or ancestry group' (22). The distinction between race and ethnicity is further complicated by the fact that the former is more commonly used in the United States and the latter in the United Kingdom and Europe. By the same token, scholars of the ancient Mediterranean have tended to prefer ethnicity as a marker of cultural identity (Hall 1997; Gruen 2011a); recent work arguing for race has come in its wake (Isaac 2004; McCoskey 2012). What might racial formation mean in an ancient Mediterranean context? It is true that we have many texts offering theories of a somewhat abstract nature (Kennedy, Roy and Goldman 2013). On the other hand, practices of social differentiation show up differently in Greco-Roman history and are only sometimes identified as race (McCoskey 2012: 81–131).

Finally, why race *and* politics? The combination is tautological if we recognize race to be a fundamentally political phenomenon. Nonetheless, the combination articulates a central argument of this chapter: that contemporary contexts necessarily intrude into and even frame articulations of ancient inter-group relations, with the result that a bifocal approach is needed. In a word, there is an unescapable (modern) political dimension to the study of (ancient) race.

HELLENES, HELOTS AND HELLENISM

What would a history of ancient inter-group relations look like? This is the challenge Haarhoff takes up in *Stranger at the Gate*, a challenge taken up also by other scholars but rarely with such an appetite for making comparison with their own worlds. In the early twentieth century such large-scale histories would typically hew a path close to literary sources, beginning with Homer. The *Iliad*, recounting episodes in the Trojan War, is *a priori* a story of inter-group contact but in practice there are no visible differences between Greeks and Trojans that correspond to modern notions of social or linguistic distinction. The Trojan War looms large in Greek tradition, as is evident from the 'Archaeology' with which Thucydides begins his *History of the Peloponnesian War* (1.2–19): before that time there was no common cause to unite the Greeks, he says, and the fact that Homer doesn't use the term *barbaros* for non-Greeks is indicative of the fragmentation of the Greek-speaking world. It is only with the development of sea-power that Greek states gained long-distance power and also a strong sense of corporate identity (Thucydides 1.3). By contrast, at the start of the *Odyssey*, we read that the hero Odysseus 'saw the cities of many men and came to know their minds' (1.3), but as the narrative progresses this supposed knowledge of people's minds turns out to be eclipsed by Odysseus' resourceful trickery. Such 'mythistory', an ancient blend of what we might call history and myth, predominates in ancient accounts and has aligned awkwardly, if at all, with modern archaeology (Cartledge 2012: 18–35; Gehrke 2014). Nonetheless, it gives evidence for ancient thinking about cross-cultural contact and the identities involved.

Colonization was a major feature of the archaic age, which lasted from 776 BCE (according to Greek tradition) to the end of the Greco-Persian Wars in 479 BCE. This process started with Euboea's establishment of satellite settlements at Cumae and Pithecousae, approximately 750–730 BCE, with other states and indeed colonies themselves following suit at a wide variety of locations. This period was characterized by state formation in the form of the *polis*, constituted in substantial measure by religious factors. Interstate relations would depend in part on warfare, which had some ritual elements. While scholars have debated the term colonization, given connections with modern history, this process is without question one involving long-distance migration. It is less clear whether the processes were haphazard or centralized. Concerning the relation of colony to metropolis there is tantalizing but limited evidence from documents such as the foundation decree of Cyrene, which survives in its fourth-century BCE form though claims (somewhat questionably) to stem from the foundation itself in the seventh century BCE. It records the resolution of the island-state Thera to send a contingent under the leadership of Battos out to make a colony in Cyrene in North Africa: among the terms stipulated is equal citizenship with Therans.

The year 776 BCE is also the traditional date for the start of the Olympian Games, which drew participants from all over the Greek world, including its colonies; three further festivals were added in the sixth century, at Delphi, Nemea and Isthmia. These panhellenic festivals continued to be celebrated until their abolition by the Christian emperor Theodosius in 393 CE. Religious festivals would be an important expression and source of ethnic identity while allowing for distinctiveness within overarching commonalities (Hall 2002).

Slavery is a major thread throughout Greco-Roman history, but its ethnic and racial elements are complex. It was common to identify slaves by their origins, for example the Scythian archers who served as a kind of police force in fifth- and early fourth-century Athens (Figure 5.2). In Aristophanes' *Thesmophoriazusae* these Scythians are marked by their non-Athenian language usage. But it is also true that this kind of identification was far from absolute or limiting. Aristotle's concept of natural slavery (*Politics* 1) does not seem to have been ethnically conceived, and the relevant passages are riddled with contradictions (for lengthier discussion of Aristotle's views on natural slavery, see Kaufman in this volume). Nonetheless, Aristotle's implication that natural slavery is unchangeable has bolstered latter essentialist approaches to group identity, and many moderns have used Aristotle to justify slavery. Thus, in the Valladolid Controversy concerning Spain's right of conquest (1550), Juan Ginés de Sepúlveda claimed that Amerindians were natural slaves: Aristotle is a central pillar along with biblical and classical sources. Aristotle

FIGURE 5.2 Attic plate with a red-figure image of an archer in Scythian dress, fifth century BCE. © Print Collector/Hulton Archive/Getty Images.

was likewise quoted by the former slave Jacobus Elisa Johannes Capitein in support of his argument, in a University of Leiden thesis of 1742, that physical slavery is indeed compatible with Christian freedom (Parker 2001) (Figure 5.3).

A little understood but intriguing part of the story involves the helots, namely Laconians and Messenians conquered by the Spartans between the tenth and seventh centuries BCE. These were state-owned, and in terms of their status 'between free persons and chattel (*douloi*)'. The sources emphasize Spartan brutality towards the helots (e.g. Thucydides 4.80), and the huge numerical predominance of helots over Spartans (Xenophon, *Hellenica* 3.3.4–11). Helots seem to have provided military capacity for the Spartan state and agricultural labour for individual Spartans. This ethnic unity of the helots seems to have been a unique scenario, whereas in city-states other than Sparta slaves seem to have come from a variety of groups.

While warfare involved violence it also had ritualistic and ideological elements, particularly around the hoplite phalanx. The Persian Wars (491–479 BCE) may have

FIGURE 5.3 Jacobus Elisa Johannes Capitein (1717–1747), illustration in his *Political-Theological Dissertation on the Compatibility of Slavery and Christian Freedom* (Leiden: Philippus Bonk, 1742). © Wikimedia Commons. Public domain.

united Greek city-states against a common enemy, but they also saw a degree of Athenian 'cultural receptivity' to Achaemenid Persia evidenced in its use of prestige goods, not only weapons but also ceramics, furniture, dress and so on. This phenomenon Miller (1997) characterizes as *Perserie*. It is in this light that a broad view of inter-group contact should inform any consideration of Alexander's expedition and the new polities it created. It is ironic that Macedonia, a latecomer to Panhellenic activities, would in the age of Alexander become a motor force for the diffusion of Greek speakers into southwest Asia. The pièce de résistance of Hellenism is Afghanistan. As French archaeologists have shown, one of its sites, Ai Khanum, shows evidence of Greek language and material culture, in the form of inscriptions and structures such as an apparent gymnasium and theatre. More recent scholarship has shied away from interpreting the site as a 'Greek city', suggesting instead that these material remains could have represented choices made by some local inhabitants to align themselves with Greek culture (Parker 2007; Mairs 2014). Racial identities are not simply imposed by some uniform sense of 'culture' as a package deal. Such newer interpretations cohere with Moya and Markus's focus on race-as-doing, in this case use by local people of the accoutrements of Greek culture to become Greek (Figure 5.4).

The Hellenistic period also saw the development of Stoicism, with its cosmopolitan elements, a process that reached its high point with Seneca, Epictetus and Marcus Aurelius in the high empire. For Haarhoff, Alexander was a hero of cosmopolitanism, his expedition motivated by a desire for the 'brotherhood of man', as articulated by his biographer W. W. Tarn (1869–1957); Isocrates' Panhellenism was an earlier step in that direction. It is against this positive vision of Alexander-the-dreamer that Ernst

FIGURE 5.4 A young Tajik soldier from the Northern Alliance shows a vestige of the ancient Greek city of Ai Khanum. © Patrick Robert-Curtis/Sygma/Getty Images.

Badian reacted, emphasizing instead the brutal nature of the expedition (Badian 1958). Alexander scholars have tended to differ as to whether he was primarily a figure of unity and cultural diffusion or rather one of violent subjugation. There is also a question of agency: by contrast to Tarn's outside-in colonial vision, A. K. Narain famously took a nationalist line: 'they came, they saw, but India conquered' (1957: 11). As we shall see further below, Alexander has been a focus for some race-focused views of antiquity.

For the Hellenistic period, there is a rich archive of evidence concerning inter-group relations. In a well-known papyrus, an unnamed non-Greek Egyptian complains in a letter, dated 256–255 BCE, to his employer Zenon that he is in straitened circumstances for want of necessities and payment:

> I am in distress summer and winter. And [my supervisor Crotus] tells me to accept ordinary wine for salary. But they have treated me with contempt because I am a barbarian (*barbaros*). I therefore request you, if you please, to order them to let me have what is owed to me / and in future to pay me regularly, so that I do not die of hunger because I do not know how to speak Greek (*hellenizein*).
>
> (*P.Col.Zen.* I 66)

To translate *hellenizein* as 'speak Greek' is reasonable, and indeed the earliest known instance of the word Ἑλληνισμός refers to language (2 Macc. 4:13). But this is by no means the only possible interpretation: to judge from related words, it might in principle mean 'act like a Greek'. Either way, this is a prima facie case of racism, in which social difference, systematically determined, results in prejudicial treatment. For all the unanswered questions this document leaves, it is a salutary reminder that inter-group relations should be considered in terms of practice no less than theory: the implications for histories of race are considerable, especially in ancient societies when we know more about their theory than their practice. As we shall see below in relation to Schachermeyr, the very matter of Hellenism has its discontents.

EMPIRE AND *IMPERIUM*

The significance Haarhoff accords 'Caesar the cosmopolitan' (1948: 249) is consistent with any overview of Greco-Roman history. (For Haarhoff, 'cosmopolitan' seems in effect a synonym for 'imperial', with a positive resonance in each case.) Caesar's campaigns in Gaul were a late but decisive chapter in the expansion of Roman power; what is more, his autocratic style, though rejected by senators, provided a template for later rulers. His successor Octavian/Augustus avoided its more explicit forms but nonetheless adapted it in order to establish long-lasting autocracy. In this sense the centralized, multi-ethnic state, ideologically united by an emperor was Caesar's legacy, formally lasting in the west until 476 CE and in the east until 1453 – and well beyond those histories as a transferable symbol. The process of Rome's expansion, especially in the age of Caesar, was closely linked to competition within the elite: the need to gain military *honour* was a major propelling factor in Roman conquests within the Mediterranean, given that they were publicly and even spectacularly celebrated in triumphs as well as their related architecture and images.

The history of conquest has typically been told from a Roman perspective, often teleologically, as if there was something inevitable in Rome's pan-Mediterranean conquest – starting with the Roman conquest of Italy in the fifth and fourth centuries BCE and later, following success against the Carthaginians, the addition of Sicily, Corsica and Sardinia in the mid-third century, finally culminating with victory over Cleopatra's Egypt in 30 BCE. The urge to explore non-Roman perspectives is a relative novelty responding to the post-colonial turn in ancient studies (e.g. on Gaul, Woolf 1998; on Spain, Johnston 2017). The cultural impact of Roman power has been characterized as a process of 'Romanization' (notably Haverfield 1906), a model that still persists despite widespread critique of assumptions about its supposedly unidirectional and top-down imposition. More recent approaches have, by contrast, sought innovative ways of addressing the problem of perspective, canvasing possibilities such as hybridity and discrepant identities in relation to Rome's contact with others (Mattingly 2011: 3–42; Schneider 2012). In contrast to scholarship a century ago, Roman imperialism has looked different now that discrepant experiences and perspectives have become part of the analysis, and agency more broadly conceived.

The late Republic, the age of Caesar, is also the period in which intensive scholarly interest was given to Rome's early past. Both Virgil's *Aeneid* and Livy's *History* (books 1–2) are mythistorical creations, articulating Rome's past for the age of Augustus (31 BCE– 14 CE). Indeed, a good deal of what we know about early Roman history comes principally from scholars and writers of the late Republic, several centuries later, very much shaped for contemporary ideologies and largely supportive of the political establishment. Such stories recount the evolution of early Rome as a clash of rival groups, including Latins, Sabines and Etruscans. While details should not be taken at face value as historical fact, what they do reflect is a sense of Rome itself as an ethnic composite. The myth of Aeneas as founder of Rome, reflected in the *Aeneid*, for one, gives privileged status to the Trojans, the defeated party in the Trojan War. Even if Haarhoff's comment with reference to the middle and late Republic that 'the Romans gave their defeated enemies a place in the state on equal terms with themselves' is exaggerated (1948: 138), it contains a grain of truth: that the growth and longevity of the empire had much to do with its power to negotiate and integrate divergent cultural identities. Indeed, even though the empire exhibited regional variations in architecture, religion and language, at the same time, shared beliefs, images, practices and identities united its subjects over several centuries.

A key part of this involved local elites, who were made to feel Roman and thus invested in the integrative functioning of the state. The result was a high degree of consensus, and the relative absence of 'nationalist' risings to challenge Roman power. One explanation that has been offered for this is the continuity of the imperial office and the charisma associated with it, even in the relatively turbulent third century CE (Ando 2000). A strong example of this dynamic is Aelius Aristides' 'Roman Oration' (155 CE), delivered before the imperial court as a virtuosic display of rhetoric. In the hyperbolic language characteristic of this kind of oratory, Aristides poetically claims his vision of a highly integrated empire, in which trade and travel are facilitated and civic discord absent. Shared adherence to the empire as a whole, a *communis patria*, inspires an overall patriotism, superseding any possible regional or ethnic loyalties. On this – no doubt exaggerated – view, Rome rules its empire via soft power which overshadows smaller-scale loyalties: 'There is no need of garrisons to hold their citadels, but the men of greatest standing and influence in every city guard their own fatherlands for you' (Aristides, *Orationes* 64; trans. J. H. Oliver).

Rome's acquisition of an empire also intensified the metropolitan status of the city, which we know to have accommodated inhabitants from far and wide (Noy 2000). Public spectacles conducted in the Flavian Amphitheatre were displays of the emperor's power, using wild animals imported substantial distances for the purpose. The negative view of the poet Juvenal, writing in the early second century CE, may be exaggerated in its own way but nonetheless indicates de facto cosmopolitanism: 'For some time now the Syrian [River] Orontes has let out into the Tiber, conveying its language, customs, pipes and harp-strings, and even its traditional tambourines, and girls forced to prostitute themselves at the circus' (*Satires* 3.62–5). Rome, as presented in the stark colours of Juvenal's narrator Umbricius, is crawling with Greek-speaking low life, so much so that Umbricius finds himself compelled to leave the city.

STRANGERS AT THE GATE

It is time to take a closer look at Haarhoff. Born to a distinguished Cape Afrikaner family, he received most of his education in English (at the University of Cape Town and Oxford), though later he took his doctorate at the University of Amsterdam. He held the chair of Classics at the newly established University of the Witwatersrand, Johannesburg, from 1922 to 1957. As a poet and public intellectual he championed the cause of the Afrikaans language, which had no official recognition until 1925. He combined scholarship with poetry in his verse translations of Catullus and Vergil's *Georgics*. As a child he lived through the Second Anglo-Boer War (1899–1902), bitterly fought between British and Afrikaners, yet his politics were moderate by the standard of their times, and he outspokenly supported General J. C. Smuts over his nationalist rivals. At several points in Haarhoff's scholarship, as in his many popular writings, he advocated harmonious inter-group relations, but on closer inspection it becomes clear that his purview was restricted to white South Africa (Parker 2010: 223).

In *Vergil in the Experience of South Africa* (1931), republished after the Second World War as *Vergil the Universal* (1949), Haarhoff simultaneously celebrates the Roman and the Afrikaner citizen-farmer, both sons of the earth. The comparison is underscored by homely examples of farmers' knowledge: thus, the scattering of a handful of dust to calm a quarrel among bees or the apparent boiling of grape juice at *Georgics* 1.295, which he equates with the Afrikaner delicacy of *moskonfyt* (Latin *defrutum*).

The Stranger at the Gate: Aspects of Exclusiveness and Co-operation in Ancient Greece and Rome, with Some Reference to Modern Times was first published in 1938 and republished a decade later. Its dedication 'To the spirit of racial co-operation' seen in the context of the book as a whole, does not extend to Black South Africans: rather, it is intended as an antidote to residual tensions from the Anglo-Boer War. In fact, where he mentions Blacks at all Haarhoff is patronizing, especially in his journalism (Parker 2010: 229). In retrospect and in contrast to more recent scholarship, it also seems surprising that the work contains only three brief references to Judaism and Jews, given that this is a group whose perspective is well attested in the Hellenistic and Roman periods.

Haarhoff's support for Smuts is strongly linked to the statesman's role in the creation of both the League of Nations and to a lesser extent the United Nations; Haarhoff himself was a delegate to United Nations Educational, Scientific and Cultural Organization (UNESCO) in 1946. He repeatedly praises Smuts's *Holism and Evolution* (1926), a mix of physics and metaphysics composed in Smuts's phase out of government. It is ironic that this highly abstract work, anti-Cartesian in its denial of a division between body and spirit, was written by a famously shrewd politician; it is even more ironic that this champion of world peace and human rights was intransigent about the rights of Black people in the country he ruled (Dubow 2008: 59). Nonetheless, Haarhoff was a public intellectual in the mould of Gilbert Murray, and readier than his colleagues to connect ancient and modern histories, even if by today's lights his blind spots were considerable.

In May 1948, the National Party under Dr D. F. Malan unexpectedly beat Smuts's United Party at the polls, ushering in the apartheid system that lasted until 1994, when Nelson Mandela's African National Congress and its allies came to power. It is not clear whether the preface to the second edition was composed before or after the election, but nonetheless the 1948 preface strikes an elegiac note. Seen in a context of its original 1938 publication, the book exhibits optimism in a time of duress by propounding the idea of Smutsian 'creative wholeness' as an answer to social crisis. Before and after the Second World War, Haarhoff's classical antiquity offers a model of inter-group harmony.

Classical antiquity shows up quite differently in a noted public lecture, subsequently published, 'The Contribution of Non-European Peoples to World Civilization'. It was composed by a different stranger at the gate: Benjamin Kies (1917–79), a teacher, lawyer, activist and founder of the Non-European Unity Movement (NEUM), a Trotskyist group that opposed racial segregation. Whereas the Population Registration Act of 1950 had named 'Coloured' as a major category alongside White and Black ('Indian' was added soon after), the NEUM became known for embracing a non-racial approach to South African and world politics. Their journal, *Torch*, started using quotation marks around terms such as Coloured, African, race, racial groups, Bantu, *Kleurling* and *Herrenvolk* (Adhikari 2005: 113). From the late 1950s the term 'so-called Coloured' became standard practice under NEUM influence, at the same time as the terms 'Colouredization' and 'Bantuization' were coined. More than twenty-five years after the end of apartheid, Coloured identity continues to be the subject of contention and a practical problem of terminology: in a key study of the topic 'the term *Coloured* is used to refer to those people who regard themselves as Coloured', even though many Coloured leaders rejected the term and category (xv).

Kies's talk was delivered as the A. J. Abrahamse Memorial Lecture under the auspices of the Teachers' League of South Africa in Cape Town on 29 September 1953. Published with fifty-three pages and ninety-seven footnotes, it became a landmark in the intellectual landscape of Black resistance in South Africa. At stake was the very notion of 'civilization' in both a world-historical and a South African sense, and one whose racial underpinnings are under attack: as Kies bracingly says, 'the term "White" as describing civilization is beneath serious consideration except as part of the epitaph on the funeral urn of the South African Herrenvolk' (1953: 30). A substantial part of the lecture is aimed at questioning the nature and status of the 'three so-called pillars of "European" or "Western" civilization: Greece, Rome and Christianity' (30). The questioning of race per se was in keeping with the anti-racist thought of the NEUM and its predecessor, the New Era Fellowship: in the opposition of those groups to apartheid racism, its members explained social difference by criteria other than race (Soudien 2019).

Fast forward to 2015 and the classical tradition again comes to the fore: Black students at the University of Cape Town (UCT) targeted a bronze statue of Cecil John Rhodes (1853–1902), entrepreneur and arch-imperialist, in their frustration at the slow pace of socio-economic upliftment and more immediately their feelings of marginalization by the university. In this case, the classical tradition is indirect but nonetheless constitutive of the landscape, in that Rhodes, himself a collector of classical objects and texts, was commemorated in classical-style bronze; the UCT campus and the nearby Rhodes Memorial reflect a classical aesthetic, using pediments and pillars to evoke ancient Greece and Rome (Parker 2017b). The Rhodes Must Fall movement turned sharply against such monumental aspects of the classical tradition, as evidenced in the defacement of statues on this campus and elsewhere. Whereas the early to mid-1990s saw a politics of reconciliation spearheaded by Mandela and Archbishop Tutu, more recent leaders have turned to ethnically or racially based nationalism, not least the Economic Freedom Fighters (EFF), a party that has risen solidly since its foundation in 2013 and is currently the third largest in parliament. Its charismatic leader, Julius Malema, was convicted of hate speech in 2010 and 2011, and has consistently expressed views that accord with some of the most hardline student demands.

True to worldwide trends, the same nationalist turn can be seen in other parties, both Black and white: the phenomenon of state capture, whereby state resources are siphoned off into private coffers via cronyism and other kinds of kleptocracy, which seems endemic in twenty-first-century South Africa. Public discourse on corruption, and indeed other matters, is typically articulated in terms of race. President Thabo Mbeki (1999–2008) made a habit of deflecting criticism of his policies and style with counter-accusations of racism, whether on the part of whites or else what he termed 'self-hating blacks'. The more tradition-minded President Jacob Zuma (2009–18) has himself made many appeals to the notion of race. It is easy to see why the concept of race, which has been such a visible part of South African history, has become saturated: one thoughtful analyst has gone so far as to suggest that South Africans agree to a moratorium on the use of the term, in hopes of clarifying what exactly is meant by the term on any given occasion, and in the process breaking the ongoing stalemate (Maré 2015). That 'non-racialism' was enshrined in the Founding Provisions of the Constitution of South Africa (1996), chapter one, section one, is of no account politically: if anything, it is viewed by student leaders and the EFF as a sign of capitulation on the part of the Mandela generation of Black leaders. Non-racialism is now a relic of the liberation movement's older, mostly deceased generation, including Mandela and Ahmed Kathrada, as evidenced in the foundations that bear their names. The very term invokes the Freedom Charter (1955), in which the principles of the African National Congress and its allies were spelled out (Figure 5.5).

Between the mid-1950s and the twenty-first century, Classics has lost much of its social and curricular status, and today it plays little if any overt role in public debate. At UCT and other South African universities, Classics continues to be taught but is subject to immense financial and political pressures. The same is true of the humanities generally, yet Classics is especially badly placed in light of past complicities, passive or otherwise (Lambert 2011: 44), and its relative lack of 'transformation' amid a larger sea change. Many departments have struggled to attract Black students, let alone develop a pipeline of Black faculty. To me as someone on the fringes of South African Classics it appears that the work of redefining the field for the post-apartheid era is a work in progress, and that identity-based campus conflicts have afforded little room for engagement and instead encouraged quiet retreat. Whereas ancient Greeks and Romans were a source of cultural pride and a touchstone of civilization in the time of Haarhoff and Kies, their presence in South African universities today is at best attenuated and at worst a source of awkwardness. If racial nationalism has merely metamorphosed after the end of apartheid rather than disappeared (Jansen and Walters 2020), the potential of Classics to address enduring divisions is far from clear.

The three examples discussed here show contrasting approaches to the matter of race: whereas Haarhoff used the concept to negotiate Afrikaner – English relations, Kies and the New Era Fellowship viewed race as a false consciousness, obscuring class differences.

FIGURE 5.5 Freedom Charter memorial in Kliptown in Soweto, Johannesburg, South Africa, 2017. © Frédéric Soltan/Corbis/Getty Images.

More recently, the EFF has embraced race as a marker of class difference, a view that holds considerable appeal to young South Africans frustrated with inequality.

HISTORY FROM THE NORTH

Haarhoff's moderate position on race, like Kies's radical one, gains perspective from comparison with a contemporary in a context very different from South Africa's. Fritz Schachermeyr (1895–1987), born three years after Haarhoff in the Austrian city of Linz, was a prolific and versatile historian of Greco-Roman antiquity and an undoubted leader in the field. His vast output in Mediterranean ancient history and prehistory, both scholarly and popular, in several ways reflects Nazi approaches to race (Chaniotis and Thaler 2006: 413).

Following studies at Graz, Berlin and Innsbruck, he held chairs at Jena (1931–6), Heidelberg (1936–41) and Graz (1941–5). From the time of his appointment at Jena – at the behest of Wilhelm Frick, then Thuringia's Minister of Education and later co-author of the Nuremberg Race laws – he participated actively in the NSDAP (National Socialist German Workers' Party), taking prominent positions in and on behalf of the party in Germany and later in Austria; in fact his appointment at Heidelberg was made possible by the removal of the Jewish incumbent. What is more, as we shall see, Schachermeyr's classical research and teaching closely reflected Nazi racial thinking. At the end of the war he was forced into retirement in view of his active participation in the Nazi regime, but he received effective amnesty when he was appointed to a chair at the University of Vienna in 1952, occupying it until his retirement in 1963. In the course of a productive career, he also received many honours and awards from the Austrian government as well as several learned academies. Later Schachermeyr would deny active participation and even claim opposition to the regime: his memoir is highly selective on his wartime activities. Even his subsequently published bibliography omits mention of his contributions to the journal *Rasse* and other writings on racial 'science', some of which were destroyed during the war (Chaniotis and Thaler 2006: 403n53).

Schachermeyr's major book on Crete (1939b), written at Heidelberg, addresses the relationship of race and culture, teasing out their implications for what he calls the 'European spirit'. This and his study of Carthage focused on the supposed presence of 'inferior' Asiatic racial types: *Indogermanen und Orient* (1944) reads like an apologia for Rome, ignoring the more brutal aspects of conquest. Overall, he takes a broad, world-historical approach, comparable with Oswald Spengler or Arnold Toynbee, but unlike their writings, his is suffused with and even formulates Nazi racial doctrine.

In so far as race grounds his conception of the rise and fall of civilizations, Schachermeyr ranks among the most prominent classicists of the Third Reich. His work connects with that of Hans F. K. Günther (1891–1968), who was appointed to a chair in social anthropology at Jena the same year as Schachermeyr's own appointment at that university. Günther's *Rassenkunde des deutschen Volkes* (originally 1922, much republished) was a foundational and influential work that made him a leading exponent of the pseudo-science of race. Günther made particular use of Tacitus' *Germania*, a treatise on the Germans dating to around 98 CE (Krebs 2011). Despite his role as the so-called 'race pope', Günther too came out of the post-Second World War legal processes almost scot-free, being classified in the least culpable category of collaborator (*Mitläufer*) despite his active support for the NSDAP and its ideology.

After evading denazification procedures, Schachermeyr retained the key views that characterized his work under the Third Reich. Thus, racial characteristics were consistent across generations according to his history of Greece, his Greeks being motivated by 'inexhaustible energy' and harder working than Semitic people (Schachermeyr 1960). His biography of Pericles (1969) presents the Athenian leader as a Hitler figure: giving purpose and discipline to Athens' overly individualistic youth via the experience of war, Pericles is here a perfected Nordic hero (Pesditschek 2005: 63–5). Schachermeyr's lack of apology is visible in his final book, *Die Tragik der Voll-Endung* (The Tragedy of Completion or Perfection, 1981), a reflective work pining for an old order. In his memoir he denies membership of the NSDAP and presents himself as an active opponent of the Nazis while simultaneously defending his racist writings of the time. The career of Schachermeyr typifies the 'Waldheim phenomenon': the Austrian state's unwillingness to address its role in the Holocaust, accompanied by a readiness to forgive war crimes beyond what their perpetrators officially acknowledged. The implications for classical studies are considerable (Lohsemann 1977).

For all their variety, Schachermeyr's writings reveal key themes (Chaniotis and Thaler 2006: 417–18). One may be labelled Nordic world history, namely an intense focus on the north as the key motor force in global history. Central to this is the idea of northern origins of the Indo-Europeans, and with it an ideal type of Nordic leader (*nordische Führerpersönlichkeit*). This element is put to work as an explanation of Rome's conquest over Carthage, and their ascendancy in general, and accords well with Nazi racial theory. To underpin all this is an essentializing sense of 'unique cultural qualities' (*das Arteigene*), as Schachermeyr spells out in a 1939 essay. These characteristics are racial and racist in that they directly link behaviour with physical attributes (Schachermeyr 1939a: 344).

Tacitus' *Germania* (*c.* 98 CE) became a bible for Nazis, and certainly was a text to which Günther returned at key times (Krebs 2011). This is not surprising, given the importance it commanded among humanists in the fifteenth and sixteenth centuries. For many, it appeared to offer a model of racial purity, based on warlike spirit and piety. The Thirty Years' War (1618–48) heightened the need for originary Germanic purity, embodied in language, so there is a broad and complex history of this text. In terms of Schachermeyr's racial-historical theory, the Nordic races exhibit *Lebensgesetzlichkeit*, to quote the title of his 1940 book: this term may be glossed as 'adherence to law', a quality lost when intermarriage supposedly destroys racial integrity.

Schachermeyr's magnum opus was his augmented biography of Alexander (1973). It gives a negative portrait of Alexander: whereas Haarhoff's Alexander was an agent of cosmopolitanism, Schachermeyr's Alexander promoted miscegenation (*Rassenmischung*) and simultaneously 'denorthing' (*Entnordung*), with the result that the cosmopolitanism of the Hellenistic age brought insufficient national and racial consciousness. In this, there is the influence of the British-born Houston Stewart Chamberlain (1855–1927), whose sweeping racial theories stoked European nationalism in the early twentieth century and directly influenced Hitler (Pesditschek 2005: 60).

Despite all this, as in the case of South Africa, it should be pointed out that classical antiquity in the Third Reich was not only used for oppressive purposes. Thus Karl Meister (1880–1963), who served one year as Rector of the University of Heidelberg (1930–1), in his inaugural speech addressed 'The Virtues of the Romans', thereby warning his audience against the consequences of National Socialism (Chaniotis and Thaler 2006: 393). While the story of Classics in the Third Reich has been extensively told elsewhere (e.g. Lohsemann 1977; Roche and Demetriou 2018), here it is significant to see the resonance of arguments made by Schachermeyr, Günther and others in the contemporary United States (Zuckerberg 2018): this will be discussed in the next section.

THE GLORY THAT WAS NUBIA

The final case study brings us back to the African continent and simultaneously to the United States. With its exhibit *Ancient Nubia Now* (October 2019–January 2020), curated by Denise Doxey and others, Boston's Museum of Fine Arts (MFA) delved into its own collection. Its excavations in the early decades of the twentieth century gave it one of the world's largest collections of Nubian antiquities, which until recently have had little prominence in the museum. Visitors faced a double question at the entry to the exhibit: 'What was ancient Nubia and what does it mean to you?' As we shall see, the second of these questions has special significance. Yet the first serves as a reminder that Nubia is little known – a cultural zone spanning the area from south of the Nile's first cataract to just south of Khartoum at the sixth. Its fate has been to languish in the shadow of Egypt, and one of the objectives of the exhibit was thus to restore Nubia to its rightful prominence within world history and African history.

The collection on which the exhibit is based owes its existence to George Reisner (1867–1942). Trained at Harvard, he began his archaeological work in Egypt before leading excavations in Nubia on behalf of the Egyptian government (1907–9). Later, holding positions of leadership at both the MFA and Harvard University, Reisner excavated at Jebel Barkal, Meroe and other Sudanese sites (1916–23) in the off seasons from his main work in Egypt. Reisner was a pioneer of archaeological method, carefully refining the scientific practices of Petrie and others. What is more, the antiquities he funnelled to his home institutions have made their collections unmatched in quality and extent anywhere outside of Sudan today. Nonetheless, Reisner has been criticized for denying African agency: he assumed that some of the finest treasures he discovered were of Egyptian origin, brought by Egyptians. One highlight of the exhibit is instructive. The statue of a seated Lady Sennuwy (1971–1926 BCE) dates to the reign of Senwosret I from Dynasty XII, in Egypt's Middle Kingdom (Doxey 2018: 140). It is a particularly well-proportioned and well-preserved statue, in grandiorite. Discovered by Reisner's team in 1913, it was surrounded by distinctively Nubian funerary wares. Reiser's deduction at the time was that its provenance proved Nubia to be an outpost of Egypt, whereas the opposite seems to have been the case: namely that Nubians had conquered Southern Egypt and had brought back the statue as booty (Figure 5.6).

The exhibit presents itself as a twofold restorative act; first, one of visibility, whereby Nubia now receives more attention than before among the MFA's rich stock of antiquities; and second, one of counteracting the denial of African agency, in which respect Reisner was not alone. To take a comparable example, the earliest Western reports about Great Zimbabwe speculated that their origins must have been Phoenician or Arab, assuming that no African people would have been capable of such monumentality (Parker 2017a: 44).

An even heavier sense of restitution hangs over the exhibit: a public petition was made to rename Boston's Dudley Square to Nubian Square. The argument against the existing name is that it honours an early governor of Massachusetts, Thomas Dudley (1576–1653), who held office at a time when laws were passed enabling slavery. By contrast, in the words of a municipal ballot, '[t]he name Nubian Square would recognize the area as a hub of the African American community and pay tribute to a former anchor business in the area, A Nubian Notion gift shop' (City of Boston 2019). This store had been a family business for more than fifty years. The name change was approved by Boston's Public Improvement Commission in December 2019.

In the months leading up to *Ancient Nubia Now*, an incident at the MFA illustrated an underlying need to find new audiences, as well as the difficulty of realizing that goal. A group of school pupils from the Helen Y. Davis Leadership Academy was involved in a racially charged incident together with security guards and two patrons who were also donors. The children were African American whereas the security guards and patrons were white. Following an urgent commission of inquiry, the MFA made additions to the museum leadership to systematically address diversity and inclusion. In what may have been another response, four free admission passes were given to every child visiting in a school group, in hopes of encouraging them to return with their families. The intention was clearly to broaden the reach of the MFA, a need sorely emphasized by a 2017 survey showing that of its three thousand visitors on a normal Saturday, only 4 per cent were African American. In one sense, in terms of museum practice, this story shows how easily the laudable intentions of administrators and curators may be undone by extrinsic factors, in this case with an apparently racial edge.

In this light, Nubia, with its pyramids, monumental statuary and fine wares, becomes a place marker for lost histories of slavery. The Meroitic language is a further element in the project of giving voice to African antiquity: the Meroitic script has been deciphered since 1909, based on the Meroitic spellings of Egyptian names, yet the language itself remains untranslated. Meroitic writing thus holds out a promise of African voices, one that is yet to be fulfilled, even as the exhibit presents the public with the longest known Meroitic

FIGURE 5.6 Statue of Lady Sennuwy. Egyptian, Middle Kingdom, Dynasty 12, reign of Senwosret I, 1971–1926 BCE. Found at Kerma in Nubia, Sudan. Photograph © 2019 Museum of Fine Arts, Boston.

inscription, namely the stele of King Tanyidamani (180–140 BCE). Found by Reisner's team at the temple of Amun at Jebel Barkal, the stele appears to record donations to the temple (Doxey 2018: 90). The visual presentation of the king, alongside the gods Amun and Mut, is in keeping with Egyptian art. The recent surge of interest in ancient Sudan suggests that the Meroitic language may receive new scholarly interest.

The exhibit included interviews with an Egyptologist, a biological anthropologist, a historian, a photographer and a young Sudanese American – the last-mentioned of these is Lana Bashir, an undergraduate at the University of Massachusetts Lowell, who speaks of the positive, celebratory tone of the exhibit, contrasting it with the predominant media image of Africa as a place of poverty. Her admiration for Lady Sennuwy, she says, stems from and bolsters Black pride. This is somewhat problematic, given that the statue is an Egyptian one that landed up in Nubia, but the general point is a crucial one: Africa (which for this purpose subsumes Egypt) is an ancient and proud civilization, possessed of monuments and writing, in a word, what nineteenth-century Germans called a *Hochkultur*.

The appeal to US-born persons of Sudanese descent is thus a significant element. It certainly addresses the pedagogic mission of museums such as the MFA to involve new generations, in this case via emic affinities. Such affinities are not necessarily racially defined, but often are; one might compare the Cyrus Cylinder at the Getty Villa in 2013, which attracted a large audience from the Iranian community of the Los Angeles area. It is possible, but no means certain, that at the MFA the younger generation of viewers might be more comfortable with US ownership of what might easily be considered Sudanese cultural property. The second of the questions greeting visitors to the exhibit, 'What does [Nubia] mean to you?', valorizes the more subjective responses such as those of Lana Bashir by emphasizing personal identity and affinities. In the process, *Ancient Nubia Now* could quietly circumvent the old quagmire of the *Black Athena* debate by avoiding the question of scientific accuracy, to which both sides appealed (Orrells, Bhambra and Roynon 2011). It also steered clear of related issues around Afrocentrism. To judge from *Ancient Nubia Now*, between the late twentieth century and the early twenty-first the focus has shifted from the origins of Western civilization to African diasporic pride.

Larger questions raised by the exhibit concern the very nature and status of African antiquity in world history, as well as the representation of blackness in art. The first of these relates obliquely to classical antiquity, which has produced an overwhelming and constricting frame of reference, and also to Egypt and the Fertile Crescent. There is no little irony in the *Wall Street Journal*'s review of the exhibit, entitled 'The Glory That Was Nubia' (Kaylan 2019), and thereby adapting the famous lines from Edgar Allan Poe's poem, 'To Helen': 'the glory that was Greece / and the grandeur that was Rome' (2nd edition, 1845). The implication of the exhibition title is that Nubia now competes with those long-established sources of power and prestige.

ANTIQUITY AND ME: BETWEEN SILENCE AND SALIENCE

Whereas Caesar's Gauls put aside their trousers and put on the broad stripe in order to enter the senate, the Economic Freedom Front parliamentarians in their red overalls today use the politics of spectacle to diverge maximally from political norms: they claim to reject assimilation to the elite and identify instead with disempowered Black South Africans. That such gestures expose the parliamentarians to allegations of hypocrisy is immaterial: at issue is the display value of social difference, in a word, of race. Spectacles of racial identity obscure arguably more pertinent questions about inequality and intergroup, including intergenerational, relations.

The case studies presented here raise questions about elisions, continuities, identities and – in the case of the Third Reich – murderous complicities. To draw boundaries of the ancient Greco-Roman world is itself a political act and reflects the makings of Classics as a field. Nubia was located at the southern fringe of the Hellenistic world, its gold mines attractive to the Ptolemies (Burstein 1993). Herodotus was familiar with Nubia (3.17–25), and from the third century BCE Meroe was a reference point in Greco-Roman geography, its location described in detail by Diodorus Siculus (1.33). The history of Nubia reaches the twenty-first century via the MFA exhibit and the excavations on which it was based. This exhibit is remarkable for the element of social outreach on the part of the museum.

It is reasonable that as the author of this chapter I should address my own subject position. My reluctance to do so is explained in relation to Coloured political identity discussed above: an uneasy relation, from my South African student years in the 1980s to the present day, between the imposed, negative nature of apartheid's categories on the one hand and positive social realities on the other, in families and other forms of community. Furthermore, non-racial ideals were central to the struggle against apartheid, only to be eclipsed by renewed nationalisms and racism of the post-apartheid era (Maré 2015). Then there is the question of my own racial legibility outside of South Africa, especially in the United States, where I studied and have lived most of my adult life. Certainly, Coloured history invites comparison with African American with regard to slave origins, but there are also problems of translation: mixed-race identities have different degrees of acceptability and appeal in South Africa compared to the United States, and furthermore Cape slave history involves the Indian Ocean world rather than the Atlantic. Though I am a historian of ideas and identities, I cannot assume that I have much power in the way in which I am perceived by significant others, and at the same time I recognize that the degree to which I choose, or others choose, to draw attention to the question is itself a political matter. In any case, the personal background I have sketched here has had at least two outcomes: a gravitation towards marginalized voices of colonialism, and a residual distrust of race as a stable and self-evident criterion of social analysis transcending history.

What antidotes to this situation are available? Reflexive awareness can go a long way, in philosophical anthropology (Todorov 1993: 341–52), towards critically reassessing scholarly themes, and in recognizing the fact that Classics as a field has yet made few inroads into under-represented minorities. This circumstance has brought countervailing pressures to bear on me as a graduate student, postdoc and faculty member at elite US institutions: a desire to establish my credentials via mainstream, canonically defined Classics that has coexisted with a different kind of need, namely to connect my studies with histories and identities that engage me on a personal level. It is one thing to define myself in terms of race; it is another to circumscribe the extent to which race defines me in a changing political landscape, while realizing that my identities are to a considerable degree determined by significant others. In my experience there has been troublesome slippage between two different questions: Does race matter? and Should race matter? The problem is far from simple.

I would like to conclude with a plea for defamiliarization: if it is true that there is much more about ancient worlds that we do not know, it follows that our knowledge of ancient race – even among societies that have left considerable verbal and material records – is necessarily limited and should in any case encourage a healthy dose of self-awareness on the part of its scholars. The examples offered here may be taken as cautionary tales about supposed historical objectivity. If Classics could take a lead in highlighting cross-cultural encounters as objects of history, redefining key concepts and otherwise sharpening tools of social analysis, foregrounding historical specificities over assumed diachronic commonalities – and in a word rethinking race beyond the modern United States, or even unthinking race – that would be no bad thing.

CHAPTER SIX

Race and Ethnicity

NAOÍSE MAC SWEENEY

CONFIGURING RACE AND ETHNICITY

Race is not the same thing as ethnicity. Sometimes we confuse the two, eliding one into the other in the lazy slippage of careless conversation. More often we conflate them, substituting the other for the one in the embarrassed pursuit of scholarly objectivity. The concepts of 'race' and 'ethnicity' do of course have much in common. Both are social constructs, despite their claims to universality and objectivity (McCoskey 2012: 2 and 28). Both can be used to categorize people on the basis of differences perceived to be essential and biological. Indeed, for many people the terms are interchangeable, with 'ethnicity' often replacing 'race' to avoid the stigma attached to this latter term after the Second World War (e.g. McCoskey in this volume). Yet there are also subtle differences in the way that these two words are used and understood. In this chapter, I will argue that it is methodologically useful to draw a distinction between 'race' and 'ethnicity' when studying the ancient world. Maintaining a sense of this distinction can help us to interrogate our own assumptions, and to view afresh the various different systems of human classification that can be found in antiquity.

It should be noted that, by and large, we already draw a distinction between 'race' and 'ethnicity' in our scholarly practice. While there is a rich and long-established body of recent academic literature on ethnicities and cultural identities in the ancient world (Malkin 2001b; Hall 2002; Roymans and Derks 2009; Gruen 2011a; McInerney 2014b), during the latter part of the twentieth century relatively little was written about race. Several notable examples bucked this trend (e.g. Snowden 1970, 1983; Thompson 1989; Isaac 2006), rising to a relative crescendo over the last ten years (Haley 2009; Lape 2010; McCoskey 2012; Kennedy, Roy and Goldman 2013). Indeed, as the publication of this volume demonstrates, momentum is gathering around the investigation of race in antiquity, and the scholarly balance may well tip within the next few years. As we enter the second decade of the twenty-first century, we may be in a moment poised between the study of ancient ethnicities and the study of ancient race.

So where does ethnicity end and race begin? For the purposes of this chapter, I define race as the classification of people according to perceptions related to (or meanings derived from) the physical form of their bodies – skin colour, hair colour and/or texture, height, shape of eyes, etc. In contrast, I define ethnicity as the classification of people according to ideas about ancestry and descent. That the two concepts are related is obvious. After all, bodily forms are both enabled and constrained by genetics. This is true, despite the important roles played by cultural and historical factors, as well as by individual choice, in the formation of physical appearances; and it remains true even when we acknowledge that our perceptions and interpretations of the body are culturally determined. Indeed, physiognomic differences have often been explained through bloodlines and ancestry. At the start of the twenty-first century, we are experiencing a revival of this idea. In particular, advancements in genetic science and technology have been used (and abused) by those seeking to advance biological explanations of human variation. Yet despite the close relationship between the two concepts, race and ethnicity may not necessarily map directly onto each other. Maintaining a distinction between them has some interpretive advantages.

Maintaining the sense of difference between the two concepts makes it possible, for example, to designate an ethnic group on the basis of distinct genealogy and cultural traits, without investing it with somatic peculiarities. An example of this might be the contemporary distinction between the English and the Welsh. Today, most people would tend to describe this as an ethnic rather than a racial difference. They would not seek to infer any major differences in physiognomy, but instead would seek to imply a separate descent, articulated and expressed through different language and culture. Similarly, conceptually separating ethnicity from race makes it possible to construct a racial group on the basis of perceived physical characteristics, without necessarily presuming their derivation from a common bloodline. An example of this might be the contemporary construction of whiteness, which is usually understood as a racial rather than an ethnic classification (Frankenberg 1997). This classification involves the arbitrary grouping of a range of human skin tones into a single category of 'white', and the equally arbitrary grouping of an even wider range of human skin tones into the category of 'non-white'. Yet despite our physiognomic category of 'white' being both historically and culturally specific (and at times regulated by notions of descent), we understand it first and foremost as depending on somatic form.

Culture is an important third point in this conceptual matrix. Whereas ethnicity relates to descent and race relates to somatic form, 'culture' is primarily concerned with *activity* – what language people speak, what religion they practice and how they practice it, what social norms they uphold, and what customs they adhere to. Culture has often been taken as the outwards expression of an underlying racial or ethnic identity – the means through which an identity is socially performed, or the evidence on which an identity may be externally ascribed. It appears with particular frequency in scholarship on ancient ethnicities, and in some instances the phrase 'cultural identity' has been used more or less interchangeably with 'ethnicity' (Lucy 2005; Tuplin 2007a; Sommer 2010; Gruen 2011a). Yet culture is distinct from both ethnicity and race, and it is possible for cultural identities to exist that are predicated on neither descent nor bodily form. For example, the collective identity of football fans relies primarily on their adherence to a set of social actions – support for a particular team, watching a particular set of sporting fixtures, wearing particular ritual garments (e.g. the football shirt), etc. None of this necessarily implies descent from a specific bloodline or a distinctive physiognomy. In this chapter therefore, my focus is specifically on ethnicity and race – culture will only be considered in specific instances where cultural performance or activity is perceived as relevant to the formation of the collective identity under discussion.

As we have seen, race and ethnicity are overlapping strategies for human categorization. In this chapter, I will nonetheless argue that there is methodological mileage in acknowledging the subtle difference in emphasis and articulation between the two. It is useful to tease out this difference in emphasis because, like the concepts of race and ethnicity themselves, the configuration between the two ideas is also socially constructed. The precise relationship between these two classificatory strategies has varied across both time and space. There are moments in history when bloodlines and genealogies have been of paramount importance, and when somatic variation has attracted less interest. Conversely, there are times when the specifics of your descent mattered far less than the shape, size or colour of your body. This chapter explores the changing configurations of this relationship in the ancient world. When – following my definitions of the two terms – was race more important than ethnicity, and when was ethnicity more important than race? When did the two concepts come together, as they often do today? And crucially, why?

As a fully comprehensive study of the topic is not possible within the constraints of this chapter, I shall present a series of brief case studies from across the chronological and geographical span of Mediterranean antiquity. My focus in this chapter is explicitly on *Mediterranean* rather than *Greco-Roman* antiquity. As explained in the introduction to this volume, our modern tendency to focus on Greeks and Romans as solely constitutive of the ancient world is largely a product of our own disciplinary history. Indeed, scholarship from Bernal onwards has demonstrated that we cannot fully understand the Greeks and the Romans if we abstract them from their own contemporary contexts; and that they were both deeply enmeshed with, and heavily influenced by, other groups and societies throughout antiquity. A key step in trying to understand race, ethnicity or identity in the ancient world, therefore, is seeing a bigger, broader and more diverse ancient world – both stretching beyond the boundaries of Greco-Roman antiquity and also recognizing that these boundaries themselves were ever-changing and permeable. Another key step is trying to think outside our own conceptual frameworks, and as set out in the introduction to this volume, attempting to understand the schemes of human classification employed by diverse people of antiquity.

In what follows, therefore, I have deliberately selected examples where the two concepts of ethnicity and race cut across and confuse each other, producing categories that might seem counterintuitive to the modern observer. I could, of course, have done the exact opposite, choosing instances where ideas about descent and physiognomy were neatly aligned, both with each other and with our modern expectations. Yet to do so would have been to reinforce these expectations, conditioned by our modern systems of human classification. Instead, my aim in this chapter is to draw out the unexpected and the uncanny, challenging us to rethink our assumptions about the configuration of race and ethnicity in the ancient world. Given the specifics of the current political and cultural moment, given our own particular histories of racial and ethnic classification, and given our tendency to read our social assumptions into genetic science, it would be easy to assume that our contemporary categories are universal. It would be easy to assume that 'race' and 'ethnicity' were synonymous throughout human history, and that descent and physiognomy were always viewed as intrinsically linked. The examples below demonstrate that this was not always the case.

THE BLUE-SKINNED GODS OF TAHARQA

In the early seventh century BCE, the Greek city-states were developing, the Homeric epics were emerging, and the Assyrian king Sennacherib was building his 'palace without rival' at Nineveh. Whilst all this was going on, the Egyptian pharaoh Taharqa erected a shrine to Amun-Re in the temple complex at Kawa, part of a grand building programme that saw new monuments springing up across Egypt and Nubia (Kitchen 1986: 388–92). The external walls of this shrine depict the pharaoh making offerings to four different sets of gods: to those of Heliopolis on the south wall, to those of Memphis on the north, to a local version of Amun-Re based at Thebes on the east, and to the Amun-Re of Kawa itself on the west (Macadam 1955) (Figure 6.1).

Photo-luminescence has recently revealed traces of pigment on some of the figures adorning this shrine, indicating that they had been painted a bright blue (Armstrong 2015). Blue is found on the hair of some goddesses, on the headpieces and dresses of others, and – perhaps most conspicuously – colouring the skin of the Amun-Re of Kawa. The blue skin of the Kawan Amun-Re is all the more eye-catching given the lack of blue pigment on the skin of his Theban counterpart. Was this a racialized representation of two incarnations of the same god? Was the Amun-Re of Kawa portrayed with blue skin to show that he was racially distinct from the Amun-Re of Thebes? At first glance, this seems possible. After all, the site of Kawa was located in Nubia (modern Sudan and southern Egypt), while Thebes (modern Luxor) was an erstwhile capital of upper Egypt. In addition, there was a long tradition in Egypt of portraying Nubians in a racialized way

FIGURE 6.1 Shrine erected by the Pharoah Tarharqa to Amun-Re at Kawa. © Heritage Images/Getty Images.

as black skinned 'Others', subservient to and in contrast with the red-skinned people of Egypt (Smith 2014).

Yet on closer inspection, it becomes evident that our modern expectations about skin colour and race do not apply in this particular instance. The shrine, and the wider temple complex of which it was a part, were built by Taharqa, a Kushite pharaoh of the Twenty-Fifth Dynasty, who themselves hailed from Nubia. The Kushite pharaohs both adopted and adapted Egyptian traditions of royal iconography, in particular borrowing from Old Kingdom models, but also adding innovations such as the cap crown with double uraeus (Myśliwiec 1988; Chimko 2003). Yet while they presented themselves with hybrid accoutrements of rule, the Nubian pharaohs of the Twenty-Fifth Dynasty did not tend to make racial distinctions between themselves and their predecessors. While earlier Egyptian art had used skin tone as a means of distinguishing Egyptians from Nubians, the art of the Twenty-Fifth Dynasty does not follow such conventions. In particular, the Nubian pharaohs are not usually portrayed as physiognomically different from pharaohs of other dynasties. How, then, should we interpret the bright blue skin of the Amun-Re of Kawa, especially in contrast to the non-blue skin of the Amun-Re of Thebes?

Blue skin was the norm in earlier depictions of the god from the late Eighteenth Dynasty onwards, especially following the re-establishment of polytheism after a brief experiment with monotheism during the Amarna period (Van de Mieroop 2011: 209–10). This blue skin was a mark of distinction, signifying Amun-Re's status as the supreme god with life-giving power, and his control over the Nile with its cycles of fertility and rebirth (Armstrong 2015: 191). The difference in skin colour between the two Amun-Res at Kawa was therefore one of status rather than one of race. The Amun-Re of Kawa is portrayed as the more powerful, his position marked out by the cerulean hue of his heavenly skin. The point being made here is not just religious but also political – the cult of Amun-Re at the Nubian city of Kawa is elevated over the cult of Amun-Re at the old capital city of Thebes, a parallel of the geographic shift of power southwards down the Nile valley (195).

But while the pharaohs of the Twenty-Fifth Dynasty may not have distinguished themselves from their predecessors racially, they did mark themselves out ethnically by emphasizing separate descent. They took care to stress that they not only belonged to a different dynastic family from those that went before them, but also they belonged to a different ethnic group that constructed genealogies in an entirely different fashion. In Egypt, genealogically driven king lists are known from the New Kingdom onwards, and interest in specifically genealogical texts grew towards the end of this period (Eyre 2013: 285–6). Egyptian genealogies were usually traced from father to son, focusing on direct descent in the male line. In contrast, Twenty-Fifth Dynasty pharaohs introduced a revolution in genealogical thinking, stressing that they were from another ancestral line that followed radically different genealogical rules.

During the Twenty-Fifth Dynasty, power was passed from king to king in a highly unusual manner. First, it was inherited matrilineally, through the female rather than the male line. Second, it was not inherited by direct descent (i.e. mothers and daughters) but instead by each king passing the throne to his sister's children (Lohwasser 2001). This radical approach to dynastic genealogy is set out in a number of texts, including several monumental stelae erected by Taharqa in the sanctuary of Kawa itself. These include two very similar stelae (Kawa IV and VI) recounting the establishment of the dynasty by Taharqa's ancestor Alara, who secured the royal line by dedicating his sister and her descendants to Amun-Re, praying for the god to 'look to the womb of my relatives for me, and establish their descendants on earth' (Gozzoli 2009: 244). A third stele (Kawa V) describes Taharqa's coronation, the climax of which is the king being reunited with his mother. This maternal meeting is played out as a piece of political theatre, with mother and son assuming the role of Horus and Isis, and Taharqa acknowledging that his own authority to rule derives from his mother (237–8). Descent, lineage and ethnicity were seen as vital marks of distinction, separating the pharaohs of the Twenty-Fifth Dynasty from their forerunners, and elevating them through the female line. This unique approach to articulating descent was a means of constructing a distinct ethnicity – not only did the Nubian pharaohs come from a different genealogical line from earlier rulers, but this genealogical line was *ethnically* different – ordered by different rules with a different genealogical logic.

There is much to be learned about concepts of race and ethnicity in seventh-century BCE Egypt and Nubia from the inscriptions and iconography at the temple of Amun-Re at Kawa. We learn that the Kushite pharaohs of the Twenty-Fifth Dynasty did not use physiognomy to articulate a distinct identity, contrary to what we, with our modern assumptions, might have expected. Instead, their distinctiveness was constructed through ideas about a unique and elevated genealogy – a genealogy that worked in ways which were also contrary to what we, with our modern assumptions, might have expected.

DARIUS' DIVERSE SUPPORTERS

A century and a half later, physiognomic characterization and genealogical exposition were brought together within a single system for human classification elsewhere in the ancient world. By the end of the sixth century BCE, the Achaemenid Persian Empire had become the largest state that the ancient world had yet seen; stretching from Thessaly in the west to Afghanistan in the east, and from Ukraine in the north to Sudan in the south (Briant 2002; Allen 2005). Holding together the diverse peoples of the empire required not only an efficient and sophisticated new system of imperial administration but also a whole new way of thinking about human diversity – a new approach to comprehending, systematizing and categorizing people (Gates-Foster 2014).

This new approach can be seen in the monuments, inscriptions and art commissioned by the Achaemenid kings (Root 1979). The tomb of one such king, Darius I (r. 522–486 BCE) features a life-size sculptural relief of the king sacrificing to Ahuramazda, the supreme deity in the Persian religion of Zoroastrianism. In Figures 6.2 and 6.3, Darius stands supported by his subjects. The platform on which he stands is held up by thirty human figures (all male), arranged in two registers. These figures represent the subject peoples of the empire, and visual stereotypes in dress, accoutrements and bodily form are deployed to make each recognizable. To avoid any possible confusion as to their identities, the figures were also labelled trilingually in Old Persian, Elamite and Babylonian. The labels read:

This is the Persian	This is the Babylonian
This is the Mede	This is the Assyrian
This is the Elamite	This is the Arabian
This is the Parthian	This is the Egyptian
This is the Aryan	This is the Armenian
This is the Bactrian	This is the Cappadocian

RACE AND ETHNICITY

This is the [Sogdian?]
This is the Chorasmian
This is the Drangian
This is the Arachosian
This is the Sattagydian
This is the Gandarian
This is the man from the Indus valley
This is the Amrygian Scythian
This is the Scythian with the pointy hat

This is the Lydian
This is the Ionian
This is the Scythian beyond the sea
This is the Thracian
This is the Ionian with the sunhat
This is the Libyan
This is the Kushite
This is the Makrian
This is the Carian

(inscription DNe, from Darius' tomb at Naqsh-e Rostam; Schmitt 2000)

The categorization of people on this monument therefore seems to have three main elements. The first is geographical, as the figures are named according to the country (*dahyu*) that they come from. The second is cultural, as the figures can be distinguished by their distinctive dress and equipment – the Persian, for example, wears a characteristic pleated skirt and bears an *akinakes* sword; the Skythians wear trousers and either pointed or round hats; and the Libyan wears a long tunic and carries a mace (Schmitt 2000). But the categories are also partly biological, as implied by the figures' different physical features. The men from Gandhara and the Indus valley (modern Pakistan and northern India) are depicted with long, straight noses and straight hair. In contrast, the Babylonian (modern southern Iraq) and the Arabian have been given medium-sized noses and hair that spirals in tight curls. The Ionian (interchangeable here with Greeks) and Thracian

FIGURE 6.2 View across Naqsh-e Rostam, showing the cruxiform tombs of Darius I (*right*) and Artaxerxes I (*left*). Also visible at the lower level are reliefs of later Sasanian kings (*right to left*): Bahram II; Shapur I; Shapur II; and Hormizd II. © Prisma Bildagentur/Universal Images Group/Getty Images.

FIGURE 6.3 Sculptural relief above the tomb of Darius I at Naqsh-e Rostam. © Werner Forman/Universal Images Group/Getty Images.

(the northern Aegean and Bulgaria) have hair that is straight once more, while the Nubian (modern southern Egypt and north-central Sudan) is depicted with a smaller rounded nose and tightly curling hair. Given that the relief would originally have been painted, it is possible that skin and hair colour were also used to differentiate the figures. The classification of people on this relief is therefore partly racial (by somatic characteristics), but it also seems to be partly cultural (by dress) and partly geographic (by regional label).

Things are further complicated if we consider another inscription from the same monument. This inscription, carved directly behind the head of the king as if it were a speech-bubble, lays out a programmatic statement of Darius' imperial ideology. In it, Darius introduces himself: 'I am Darius, the great king, the king of kings, king of the countries of all the people, king on this great earth far and wide, the son of Hystaspes, an Achaemenid, a Persian, the son of a Persian, an Aryan, of Aryan lineage' (DNa, lines 8–15). In this inscription, Darius makes two claims. The first is to universal kingship and the second is a claim about his own lineage and descent – in other words, his ethnicity. Darius' statement of ethnicity begins with his immediate genealogy (he is the son of Hytaspes), before going on to make some broader claims about his lineage.

He is first said to be descended from Achaemenids, the clan of Cyrus the Great who founded both the royal dynasty and the empire. This is immediately problematic, as Darius had taken the throne in a violent coup (although Darius presents this as a counter-coup against the murderers of Cyrus' son), marrying Cyrus' daughter Atossa to bolster his legitimacy. Darius' next statement is that his ancestors were Persians and Aryans. This is also problematic, as according to Darius' own classification system Persians and Aryans were distinct and separate racial-cultural-geographical groups. Specifically, Persians were linked to the region of Fars in southwest Iran, while Aryans were associated with parts of eastern Iran. (It is important to note that in this period, the term 'Aryan' did not have the same connotations of white supremacy as it does today.) Yet Darius' own grandfather, it seems, was both a Persian *and* an Aryan simultaneously.

It seems that in the Persian world, clear racial categories were constructed, using a framework for defining identity which places an emphasis on somatic as well as cultural and geographic markers. Yet ethnicity and descent could cut across racial lines, and racial categories were permeable. It was evidently possible for Darius' grandfather to belong to more than one race – not to be of mixed race, as we would understand it, but to have complete and full possession of two racial identities simultaneously. This racial flexibility may not, of course, have been possible for all subjects of the empire in the same way as it was for members of the royal family, but it is still evident that in Achaemenid Persia, no less than in Egypt and Nubia, our modern assumptions about race and descent do not necessarily apply.

PRAXITHEA AND HER EARTHBORN DAUGHTERS

In the late fifth century, a generation or so after the death of Darius, the playwright Euripides staged a new trilogy of tragedies in his home city of Athens. Among them was the *Erechtheus*, a play that today survives only in fragments. The play was set in the mythical past and told the story of how, when Athens was under attack by Thessalians, the Delphic oracle declared that victory could only be won if the king were to sacrifice one of his daughters. The king in question was the eponymous Erechtheus, a local hero said to have been 'born from the earth' (*gēgenēs*) of Attica itself (*Iliad* 2.546–51; *Odyssey* 7.80–1). In response to the prophecy, Erechtheus's wife, the queen Praxithea, makes a long and impassioned speech arguing in favour of killing her daughter. She begins this speech by claiming:

> I have many reasons, the primary one being
> That I could have no better city than this.
> Firstly, we are not an immigrant people from elsewhere,
> We are born autochthons, while other cities
> Are founded by moves like a board game,
> Different people brought in from different places.
>
> (Euripides, *Erechtheus* F360 lines 5–10)

The speech continues in the same vein, with Praxithea weighing the grief of one family against the good of the city as a whole; and arguing that since she would not have hesitated had she been asked to give up a son in combat, she should not quail at losing a daughter. As well as being dramatic and full of emotion, the speech also tells us something about contemporary attitudes to ethnicity and how concepts of Athenian identity were articulated in relation to descent. Praxithea's emphasis in this speech is clearly on Athenian autochthony, and the idea of being native or indigenous to the soil that one inhabits. She contrasts this favourably with the populations of other Greek cities, whose origin stories often relied on mythic migrations.

The idea of being autochthonous was unusual in the ancient Greek world, and the Athenians were one of only a handful of groups who claimed to be 'earthborn' (Roy

FIGURE 6.4 The Erechtheion (Temple of Erechtheus) on the Acropolis of Athens. © De Agostoni/Getty Images.

2014). After all, a claim of autochthony contradicted the traditional model of Greekness as determined by common ancestry, articulated most clearly in the sixth-century Hesiodic poem *The Catalogue of Women* (J. Hall 2002; Vlassopoulos 2013a: 174–5). If the Athenians were descended solely and purely from an indigenous line, this meant that they could not also be descended from the eponymous common ancestor of the Hellenes, the mythical Hellen (J. Hall 1997: 51–5). Claiming a pure autochthonous ancestry, therefore, called into question the Athenians' fundamental Greekness.

Euripides was not, however, the first to tap into this idea of Athenian genealogical exceptionalism. In 451 BCE the statesman Pericles passed a radical new law, stating that Athenian citizenship could only be claimed by those who had two citizen parents – previously, it had been sufficient only to have had a citizen father (Lape 2010). While the motivation for this law may have been economic and organizational, its institution had implications for how Athenians understood their civic identity, and how they viewed their ethnicity in relation to other Greeks. Around this time, Athens was exercising hegemonic rule over hundreds of other Greek cities under the aegis of the Delian League (Low 2008). The Athenians justified their imperial power in a range of ways – they argued that an alliance was necessary to keep the Persians at bay and constructed a rich rhetoric around the barbarian 'Other' in order to support this argument (E. Hall 1989; J. Hall 2002); they manipulated myths to argue that many of the Ionian cities were originally founded by Athenian migrants and that these cities therefore owed Athens their allegiance (Mac Sweeney 2017); and they also encouraged a discourse of Athenian exceptionalism, creating an image of Athens as unique, predestined for hegemony.

The myth of autochthony fed into Athens' self-image, and unlike other strands of Athenian imperial rhetoric was primarily designed for internal rather than external consumption (Rosivach 1987; Blok 2009). In particular, it offered a founding myth for Athenian democracy, stressing commonality between citizens (Loraux 2000). Indeed, the idea remained powerful throughout the second half of the fifth century with the rebuilding of a major new temple to Erechtheus on the Acropolis (Figure 6.4). About ten years after the *Erechtheus* was staged, Euripides went on to rewrite another of Athens' origin myths in the *Ion*. The eponymous hero of this play was another mythical king of Athens, traditionally held to be a descendant of Hellen on his father's side, and of Erechtheus on his mother's side; and the purported ancestor of 'Ionian' migrants who later set out from Athens to found a series of Greek cities in the central and eastern Aegean. Euripides revised the story to make Ion the son of Apollo, effectively removing his Hellenic ancestry and making him into a pure autochthon. By the end of the fifth century then, Athenian ideas about their own exceptionalism had gone so far as to deny their basic Greekness.

Was this necessarily a problem? Modern scholars tend to assume that Greekness was consistent in its definition – that it was either a racial or an ethnic category, in line with our own expectations (Vlassopoulos 2010b; Luraghi 2014). Yet as we have seen here, several ancient texts problematize the idea of Greekness based on descent (i.e. ethnicity), while others texts problematize the idea of Greekness as based on somatic features (i.e. race). In the latter case, in some ancient texts, some of the crucial factors governing bodily form and physiognomy are climate and environment. For example, in the well-known Hippocratic *Airs, Waters, Places*, is it stated that: 'you will usually find that the nature and the physical form of people follows that of the place they live in' (*Aer.* 24: for more on this work, see Kaufman in this volume). So if – contrary to modern assumptions – Greekness was neither consistently ethnic nor consistently racial, then what was it?

The answer is that the definition of Greekness was changeable, and that over the course of the classical period, 'Greek' increasingly became a cultural rather than an ethnic category (J. Hall 2002: 2; Kim 2009; Vlassopoulos 2013a). Cultural identities, as defined at the start of this chapter, focus primarily on what people *do* – on action and social practice, rather than bloodlines (ethnicity) or bodily form (race). We have already seen in the works of Euripides how the idea of Greekness as related to shared descent was eroded in fifth-century Athens. The fourth century saw the rise of an idea of Greekness predicated instead on shared culture, with the Athenian orator Isocrates claiming that: 'the name "Hellene" no longer denotes a race but a frame of mind, and people are called Hellenes for sharing our culture rather than for sharing a common blood' (*Panegyricus* 50). For Isocrates, Greek was not something you automatically *were*, it was something that you could *become*.

The potential for change is crucial to understanding classical Greek conceptions of race and ethnicity. Race was like culture – changeable. One could transform one's bodily form through a combination of effort and environment (e.g. training one's body through athletics and exercise), just as one could transforms one's customs and culture. In contrast, descent was not thought to be changeable in the same way: one's ancestors and bloodlines were assumed to be predetermined. This idea of ancestry as fixed and therefore especially powerful goes some way towards explaining the prevalence and popularity of genealogies in the ancient Greek world – genealogical exposition is found not only in historiography and drama, but also in epic and lyric, philosophy and epigram, and inscriptions from across the ancient Greek world (Fowler 1999; Varto 2015). The irony of this position should be immediately obvious, given Euripides' rewriting of Ion's genealogy. An ostensible belief in the fixity of ancestry went hand in hand with the near-constant revision and reworking of that ancestry. Whatever the Greeks may have *said* about ethnicity being fixed while race and culture were changeable, it is evident that *all* of these forms of identity were up for negotiation.

RACIALIZED GAULS AND ETHNICIZED GERMANS

Almost a century after Euripides wrote his plays in classical Athens, a new era opened following the Achaemenid Empire's conquest by Alexander of Macedonia (also known as Alexander the Great) and the subsequent collapse of the empire following his death. The hybrid world of the Hellenistic empires disrupted earlier ideas about the categorization of people. The contested relationship between Greek and Macedonian identities (Engels 2010) developed into even more complex triangulations under Seleucid rule based in Mesopotamia (Kosmin 2014; Stevens 2019) and Ptolemaic rule based in Egypt (McCoskey 2002; Fischer-Bovet 2018). Perhaps the best-known debate on the nature of Hellenistic hybridity is the long-running and fiercely contested dispute over whether Cleopatra was 'White' or 'Black', often carried out without acknowledgement that Cleopatra herself may not have recognized these categories at all (Ashton 2008). Comparatively less attention is paid to a group of people who became the ideological bogeymen of the Hellenistic world, cast as a racialized Other by the Ptolemies of Egypt, the Attalids of Anatolia, the Aetolians of southern Greece, the Etruscans of Italy and even by the expanding state of Rome: the Gauls (Gruen 2011a: 141–58).

This othering was driven by an immediate and intense fear. Groups referred to as 'Gauls' or 'Celts' sacked Rome *c.* 387 BCE; swept through peninsular Greece in the early third century, famously attacking Delphi around 279 BCE; and raided the coast of Anatolia, eventually settling inland after their defeat by Attalos of Pergamon *c.* 230 BCE (Mitchell 1993; Shipley 2000: 52–4). Scenes rapidly began to appear in both visual art and literature that depicted Gauls in stereotyped ways, casting them as the barbarian enemies of civilization. In his *Hymn to Delos*, the Alexandrian poet Callimachus referred to the attack of Delphi, deriding the Gauls as 'like snowflakes' before ascribing their defeat to his patron the Egyptian pharaoh Ptolemy II Philadelphus (lines 171–90). Over the next century, a new type of combat scene entered into the artistic canon, supplementing the Gigantomachy (battle between the Olympian gods and the giants) and the Amazonomachy (battle between male warriors and Amazonian warrior women) – the Celtomachy. In such scenes, the viewer was invited to associate with Us – the 'normal' male combatant – in contrast to Them – the uncivilized Other. Celts or Gauls, like the monstrous giants or the barbaric Amazons, were cast as the inhuman opposites of civilization (Woolf 2011: 23; Rebeggiani 2018: 71–3).

The characterization of the Gauls included several racial elements, creating a sense of a distinctive physiognomy (e.g. Strabo 4.1.1). One key feature of this was unnaturally pale skin. Callimachus' snowflake is a reference not only to the Gauls' chaotic fighting style but also to the strange colour of their bodies; when Virgil describes a scene of Gaulish warriors on the shield of Aeneas, their skins glow a milky-white (*Aeneid* 8.660; see also Ammianus 15.12.1 and Isidore who suggests that the word 'Gaul' is derived from the ancient Greek *gala,* meaning 'milk': *Etymologies* 14.4.25). Great height was another point of frequent comment (Diodorous Siculus 5.32.2; Strabo 5.5.2–3; Caesar, *Gallic Wars* 2.30; Ammianus 15.12.1). Another physical feature that was sometimes highlighted was the Gauls' unusual hair. In terms of colour, it was yellow or gold; and in terms of nature, it was abundant (Diodorus Siculus 5.28.1; Ammianus 15.12.1). In visual representations of Gauls, hair is sometimes conspicuously modelled, appearing thicker, fuller, and more prominent than the hair of other groups. This was true not only of the hair on their heads but of their bodily hair too – and in particular pubic hair. This idea of a characteristic Gallic physiognomy (Woolf 2011: 20 and 32) is perhaps best encapsulated in a short passage written by the first-century BCE historian, Diodorus Siculus: 'The Gauls are tall of body, with rippling muscles, and milky-white skin. Their hair is golden not only by nature, as through artifice they seek to augment the unusual colour that nature has given it' (5.28.1) (Figure 6.5).

FIGURE 6.5 The 'Dying Gaul', Roman marble statue based on a Hellenistic bronze original, commissioned at Pergamon. © Karen Bleier/AFP/Getty Images.

The racialized description of Gauls stands out if we compare it with the treatment of another northern European group – the Germans. During the early and high Roman Empire, these two groups were often discussed alongside each other, and elements of their characterization were often shared (Gruen 2011a: 159–78; Woolf 2011: 40–55). Interestingly, while the Gauls were often associated with a distinct set of somatic features (see above), texts discussing the Germans were less concerned with their physical appearances. Perhaps the best illustration of this is Tacitus' *Germania*. Like other early Roman ethnographic texts, the *Germania* primarily focuses on lifestyle and culture, with a particular interest in political organization. At the start of the treatise however, Tacitus devotes just over two full sections (*Germania* 2–4; 296 words of Latin) to a discussion of the genealogical origin of the Germans. Although he mentions several different divine genealogies, as well as alternative stories that incorporated ancient Greek heroes into the Germany genealogical pool, Tacitus clearly states his own view of the Germans as ethnically (i.e. genealogically) distinct:

> I would argue that the Germans themselves are indigenous, and not at all mixed with other peoples through travel and immigration …. In their ancient songs, which are their only way of keeping records and memories, they claim that their people are descended from the earth-born god Tuisco. They say his son Mannus is the progenitor of their people, and they assign to Mannus three sons, from whose names they say that those near to the Ocean are called Ingaevones, those in the middle Herminones, and the rest Istaevones. Some, given the freedom of talking about ancient things, say that the god had several offspring and these created several tribal names – the Marsii, the Gambrivii, the Suevi, the Vandilii – and that these are true ancient names.
>
> (*Germania* 2)

Later, in an ominous foreshadowing of twentieth-century Nazi rhetoric, Tacitus notes, 'I myself agree with those who think the peoples of Germany are uninfected by intermarriage with other races, pure and particular to themselves' (*Germania* 4).

In contrast, Tacitus devotes a far shorter passage (only thirty-nine words in Latin) to a physical description of Germans, claiming: 'They have fierce blue eyes, red hair, and big bodies suitable for strong force' (*Germania* 4). At this point, it is worth reiterating that ancestry and physiognomy were often closely related in ethnographic texts such as Tacitus' *Germania*. Indeed, Tacitus himself suggests that the reason why all Germans look alike is because of their pure ancestry and inbreeding, and as discussed in the introduction to this chapter, race and ethnicity are very closely related. Yet in the *Germania* there is a distinct emphasis on ethnicity rather than race – on bloodlines rather than bodies. Tacitus is simply more interested in ancestry than he is in physiognomy.

The different ethnographic treatment of Gauls and Germans requires further research and explanation. Why should there be a tendency to discuss the Gauls in terms of racial characteristics, and Germans in terms of genealogy and descent? Why should two otherwise similar groups be approached from these different perspectives, and described with this difference in emphasis? The inter-relationships between race and ethnicity in antiquity were complex and ever-changing, creating configurations that we may not necessarily expect.

CHANGING SKINS IN HELIODORUS

Sometime in the third or fourth centuries CE (our sources are unclear about the precise date), a scholar called Heliodorus sat down in his hometown of Emesa to write a racy (and indeed also a race-y) tale about two young lovers. The text is known as the *Aethiopica*, a romantic fiction telling the story of Chariclea and Theagenes, and is one of five surviving ancient Greek novels (Whitmarsh 2008). As the *Aethiopica* has been treated fully elsewhere (see Derbew and Haley in this volume), I shall discuss it only briefly here, focusing on one aspect that is particularly important for this chapter – the relationship between ethnicity and race, between the genealogical and the somatic.

The basic plot of the story is similar to those of other Greek novels. The protagonists meet, fall in love and eventually live happily ever after: but only after a series of exciting adventures and frightening misfortunes. Before they can retire into romantic bliss, Theagenes and Chariclea must first encounter pirates and bandits; stand firm through trials of sexual threat and temptation; and make a number of perilous journeys, from Delphi to Egypt, and from there to Ethiopia. The final dramatic episode sees Theagenes and Chariclea held as the prisoners of the Ethiopian king Hydaspes, who decrees that they are to be sacrificed to the gods Helios and Selene. It is at this point that Chariclea reveals her true identity as Hydaspes' long-lost daughter and a princess of Ethiopia. The story ends with King Hydaspes and his queen Persinna agreeing to outlaw human sacrifice, and the joyful union of Chariclea and Theagenes.

One of the key moments in this tale is therefore the unveiling of Chariclea's identity. We learn of the circumstances surrounding her conception and birth, and of the exile that resulted in her being brought up by a priest at Delphi. Several tokens are produced to confirm Chariclea's identity, including Persinna's engagement ring and a ribbon inscribed with a note in the queen's own handwriting (*Aethiopica* 10.12–13). Hydaspes is almost convinced by these tokens, but then voices his concern that while he and Persinna are, like most other Ethiopians, dark skinned, Chariclea's skin is pale (*Aethiopica* 10.14). An unusual explanation is offered for this somatic difference: in the moment of Chariclea's conception, Persinna gazed upon a picture of Andromeda, and as a result the embryo took on the physical form of the mythological heroine. (Andromeda was herself an Ethiopian princess, and her skin colour was portrayed in various different ways in antiquity, see McCoskey 2012: 146–8.) When the picture in question is produced, the assembled crowds gasp to see the likeness between the painted Andromeda and the living Chariclea (*Aethiopica* 10.14).

In the case of Chariclea, a common ancestry does not necessarily result in a common physiognomy, and ethnicity does not necessarily match with race. Crucially, when it comes to governing bodily forms and racial characteristics, genealogy seems to matter somewhat less than visuality. It is the power of sight, and specifically the power of the image burned into Persinna's mind, that determines the physical form of her daughter. This emphasis on the visual is central to the *Aethiopica*. The novel is full of lavish description, employing sophisticated strategies of *ekphrasis* (using words to describe visual art), and playing complex games with the idea of seeing and being seen (Bartsch 1989). Individual works of art feature at several points in the story, not least the painting of Andromeda.

This interest in visuality is common to other literary works of the time. Indeed, it is one of the key characteristics of Greek literature written under the Roman Empire from the second century CE onwards. This body of literature is usually described as the 'Second Sophistic' – a term that refers to the use of deliberately archaic and highly stylized literary forms (Whitmarsh 2009). Another common theme within the literature of the Second Sophistic is the fluidity and constructed nature of identities (Dench 2017) – a theme that seems to have permeated not just the stories these authors told but also their own lives. In the final words of the novel, Heliodorus describes himself. 'This [book] was written by a Phoenician man from Emesa, of the people/tribe (*genos*) of Helios, the son of Theodosius, Heliodorus' (*Aethiopica* 10.41). There seems to have been no contradiction in a Greek literary figure claiming a Phoenician ethnicity, while likely also enjoying the benefits of Roman citizenship. For Heliodorus, your *genos* was in your bloodline. Yet in the *Aethiopica*, race, like beauty, was very much in the eye of the beholder.

CONCLUSION

In this chapter, I have argued that race and ethnicity are not necessarily the same. It is true that 'ethnicity' has sometimes stood in as a more polite and socially acceptable synonym for 'race', but this should not mask the subtle yet significant differences that the two concepts can be used to connote. In this chapter, I have argued that while they often overlap and reinforce each other, racial discourse and ethnic discourses can be employed in ways that shed light on the different emphases and directions of different identity formations. The former I take as primarily concerned with physical differences and somatic variation, while the latter has its primary focus on ancestry and bloodlines. And while we tend to conflate these two things in our own matrix of sociological thought, people in the ancient world did not necessarily see things in the same way.

We have seen that around the same time as the Homeric epics were spinning tales of the 'blameless Ethiopians' (*Iliad* 1.423–4; 23.205–7), in Egypt under the pharaoh Taharqa the physiognomic marker of skin colour was used to communicate divine power rather than racial difference, and Nubian identity was instead constructed through an unusual matrilineal genealogy. We have seen how the Achaemenid Persian kings divided their empire into subject peoples, defined partly by perceived physical markers, but that these same kings themselves claimed genealogies that cut across racial boundaries. We have seen an outright denial of ethnic Greekness in Athens during the classical period, and how this was a step on the way to a more cultural conception of Greek identity, alongside which emerged the idea that ethnicity was a more fixed and stable form of classification than race. We have discussed the racialized characterization of the Gauls in the late Hellenistic period and at the height of the Roman Empire, and questioned why the comparable category of Germans was often discussed more in ethnic than in racial terms. Finally, we have seen how in late antiquity it was possible to construct a world where racial characteristics did not stem from ethnicity and bloodlines, but could instead be formed through the power of human perception.

And this is, of course, where we must necessarily conclude. In all of these snapshots from antiquity, it has been human perception that has shaped racial and ethnic categories – perception that is deeply rooted in its specific social and historical context. We must not, therefore, assume that the peoples of antiquity shared in our own contemporary modes of perception. In today's world, ethnicity is thought of as mapping onto race, and descent is assumed as crucial in constituting bodily forms. In the many worlds of antiquity, there were other ways of thinking.

CHAPTER SEVEN

Race and Gender

SHELLEY P. HALEY

SOCIAL CONSTRUCTS, ANCIENT AND MODERN

Our understanding of race and gender in the ancient world is situated within the frameworks we employ, knowingly or unknowingly, to analyse these social markers of identity. In recent years, feminist scholars and scholars of race studies have abandoned the approaches of positivism and turned to those of social construction and intersectionality. The term 'intersectionality' was coined by the legal scholar Kimberlé Crenshaw in a 1989 article, and she defined it in a more recent interview as 'a lens through which you can see where power comes and collides, where it interlocks and intersects' (Crenshaw 2017). However, as a concept, intersectionality is rooted in the earlier *Combahee River Collective Statement* (1977) by Barbara Smith, Beverly Smith and Demita Frazier, which articulates very clearly the simultaneity of oppressions that women of African descent endure.

Intersectionality is a critical intervention against the essentialism of critical race theory and is a core concept of critical race feminism (hereafter, CRF). The anti-essentialism of CRF has 'provide[d] a critique of the feminist notion that there is an essential female voice, that is, that all women feel one way on a subject .... CRF highlights the situation of women of color, whose lives may not conform to an essential norm' (Wing 2003: 7). Since Crenshaw's articulation, intersectionality has spread as an analytical tool beyond disciplines and borders. Intersectional projects and methods exist in a wide range of fields, expanding from its origins in jurisprudence to sociology, education, history, psychology and even business. Margaret Conkey (2005) has explored intersectionality as an analytical tool in her discussion of the intersection between feminist archaeology and indigenous archaeology. As Carbado et al. state, 'Very few theories have generated the kind of interdisciplinary and global engagement that marks the intellectual history of intersectionality' (2013: 303–12). While scholars of the ancient world are finding intersectionality a useful tool for examining ancient societies, they engage with it in a limited way. For instance, often, classicists neglect the core axis of race in their application of the concept.

For some time now, the concept of social construction has also proved fruitful in the efforts to uncover the operation of race and gender in ancient societies. Wing notes that defining race as a social construction helps us realize that 'biological races do not exist, as recent science has clearly shown. There is more genetic difference within so-called races than between them. Instead, races have been socially constructed and the legal system reifies that construction, privileging some races over others' (2003: 5) A sterling discussion of the social construction of race in the United States comes to us from Ta-Nehisi Coates:

> But race is the child of racism, not the father. And the process of naming 'the people' has never been a matter of genealogy and physiognomy as much as one of hierarchy. Difference in hue and hair is old. But the belief in the preeminence of hue and hair, the belief that these factors can correctly organize a society and that they signify deeper attributes, which are indelible—this is the new idea at the heart of these new people who have been brought up hopelessly, tragically, to believe that they are white.
>
> (2015: 34)

The same analysis applies to the social construct of gender and the intersection of race and gender. While both these 'modern' approaches can get us closer to understanding what Tim Whitmarsh has described as 'hybridized ancient Greek and Roman worlds' (Whitmarsh and Thomson 2013: 4–5), they still are flawed by the exclusive binaries (i.e. 'either/or') inherited by Western epistemological frameworks and arguably first expressed by Aristotle.[1] For race, recasting Whitmarsh's concept of 'hybridization' as 'creolization' is a first step in dismantling these binaries. Creolization is a process of cultural and linguistic blending which creates a new culture.[2] Furthermore, such reframing aids in breaking down the influence of modern social constructs of race and gender which undergird our reception and perception of race and gender in antiquity.

Historically, the Western construct of gender goes back to the nineteenth century, when the rise of eugenics and the 'cult of true womanhood' were the scaffolding upon which the gender construct was based. As Narayan points out, intellectual discourse 'divided "healthy", "normal" bodies into one of two sexes. This sexual binary was used to normalise and elevate European bourgeois patriarchal formations over all other gendered configurations and played a central role in inventions of Englishness and other forms of European nationness' (2019: 1231). The concept of racialized gender provides a fruitful way of moving beyond the kinds of Eurocentric assumptions embedded in conceptions of gender that arise from the 'cult of true womanhood'. As Eileen Boris states,

> Race and gender exist in tandem to transform profoundly the ways that each works alone. ... Constructed through gendered representations, race in turn reconstructs gender identities .... The concept of racialized gender reflects this interaction.
>
> (2003: 10)

In addition, racialized gender aids in dismantling the simplistic binary that 'men have race and women have gender' (Boris 2003: 10). Up to now, it has been Marxist feminists who have applied the concept to labour movements and labour history where the intersection of race, gender and class has been paramount to the discussion. However, the concept can also shed light on past societies, including those of antiquity.

Sarah Derbew in her chapter for this volume discusses skin colour and Aithiopians in the Hellenic world. Both the Hellenic peoples (i.e. people living in the Greek-speaking world[3]) and the Romans noticed skin colour. Given Rome's significant political and, in imperial times, cultural contact with Africa, the issue of whether skin colour had a role in how Romans valued others is a valid question: was there a skin-colour 'norm' in Roman society? There was, in fact, a range of skin hues and this is reflected in Latin skin colour terminology. *Albus, ater, candidus, fuscus, niger* are all used by Roman authors to describe the skin colour of peoples with whom they came in contact. However, it is equally important to note that there are many, many contexts where skin colour is not mentioned or described. For example, there is no skin colour given for Aeneas, Dido or Iarbas, characters in Book 4 of the *Aeneid* whose representations I will return to later. In these contexts, character – or characterization – was not dependent on skin colour. When the Romans did apply a skin colour descriptor to themselves it generally was *albus*.

What did *albus* mean to a Roman? Nineteenth-century lexicographers render *albus* as 'white' and the related term *candidus* as 'shiny or glistening white'. The opposite of *albus* is *ater* ('black' or 'lustreless black') and opposite to *candidus* is *niger* ('black' or 'shiny or glistening black'). Lloyd A. Thompson in *Romans and Blacks* persuasively argues against translating *albus* as 'white', which for the modern reader in the United States connotes a Nordic or northern European colouring (1989: 10–11). If, then, the reference point for *albus* is pale brown, not the white of a Nordic consciousness, then it transforms the interpretation and reading of other skin-colour terminology. *Ater, candidus, fuscus, niger* all become degrees of brownness. However, it cannot be stressed enough that often skin colour is not mentioned, making it clear that it was not the chief component in the construction of racial difference.

To explore how the lens of racialized gender might work when applied to the ancient societies of Greece and Rome, I will examine several case studies. This lens entails taking a broad view of race to break out of traditional binaries (such as Black/white) and to challenge language which too often erases race (such as 'ethnicity'). In the case studies, I try to stress that the perception and reception of women *and* men is influenced by racialized gender. For the Hellenic world, I employ this lens while examining metic (that is, immigrant) women such as Aspasia in Athens, Helots and Spartiates in Sparta, and mythical characters such as Circe and Medea in cultural representations. The Roman case studies include Dido as represented by the Latin poet Vergil (70–19 BCE) and Sophoniba, Massinissa and Scipio as represented by the Roman historian Livy (*c.* 64–59 BCE–12 CE). I then explore the multiracial context of Heliodorus' *Aethiopica* and end with examples of racialized gender in the graffiti of Rome and Pompeii. I hope to show that the intersection of race and gender in antiquity reflects the transformative nature of racialized gender that Boris describes (2003: 10).

Before discussing the details of the intersection of race and gender in the ancient world, it is important to set out the operating principles of the discussion. First and foremost, the social constructs of race and gender in antiquity were *not* the same as modern times, but, nevertheless, they existed in forms which we have to apprehend on their own terms. However, it cannot be stressed enough that reception of the ancient constructs of race and gender in later times is profoundly influenced by the hierarchal framing described by Coates and Narayan. Pushing against that framing to arrive at a more plausible analysis of race and gender in antiquity is the intellectual and moral imperative of this chapter.

HELLENIC PEOPLES

Ancient formulations of race and gender, like their modern counterparts, were not static; nor were they immutable. Jonathan Hall notes in his work on 'ethnic groups' in Hellenic society that '[e]thnic groups are not static or monolithic, but dynamic and fluid. Their boundaries are permeable to a degree and they may be subject to processes of assimilation and differentiation' (1997: 33). Notably, the Hellenic people enshrined different racial categories in their mythic foundations.⁴ In this regard the narratives concerning racial genealogies are forms of social construction that ancient societies used to explain their racial differences through ancestry. In the myths surrounding the genesis of Hellenic peoples, the ancestors of the three major racial groups are depicted as descendants of Zeus or of Hellen; these figures, Aeolus, Doros and Ion, became the eponymous founders of the Aeolian, Dorian and Ionian races, each of which had distinct linguistic and cultural traits.

So, too, gender and certainly gender relations could and did intersect with these racial distinctions, making racialized gender a useful analytical tool. The Ionian people, best represented by Athens, constructed gender and gender relations along rigid lines especially after the legislation of Solon in the sixth century BCE; the Dorian people, represented by Sparta, also established rigid standards but afforded women more agency than the Ionian people; and the Aeolian group, represented by Lesbos and Corinth, favoured a more egalitarian framing of gender and gender relations. While we can argue that there were relatively uniform 'Roman' constructs for race and gender, we cannot say that there were monolithic constructs in ancient Hellenic societies. These were tied closely to ethnic groups in different city-states around the Aegean Sea.

For Hellenic societies, race itself, as well as racialized gender, becomes more nuanced and complicated because of colonization. A case in point here is Aspasia, an intellectual and partner to the fifth-century Athenian statesman Pericles. Aspasia was born and raised in Miletus, a city-state located in the modern-day Aydin Province in Turkey. It was colonized by Athenians *c.* 1000 BCE and is described as an Ionian 'Greek' city to distinguish it from its indigenous roots in Anatolia. Although it is called an Ionian city, by the time of Aspasia, Miletus was a multicultural city which framed gender in the mould of the Aeolian people which allowed Aspasia to develop as an intellectual. When she emigrated to Athens, she held the status not of an Athenian woman, despite Athenian colonization of her native city-state. Instead, she held the citizenship status of a *metic*, a foreign resident. Her relationship with Pericles did not exempt her from the stipulations of his citizenship law of 451 BCE. This law enforced racialized gender by effectively proscribing legitimate marriage as one between an Athenian man and an Athenian woman. Only their children were considered legitimate heirs and citizens of Athens. Aspasia, because of racialized gender, could never achieve the status of an Athenian wife and had to settle for concubinage, which Konstantinos Kapparis defines as cohabitation without the benefit of lawful marriage; he further points out that before the citizenship law of 451 the 'dividing line between wives and concubines was quite blurry' (2018: 152). After 451, that line became more distinct.⁵

For Sparta, racialized gender comes into stark relief because of the apartheid system which existed there. The indigenous people living on the Argive peninsula were invaded and colonized by a Dorian population. There is not much information about the racial identification of the subjugated people; they are now called Helots, from the name given them by the Spartiates, their colonizers. Because the Helots greatly outnumbered the Spartiates, they were kept in check through means of enslavement, surveillance, torture and murder. They were not permitted to be educated, but they were expected to have children, and had to adhere to the same eugenics protocol as the Spartiates. Indeed, Helot women were often used as wet-nurses. Furthermore, if the population of Helots fell, Spartan men could and would have children with Helot women to increase the numbers of the city-state's enslaved population.⁶ Male children from such a union were caught between the status of free and enslaved; girl children were the victims of infanticide.⁷

Racialized gender had an impact on Spartiate women as well. Plutarch, in his treatise, *Sayings of Spartan Woman*, exoticizes Dorian femininity by attributing bravery, emotional distance and patriotism to Spartan women. Since the men were trained to be full-time warriors, women were reared to administer the non-military spheres. Following the policy of eugenics, they were also expected to produce warriors for the race.[8] To that end, Spartiate women were allowed a better diet, a strict exercise regimen and an education. Marriage occurred later for young Spartiate women, giving their bodies a chance to mature and be better disposed for childbirth. Maternal mortality rates were lower for Spartan women than for Athenian women who tended to marry very soon after the onset of menstruation.[9]

Since racialized gender is at the centre of the construction of identity for Hellenic peoples, it is not surprising to find it illustrated in cultural production, especially literature. Epic poetry, arguably the earliest genre, offers several examples of racialized gender. Indeed, racialized gender can be said to drive the plots of Homer's *Iliad* and *Odyssey*. In the *Iliad*, the characters of Briseis, Helen and Andromache are exempla of the intersection between race and gender. Briseis was seized as a prisoner of war by Achilles after the occupation of her city-state Lyrnessos in Dardania (modern-day Turkey), which was inhabited by Cilicians.[10] Because of racialized gender, Briseis becomes a war-prize, the literal possession of her oppressor. Most people would agree that Helen's rape and abduction occur because of her gender. However, her race is a factor as well, making her exploitation possible because of racialized gender. Andromache, too, will suffer enslavement because of her race and gender. The bondage of each of these female characters is tied directly to the racialized gender of their male counterparts: Achilles, Paris, Agamemnon and Hector. In the case of Achilles, Agamemnon and even Memnon, the Ethiopian warrior, their racialized gender is often presented as the embodiment of the heroic or warrior code (Figure 7.1). Paris and Hector, as Trojans, also demonstrate elements of their racialized masculinity when they either exhibit cowardice (Paris) or embrace heroism (Hector). Reframing their actions as performances of racialized gender helps to illustrate how the concept applies to men as well as women.

The *Odyssey* offers up more representations of the intersection of race and gender. The power of Odysseus' character itself, as the male ruler of Ithaca, as a trickster figure and as a warrior rests on his racialized gender. His race and gender are honed by his encounters with women of different races. For example, Odysseus' reaction to Calypso, the daughter of two Titans, Atlas and Pleione, is the result of her racialized gender as well as her status as a demi-god. The intersection of Odysseus' race and gender – as well as that of his men – is highlighted when they meet Circe. As the daughter of Helios, Circe has ties to the race of the gods, but also to people of African descent.[11] Her racialized gender is particularly threatening to Odysseus and his men because of her ability to expose their racialized genders as animals which reflect their true 'natures'. In this way Circe's power stems from her racialized gender; subjugating this to Odysseus' own is crucial to his development as an epic hero. His later cruelty towards the enslaved women of Penelope's household is stoked by racialized gender; women of other races must be controlled by Odysseus as a way to assert his power.

Circe's race also establishes the race of another mythic character who has become the epitome of racialized gender: Medea. As the daughter of Circe's brother Aeetes of Colchis, Medea is both a niece to Circe and a granddaughter of Helios. Herodotus informs us that Colchis, a kingdom at the eastern end of the Black Sea, was colonized by an Egyptian pharaoh, probably Sesostris II:

FIGURE 7.1 Amphora featuring the Ethiopian hero Memnon and his attendants, *c.* 530 BCE. © Metropolitan Museum of Art (creative access).

> The Egyptians did, however, say that they thought the original Colchians were men from Sesostris's army. My own idea on the subject was based first on the fact that they have black skins and woolly hair (not that that amounts to much, as other nations have the same), and secondly, and more especially, on the fact that the Colchians, the Egyptians and the Ethiopians are the only races which from ancient times practiced circumcision.
>
> (Herodotus 2. 104–6; trans. Aubrey de Sélincourt)

This information comes within the context of Herodotus' construction of peoples other than Hellenic as 'barbarian'. Later, Euripides capitalizes on this construction to create his version of the character of Medea. In Euripides's hands, Medea's 'Otherness' and the reactions of other characters to it are rooted in her racialized gender. Her ancestral genealogy establishes Medea as racially and culturally different and sets her up as the foil to her Hellenic husband Jason's racialized gender, one that is constructed as more civilized and hence superior. Yet Jason cannot succeed without Medea's knowledge and skill.

It is notable that in Euripides' *Medea* it is the chorus of Corinthian women who express the injustice of women's position to Euripides' Athenian audience. These female members of the Aeolian demographic demonstrate their different construction of gender when they reflect on the historical treatment of women. In lines 412–22, the chorus decries the spurious perceptions men hold of women and predict a day when the truth will be revealed and history and literature will correct the biased views of women. Despite this plea for equality of representation, the *Medea* seems to concretize the binary between foreign-born and native women in the Hellenic male consciousness (Figure 7.2). However, racialized gender provides a lens to reframe the tragedy as one centred on all womankind.[12]

ROME

Before discussing racialized gender as constructed by the Romans, we need to establish their gender 'norm'.[13] Just as in the United States when we say 'African Americans' we mean Black men and when we say 'Americans' we mean white men, so for the Romans, *Romani* meant Roman men. Roman masculinity (racialized gender in and of itself) was the norm in Roman literature. Roman society was patriarchal and androcentric; the authorship of the texts under examination – being for the most part all male – reflects that. Gender difference is filtered through a male lens and that lens is the framework for gender difference.

Racialized gender was central to the founding of Rome. From whatever starting point one takes, whether the legends of Aeneas, the Trojan hero upon whom the Romans constructed a national identity, or those of his descendants Romulus and Remus, the intersection of race and gender form the foundation of Rome's origins. Perhaps more than any other, the story of the rape of the Sabine women, when interpreted through the lens of racialized gender reveals a more nuanced analysis of the role of women in the founding of Rome (Hemker 1985). According to the legend, none of the neighbouring races wanted to intermarry with the Latins, which would have doomed them to extinction. Romulus and the other men of Latium organized a festival and invited the Sabine people to join them. At a prearranged signal, the Latin men abducted the Sabine women, distributing them among the Latin men according to class and made them wives through force and coercion.

Any discussion of racialized gender as it appears in the literary production of authors such as Vergil and Livy would be remiss without explicit attention paid to Cleopatra VII of Egypt. Indeed, her defeat alongside Marc Antony at Actium in 31 BCE provided the foundation for the reign of the young Octavian, who would eventually become known as Augustus and remake Rome's political institutions on his way to becoming Rome's first emperor (27 BCE–14 CE). As we will see, Cleopatra is the inspiration for Vergil's

FIGURE 7.2 Red-figure mixing vessel (calyx-krater) showing Medea in her chariot, *c*. 400 BCE. © Cleveland Museum of Art (creative access).

Dido in the *Aeneid* and Livy's retelling of the tragedy of Sophoniba. The intersection of Cleopatra's race and gender was paramount to the treatment the historical Cleopatra received from prominent Romans such as Cicero and Augustus himself.[14] Consequently, it should be no surprise that it weighed heavily on the literary imagination of writers of the Augustan period.

VERGIL'S *AENEID*

The foundation myth of Rome is the focus of Vergil's national epic, the *Aeneid*. Commissioned by Augustus, the poem showcases the intersection of race and gender. In

Book 12, when Juno acquiesces to a compromise which erases the name of Troy but gives rise to a new biracial/bicultural people consisting of the joining of Trojans and the Latins, it not only establishes the Romans as a mixed-race people but it also glorifies that status (12.834–40). At the same time, the concept of racialized gender affords the opportunity to examine characters such as Dido and Iarbas, a native African prince, in a more nuanced way. The main component of Dido's 'Otherness' comes from the intersection of gender, culture and geographical location rather than the somatic trait of skin colour. Forced to flee the Phoenician city of Tyre, Dido is a Semitic queen now founding a new city, Carthage, on the northeastern shores of Africa. By so doing she embodies the racialized gender which pervades all the fears of Roman ruling class men: a foreign woman with political power in a geopolitical area which, historically, produced Rome's most tenacious and feared rivals, including Hannibal, whose coming is prayed for by Dido (4.625–630), and Cleopatra. Dido through her conflation with Cleopatra triggered the most recent racialized gender threat in the memory of Vergil's contemporaries. By having Aeneas abandon Dido, Aeneas demonstrates the moral supremacy of the racialized gender of the Romans, best expressed by *virtus* and *pietas*. In this regard, Aeneas stands in stark contrast to Marc Antony who – according to the propaganda – surrendered to the wiles of a foreign seductress and enmeshed Rome in a messy war, thereby betraying both his race and his gender.

Vergil heightens Dido's racialized gender by first endowing her with the traits of ideal Roman femininity and then stripping them away. When readers first encounter her towards the end of Book One, Dido is the model *univira* – a one-man woman – having taken a vow of celibacy and fidelity to her dead husband. She sublimates her sexuality and diverts her energy and attention to the founding of a city for her people. In the beginning, she embodies the solid moral and asexual character of a Roman *matrona*. Furthermore, like Livy's Lucretia, she is industrious and works hard for the welfare of those dependent on her. Vergil reinforces the parallel by using a metaphor of bees in June to describe the activity of the city builders (line 430).[15] Before Aeneas arrived, Dido had rejected an offer of marriage/political alliance from Iarbas, showing that she could remain true to her vow to her dead husband.

Clearly, Dido had to change. As she stands at the beginning of the episode, she represents the ideal Roman woman. Within the frame of a misogynistic lens, what destroys the moral fabric of women, even seemingly good women? What is the *essence* of foreign women that makes them especially alien to Romans? The answer, of course, is passion and control of their sexuality. Passion was a cultural stereotype projected upon Africans by Romans and Greeks. In this way, Vergil moves Dido further away from Rome and closer to Africa by implicating her in the flaw of passion. Feminist scholars have noted that in a Roman male mindset the intersection of race and female gender is seen as an imbrication of the categories of female and foreign. Regarding the essentialist category of 'female', Suzanne Dixon states that it has been employed as 'a category of discourse, *the other*, against which to define the insider qualities of the normative, hypothetical male' (2001: xi; emphasis in the original).

However, when the concept of racialized gender is broadened to include foreign men, the same overlap occurs and they become feminized. For example, Iarbas (who may have looked like Figure 7.3), upon learning that Dido had entered a relationship with Aeneas after rejecting him, prays for redress from his father, Jupiter Ammon. In that prayer, he chastises his father for seeming to show preference for the Trojan prince and his people over his own offspring. In Book Four, Iarbas describes Aeneas as '[t]hat Paris with his

FIGURE 7.3 Mummy portrait of a bearded man, *c.* 150–70 CE. © The Getty Centre (open content programme).

half-man entourage, wearing a Phyrgian cap tied below his chin and hair dripping with perfume' (*ille Paris cum* semiviro *comitatu/Maeonia mentum mitra crinemque madentem/ subnexus,* 215–17; my emphasis). Iarbas endows Aeneas with a racialized gender that, based on his ethnic clothing, hairstyle and the company of fellow Trojans, is not fully masculine. Iarbas expresses an implicit bias that Aeneas' construct of masculinity is inferior to his own. It is that bias which is at the core of his frustration that Dido prefers Aeneas to him.

However, Iarbas is not the only character to share a prejudiced view of Trojan masculinity. Later in the epic, Turnus, a leader of the Rutulian people and Aeneas's chief opponent, applies the same epithet and hairstyle to Aeneas. Early in Book Twelve, Turnus pumps himself up with an exhortation for his imminent one-on-one confrontation with Aeneas: 'allow me to throw his body down and to rip off the corselet torn by my strong hand and to befoul in the dirt the Phrygian *half-man's* hair crimped by hot iron and dripping with myrrh' (*da sternere corpus/loricamque manu valida lacerare revulsam*/semiviri *Phrygis et foedare in pulvere crinis/vibratos calido ferro murraque madentis*, 99–100; my emphasis). It is worth noting that Vergil only employed '*semivir*' in these two instances where native born leaders have been supplanted as suitors by an immigrant whom they view as an occupier and colonizer. This is especially true for Turnus who was already betrothed to Lavinia, the daughter of the Latin rulers, Latinus and Amata. While Dido's racialized gender gave her agency in rejecting Iarbas, Lavinia reflects the status of ruling-class Roman daughters: tools to further their fathers' political ends. Lavinia never speaks and does not have a say about the choice of her future husband. Although Turnus dies, his racialized gender construct triumphs over that of Aeneas, the temporarily victorious *semivir*, due to the promise Juno received from Jupiter that the customs, language and very name of the Trojans would disappear, having been assimilated into a new race of people: Romans. In cultural terms, Turnus survives and Aeneas fades away.

SOPHONIBA

In the genre of historiography, there is one episode in Livy's narration of the Second Carthaginian War which lends itself to analysis via racialized gender and offers insight into the racial ruptures of Roman history: Livy's 'tragedy' of Sophoniba,[16] which delineates the racialized gender not only of Roman men but also that of men and women of African descent. Further, the character of Sophoniba can be seen as the crucible for the formation of racial and gender identities for the Roman male elite in the age of Augustus. Therefore, Roman racial formation and racialized gender formation are constructed on the bodies of two exotic 'Others': Sophoniba and Massinissa. The result, then, is the social reproduction of 'ideal' Roman masculinity through the transformation of Masinissa's racialized gender from that of a Numidian to that of a Roman. However, none of this is possible without Sophoniba who undertakes an equally transformative racial and gender performance, moving from a Cleopatra-esque figure to a Lucretia-esque one, namely, from African to Roman, mirroring as well as enabling the performances of Masinissa.

It is best, perhaps, to begin with a brief summary of the story of Sophoniba, since the story is not a familiar one and full of twists and turns. The ancient sources for her story are Polybius (who never mentions her by name), Livy (who gives the most fulsome account), Diodorus, Cassius Dio and Zonaras (Polybius 14.4–7; Livy 29.23.3–10; 30.12.11–15.11; Diodorus 27.7; Appian, *Punic Wars* 27.7; Cassius Dio, Frag. 17.57.51=Zonaras 9.11–

9.13). Sophoniba was the daughter of the Carthaginian leader Hasdrubal, the son of Gisgo – to distinguish him from Hasdrubal Barca, the brother of Hannibal. Although Sophoniba had been betrothed to Masinissa, the son of the leader of the Eastern Numidians, as a way to cement a diplomatic alliance between the Eastern Numidians and Carthage, Masinissa began to reconsider his alliance with Carthage after witnessing how Scipio and the Romans successfully drove the Carthaginians out of Spain. When Syphax, the leader of the Western Numidians, was able to conquer Eastern Numidia, Masinissa (whose father had died) now switched his allegiance to Rome. Needing a new Numidian alliance, Hadrusbal then married Sophoniba to Syphax. When the Romans invaded Africa, under the command of Scipio and Laelius, they, with the help of Masinissa, were able eventually to defeat Syphax and Hasdrubal. After Masinissa captured Cirta, Syphax's capital, he met Sophoniba and impulsively married her to prevent her from falling into Roman hands. When Masinissa was persuaded by Scipio that Sophoniba was the property of Rome, Masinissa sent poison to his wife. In heroic fashion she drank it and died.

The story, of course, is much more complex and nuanced than this simplified summary can relate. For instance, each of the two significant ancient sources for the story of Sophoniba relies on racialized gender stereotypes in the characterization of Sophoniba and Masinissa. For instance, Polybius relates that Scipio thought it likely that Syphax had grown tired of his young bride (whom he never names) and hence of his alliance with the Carthaginians. The reason Polybius attributes to Scipio for thinking this is what is important here. For Polybius says it was 'because of the *natural fickleness of the Numidians and their perfidy* towards the gods and men' (διά τε τὴν φυσικὴν τῶν Νομάδων ψικορίαν καὶ διὰ τὴν πρός τε τοὺς θεοὺς καὶ τοὺς ἀνθρώπους ἀθεσίαν, 14.1.4; my emphasis). Later, Polybius does give a hint of Sophoniba's charming and persuasive personality when he depicts Sophoniba begging Syphax not to desert the Carthaginians and he is moved by her entreaties (14.7.6).

Livy is the source who spends the most time on Sophoniba. We learn from him that Sophoniba was a 'maid of marriageable age' (*nubilis erat virgo*, 29.23.4). Livy then describes how Hasdrubal took advantage of her beauty and charm and Syphax's passion to bind the Numidian leader more closely to the Carthaginian cause (29. 23.6–10). Livy's portrayal of Sophoniba is taken up again when Masinissa captures his rival Syphax's capital of Cirta (30.11–12). He is spotted by Sophoniba, now named by Livy, who begs the Numidian leader to save her from the Romans (30.12.11–16). In the act of naming her, Livy gives Sophoniba not only agency but also accountability. She is no longer the dutiful '*nubilis virgo*' doing her father's bidding. She now has the potential to act in her own name and on her own behalf. Captivated, Masinissa agrees to help her, and impetuously marries her (30.12.18–20). None of this is pleasing to Scipio who pedantically reminds Masinissa that Sophoniba is the property of Rome and he must turn her over to him (30.14.4–11). Masinissa, like the good student of Roman ideals that he is, goes off to consider the advice and admonition of Scipio and resolves to send Sophoniba a cup of poison which she bravely accepts (30.15.1–9).

All of the later sources – Diodorus, Cassius Dio, Zonaras – give notice of Sophoniba's beauty and education, noting that she was well versed in grammar and music. These authors go on to say that Sophoniba was clever, ingratiating and altogether so charming that the mere sight of her or the sound of her voice sufficed to vanquish everyone – even the most indifferent. Through such qualities these later sources, no doubt because of their distance from the events of the late Roman Republic, make the conflation with Cleopatra more explicit than Livy needs to. There is a strong parallel to Plutarch's description of Cleopatra in his *Life of Antony* at section 27.

Whereas the later sources seem to be retelling a touching story, Livy's agenda is very different: re-establishing the Roman moral fabric of old, one which has become badly frayed. His main vehicle for this is racialized gender. As a result, each of the male characters has his own political and/or moral crisis and each crisis gets resolved by reasserting the normative racialized gender. For instance, earlier in Book Twenty-Nine, Livy describes Scipio's crisis surrounding the subjugated city of Locri in Magna Graecia. There had been a senatorial investigation into the Locrian complaints and Scipio's role in them. Livy recounts the following charges against Scipio revealed during the Senate's deliberations:

> Much was also said against the commander-in-chief himself – *his dress and bearing were unRoman, and not even soldierly; he strolled about the gymnasium in a Greek mantle and sandals and wasted his time over books and physical exercise* .... The discipline of the whole army had gone to the dogs, just as at Sucro in Spain and again at Locri, so that it was more of a menace to its friends than its enemies
>
> (29.19.10–13; my emphasis)

While many or even most of these charges were untrue, Scipio does have an image problem and he must reclaim both his moral position as the exemplar of 'ideal' Roman masculinity and his political reputation as a military commander. Masinissa and Sophoniba are the tools to his success in this reclaiming. When Masinissa conquers Cirta and defeats Syphax, he is an ally of Scipio and becomes his proxy in terms not only of military success but also Roman racialized gender. However, Livy makes very clear that Masinissa is racially different from the Romans he is emulating. Sophoniba is the vehicle through which Livy reminds us that our Numidian hero is a non-Roman hero. The beautiful Carthaginian woman will seduce him and cause him to slip back into his 'natural' racialized gender and stereotype of the Numidian.

A quick review of Masinissa's encounter with Sophoniba in Livy supports this interpretation. When Livy first mentions Sophoniba (29.23), it is clear that Hasdrubal is the architect of the scheme to win over Syphax from the Romans; Sophoniba is a pawn in a political move. Hasdrubal is relying on his daughter's beauty and Syphax's *passionate* nature. However, when Sophoniba is an agent of her own destiny and comes out to greet Masinissa, Livy gives her a speech that demonstrates her persuasive power as well as the racial rupture caused by the Roman invasion of Africa:

> If I had been nothing other than the wife of Syphax, I would have preferred to trust the honor *of a Numidian and one born, like me, in the same Africa* than that of an alien and outsider. What a daughter of Carthage, not to mention a daughter of Hasdrubal has to fear from a Roman you do understand. If you are able of nothing else, then I beg and beseech you to save me through death from the Romans' will.
>
> (30.12.15; my emphasis)

Livy overshadows Sophoniba's appeal to Masinissa's race loyalty by again repeating the racial stereotype of the Numidians as hypersexualized. Following Sophoniba's speech, he describes her as 'outstanding in beauty and at a blooming age' (30.12.17). From Livy's perspective, Masinissa heard Sophoniba's speech more as blandishments of a lover rather than entreaties of a suppliant, because he is a Numidian and 'the race of Numidians is inclined toward passion' (30.12.18). As a consequence, Livy says, 'the victor is captured by the love for the captive' (30.12.18).

The subsequent marriage between Sophoniba and Massinissa also gives Livy the context in which to contrast the 'recklessness' of Masinissa and the 'self-control' of Scipio. Livy focuses on Scipio, showing his controlled handling of Syphax's defection as well as his disappointment and even anger over Masinissa's yielding to his 'baser' instincts (30.14). When responding to why he turned from his alliance with Rome, Syphax places the blame on his having wedded a Carthaginian woman (*Carthaginiensem matronam,* 30.13.11). It was madness bred from passion (30.13.12). More worrisome to Scipio – but consistent with Livy's view that lack of restraint has unfortunate consequences – is Syphax's observation that Masinissa was neither more prudent nor restrained than he. In fact, he is less cautious because of his youth. Masinissa's hasty, impulsive marriage to Sophoniba supports Syphax's image of Masinissa and provides the most telling evidence to support Scipio's growing anxiety (30.14.1). Scipio sees clearly the possibility that Masinissa, although he had been very loyal up to this point, might now turn to the Carthaginian cause due to the influence of Sophoniba. In addition to his anxiety, Scipio is disgusted because, following *mos maiorum*, he practiced self-control and resisted the beautiful female prisoners when he was in Spain (30.14.3).

When Masinissa arrives, Scipio receives him warmly and lavishes public praise on him for his military accomplishments. There follows, however, a private tongue-lashing:

> But of these virtues for which I would seem to have been sought out by you, I should have been prouder of none as much as my self-control and my resistance to bodily lusts. How I wish that you had added this also to your other outstanding virtues, Masinissa! There is not – absolutely not, believe me, as much danger to men of our age from armed enemies as from the constant presence of sensuality all around us. The man who reins these in and tames them with his own self-control has earned for himself more honor and a greater victory than we have with the conquest of Syphax.
>
> (30.14.5–8)

Livy demonstrates that Masinissa, passionate Numidian though he may be, is really more Roman than the Romans and shares many of their ancient values. However, Masinissa, like Livy's contemporary Romans, has lost sight of these virtues; Scipio's exhortation to Masinissa not to destroy the many good qualities with the one defect of passion could well be Livy's words to his fellow Romans.

Masinissa fully grasps the logic of Scipio's speech and like many colonized people is caught between two worlds. Does he abandon the colonizer and lose all the political advantages that might flow from that alliance? Or does he become a race traitor and turn over the woman he loves to Rome? After privately venting his grief he hits upon a compromise (of sorts) and provides Sophoniba with the opportunity to commit suicide. When she accepts the cup of poison she reverts back to her previous gender performance of the obedient woman. By moving from a passive, silent and obedient daughter to a forthright vocal agent of her own sexual and political destiny, she violates the norm of Roman femininity and becomes the Cleopatra-esque exemplar of the corrupting foreign beauty. When she accepts the poison, she moves back to the obedient (although certainly not passive or silent) wife and restores authority to the Roman male view of gender norms in the time of Livy. The speech that Livy gives Sophoniba as she receives the poison places her in the tradition of Lucretia, the noble Roman woman who commits suicide for honour: 'I receive this wedding gift, one not unwelcome, if a husband is able to offer his wife nothing greater. But tell him this: I would have died a happier death if I had not wed on the day of my funeral' (30.15.7). For this she earns praise from Livy: 'She spoke calmly as she drained fearlessly the received cup, with absolutely no indication of any trepidation' (30.15.8).

Even though Scipio loses a trophy to be paraded in his triumph, he gains so much more because of Sophoniba. His crisis of masculinity is resolved by the assimilation of an African man who becomes a shining example of Roman racialized gender and by the suicide of an African woman whose beauty might have dismantled the Roman imperial agenda.

As the Roman Empire expanded, imperial literature provided opportunities to interpret the interplay between race and gender. In the fourth century CE, Heliodorus of Emesa composed the novel *Aethiopica*, a work also discussed by Derbew and Mac Sweeney in this volume. However, for our purposes in this chapter, the *Aethiopica* is as much about gender as it is about race and so represents the 'perfect storm' for the thesis of racialized gender. Suzanne Lye remarks that 'Heliodorus recasts the figures from myth to fit his novel's version of ethnic and gender dynamics, thereby "contesting the narratives which structure Greek society's mythic vision of itself"' (2016: 242). Heliodorus inverts and subverts the performance of race and gender throughout the novel and the whole premise of his plot turns on deconstructing race through the main character's birth. When Charicleia, daughter of the Ethiopian rulers Persinna and Hydaspes, is born, her skin tone takes after a pale representation of her ancestor Andromeda, another Ethiopian princess who was rescued by and later married to the hero Perseus. During Charicleia's conception, Persinna fixates on the representation of Andromeda (perhaps a painting), causing, she believed, her daughter to be born so pale. The underlying assumption is that as Ethiopians, Persinna and Hydaspes are dark skinned. Persinna, concerned that her husband would suspect adultery on her part upon viewing the colouring of his child, gave her daughter away and claimed that she was stillborn.

Through the character of Charicleia, Heliodorus problematizes the construction of race and gender in the multiracial milieu of the late Roman Empire. Furthermore, by centering the female characters of the novel, Heliodorus urges the reader to confront the intersectionality of race and gender. In her analysis of Arsake, another central female character in the novel, Lye states:

> While sharing attributes with many female characters in the novel, Arsake ultimately and most emphatically embodies the antithesis of the novel's heroine, Charicleia. Both are foreign women educated in Greek culture, whose ethnicities are constructed in such a way as to orient the audience and predict whether they will take a positive or negative course. ... Heliodorus creates a hierarchy of ethnic identity informed by gender, which is used as a code for readers to typecast positive versus undesirable traits and behavior. By choosing to act more female or more male, a character moves along the scale of their assigned ethnicity's stereotype.
>
> (2016: 244)

Lye demonstrates Arsake's racialized gender more explicitly when she remarks that 'it is difficult to distinguish which stereotype is more prominent in the character of Arsake because they line up so closely – the qualities which Heliodorus uses to mark her identity as a woman are almost interchangeable with those that mark her identity as a Persian ruler' (2016: 251).

In this way, Heliodorus represents the evolution of thinking about racialized gender and how it can be a tool to interpreting the social context of his time, a context which was complexly multicultural and multiracial. It is the culmination of Roman imperialism and colonization and affords an opportunity to examine how racialized gender operated in Roman history and literature.

THE *MORETUM*

Nowhere in Roman literature is the intersection of colour, ethnic origin, gender and class better represented than in the Pseudo-Vergilian *Moretum*. In this poem of 123 dactylic hexameters, an African woman of the peasant class is given a detailed physical description. Most scholarly attention has centred on the authorship of the piece (see e.g. Todd 1925), and once its attribution to Vergil was deemed implausible it was forgotten and received little attention. Needless to say, the *Moretum* is not part of the classical canon, but recently whenever the racial composition of ancient Greece or Rome is discussed, scholars always find it.[17] The text reads:

> erat unica custos,
> Afra genus, tota patriam testante figura
> torta comam labroque tumens et fusca colore,
> pectore lata, iacens mammis, compressior alvo,
> cruribus exilis, spatiosa prodiga planta.
>
> (*Moretum* 31–5)

> (She was his only companion,
> African in her race, her whole form a testimony to her country:
> her hair twisted into locks, her lips full, her colour dark, her chest broad,
> her breasts flat, her stomach flat and firm, her legs slender, her feet broad and ample.)[18]

In *Blacks in Antiquity*, Frank Snowden praises the author of the *Moretum* for the congruence of his/her description with the racial characteristics delineated by modern physical anthropologists, remarking that '[t]he author of the *Moretum* who described Scybale would be rated today as a competent anthropologist' (1970: 9).[19]

For the purpose of this chapter, the passage illustrates one very crucial point. Whoever the author of the *Moretum* was, he/she had detailed physical knowledge of Africans, in particular, African women (Figure 7.4). The author also assumes that his/her audience has had enough contact with Africans to appreciate Scybale's racialized gender. We can make the important inference that Africans were not a rare spectacle for at least some portion of the Roman populace. While Scybale is a fictional character, she is sympathetically drawn. Every indication is that Scybale is the equal of the peasant Simylus with whom she lives and for whom she cares. It is also interesting that Scybale's racialized gender does not result in her being hypersexualized like Dido, Sophoniba or Masinissa.

FIGURE 7.4 Fayum mummy portrait of a young woman. © AGIS/Alamy Stock Photo.

CONCLUSION

The intersection of race and gender succinctly expressed in the concept of racialized gender is a useful tool in analysing the ancient societies of the Hellenic and Roman peoples. Donna Haraway, in her article that aims to construct a new mode of analysis based on feminist, anti-racist discourse, argues that

> 'racialized gender' [is] a practice that builds worlds and objects in some ways rather than others ... neither gender nor race is something with an 'origin' ... that then travels out into the rest of the social world, or from nature into culture, from family into society, from slavery into conquest .... Rather, gender and race are built into practice.
>
> (1994: 67).

This was as true in antiquity as it is today.

Up to now, my case studies have dealt with the cultural production of the elite in both Hellenic societies and Rome and its empire. However, I would like to conclude with a genre where we can explore the standpoints of non-elite populations of the Roman Empire. Extant graffiti, particularly from Pompeii, provides an opportunity to demonstrate how racialized gender was expressed by non-elite women and men in the Roman Empire, outside of the cultural production of literature by the elite. For example, a graffito found at Pompeii makes racialized gender differences explicit:

Candida me doCuit nigras
OdIsse Pvellas; odero; sepotero; sed non InvItvs
Amabo
SCripsit Venus Fisica Pompeiana.

(CIL 4.1520)[20]

(A bright pale-brown woman taught me to hate bright black women
I would hate them if I could; but not unwilling I will love them.
Pompeian Venus Fisica has written this.)

Furthermore, the author of another graffito seems to believe that dark-skinned women provoke a burning passion in their lovers and relies on racialized gender to make her/his point:

Quisquis amat nigra(m) nigris carbonibus ardet
Nigra(m) cum video mora libenter <a>ed<e>o.

(CIL 4.6892)

(Whoever loves a bright black woman burns with black coals
When I see a bright black woman, I gladly eat blackberries.)

Based on the case studies I have presented here, it is clear that Hellenic and Roman societies reacted to the intersectionality of themselves and others in a holistic way. Viewing these societies through the lens of racialized gender is a step in fulfilling the intellectual and moral imperative I set out at the beginning of the chapter.

CHAPTER EIGHT

Race and Sexuality

Racecraft in the Odyssey

JACKIE MURRAY

INTRODUCTION

Predictably, when the BBC/Netflix series *Troy: Fall of a City* was released in 2018, the production's bold casting choices triggered a White supremacist backlash on social media. The series featured a multiracial cast with Black actors playing prominent roles as gods and heroes. What enraged the racists in particular was the portrayal of Achilles by the Black London-born actor David Gyasi (Figure 8.1). As the 'know-it-alls' on social media assured everyone – often with paroxysms of expletives – the original Achilles, namely, Homer's Achilles, was White.[1]

Classicists were swift to respond to this backlash against the creative license taken by the production. In particular, Tim Whitmarsh in his article for *Aeon* (2018) and the contributors to the website *Pharos: Doing Justice to Classics* (Ball et al. 2018a, b, c, d) assembled a vast array of ancient evidence demonstrating that a White supremacist vision of antiquity has no basis in how ancient Greeks and Romans actually viewed themselves racially or how they understood the social value of skin colour. Whitmarsh made a crucial observation that upends most contemporary racialized readings of the ancient sources: 'No one in Greece or Rome ever speaks of a white or a black *genos* ("descent group")' (2018). Distinctions in pigmentation had little to do with how racial categories were constructed in the ancient world. In fact, if skin colour had any social meaning to the Greeks and Romans, it tended to signify a gender distinction. In art and literature, white skin was closely associated with women, and given the principle of female inferiority within the patriarchal ideology, white skin in men was a mark of effeminacy. If a Greek hero were to have white skin, he would have been eroticized (Figure 8.2).

To the extent that some ancient writers show any interest in the potential for skin colour to mark racial distinctions,[2] they use them to mark peoples with very dark and very light complexions as morally inferior to themselves and locate them on a continuum at opposite extremes from their own light- to medium-brown complexion: the somatic

---

I would like to thank the editor, Denise McCoskey, for all her hard work and patience in putting this volume together during challenging times, as well as Rebecca Futo Kennedy for reading a version of this paper and offering comments. I am also very grateful to Hilary Martin and David Kaufman for their help hashing out the idea and proofreading numerous drafts.

FIGURE 8.1 David Gyasi attends a preview screening of *Troy: Fall of a City* on 29 January 2018. © David M. Bennett/Getty Images Entertainment/Getty Images.

norm (Figure 8.3). In other words, ancient Greeks and Romans did not consider themselves (and by extension their mythical heroes and gods) to be racially Black or White (Whitmarsh 2018). This is not to say that the ancient Greeks and Romans did not have their own constructions of race or racism. On the contrary, they certainly did.

This discussion explores one ancient construction of race and how it is reproduced in Homer's epic poem the *Odyssey*. Dated to around the end of the eighth century BCE, the *Odyssey* had widespread cultural influence throughout the Greek world for centuries and so it offers opportunities for analysing racecraft in ancient storytelling.[3] The *Odyssey* features Odysseus' interactions with 'alien' peoples, who are racially 'othered' in the mythical world of the narrative. Later authors recruited these constructions, making them correspond to racializable 'others' in the real world. Euripides' reworking of *Odyssey* 9 in his satyr play *Cyclops*, recruits the Odyssean construction of race to address the immediate concerns of the Athenian audience around the time of the Sicilian expedition.

In the first part of this chapter, I discuss the role storytelling plays in reproducing the racial ideology of a society. I offer a brief analysis of the racecraft involved in the reception of the classical world in film and television, including how it adapted to societal

FIGURE 8.2 Black-figure amphora by Exekias depicting Achilles and Penthesilea. © DEA Picture Library/Getty Images.

pressures to keep reproducing White supremacy. The next section provides a definition of race that enables an analysis of the social construction of racial difference that is both transhistorical and historically contingent. To interrupt the dangerous tendency to rely on skin colour or physical differences as *sine qua non* criteria of race,[4] I use the spatial metaphor of a continuum and the distancing of sameness and otherness to describe race as a socially constructed category determined by an ideology of oppression. These two sections provide the theoretical framework for analysing the racecraft of the *Odyssey* and its recruitment in the fifth century BCE by Euripides in his *Cyclops*. I conclude by

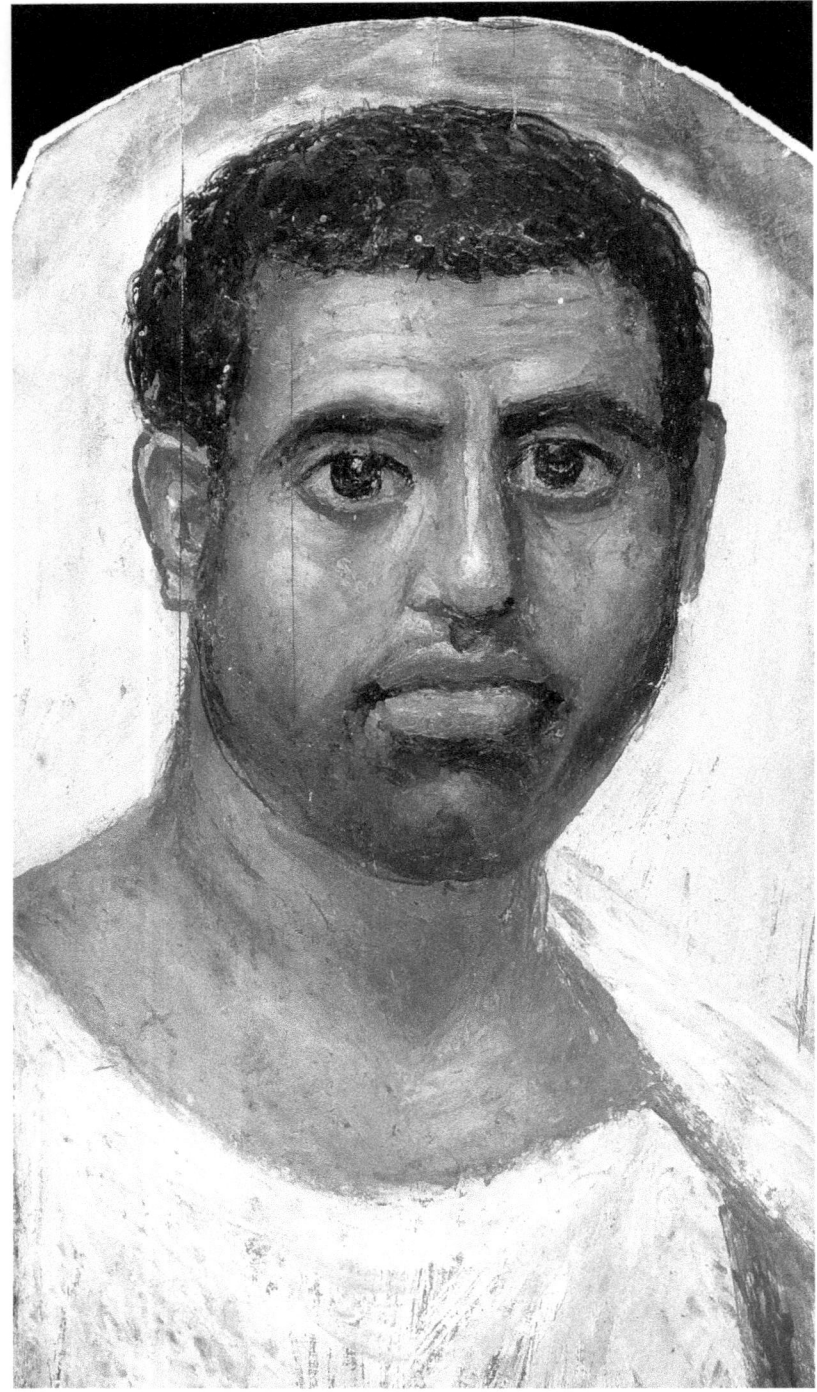

FIGURE 8.3 Mummy portrait from Greco-Roman Egypt showing the ancient somatic norm for men. © Photo 12/Universal Images Group/Getty Images.

discussing translation as a form of reception and racecraft, focusing on its dangerous tendency when treating terms referring to skin colour to reproduce the same kind of White supremacist biases and distortions that classicists have recently railed against in defence of *Troy: Fall of a City*.

RACECRAFT AND THE POWER OF STORYTELLING

For over a century, the mainstream North American film and television industry has contributed to the social construction of race through the maintenance of a Celluloid Classical World,[5] a *lieu de mémoire* of White supremacy and White nationalism in the popular imagination by representing the ancient Greeks and Romans as White.[6] In other words, through 'the magic of the movies' the world of the ancient Greeks and Romans has been recruited to mirror contemporary racist ideology of White European racial, cultural and moral superiority. The recent controversy over *Troy: Fall of a City* is the perfect, contemporary place to begin since it is an excellent example of precisely this process of racecraft in a specific cultural context, through the creation of narrative worlds. Racecraft, as I will use the term, refers to the processes and mechanisms used to socially construct race. Contemporary film provides an entry point for describing the ways racecraft produces a transhistorical conception of race, a process that we will also see in ancient epic, even as both film and epic illustrate the power of cultural storytelling.

Storytelling offers an efficient soft power mechanism for reproducing dominant narratives, so it is to be expected that the dominant group in a society will recruit storytelling to impose their legitimating ideologies onto the larger society. Moreover, when necessary, storytelling has the endless capacity to adapt itself to competing narratives that threaten to replace it. For example, at key moments in the history of racism in the United States, societal pressures forced the film industry to adapt the Celluloid Classical World, which contributed to normalizing the controlling narrative of White supremacy.[7] Film was popularized during the Jim Crow era, when laws denying equal justice, mob violence spectacularizing the dehumanization of black bodies and the normalization of anti-Black hatred reinforced Black racial inferiority.[8] Legally sanctioned racial discrimination in casting meant that White actors always played the significant roles – the historical figures, the heroes and heroines, the gods and goddesses, etc. The occasional depictions of Black slaves, Black prisoners and Black savages – all played by White actors in blackface at times interrupted this systematic erasure of Black people from the Celluloid Classical World (see Fain 2015). The general stereotyping of Blacks as violently subjected racial inferiors or terrifyingly violent threats – usually to White women and girls – also occurred in the Celluloid Classical World. These images mirrored the ubiquitous depictions of Blacks in the wider US society and helped to legitimize the violence against them at the time.

During the late 1960s, the movement for civil rights and racial justice in America posed a serious challenge to past depictions of Black lives as inferior, unequal and inherently violent and threatening. Colour-blind racial representations of Black characters and their lives was the industry's adaptation. Nevertheless, the mere appearance of racial equality and the absence of real structural inequities maintained White supremacy in film-based cultural storytelling.[9] The pressure to relax racist hiring practices led Hollywood's stories to feature more Black actors. But this change in policy simply recalibrated the way mainstream films reproduced the racial hierarchy. In this historical context, films depicting classical stories, comprising the Celluloid Classical World, continued to reproduce images of Black racial inferiority, albeit now strengthened by realism. Black actors played the roles of the Black slaves, Black prisoners and Black savages (Bell 1992; on Black characters in epic films, see also Bâ 2011; Blanshard and Shahabudin 2011: 226).

Until about a decade ago, the White supremacist character of Hollywood's ancient Greeks and Romans rarely received serious oppositional critique from any quarter. The lack of anti-racist pushback was directly related to the dominance, and therefore invisibility, of White supremacist ideology in society. Historically, the discipline of Classics, while it has always had the authority to challenge White supremacist recruitment of ancient texts and culture, has never been a bastion of anti-racism. Rather, Classics has far too often been complicit in the perpetuation of racist receptions of the ancient world.[10] Against the backdrop of ancient evidence that does not align with modern ideas about race, White supremacist resistance to a multiracial cast with Black actors playing prominent roles as gods and heroes in *Troy: Fall of a City* can be clearly understood as an anachronistic projection of present-day racial categories onto the ancient world. Anti-racist interpretation, based on close reading of the ancient texts is both possible, and crucial. The contest over who gets to analyse textual and cultural meaning highlights the tendentiousness of the classical world's reception, whether in the form of adaptation, interpretation or translation.

As I argue in the next section, racial constructs are complex and historically contingent, and they cannot be understood apart from the racial discourse of the society that is recruiting these constructs. Hence, the controversy over *Troy: Fall of a City* brings to the surface just how inextricable the racecraft of a cultural product is from the racial politics and ideology embedded in its reception. For the racecraft in the *Odyssey* to be legible outside the poem, the historical context of reception must be considered. Put differently, just as literary meaning is constructed at the moment of reception for any text, so too racial meaning cannot really be grasped without contextualizing the social power relations in the receiving society. Close reading of the texts will show how this storytelling racework is done not in relation to skin colour as might be assumed from a contemporary, specifically, post-fifteenth-century perspective, when skin colour became the dominant marker for race in European colonial empire-building,[11] but in relation to frameworks for reading the body and sexuality that are rooted in contemporary ancient Greek social hierarchies and power dynamics.

A TRANSHISTORICAL DESCRIPTION OF RACE

Thanks to the debate around *Troy: Fall of a City* there is growing recognition in the popular (and scholarly) consciousness that the ancient Greeks and Romans would not have considered themselves to be part of what our modern racialized system designates as the 'White race'. It is a historical fact that our skin-colour-based racial categories started to emerge in the fifteenth century in discourses justifying the permanent enslavement of Africans. White supremacy/anti-Black racism did not exist before the need (political and economic) to identify specifically Africans as opposed to other conquered peoples as 'natural slaves' (see Fredrickson 2002: 49–96; Kendi 2016: 22–30). However, just because the racial categories we know had not yet been constructed does not mean that the ancient Greeks did not have a concept of 'race'. On the contrary, since group-based social hierarchies seem to be a feature of all human societies, it is far more likely that the racial categories of the ancient Greeks and Romans were based on other criteria (Sidanius and Pratto 1999: 31–2).

Although sociologists, geneticists, historians and philosophers agree that races are historically contingent, socially constructed categories,[12] the belief that the perception of physical difference causes racism is a widely held misconception nevertheless (see e.g. Watts 1976; Goldenberg 2009). The root of this erroneous conclusion is in a misapprehension about what races are and how they come into being. Theodore Allen points out, 'However one may choose to define the term "racial", it concerns the historian only as it relates to a pattern of oppression (subordination, subjugation, exploitation) of one set of human beings by another' (2012: 27). It is the desire or need of dominant groups to oppress or conquer and exploit other groups that provides the impetus to create categories of group-based sameness and otherness, such as race or ethnicity. Adolph Reed Jr noted the dynamic that binds racial and ethnic oppression together,

> I said that race and ethnicity are simply categories of social hierarchy; they are just labels for different magnitudes of distance from the most desirable status on a continuum of 'okayness'. The farther out a population is on the continuum, the more likely it will be seen as a 'racial' group; if it's somewhat nearer in, it'll more likely be understood as an 'ethnicity'.
>
> (Reed 2000: 139)

The crux of Reed's 'continuum of "okayness"' is the concept of alienable humanity: along the continuum of sameness and otherness, the humanity of groups moves from alienable to alienated. For the purpose of this chapter, alienable or alienated humanity means that the humanity of members of that group is not recognized, and can be violated without any social, legal, moral or divine consequences.[13] This continuum is tendentious because the dominant group, whose humanity is absolutely inalienable, occupies the pole of 'sameness', and proximity to this group determines whether subaltern groups are constructed as ethnic or racial others. The dominant group deems 'ethnic others' to be subaltern groups with a high sameness quotient, whereas they deem subaltern groups with a low similarity quotient 'racial others'. So, 'ethnic others' are closer to the sameness pole on the continuum than 'racial others' who are at the otherness pole (on the relationship between race and ethnicity, see also Mac Sweeney in this volume).

The quality of humanity that the dominant group grants to a subaltern group determines both its quotient of sameness and where it is located on this sameness–otherness continuum. The dominant group grants to itself *inalienable* humanity. To ethnic others, they grant *alienable* humanity, namely, they recognize the humanity of specific subaltern groups only insofar as this recognition serves their own interests. But to racial others the dominant group withholds the recognition of humanity. Alienated humanity refers to the dominant group's refusal to recognize the same quality of humanity in a subaltern group it considers racially other.

Hence, race as I have theorized it, is always relational: races exist on opposite poles of a continuum of sameness and otherness. This means also that the social construction of a race that has alienable or alienated humanity is simultaneously the construction of a race that enjoys inalienable humanity. This description accords with Whitmarsh's observation about the role that representations of skin colour played in the ancient world as a mechanism to construct gendered attributions of inequality and power not based on sex, but on dark or light as extremes (otherness) defined in relation to the median position of light to medium brown complexion.

The racial relationship only becomes explicit as the racial ideology is practiced by societies. Wartime atrocities, human trafficking, enslavement and so on are racial practices that make alienated humanity most visible. But horrific racial practices are not the only ways that race is socially produced. Race is also produced 'in the ordinary doing of things' in the various and sundry arenas of social interaction whenever double standards are applied that make the racial hierarchy visible (Fields and Fields [2012] 2014: 25). In what follows I lay out six double standards that are the mechanism of racecraft; these will form the framework for my close reading of the *Odyssey* and the *Cyclops*.[14]

1. *Monstrification* is a double standard that socially constructs the subaltern group as so physically different that alienating their humanity can be morally justified. The bodies of members of the subaltern group, regardless of their actual physical features, are homogenized and deemed monstrous. A subaltern group with the same phenotype as the dominant group may be racialized by metaphorical association with monsters, whereas a group that is a different phenotype may have their physical features deemed monstrous.[15]
2. *Sumptuary codes* are double standards regarding 'what' kinds of material goods and comforts go with 'whom'.[16]
3. *Kinship restrictions* are double standards regarding where kinship begins and ends. They police the borders of inalienable humanity using laws, norms or violence. Kinship restrictions socially construct race by preventing bonds between the races that would force the recognition of the subaltern group member's inalienable humanity from forming.[17]
4. *Centring* refers to double standards that construct race by giving more authority or attention to the dominant group's experience of the racial relationship. Centring maintains the dominant group's perspective and ensures that even critiques are expressed in ways that reinforce the racial hierarchy by, for example, dismissing the point of view of the subaltern group.[18]
5. *Ritual deference* refers to double standards regarding how people treat one another. Ritual deference requires racial subalterns to *display* their obedience and submission to members of the dominant group. The point of ritual deference is to make the power dynamic between the races visible in social interactions.[19]
6. *Sexual asymmetry* is a different double standard from kinship restrictions, which has to do with maintaining the racialized group on the otherness pole. Sexual asymmetry has to do with whose bodies must be available to whom to be used for sex. Whereas the bodies of a racialized group should always be available to the dominant group, the bodies of members of the dominant group are never to be available to the subaltern group.[20]

As W. E. B. Du Bois famously pointed out about the criteria for being racialized as a Negro in America, 'The black man is a person who must ride Jim Crow in Georgia' (1940: 77). Race is often socially constructed with other forms of group-based oppressions and so it exists in a web of intersecting mutually intensifying social forces.

In my reading of the *Odyssey*, I will focus on the relationship between the enslaved herders and their enslavers, the heroes. However, since this relationship could be mistaken for a strictly class dynamic, I pause briefly to distinguish between the two oppressions.

Class oppression, in particular, when it coincides with race in the same individual, can be hard to disentangle. However, in this model, where race is crucially defined in terms of inalienable and alienated humanity, the gap between race and class is evident where the two do not coincide in the same individual. Moreover, since class is not the same kind of social difference as race, members of the same race can be in different classes and members of the same class can be in different races.

RACECRAFT IN THE *ODYSSEY*

Recalling the Celluloid Classical World in relation to the power of stories outlined in the first section and the six double standards of racecraft outlined in the previous section, I now consider racecraft in both the *Odyssey* and a text that builds on the *Odyssey*. Like the Celluloid Classical World, the *Odyssey* serves as a cultural vehicle for the dominant group's narrative about social hierarchy, hence it presents the dominant group's narrative about race. Ancient epic reproduced the racial ideology of ancient societies in the *lieux de mémoire* of the mythic world. The racialized subaltern group are herders, a group socially constructed as the racial opposites of the heroes, who are seafaring city-dwellers. Herders' status vis-à-vis heroes in poetry seems to mirror their status vis-à-vis real city-states in the ancient world.[21] My focus, however, will not be on *whether* herders are a race: they are. Heroes treat the herders as having alienated humanity. They oppress, enslave, traffic and generally exploit herders. Instead, I will explore *how* epic reproduces this racial ideology by poetic processes. I will concentrate on the two most effective ways that race is socially constructed: monstrification and double standards in social interactions.

The *Odyssey* establishes the racial relationship between herders and heroes as an important feature of the epic world, and subsequent poets accept this feature as given. In the *Odyssey*, herders are alienated from their humanity by the double standards that operate in the epic world and also by their association with monstrous herders, the Cyclopes and the Laestrygonians. Although they are not part of Odysseus' 'real' world, the Cyclopes and the Laestrygonians nevertheless serve as monstrified proxies for the herders who are. Significantly, the Cyclopes and Laestrygonians are herders who neither have ships nor engage in agriculture; and although they are superior in terms of physical strength (βίη), they are inferior in terms of cunning (μῆτις), Odysseus' peculiar heroic excellence.

The stories Odysseus tells to the Phaeacians about his encounters with the Cyclopes and Laestrygonians maintain the racial continuum created by the narrative as a whole. So, too, the attitudes of Odysseus' listeners, who are predisposed to enjoy his story, help reinforce this interpretative framework. For the Phaeacians' physically inferior and city-dwelling ancestors were once driven from their homeland by the Cyclopes, and so they derive pleasure from the vicarious revenge they can take in Odysseus' account of the blinding of the mightiest of the Cyclopes (Figure 8.4). In this way, while the stories Odysseus tells construct herders as a race within a discourse of 'ethnography' that transmogrifies their alienated humanity into terrifying alien monstrosity, the Phaeacians' approbation of such storytelling encourages the poem's primary audience to align with such a view, making them willing to take on the racialization of herders that the monstrification produces on the metaphorical level. Moreover, the superior strength of the Cyclops and the Laestrygonians does not cancel out the racialization of herders along the 'continuum of "okayness"', for attributing such physical superiority to herders incites a terror that reinforces racial ideology.

FIGURE 8.4 Detail of the blinding of the Cyclops, Roman copy of a Hellenistic statuary group. © DEA/S. VANNINI/Getty Images.

Terror, especially the terror caused by the potential loss of social dominance, is a powerful incentive for, and justification of, racial hatred and violence (see e.g. Anderson 2016; DiAngelo 2018). The White supremacist backlash to *Troy: Fall of a City* is a useful example of this phenomenon. The series threatens the modern anti-Black racist narrative that says the ancient Greeks were the glorious ancestors of the White race. The production not only refused to 'phenotype cast' the Black actors as slaves, prisoners, brutes or sidekicks, it also created a terrifying racial counter-narrative of lost White supremacy in a classical world of racial equality. In a similar way, Odysseus' stories accord perfectly with an anti-herder racial ideology by drawing on the fear of lost dominance. His violent encounters with the Cyclopes and Laestrygonians mirror how heroes would see an inversion of their relationship with herders, namely, as a terrible nightmare.

However, monstrification is not the only mechanism of racecraft in the epic poet's arsenal. Depictions of anti-herder racism in the ordinary doing of things reinforces the racial othering constructed within the epic. Mundane social interactions between the herders and heroes expose the double standards that solidify their relationship as racial. Sumptuary codes, kinship restrictions, centring, ritual deference and sexual asymmetry all operate in the mythical world to reinforce the herders' alienated humanity.

Sumptuary codes in the *Odyssey* govern the double standards in living conditions that socially construct herders as a subaltern race vis-à-vis heroes. When they first meet, Eumaeus assumes the disguised Odysseus is like himself, a non-hero who is liable to enslavement and other kinds of predations by heroes. Offering him food he says: 'Eat up now, guest friend, this pork is for us slaves; the suitors get to eat succulent sows' (*Odyssey* 14.80). Throughout Odysseus' stay, Eumaeus complains about the suitors eating food that is both different in kind and quantity from that consumed by the enslaved herders, like himself.

His complaints help to emphasize the wickedness of the suitors, who usurped Odysseus' position as master and are devouring his possessions. But Eumaeus is not acknowledging the real reason the herders must constantly take the best animals from Odysseus' herds to feed the suitors: it is perfectly appropriate for the suitors, as guests of the dominant racial group, to be fed the best and for the slaves to have inferior quality food. The problem is that there are too many suitors and they have all overstayed their welcome.

A similar sumptuary code dictates that slaves must not wear the kinds of garments heroes wear; they can only wear humble clothing or rags. In the false backstory that Odysseus tells Eumaeus and the other herders, he mentions that in their preparations to sell him into slavery, the Thesprotians stripped off the decent clothes he had been wearing and put him in the filthy rags he has on (14.339–42). And when Odysseus tries to wheedle Eumaeus out of his cloak, Eumaeus only agrees to let him have his cloak for the night, pointing out that:

> There aren't many cloaks and tunics to change into here, there is only one cloak for each man. But whenever Odysseus' dear son comes, he will clothe you in a tunic and cloak, fine garments. And he will send you wherever your heart's desire bids you.
>
> (14.513–17)[22]

Eumaeus advises Odysseus to ask Telemachus for better clothes, not just because he has none to spare but also because as a hero Odysseus *should* wear better clothes. At the beginning of their acquaintance, Eumaeus has no way of knowing whether he and Odysseus are the same race. But Odysseus makes things clear by presenting himself as a down on his luck *hero*. He has come close but has never been a slave. Even though his fictitious mother was a slave, Odysseus is sure to make his fictitious father acknowledge him as one of his sons.

Kinship restrictions emerge when Odysseus questions Eumaeus about his parents and he answers by describing his relationship with Odysseus' mother and sister:

> She raised me herself together with Ctimene with the flowing gown, her stately daughter, whom she bore last of all her children. I grew up with her, but I was held in a bit lower esteem. And when we both reached the prime of youth that is full of desire, they then gave her away in marriage to a Samian and they got countless gifts. But as for me, that lady dressed me in a cloak and tunic, very fine garments, and putting shoes on my feet she dismissed me to the field. She really loved me in her heart.
>
> (15.363–70)

Through the fog of Eumaeus' fond feelings, it is evident that he was never really considered part of Odysseus' family. He describes Ctimene with epithets appropriate to a heroine: 'flowing gown' (τανύπεπλος) evokes Helen (*Iliad* 3.228; *Odyssey* 4.305); 'stately' (ἰφθίμη) is regularly used of heroes and in the *Odyssey* it is applied to the legendary beauty Pero (11.287). However, his eroticized description of their arrival at youth, 'full of desire' (πολυήρατον), emphasizes that he was never considered a possible marriage partner for Ctimene. Rather, Eumaeus was probably brought up with Ctimene to be her playmate, and once she was married off to someone of her own race, he was sent to where he belonged: in the fields tending the herds.

Epic necessarily *centres* the heroic experience. Nevertheless, there are moments in the narrative where this centring contributes to the double standards that racialize the herders.

The clearest examples are when centring the hero obscures, minimizes or normalizes the true brutality of the herders' experience of their enslaved condition. Centring occurs when Odysseus asks Eumaeus about how he ended up as a slave on Ithaca:

> O wow, you were really little, swineherd Eumaeus, when you were carried away from your fatherland and parents! But come now, tell me your whole story in all its details. Was your city laid waste, its people and streets utterly destroyed, the city where your father and noble mother used to dwell? Or were you all by yourself with your sheep or cows when hostile men with ships seized you and sold you to the household of this man who paid a worthy price?
>
> (15.381–7)

As a hero, Odysseus only knows slavery from his dominant group's perspective. So, he frames the question in terms that centre the heroic experience. To Odysseus, children are enslaved when heroes take them as captives in war or with herds and other goods in raids. Even in his lies about his own brush with slavery, his cunning and trickery, his heroic excellence, are centred. Scheming Phoenicians and Thesprotians, whose morality and activities are difficult to distinguish from his own, were responsible for Odysseus *almost* ending up a slave.

However, as Eumaeus explains, there are other ways to fall into slavery. In his own true story about how he was trafficked as a child, the main agent was a female slave who wanted her freedom (15.403–84). This Phoenician slave girl, who was charged with his care, was convinced that she could escape and return home. She took Eumaeus along with her intending to sell him into slavery, but she died on the journey. The Phoenicians threw her body overboard and sold Eumaeus to Laertes when they came to Ithaca. Although the story itself does not centre heroes, Odysseus' reaction does. He expresses pity briefly and then minimizes the exploitation of slavery:

> Eumaeus, by telling me the details of all the suffering you have experienced, you have really stirred sad feelings in my heart. But look, Zeus gave you good as well as bad, because when you arrived after much suffering at the palace of the kind man who provided you with regular meals and drink, you lived a good life. But look at me, wandering to many cities of mortals I come here.
>
> (15.486–92)

Odysseus' change of focus from Eumaeus' experience to the fictitious experience of his disguised persona alludes to the theme of the entire epic: Odysseus' wanderings.

Eumaeus' reflections on the hardships of slavery often transform laments about his condition into laments about Odysseus' absence. When he first meets Odysseus and expresses relief that the dogs did not maul him, he says:

> Old man, surely my dogs almost mauled you to death in an instant, and you would have poured down curses on me! The gods gave me other pains and woes to sit here weeping and wailing about – my godlike king, I nourish his succulent sows for others to eat! Meanwhile, I guess, he longs for food and is wandering to the countryside and city of alien men, if he is even still alive and sees the light of the sun.
>
> (14.37–44)

Again, Eumaeus centres the heroic experience when he laments the lot of the slaves under the suitors:

> Strangers and beggars are all from Zeus. Small but friendly is our generosity, because this is the custom of slaves, always dreading when lords oppress us, especially the young ones. For surely the gods have locked away *his* homecoming.
>
> (14.58–62; my emphasis)

Eumaeus' complaints regarding the lot of slaves often hint at a critique of the whole system that oppresses him and his fellow herders. However, under Odysseus, herders would still be exploited. Eumaeus' complaints, which are designed to characterize him as a faithful slave, obscure that fact.

Particularly egregious is Eumaeus' comparison of the suitors to pirates. He makes the comparison immediately following his complaint about the quality of the pork available to slaves (quoted above). By claiming that the suitors are worse than marauding pirates, he centres the heroic experience.

> In their hearts they take no thought of the gods nor have pity! Well, the blessed gods don't like wicked deeds, but they reward justice and men's righteous deeds. Even enemies and foes – if they attack a foreign land and Zeus grants them plunder, when they have filled up their ships and boarded to go home – even to their minds a mighty fear of the gods occurs!
>
> (14.82–8)

Odysseus, of course, is the kind of hero who raids and plunders foreign lands with his ships. The irony here is a species of centring that makes the suitors' abuse of hospitality a greater crime than piracy, one of the activities that heroes engage in when they enslave herders.

Ritual deference is at the heart of Eumaeus' complaints about the suitors. In general, in a racial power relationship, just as slaves owe personal deference to their masters, so the subaltern racial group owes public submission and obedience to the dominant group. In the *Odyssey*, the personal and public requirements for deference are in conflict because Odysseus has been absent and the suitors have taken advantage of their membership in the dominant group to usurp his position over the herders. Eumaeus' grudging obedience to the suitors is a compromise that satisfies the conflicting demands on him for deference. It should be observed that Eumaeus had some help arriving at this compromise. His loyalty reciprocates the special treatment he received as a child growing up with Odysseus' sister and the special status it granted him among the herders. Not all herders have this extra moral duty to induce them to stay loyal to Odysseus. The consequences of Melanthius' choice to show complete deference to the suitors, minimal deference to Telemachus and no deference to the memory of Odysseus exposes the violence inherent in the relationship between herders and heroes. For, just as when the gods visit mortals in humble disguise to test them, Odysseus demands deference, at least to his memory, from his slaves, and he metes out bitter punishment to those who defy him. So, when Melanthius insults Eumaeus and Odysseus disguised as a beggar, Odysseus' anger almost forces him to break character.

Odysseus debated within himself whether he should rush at him and beat him to death with his staff or lifting him up by the middle drive his head into the ground. But he endured it and checked his rage-filled thoughts.

(17.243)

Odysseus' reaction reflects his status as a hero confronted by a slave refusing to show deference. Were it not essential for Odysseus to maintain his disguise as a beggar, he would have murdered Melanthius then and there for his defiance of ritual deference. When the time comes to finally punish Melanthius, significantly it is the moment when he is about to bring out weapons to the suitors. His deference to the suitors has led him to outright rebellion against Odysseus. Eumaeus offers to take him down and kill him for the crime of overstepping his place (ὑπερβασία, 22.168). However, Odysseus orders Eumaeus and the other herders to string him up and hoist him to the rafters of the storeroom so that he can dangle in agony while still alive (ὥς κεν δηθὰ ζωὸς ἐὼν χαλέπ' ἄλγεα πάσχῃ, 22.177). In other words, Melanthius is to become a cautionary reminder of the violence that enforces the racial relationship between heroes and herders. It is also significant that Odysseus does not grant Eumaeus the right to kill Melanthius in a heroic struggle. Instead, he gives Eumaeus and the other herders the task of torturing their fellow herder, which enacts his and their own alienated humanity. As Melanthius' refusal to offer deference to Odysseus as a member of the dominant group is punished, Eumaeus' loyalty to Odysseus does not lead him to open defiance of the ritual deference he owes the suitors. So, both Eumaeus' adherence to, and Melanthius' defiance of, ritual deference uphold the racial ideology established in the earlier passages within the narrative.

Sexual asymmetry is related to but quite distinct from kinship restrictions. While kinship restrictions produce race by controlling who is allowed to *marry and have children* with whom, sexual asymmetry creates race by controlling who is allowed to *desire and have sex* with whom, who is allowed to *force whom to have sex* and who is allowed to *refuse to have sex* with whom. In this respect, herders are racialized because they have no control over their sexuality. Not only are they forbidden to desire, much less have sex with heroines, but they also need permission from the dominant group to form and engage in sexual relationships with women of their own race. In Eumaeus' account of his relationship with Ctimene, Odysseus' sister, he is careful not to say what his feelings were. As noted above, his language only hints that he may have desired her. At another point, Eumaeus says that Odysseus, had he been around, would have given him a wife. This implies that he could not make the decision to marry for himself. Sexual asymmetry intersects with kinship restriction here to doubly prevent Eumaeus from marrying.

Substituting the herders for the suitors helps to clarify how sexual asymmetry creates race. First, the presence of the suitors on the scene guarantees that the herders will not have sexual access to any of the slave women, whereas the presence of the herders does not prevent the suitors from doing whatever they want with the slave women (from more on the position of slave women in the *Odyssey*, see Thalmann 1998). As the dominant group, their claim to the women's bodies takes precedence – so long as Odysseus' authority is absent. To be sure, whoever had sex with his slave women, regardless of race, Odysseus was going to murder. However, it is race that dictates whether he can murder them without consequence. If the suitors had been herders, there would have been no need to hide their slaughter by pretending there was a celebration. The relatives of the herders would not be able to threaten a civil war. Thus, sexual asymmetry lays bare the herders' alienated humanity: they can be murdered without consequence, whereas the suitors cannot.

Sexual asymmetry is slightly more complicated with women because in a rape culture, such as that of the mythic world in epic, there are very few scenarios where legal or moral consequences can be brought to bear when women and girls have been subjected to non-consensual sex. In the heroic world of the *Odyssey* rape is normalized, so sexual asymmetry constructs race by dictating who can and cannot refuse access to her body for sex outside marriage. Despite their otherwise lawless behaviour none of the suitors' attempts to rape Penelope, whereas many of them have taken concubines from among the slave women. As a heroine, Penelope can refuse to be forced into sex outside marriage and the suitors can expect serious consequence to follow if they violated her. Penelope's marriageability staves off the threat of violation. However, the slave women are not marriageable. They, therefore, have no power to refuse the suitors their bodies without risking violence. Race dictates which woman can be raped without consequence. Proof of the racialized women's alienated humanity is that they cannot meaningfully prevent their bodies from being violated without risking violence.

In the foregoing I have presented some of the ways that the *Odyssey* reproduces the social construction of herders as a race. I have focused primarily on monstrification and other double standards. There are certainly other ways in which herders are socially constructed as a race that may be identified in the epic, but these should be sufficient since they underscore their alienated humanity. In the next section, I will turn to the reception of the Odyssean race construct in Euripides' satyr play *Cyclops*.

EURIPIDES' *CYCLOPS* RECRUITS THE RACECRAFT OF THE *ODYSSEY*

Euripides' *Cyclops* is a retelling of *Odyssey* 9 with a subplot about satyrs that is based on the *Homeric Hymn to Dionysus*. Although the exact date of the *Cyclops* is unknown, most scholars believe it is closely related to the Sicilian expedition (415–413 BCE), especially since the island and Mount Aetna feature prominently as Polyphemus' home (Seaford 1982). The *Odyssey*, of course, does not identify Sicily as the homeland of the Cyclopes, but by the fifth century poets from Sicily and Magna Graecia, such as Ibycus, Steisichorus and the comic poet Epicharmus had made Sicily the home of the Cyclopes and possibly the Laestrygonians too. Thucydides observes that at the time of the Sicilian expedition, the Athenians did not know much about the island. So, it is likely the *Odyssey* influenced their views about Sicilians (Thucydides 6.1.1–2). The Sicilian expedition was an unmitigated disaster and at one point over seven thousand Athenians were imprisoned in the quarries near Syracuse and left to die of starvation or disease. The few who escaped eventually made their way back to Athens and reported the disaster. Euripides' version of the Cyclops episode of the *Odyssey* may be speaking to this situation and recruiting the racial ideology of the *Odyssey* to reflect on the treatment of the Athenians by the Sicilians. It is hard to say for certain without knowing the exact date of the play. Nevertheless, it is still possible to analyse what Euripides has done with Homer's racecraft.[23]

In Euripides' version of Odysseus' encounter with the satyrs, Silenus and his sons, were shipwrecked on Sicily when they rounded Cape Malea while pursuing the pirates who had abducted Dionysus. The satyrs are soon enslaved by Polyphemus who makes them tend his herds while he goes hunting. When Odysseus and his men arrive, the play follows the Homeric plot closely with misbehaving satyrs added in the mix.

Sexual asymmetry is the double standard that I will focus on in the *Cyclops*. As noted above, in the *Odyssey*, rape is always euphemized and the racialized victim is presented as consenting. In the *Cyclops*, the violence inherent in the power imbalance is laid bare. When the intoxicated Polyphemus decides that he wants to have sex with Silenus, it is clear that the old satyr is unwilling:

SIL: Wait? Am I Zeus' Ganymede, Cyclops?
CY: Yes, by Zeus, the one I am seizing from the land of Dardanus.
SIL: I'm done for, boys! I'm about to suffer something atrocious!
CY: Are you finding fault with your lover and are you contemptuous of a drunk?
SIL: O my god! I will soon see wine as the bitterest thing.

(*Cyclops* 585–9)

Similarly, the chorus of young satyrs – notorious rapists themselves – are clear-eyed about what happens to women when a host of heroes is around. So when they hear that Odysseus is on his way back from Troy, they imagine that all the Greeks must have taken turns raping Helen.

So, when you seized the young woman, you all fucked her in turns. After all, she enjoys having sex with many men, the traitor! As soon as she saw him wearing his fancy trousers round his legs and his gold collar around his neck, she got all excited, abandoning Menelaus that excellent fellow. I wish womankind had never been created anywhere at all – except, of course, for me alone!

(*Cyclops* 179–87)

The satyrs are projecting the logic of their sexual fantasies onto the heroes: if they themselves were heroes and they had captured Helen they would have used her sexually. The satyrs' rape fantasy is racially transgressive in several ways. As observed above, the racial double standard of sexual asymmetry forbids herders from having sex even in their minds, and especially with heroines. Race also forbids heroes outside the context of marriage from raping women of their own race. Non-spousal rape puts the heroine body on par with the slave body. As an intertext of the *Odyssey*, the satyrs' remarks bring into relief this dimension of the situation on Ithaca between Penelope and the suitors. The sexual asymmetry of racecraft is the reason that the unruly suitors – over a hundred of them, who have no problem having non-consensual sex with the slaves – balk at taking the obviously unwilling Penelope by force. Instead they maintain the fiction that her choice is tantamount to her consent, all the while threatening to send her back to her father who will choose for her.

The satyrs close their obscene remarks by adding an exception to the oft-repeated misogynist counterfactual wish that women had never been created. Each satyr wishes women existed only for him. Significantly, this exception is the essence of female objectification in the myth of Pandora: woman was created for man. In terms of gender, the satyrs affirm the patriarch's sexual dominion over the bodies of all the women and girls in his household. In terms of race, however, the satyrs' wish is transgressive: it attributes to the herder views about women's bodies that are only appropriate for heroes.

As in the *Odyssey*, the herders are racialized through monstrification and other double standards, but here these processes are on the surface. For example, whereas in the epic the herders are monstrified metaphorically by association with monstrified herders, the herders in the play are actual monsters, men with bestial facial features, excessive hairiness, equine legs, tails and ears, and large erect phalluses. The satyr-play adds its own twist as well: Polyphemus is no longer a herder. He is the slave master, and when the play begins he is away hunting, a heroic activity. In other words, through the racecraft of the *Cyclops*, Polyphemus is a hero, which is reinforced when Odysseus supplicates him, not on the moral ground of *xenia* the guest-host relationship between strangers, as in the *Odyssey*, but in terms of *philia* friendship and family:

> O noble son of the Sea God, we beseech you as suppliants and speak as free men. Do not allow yourself to kill us and make us an impious meal for your jaws, us your friends who have just arrived as visitors at your cave. O lord, we protected from plunder the seats of father's temples in the innermost nook of Greece. The harbour of holy Taenarus remains intact, as well as Cape Malea's caverns. And divine Athena's silver veined rock of Sunium is safe, and so are the refuges of Geraestus. We did not surrender what belongs to Greece to Phrygians, †a senseless disgrace†. And you also have a share in them because you live under Aetna – in the innermost nook of Greece – the fire streaming rock.
>
> (286–97)

In fact, Odysseus supplicates Polyphemus as a fellow Greek. He points to temples and locales sacred to Poseidon and Athena as common religious sites and to the Phrygians as their common enemy and the Trojan War against them as their common endeavour. Odysseus even constructs the slopes of Aetna, Polyphemus' homeland, as the centre of Greece.

This construction of Polyphemus as a hero reproduces the same dilemmas for the herders around ritual deference that are present in the *Odyssey*. In the *Cyclops*, the herders owe personal deference to Polyphemus, their slave master, and public deference to Odysseus, a member of the dominant racial group. This tension is played out along generational lines. While the Cyclops is away, all the satyrs offer ritual deference to Odysseus, but as soon as the Cyclops returns, Silenus quickly changes his tune and shows his deference to Polyphemus. He drinks with him and even encourages him to eat Odysseus. Meanwhile, his sons remain loyal to Odysseus, and criticize their father for submitting to the Cyclops. Interestingly, Euripides' Odysseus does not hold Silenus' pusillanimity against him; he rescues him with his sons all the same. Of course, this was not Odysseus' attitude in the *Odyssey* towards Melanthius' show of deference to the suitors, even though they were stronger in numbers.

As transgressive figures, the satyrs can take the moral high ground in open rebellion to the racial order, even as they uphold it. On the other hand, their defiance exposes the violence that produces their alienated humanity. Polyphemus is physically stronger than Odysseus. Silenus acts out of self-preservation, whereas the sons choose morality. So, the threat of violence that enforces ritual deference to him puts morality in tension with life itself. In the presence of violence there is no way for racialized others to maintain their human dignity and their lives: either they must abandon morality to ritual deference and thus maintain their paltry existence or they maintain morality and lose their lives. Euripides' *Cyclops* reflects *Odyssey* 9 in the carnival mirror of the satyr play, but it actually removes the distortions around the epic's racecraft. Because satyrs are transgressive figures they are able to expose the dehumanization inherent in racecraft.

CONCLUSION

In this chapter, I have offered a close reading of the *Odyssey* and *Cyclops* focusing on how race is socially constructed through storytelling. Race in the *Odyssey* is not determined by skin colour; rather, the seafaring city-dwelling heroes are constructed as a dominant group against the racialized subaltern group of enslaved herders. This reading was based on a continuum of sameness–otherness involving six mechanisms, detailing *how* and *by whom* racial difference is produced and maintained. Physical features *become* racialized through racecraft, specifically monstrification. They are not essential starting criteria or motivation for racial categories. Importantly, *race* as a category cannot exist without the ideology of *racism*, which, in turn, is continually produced through narrative mechanisms richer and more subtle than a White or Black *genos*, legible from the colour of a character's skin. Races are the 'who' and the 'whom' of a particular kind of group oppression, and power determines the direction of the oppression. When we put aside skin colour as a demarcation of race in the ancient world, we must also push away the assumption that oppression is based on skin colour. However, the classical world currently functions as a *lieu de mémoire* for White supremacy, and the *Iliad* and *Odyssey* have long been recruited in support. In White supremacy, skin colour – Black or White – is not neutral but is the primary organizing principle of who is endowed with humanity, and whose humanity is alienable or alienated.

Accordingly, I will close this section with a critique of Emily Wilson's translation of the *Odyssey* (2018). Given what is at stake when the White supremacist racial construct is imported into the Homeric epics, I will foreground her handling of 'black skin' in the *Odyssey*. Wilson's translation is important to reconsider through the reading of race offered in this chapter because it is the most recently published translation of the *Odyssey* and has received much attention for its feminist approach, also because there is the danger that it will become the translation most assigned to students.

Black skin occurs twice in the *Odyssey*: μελαγχροιής at 16.174 and μελανόχροος at 19.247. In the first instance it refers to the colour of Odysseus' skin when Athena changes him back to his true appearance and in the second it refers to the skin of another hero, Odysseus' herald (κῆρυξ) whom Odysseus describes to Penelope to remind her of what Odysseus looks like. These are precisely the kinds of passages that, if not interpreted from an anti-racist perspective, end up reinforcing prevailing White supremacist appropriations of the classical world.[24]

Wilson's translation falls into the trap and produces a translation that is White supremacist racecraft. At 16.174–6, she translates μελαγχροιής in reference to Odysseus' skin colour as 'tanned', but at 19.244–9 in reference to Eurybates' skin colour she translates 'μελανόχροος' as 'black skin'. Semantically, μελαγχροιής and μελανόχροος are interchangeable, both mean 'black-' or 'dark-skinned', and their metrical shape and position in the line can easily explain the two forms. So, it seems arbitrary to translate them so differently. For comparison, Fagles translates μελαγχροιής as 'ruddy tan' and μελανόχροος as 'swarthy', and Lattimore 'dark colour' and 'black-complexioned', respectively (see also Dee 2003–4: 161–2, on translation of these passages). Wilson seems to be following their lead in making her translation different each time and making Odysseus' skin colour lighter. Giving Odysseus lighter skin than Eurybates, however, implies a physiological difference between the two men that aligns with a White supremacist interpretation: Odysseus is a White man with a tan and Eurybates, his subordinate, is a Black man. But why not simply translate both terms as 'black skin'? I would argue that the point of Odysseus' physical description of Eurybates in the context is to remind Penelope of *himself* by painting a picture in her mind of someone whom he very much resembles. Translating μελαγχροιής/μελανόχροος differently obscures the rhetorical purpose of Odysseus' speech.

But Wilson's translation becomes overt White supremacist racecraft in her handling of the language around Eurybates. Black-skinned Eurybates also has 'wooly' hair (οὐλοκάρηνος), which is a White supremacist monstrification of the curly texture of Black hair. Moreover, without any linguistic justification, she translates κῆρυξ (herald) as 'valet', which according to the *Oxford English Dictionary* refers to 'a man-servant performing duties chiefly relating to the person of his master' (*Oxford English Dictionary* 1989). With these two translation decisions, Wilson has demoted Eurybates from his heroic position as Odysseus' herald or messenger to his manservant, evoking the image of an antebellum Black butler serving Odysseus mint julips on the veranda.

I began with the controversy over the historical accuracy of casting a Black actor (David Gyasi) representing Achilles in *Troy: Fall of a City*. That the response of the

FIGURE 8.5 Brad Pitt at a photo call for *Troy* (2004) in Cannes, 13 May 2004. © Pool Catarina/Deroubaix/Getty Images.

Classics community defending the casting decision, based on the historical sources, was considered anti-racist indicates the extent to which White supremacist racecraft is a live issue in the field. Subtle, detailed attention to these texts is required, given the transhistorical nature of racework and the role of classicists in this work. Brad Pitt's white skin stirred no controversy when he played the same character over a decade ago, highlighting the alignment between the film's racecraft and contemporary White supremacy in the reception of classical texts (Figure 8.5). If Achilles can finally be Black in the Celluloid *Iliad*, certainly μελαγχροιής Odysseus can be Black in the *Odyssey*.

CHAPTER NINE

Anti-Race

Anti-Racism, Whiteness and the Classical Imagination

DAN-EL PADILLA PERALTA

This chapter's title masks a paradox. By framing this contribution as an exercise in thinking against race and racism, I am in the first instance acknowledging and lifting up those contemporary scholar-activists who have modelled how to align investigations into the historic and ongoing significance of race with explicitly anti-racist programmes for reparative justice (purely, e.g. Kendi 2019). At the same time, I am also gesturing to a fundamental dilemma faced by historians of race. Most investigations into the cultural history of a concept presuppose that the concept's antithesis lurks somewhere in the wings, never far from the action; that this antithesis can be identified, and its trajectory over time followed, with some degree of accuracy; and that concept and antithesis alike exist as stable objects, accessible under the right conditions by the 'objective' scholarly practitioner. But what if the concept has enjoyed such spectacular success in infiltrating the procedures of (Western) scholarly discourse – those usually marshalled to write the cultural histories of this Bloomsbury series – that any attempt to locate its antithesis is imperiled from the outset? What if the concept has insinuated itself into these procedures so effectively as to obstruct their capacity to produce forms of knowledge that are cleanly dissociable from the concept itself? And what if the concept is so ubiquitous in the (re)production of individual and collective scholarly identities as to give the lie almost immediately to any pretense of objective handling? These are the challenges thrown up by race – whose material and metaphysical projections, accelerated and amplified by modernity's triple bundling of North Atlantic empire formation, the transatlantic slave trade and global settler-colonialism, have burrowed deep into the humanistic disciplines.

As the terms 'anti-race' and 'anti-racism' presume the existence of race and racism but do not clarify them, it is important to linger for a moment on some issues of definition. Following the lead and inspiration of Karen and Barbara Fields, this chapter is grounded in the understanding that race and racism are related but distinguishable. Race 'stands for the conception or the doctrine that nature produced humankind in distinct groups, each defined by inborn traits that its members share and that differentiate them from the members of other distinct groups of the same kind but of unequal rank', while racism 'refers to the theory and the practice of applying a social, civic, or legal double standard based on ancestry, and to the ideology surrounding such a double standard' (Fields and Fields [2012] 2014: 16, 17). These constructs are activated and disseminated through a social process that will be foregrounded in this chapter: what Karen and Barbara Fields term *racecraft*, the 'pervasive belief' and intersubjective imprinting that leave in their wake 'a kind of fingerprint evidence that *racism* has been on the scene' (16–19; emphasis in the original). Uniting these intellectual operations and their real-life instantiations is one core function, pithily specified by Michel Foucault: 'race or racism is the precondition that makes killing acceptable' ([1978] 2013: 75; cf. Mbembe 2019: 70–4, for a refinement). Race and racism work in conjunction to open the door to the subjection and death of differentially marked communities; racecraft is the mystification that covers up the tracks.

The argument to be taken up in this chapter is that the discipline of 'Classics' is a bustling performance site for racecraft. The fact that there is race in Greco-Roman antiquity is not nearly as important as the fact that this antiquity has been and continues to be raced in scholarship and pedagogy. Note that this is not the same as stating that the discipline of Classics is racist. Nor am I speaking about the long-running and highly racialized tendency to imagine and fetishize Greco-Roman statuary as white, disregarding ancient polychromy in the process (Bond 2017). What I have in mind is the 'racial formation' (Omi and Winant [1986] 2015) of Classics as discipline, a process more internal to the field's self-realization than those twenty-first-century phenomena of 'claiming the classical' scrutinized in recent publications (Zuckerberg 2018; Mac Sweeney et al. 2019, for one case study). This chapter cannot supply a full history of racial formation in Classics, let alone reap the fruits of that history's consummation (see Rankine 2019; Umachandran 2019, for some pointers). Instead it will outline some areas where a history of this kind would have the greatest impact.

This chapter is organized into a programmatic introduction and three main sections. I begin with some orientating remarks on the racecraft of Greco-Roman antiquity. The first section then turns to the work of twentieth- and twenty-first-century scholars of race in antiquity, zeroing in on Frank Snowden and Erich Gruen. Keeping a close eye on the interpellation of these scholars themselves within hierarchies of racial domination, this section also makes use of autoethnography to illustrate the percussive force of these hierarchies. The second section assesses the responsibility of two disciplinary practices – histories of classical scholarship, a peculiarly hidebound and doxographic genre; and classical reception studies, pitched originally as highly versatile but shown recently to be in serious need of critical re-examination – in institutionalizing the idea that race-thinking is external and therefore marginal to research into Greco-Roman antiquity, with particular emphasis on the lessons to be learned from the writings of Frantz Fanon. The third and final section marks out some directions for an anti-racist classics. Throughout, I reach for critique not so much for critique's sake (cf. Felski 2015, on critique as 'thought style'), but in the hope of modelling the 'critical classical reception' called for by Johanna Hanink (2017).

'ALL WHITE LIKE I GOT THE WHOLE THING BLEACHED'

Immediately preceding an allusion to Plato's *Euthyphro*, the verse from Jay-Z's 'No Church in the Wild' that stands at the head of this introduction stages the (re)production of whiteness as a luxury item (for commentary on this song, see Padilla Peralta 2015a). Far from being extrinsic to the study of Greco-Roman antiquity, the production of whiteness turns on closer examination to reside in the very marrows of Classics. The discipline's racecraft, dependent as much on selective omission and obliquity as on explicitly racist acts, penetrates deep into the institutional and psychic history of the field, showing its hand not only in the ferocious backlash to Martin Bernal's *Black Athena* but also in the timidity of classicist handling of that backlash in the years since (McCoskey 2018b).

With this chapter's subtitle 'whiteness and the classical imagination', I am channelling both Toni Morrison's William Massey Lectures – published in 1992 as *Playing in the Dark: Whiteness and the Literary Imagination* – and a number of more recent efforts to apply Morrison's insights to the excavation of race-thinking and race-making in Classics (Haley 2009; McCoskey 2012: 32–5). These efforts have not yet ushered in a large-scale collective reorientation around the racing of Classics, and the nuances of race-thinking have been only imperfectly grasped by those classicists who are accustomed to earning material and academic wages from white privilege.

If modernity can be gendered (Felski 1995), antiquity can be – and, as I will explain, most certainly has been – raced. Specific racial configurations may not always travel across time, but racial thinking does (refining Michael Root's aphorism, see Taylor 2004: 8–17; McCoskey 2012: 3–5), and its intersectional and multidimensional properties have been mainlined directly to the heart of antiquity's study. Like any 'invented tradition', Classics drills a set of values and habits through repetition, the cumulative force of which is then interpreted as a summons from the distant past (for the concept, see Hobsbawm and Ranger 1983; for its application to classics, see Bernal 1989: 69). One of these conditioned habits is so indexical of the implication of Classics in racecraft as to justify comment here: the untiring gaze of the discipline not only on a closed set of authors and texts from Greco-Roman antiquity but also on a racially bounded set of modern scholarly interpreters.

The allegation that Classics consists of works by dead white men studied by white men is true *if* we take the 'works by dead white men' to be not the canonical authors (for whom whiteness was not an accessible identity, as the other contributions to this volume make clear) but the compulsively self-referential scholarly industry of mostly white men since early modernity. On this refinement, Classics has consisted of white men (and, as institutions of higher learning were opened to them, white women) citing and bickering with other white men and women over the meanings of Greco-Roman antiquity. These meanings inevitably orbit around whiteness as their sun because, in the absence of any sustained and institutionalized interest in scholarship by people of colour, alternative hermeneutic perspectives are assumed not to exist. One does not have to be a Tenney Frank writing with evident racial relish about race mixture in the Roman Empire to bolster white supremacy (1916; cf. Linderski [1999] 2007, for the euphemistic cloaking of Frank's racism as 'Darwinian and Mendelian principles').

Recent studies of publication trends in journals and edited volumes have documented their disturbing entrenchment of white male privilege (on US-based journals, see Padilla Peralta 2019a; Stewart and Machado 2019; for the situation in the UK, see Quinn 2019; on gender and editorial bias, see Thonemann 2019). The anonymizing strictures of peer review, whose connivance with the reproduction of whiteness deserves further study (Bal 2018), are partly responsible for this; but there are other culprits as well. Citational practices in scholarship are the primary front along which the war to preserve disciplinary whiteness is waged (on citation as reproductive technology, cf. Ahmed 2013; Kim and Mackrandilal 2014). Under the banner of 'black scholarship matters', Tat-Siong Benny Liew has encouraged colleagues in biblical and early Christian studies to ask: 'Whose scholarship counts as scholarship in my guild?' (Liew 2017). To judge from bibliographies and reading lists in Classics, scholars of colour do not matter and are even in many cases to be shunned, except when they hold forth on race (and even then …). The persistence of this enforced irrelevance, despite Shelley Haley's regular recourse to critical race theory over the years to displace 'the experience of whites as the norm' and re-centre Classics 'in the experiences of people of color' (Haley 2009: 28), imposes a ceiling on the discipline's epistemic range.

Because racial identities, inasmuch as 'they are fundamental to ourselves as knowing, feeling, and acting subjects', delimit our cognitive horizons – 'differently identified individuals do not have the same access to points of view or perceptual planes of observation or the same embodied knowledge' (Alcoff 2006: 126) – the continuing inability of classicists to cite or seriously engage with the scholarship of people of colour leaves the field as a whole intellectually impoverished. This impoverishment brings about epistemic injustice (for the concept, see Fricker 2007; for its relevance to Classics, see Chae 2018; for an egregious instance of non-citation, see McCoskey 2018b), or what anthropologists critical of citational practices in their discipline have termed 'epistemological apartheid' (Faye Harrison quoted in Beliso-De Jesús and Pierre 2019: 7–8).

Classicists have a long way to travel when it comes to documenting and rectifying their own 'racial politics of citation' (for the phrase, see Ray 2018). Of course, the work will not end with a wholesale reimagining of citation's capacity to '*broaden* the possibility space for what our research and engagement could be' (thus Graham 2018: 6, on 'punking' citation). If the field is to achieve some separation from its history of racial self-referentiality it will have to create space for scholars whose embodied experiences of difference position them to target and deconstruct white-identitarian epistemics (thanks to M. Umachandran for this formulation). But to create this space, we will also need to ask some hard questions about the discipline's incubation of racial violence.

BLACKNESS: THE GATHERING

Maybe African studies would suit you better if you can't hope [*sic*] with the reality of how advanced Europeans were. You could figure out why the wheel had never made it sub-Saharan African [*sic*] you meathead. Lucky for you, your black [*sic*], because you have little else on offer.

—Email to author, 9 March 2019

To the question 'Did racism exist in Greco-Roman antiquity?' various answers have been mooted: that colour prejudice and biological racism did not (Frank Snowden); that cultural prejudice (A. N. Sherwin-White) or somatic ideals (Lloyd Thompson) or a species of proto-racism (Benjamin Isaac) did. But what if the repetition of this question in twentieth- and twenty-first-century scholarship betrays an abiding anxiety not about race and racism in antiquity but about the racing of ancient Greece and Rome within the history of the discipline? Forced to contend with a new generation of white-supremacist appropriations of Classics, progressive champions have poured themselves into identifying and where possible debunking these appropriations (see e.g. the *Pharos* Project). But these corrective and reparative efforts will be of very limited value if they do not attend to the modes of disciplinarity that make Classics such an enticing target for white supremacists in the first place. This section considers how Classics and classicists fashion practitioners of the discipline into racial subjects.

White supremacy has historically dictated the terms of engagement with Greco-Roman antiquity by ruthlessly interpellating all participants in its knowledge production in one of two ways: as worthy white heirs to the classical tradition, or as Black and brown interlopers. As several of the contributions to this volume detail, perhaps no scholar did more to elevate race into a category of analysis for the cultures of Greco-Roman antiquity than Frank M. Snowden Jr (1911–2007). Having sought for much of his professional career to be known more as a classicist than as an African American classicist, Snowden achieved a dubious honour after his death: admission into the pantheon of overcomers. I quote from his obituary in the *Washington Post*:

> His appointment [as cultural attaché to the US Embassy in Rome] did not prevent condescending attitudes from occasionally emerging. According to a news attaché at the embassy, one visiting congressman appeared to criticize Dr. Snowden for writing his doctoral thesis on slavery in the Roman Empire.
>
> 'Well, since you are a Negro, I suppose that was of special interest to you,' the congressman said.
>
> 'Actually, my special interest was in the fact that nearly all of the slaves in ancient Rome were white,' Dr. Snowden said.
>
> The congressman stormed off.
>
> (Bernstein 2007)

This anecdote maps Snowden's lifelong programme of research to his lived experiences as an African American classicist with the help of several rhetorical strategies. The first is the reminiscence of the exchange as having provided Snowden with the perfect opportunity to recapitulate one of his major research findings: that colourism of the kind all too familiar to him and to his congressional interlocutor did not order or buttress the relationship of slavers and enslaved in Greco-Roman antiquity. The second is the euphemistic rendering of racism as 'condescending attitudes': whether out of deference to Snowden's own complicated relationship to the politics of racial identity or from a resolve to hew closely to a standard obituary template that takes little to no cognizance of structural adversity, it is revealing that neither the *Washington Post* obituary or its *New York Times* counterpart (Fox 2007) tackle the pervasiveness of racism in Snowden's life directly. The *Washington Post* opted instead simply to reference Snowden's objections to Afrocentrist critics and historians, which culminated in his negative assessment of *Black Athena* and Bernal's disparagement in response (McCoskey 2018b; on the ironies of the antagonism, see Keita 2000: ch. 7). Even if he may have relished the memory of the fray in his final years, Snowden's own autobiographical materials make the existence of other instances of his racial subjectivization painfully clear (Snowden 2002) (Figure 9.1).

The third strategy builds on the camouflaging of racism through prim periphrasis. In the person of Snowden, the encounter with racism is plotted as a triumph: the African American scholar overcomes it, with the clever riposte chosen deliberately to signal metonymically how Snowden habitually overcame racism – through inoffensive, non-violent forbearance and grace. That such forbearance and grace were what racial hegemony expected of him (since to slap or punch the congressman in retaliation would have cost Snowden his job and so much more) is left for the renegade reader to discern. Racial hegemony similarly veils its prowess in the adverb *occasionally*: the assumption that behaviours such as that of the congressman only infrequently make their appearance is heart-warming material for readers not preoccupied by or concerned with the iterative and repetitive systemic force of racism – in other words, readers accustomed to benefitting from white privilege. This privilege bleeds into the fourth and final strategy disclosed by the anecdote: the anonymizing of the congressman. Even when victorious at the site

FIGURE 9.1 Frank Martin Snowden Jr (1911–2007), Professor of Classics at Howard University, with presidential press secretary James Hagerty. © Bettmann/Getty Images.

of resistance, the victim of racism remains a named and interpellated Black man. The perpetrator of verbal racist violence, on the other hand, indulges even after death in the comforts of reputational security.

In this manner, the obituary retrieves blackness only then to conceal it – in much the same way that Snowden's lifelong project of compiling and sifting through the literary and material evidence for antiquity's 'Ethiopians' in order to vindicate Greco-Roman antiquity as not racist, or at the very least as not characterized by a distinctively modern conjuncture of heritable biological race and skin colour, enacts the appearance and disappearance of blackness (for Snowden's faith in comprehensiveness as an antidote to 'modern racial prejudice', cf. Keita 2000: 133–4). The escapist aspects of Snowden's research programme have lately been noted (Derbew with Giusti 2018); we will revisit the interplay of the personal and the scholarly in a moment. For now, let me turn briefly to the vindication of antiquity as a means of ghosting the production of blackness.

Even as scholarly modifications to Snowden's thesis multiply, the zest for vindicating the Greeks and Romans persists. Few publications confirm the thirst for vindication more than Erich Gruen's *Rethinking the Other in Antiquity* (2011a), which goes several steps further than Snowden in contending that Greeks and Romans, far from embracing static and uniformly negative prejudices about cultural Others, selectively appropriated and occasionally even plugged themselves into the identities and practices of those they branded as 'barbarians'. But despite its tips of the hat to Edward Said – who is cited on the opening page – Gruen's book is curiously uninterested in several of the core findings of *Orientalism,* or *Culture and Imperialism* for that matter (for the very limited impact of Said in Classics, cf. Vasunia 2003: 7; on recovering Said as a critic of European philology's connivance with Orientalism, see Hui 2017: 141). The most relevant one for our discussion is Said's insistence that knowledge of the Other is reproduced through institutions. This knowledge's reproduction depends not just on the information-hoovering of empire but on specific subjugating practices that make the acquisition of particular types of knowledge possible, in many cases as a preliminary to the violent extraction of wealth (on the 'material dimensions' of Roman Orientalism, see McCoskey 2012: 19–20).

Moreover, *Orientalism* also documents how imperial devices for the commandeering and warehousing of knowledge about the Other, and the contents of that knowledge, do not lend themselves to tidy packaging as a parcel from the past that can then be posted to the present. For this reason alone, Gruen's enterprise of heroically lining up as many bits of evidence as conform to his thesis while pleading away the rest is quixotic; and his rehabilitation of the Greeks and Romans as multiculturalists *avant la lettre* simply sanctifies the ancient Mediterranean so as to enable it to retain its pedigreed (whitewashed) prominence. Even the particular model of historical positivism to which *Rethinking the Other* subscribes can only with strenuous effort be pried from the grip of race-thinking, inasmuch as both this positivism and its classicist reflexes emerged in a period of intensely racializing disciplinary practice: the late nineteenth- and early twentieth-century convergence of race and historiography (Keita 2000: ch. 1; on objectivity's enthronement in American historiography, cf. Novick 1988: chs. 1–4).

Gruen's writings on race and ethnicity are theoretically underpowered for other reasons that would take too long to detail here (for a compact assessment, see Kennedy 2019). But my interest is less in the individual scholar or his output and more in the structures and habits of knowledge that he chooses to replicate and amplify. To appreciate the solidity and durability of these structures, we will need to return to Snowden once again.

'During my last visit to Athens', he wrote in the preface to *Blacks in Antiquity: Ethiopians in the Greco-Roman Experience*, 'the taxi driver who drove me from the airport, upon observing my dark color, exclaimed with confidence "Αἰθίοψ!" (Ethiopian) – a happy coincidence and an encouraging introduction for an investigator in pursuit of classical representations of Ethiopians in Athenian museums' (1970: ix). That Snowden was scanned and read into Greco-Roman antiquity by his taxi driver's gaze brought him not only joy but also the option of a winking manoeuvre around those routines of epidermal interpellation (see the discussion of Fanon in the next section) that circumscribed his life as a racial subject in the United States. What normally sufficed to discredit him, especially by comparison to those colleagues and adversaries who benefitted from institutionalized white privilege (such as Bernal; Derbew with Giusti 2019), in this specific research context gave him an invigorating boost. But as with the obituary anecdote, this episode can be made to speak beyond the bounds of the individual life, in ways that undercut the fleeting sense of empowerment attached to it by Snowden himself.

Snowden tapped the reminiscence to justify his claim of 'similarities between the ancient and modern views of colored peoples' in Egypt, Greece and Italy (1970: ix; for contextualization of this incident, Parmenter 2021: 4–5), a proposition not entirely reconcilable with the book's argumentation around the absence of biological racism in the ancient Mediterranean. More significantly, both this anecdote and a second one about a Sicilian's mistaking him as Chinese expose the work of travelling to conduct research into race and race-thinking as *race-making* work (for travelling classic[ist]s and border politics, cf. Padilla Peralta 2017a). The disciplinary endeavour that pitches itself as a venture into a distant past removed from the racial turbulences of the scholar's present turns out on closer examination to be inextricable from racecraft, one diagnostic marker of which is wariness or evasion when it comes to specifying one's own location within hierarchies of domination and subjection. The practice of acknowledging one's skin in the game, introduced and harnessed to clarifyingly powerful effect by feminist scholars over the past several decades, still sits uneasily with many students of ancient Greece and Rome, with the partial exception of those working on race (in addition to Snowden, Haley 1993; McCoskey 2012: 200–1; cf. Isaac 2004: 50–1, who is candid about experiences of anti-Semitic discrimination but silent about racialization in Israel-Palestine).

This hesitation ensues in part from classicist discomfort with and lack of sophistication around race (Kennedy 2019), most conspicuously manifest in a near-total absence of critical attention to histories and morphologies of whiteness (for first steps in Classics, see Dee 2003–4; for whiteness studies, see Wiegman 1999; on the transnational reproduction of whiteness, see Lake and Reynolds 2008; for a history of 'white people', see Painter 2010); a comprehensive failure to take up concepts of racial affect, subjectivity or queerness (McCoskey 2012: 100–5, on 'racial subjectivity' in Ptolemaic Egypt is an exception); and a recurring habit of confusing colour-thinking with race-thinking (see e.g. Whitmarsh 2018). When paired with decades of professionalization that aim to remove the body of the scholar from view as a precondition for the assertion of authoritative knowledge (for a critique of this practice, see Hallett and Van Nortwick 1997), the end result of these omissions is a hard-baked indifference to the ethics of racialized knowledge. Such indifference swings the doors wide open to racecraft, as a brief sojourn into autoethnography will now attempt to demonstrate.

My undocumented Dominican American family spent the winter of 1993 in a New York City homeless shelter. As a diffident and anxious nine year old, I puzzled over the sequence of events that, beginning with our immigration to the United States four years earlier, had culminated in my parents' separation and, some months afterwards, my family's eviction from its apartment (Padilla Peralta 2015b). The otherwise spartan shelter to which we had been assigned by New York City's Department of Homeless Services sported one luxury: a library, the relic of the shelter's previous incarnation as a public school. At the time, I was growing increasingly curious about Dominican history and badgering my mother with questions about our native country's culture and politics. I could not find any books with answers to these questions in the shelter library. What I did find, however, was an illustrated textbook entitled *How People Lived in Ancient Greece and Rome* (Reuben and Schwartz 1974). Its opening sentences brought me, and my desperation to leave the shelter in mind and body, under Western eyes:

> Western civilization was formed from the union of early Greek wisdom and the highly organized legal minds of early Rome. The Greek belief in a person's ability to use his powers of reason, coupled with Roman faith in military strength, produced a result that has come to us as a *legacy*, or gift from the past. This legacy has grown and blossomed into a smooth, colorful way of life – covering equally the arts and the sciences, the one and the many.
>
> (Reuben and Schwartz 1974: 7)

With the book in my hands, I time-travelled to a new world, millennia removed from the shelter. But the book that spurred the imagination also raced me. Years before I could even verbalize what had occurred in this moment of encounter with the classical, I somehow grasped that Classics was a cheat code for mastering whiteness (cf. Chae 2018). What took me a long time to perceive, and still longer to articulate, was that mastery of this cheat code would entail shelving interest in the complex configurations of Afro-Latinx identity that I inhabited but that were not celebrated or even represented in any of the books available to me, at the time or for many years afterwards.

The offer of imaginative matriculation into a 'smooth, colorful way of life' had been made accessible between the covers of a textbook, when so many other knowledges were not. Knowledge and pursuit of the classical in the years after that encounter came at the cost of 'cultural bleaching' (H. Wong 2018): internalization of the sense that my own personhood, and the histories that pulsed through it, had to be subordinated to a body of knowledge that radiated Western authority. The nagging and ever-insistent question in the wake of this realization would be whether I, as an Afro-Latino scholar, could contend on equal terms with an institutionalized system of thought that snared me in its charismatic web at the moment of my family's most profound vulnerability – the direct consequence of structural and racial inequity.

This is the ethical dilemma of Classics as racecraft.

FROM MARGIN TO SHINING MARGIN

Most black people aren't interested in the classics because they are self-absorbed and only want to 'learn' about black people. And most hate 'Western Civilization', which the Classics are the basis of. And just as a practical, statistical reality, how could more black people study and be published in the Classics without reducing the number of black people studying and being published in African studies or all the numerous leftist indoctrination fields like Sociology? It's a zero-sum game, and you want future America-haters to be turned into people who have respect for Western civilization by studying the Classics?

—Email to author, 27 February 2019

The quotations selected as epigraphs for this chapter's main sections capture the steady current of racist aggression in the Black classicist's being-in-the-world. They also showcase the glorification of the discipline of Classics as a racial instrument. This glorification, which is regularly infused with appeals to 'Western civilization' (Kennedy 2017; Wenger 2017), is possible only because classicists have failed to model or exemplify a species of disciplinarity that attends rigorously to the ethics of knowledge. Although this inattention occupies the leading role in classicist racecraft, a host of disciplinary practices are responsible for buffering this studied disregard from any jolting shocks. The racialized sentimentalities of philology have lately come in for a well-deserved drubbing (Rankine 2019; on philology's colonial underpinnings, cf. Ahmed 2018). This section will therefore evaluate two other practices: histories of classical scholarship and classical reception studies.

To look for the constitutive agency of race in the discipline's meditations on its own history is to be confronted almost immediately by silence. That these histories are often arranged in the form of concatenated biographies, suffused with the 'pious antiquarianism' that Regius Professor of Greek Sir Hugh Lloyd-Jones once confessed to indulging in a lecture on his Oxonian predecessors, is part of the problem (Lloyd-Jones 1982: 14; on Turner's 2014 'celebration of polymaths', cf. Hui 2017). With their pious focus on the individual classicist's institutional pedigrees and *res gestae*, these histories for the most part do not discern or so much as acknowledge the benefits that many of their protagonists derived, directly and indirectly, from the conjoined forces of white supremacy and Euro-American settler-colonialism. 'Politics, religion, ideas shape the individual' (Calder in Briggs and Calder 1990: xiv); but apparently not race. Not one biographical entry in the *Biographical Dictionary of North American Classicists* (Briggs 1994) even so much as mentions the structural force of racism in the antebellum and postbellum United States; the *Dictionary of British Classicists* performs the same work of silencing for the United Kingdom (Todd 2004). The logical inference is that every single person profiled in these dictionaries gleaned the rewards of white supremacy, or that the final status of both projects is a direct reflection of the racial myopias of their respective editors and contributors – or both.

The American dictionary's introductory essay, with its punt on any direct responsibility for building a more racially inclusive Classics, in the process also models how not to practice a racially inclusive intellectual history of the discipline: 'It is the task of the next generation to attract blacks and Asians into classics' (Calder in Briggs 1994: xxxvii), as if people of colour had not been contributing to the discipline for generations (Haley 1993; *Black Classicists* 2018; Rankine 2019). This dictionary's omission of the African American classicist William Sanders Scarborough (for an edited autobiography, see Ronnick 2005) goes hand in hand with its deliberate cloaking of Basil Lanneau Gildersleeve's racism, finessed away through discrete reference to his defence of the Southern cause (for the full hagiography, see Briggs in Briggs and Calder 1990: 93–118; for correction, see Lupher and Vandiver 2011).

Synthetic treatments of the discipline's past and present prospects that ditch biography in favour of topic- or theme-based historical reconstruction have not fared much better. Neither the legacies of Greece (Finley 1981) or Rome (Jenkyns 1992) nor 'the future of the classical' (Settis 2006) have been understood to intersect in any meaningful way with globe-spanning systems of race. The latter publication's 'stark opposition between "our" culture and those of "others"' (thus Graziosi 2005) is studded with racial subtexts, for those who have eyes to see them. By and large, the invocation of futurity as a horizon of possibility for proselytizers of ancient Greece and Rome is thick with such racial subtexts (Padilla Peralta 2019b on Beard 2019).

Not only the future but also the past of the past has been subjected to searching scrutiny in twenty-first-century histories of the discipline. Yet even here, the romance of ancient Greece and Rome's production of pastness and future perfectness tiptoes around race or racism, if the near-total absence of these terms and their conceptual appurtenances from an otherwise wide-ranging collection of essays on the topic (Porter 2006) is any indication. Most confoundingly of all, not only are there no entries for either topic in *The Classical Tradition* (Grafton, Most and Settis 2010), 'race' is mentioned in exactly three entries, only one of which (on fascism) engages with the deployment of race as a technology of structural violence; 'racism' is mentioned a grand total of three times in the volume's 1,067 pages.

As Martin Bernal's *Black Athena* and its acrimonious rejoinders became a lightning rod in the American 'culture wars' (McCoskey 2012: 171–81; cf. Adler 2016: ch. 4, taken to task in McCoskey 2018b; on Bernal's face-off against Snowden, see Parmenter 2021), several critics both within and beyond Classics did their best to don the mantle of discipline- and rigour-bound objective scholarship in their reviews. One of the least outwardly partisan of these reviews opened with a confession of admiration 'for the precise and rigorous scholarship practiced by classicists' (Marchand and Grafton 1997). Not just in Classics but in the adjacent fields of classical archaeology and historical linguistics, the exaltation of disciplinary rigour in response to Bernal was arguably more revealing than the nakedly racist responses of those critics for whom an Afrocentric account of Greco-Roman antiquity triggered an acute case of dyspepsia. While some of Bernal's more ostensibly dispassionate readers were alert to the presence of race and racism in the disciplinary histories of Classics and classical archaeology (see e.g. Marchand 1996: 181–7 and *passim*), attempts to pursue reparative work on this front sputtered. A comprehensive sociology of knowledge in Classics is still needed.

In the aftermath of Bernal, classical reception studies have emerged as one site for the study of race's projection into Greco-Roman antiquity and its legacies (see e.g. Orrells, Bhambra and Roynon 2011), offering a lifeline to classicists of colour (Rankine 2019: 353–7). But confusion has attended the subfield's attention to race from the very beginning. For one, classical reception has mostly trained its eyes on elite and almost always white Euro-American literary and artistic practices; to a significant degree, the study of non-white receptions of ancient Greece and Rome remains on the margins of classical reception itself (to the references in Richardson 2019: 184n14, add Moyer, Lecznar and Morse 2020). Even when non-white bodies are centred, the terms of inquiry are sometimes muddled. To cite only the most well-known example, 'black classicism' is variously understood as research into blackness in classical antiquity, in the manner of Snowden and his heirs; the historical engagements of Afro-descendant artists and communities with Classics; or strategies for animating and representing 'the presence of blackness in a composite, classical tradition' (thus Greenwood 2009: 88, commenting on these strands; on *classica Africana*, see McCoskey 2012: 194–7; for studies of literary Black classicism, see Rankine 2006; Cook and Tatum 2010; and Barnard 2014; for a group-centred infrastructure for future studies, see the *Eos: Africana Receptions of Ancient Greece and Rome* collective).

Precariously positioned within the employment and tenuring hierarchies of the discipline (Richardson 2017; Rankine 2019), classical reception has not enjoyed great success in bringing race theorists to the attention of classicists, let alone in forcing a conceptual overhaul of the discipline as a whole. Let us take, as one example of a theorist with a great deal to offer, Frantz Fanon (1925–61) (Figure 9.2), the Martinique-born psychiatrist whose anti-colonial writings have inspired calls for intellectual decolonization in Classics-adjacent fields (e.g. political philosophy; Mills 2015). In *Black Skin, White Masks (Peau Noire, Masques Blancs)*, Fanon plangently evoked the psychic fractures that characterize the embodied experience of colonial blackness: the paralysis of forever always being relationally constructed by reference to whiteness; the disorienting shock of recognizing that – in the Black body and within the epidermal logic of blackness – one does not exist in and for oneself, but instead as an object of a cultural domination that is ceaselessly reinscribed. 'I was responsible not only for my body but also for my race and my ancestors. I cast an objective gaze over myself, discovered my blackness, my ethnic features; deafened by cannibalism, backwardness, fetishism, racial stigmas, slave traders, and above all, yes, above all, the grinning *Y a bon Banania*' (Fanon [1952] 2008: 92).

In continuous dialogue his entire life with scholars and scholarly practices whose preoccupations with Greco-Roman antiquity are very well documented, Fanon would seem to merit more sustained engagement by classicists, and not only because of his connections to Jean-Paul Sartre and Simone de Beauvoir, iconic figures in existentialism and feminism. His writings supply a critical vocabulary for diagramming the psychic force

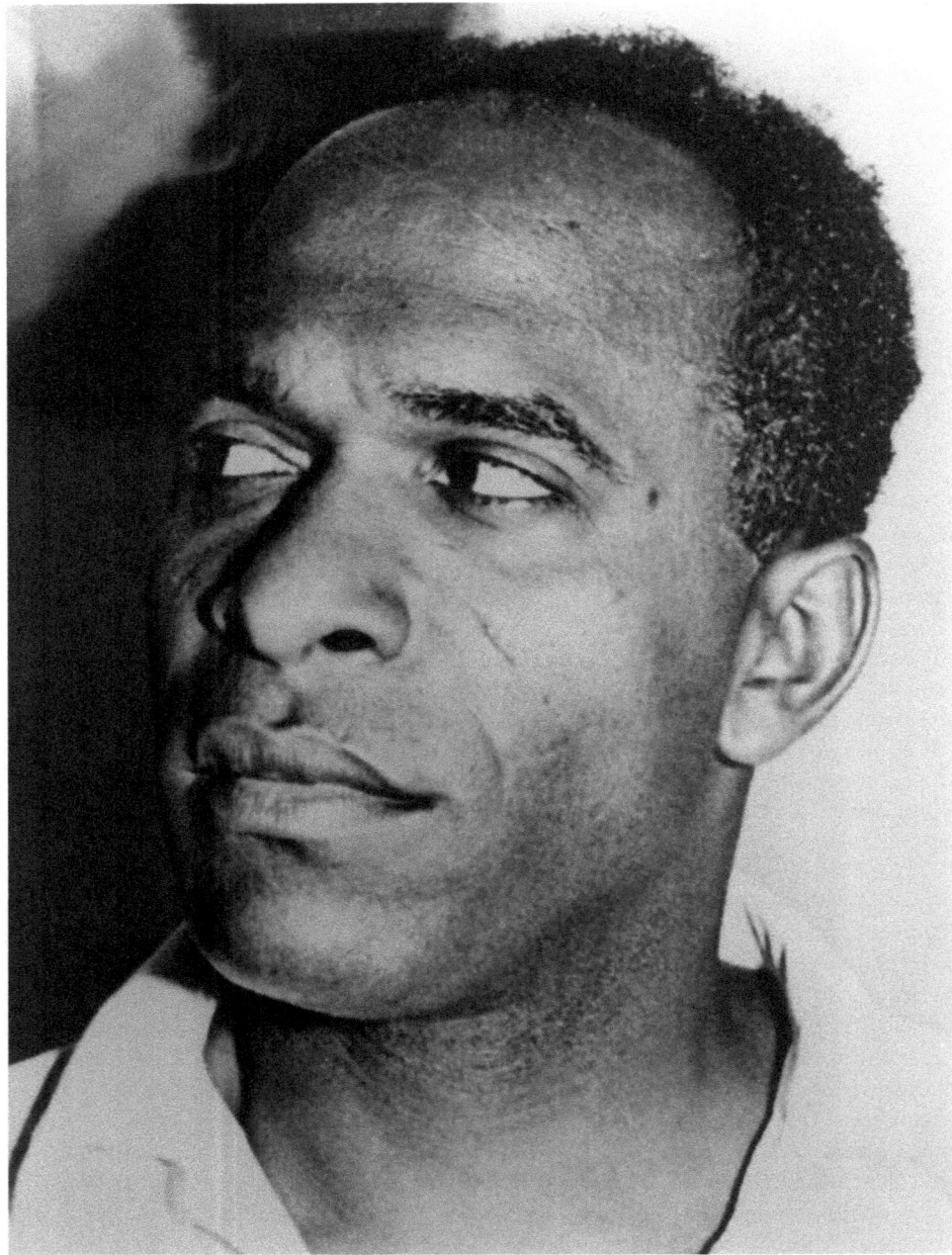

FIGURE 9.2 Frantz Omar Fanon (1925–61): psychiatrist, political philosopher, revolutionary.

of subjection that could quite easily be purposed for a study of 'complex inferiorities' in Greek and Latin literature (along the lines of Matzner and Harrison 2019) or ancient history or any of the traditional subfields – or even classical reception. But Fanon appears on the radar of classicists only when the spectre of contemporary racial blackness enters the room; otherwise, he furnishes them with no affordances of theory, no capacious worldview with or against which to struggle and strive.

Recourse to postcolonial and critical race theory would sharpen the discipline's attention to the signifying pluralities of differential raciology, another pronounced shortcoming of classicist approaches to race at the moment. Asian-identifying classicists have lately observed that the gridding of US and UK racial discourses along the axis of blackness and anti-blackness denies visibility to their own complex racial identities (Chae 2018; Umachandran 2019). This denial is significant, both as an index of white supremacy's drive to create gradients of 'not quite, not white' (the title of Sen 2018) and as an obstruction to the full enactment of an anti-racist programme pairing theory and praxis that would attend to the embodied knowledges of all non-Black classicists of colour. This programme would take on board research into the distinctive contours of anti-Asian racism in the Global North and its expression in Classics (S. Wong 2019). One exemplary model for such research is Anne Cheng's concept of ornamentalism (2019), with its attention to the habituating force of dress and make-up in the sexualized commodification of Asian women as yellow bodies. Cheng provides a much-needed counter and augment to theories of race that accord primacy in the history of race-making to the epidermalization of blackness. As such, it brims with potential for reception scholars and intellectual historians interested in tracking the sinuous movements of race as style in the logic of classicism, several source-texts for which have already been identified (e.g. Aeschylus, *Suppliants* 234–45, with Kennedy 2019 on clothing as racial hexis).

Circling back to Fanon, one can only hope that recent calls for decolonizing the discipline (Christensen 2019; Derbew with Giusti 2019) result not only in the opening up of classicist frameworks to underutilized authors and approaches, but in the realization that these frameworks have historically snapped together around a race-making logic that is premised on amassing normative positive value for itself at the expense of those practices and communities that it simultaneously classifies, marginalizes and exploits as Black and brown. But, if it is to be more than a mere buzzword, this decolonization will have to ruffle some feathers.

HOOD(ED) FUTURES

You know you're a third-rate thinker and a racial narcissist. If classics is so horrible that, as you bemoan it, we need 'reparative intellectual justice—including the demolition of the discipline itself,' why don't YOU leave the discipline and go back to the rabble-rousing and muckraking you apparently love so much? Face it: you were always a curiosity, and your only accomplishment has been the philological equivalent of being an organ-grinder's monkey. Have some character for once in your life and admit that YOU ARE NOT A SCHOLAR. YOU ARE AN ACTIVIST. GO BE AN ACTIVIST. And last, but certainly not least, go fuck yourself.

—Email to author, 7 January 2019

For the classicist of colour, the mere fact of *existing* in the study of Greco-Roman antiquity is a form of political labour (for the concept, see Ahmed 2017: ch. 5). Racecraft regularly discloses itself in the disproportionate amount of labour that is extracted from scholars of colour, and in the widening chasm between idle chatter about diversity and the punishing slog of institution- and coalition-building (see the comments of Echeverría-Fenn 2020). Although the necessary work of dismantling white supremacy within Classics will require the empowerment of these and other scholars from historically marginalized backgrounds and differentially embodied perspectives, that empowerment would require disciplinary gatekeepers to grant authority and belief to the variety of mechanisms by which these scholars have been sidelined from the production of knowledge deemed legitimate or acceptable – the mechanisms of racecraft. It would also require these gatekeepers to make an honest commitment to 'decolonial healing' (for the term and its explication, see Ureña 2019) as part of 'rethink[ing] the experience of what it is to be a classicist' (Ram-Prasad 2019).

While Classics is by no means the only academic discipline to bear a responsibility for remediation and rectification (for the case of anthropology, see Fuentes and Rouse 2016; Beliso-De Jesús and Pierre 2019), its historical pedigree presents some unique challenges and opportunities. Scholars in a field whose valuation as *classical* rides the coattails of white supremacy could do worse than to heed Walter Mignolo's call for 'projects imagining and working toward a society no longer based in models emerging in the Western tradition, from Greece to western Europe in all its imperial faces, since the sixteenth century, to the U.S., but in the activation of categories of thoughts and ways of life that have been disqualified since the sixteenth century' (2005: 140). In the absence of a genuinely reparative acknowledgement of the epistemicide that has been and continues to be perpetrated under the guise of enshrining Greco-Roman antiquity as a model of universal human values, exhortations to transcend race/racism or to strive for a post-racial world are at best ineffectual, if not downright disingenuous (on epistemicide, see Sousa Santos 2014; Hall and Tandon 2017; on the psychic toll of universalist rhetoric, see Haley 1989a: 334–5; Padilla Peralta 2017b; and Choi 2018). These exhortations, which regularly appeal to the ideal of colour-blindness in a fumbling effort to paper over targeted acts of racism, are among the most devious instruments of racecraft (on colour-blind racism, cf. Burke 2019).

Humanistic discourses are 'continually used as a smokescreen for oppression, to divert attention away from discriminatory practices and identity-based patterns of segregation and exclusion' (Alcoff 2006: 290). These practices and patterns are everywhere in evidence in the study of Greco-Roman antiquity on both sides of the Atlantic, from the fixation on 'mastering' ancient Greek and Latin – which slots right into long-standing barriers to foreign language instruction for historically and currently exploited communities – to the systematic under-representation of people of colour at all levels of institutionalized knowledge production and their over-representation in contingent and short-term teaching and research positions. 'Well, we don't believe you, you need more people' (Jay-Z, 'Takeover'): scholars of colour are repeatedly told that the pipeline is the problem, as if the pipeline were not an epiphenomenon of a species of disciplinarity that is designed to call their authority as knowledge producers routinely into question.

Drawing inspiration from community-based approaches to decolonization in other fields, classicists of colour are patiently and steadily building up platforms for equitable knowledge production and interpersonal support (for the Sportula's Naked Soul conference, see Mansukhani and Nowbahar 2019; on the Asian and Asian American Classical Caucus, see S. Wong 2019). As for the fatalistic notes being sounded lately about the introspective and self-reflexive turn of Classics and adjacent disciplines, it does not require much effort (for this author at least) to locate the roots of this concern-trolling in a thirst for maintaining ancient Greece and Rome's cultural cachet as bastion of exclusivist privilege. If Classics and ancient history in their nineteenth- and twentieth-century disciplinary incarnations are dying, they are dying not only, or even primarily, because of the internal pressure being brought to bear on their historical collusion with white supremacy by those practitioners who have some awareness of critical race theory. These fields are dying because, having fought tooth and nail against the emancipatory prospects of anti-race and anti-racist thinking for far too long, their toxic reproduction of whiteness has finally caught up to them: the unthinking veneration of textual criticism and traditional philology; the uninterrogated commitment to mastery of ancient Greek and Latin as prerequisites for legitimate professional standing in the discipline; the decision to turn a blind eye to the ravages of capital and racism (summarizing a roundtable discussion of these issues, see *Pharos* 2020; on a decolonial archaeology resistant to capitalism, cf. Hamilakis 2018; on the therapeutics of language-learning, note Echeverría-Fenn 2020).

I do not suppose that the death of these epistemic formations will yield something more emancipatory; after all, racecraft is fiendishly inventive and metamorphic. But in anticipation of the revolution to come, I will come prepared with a hoodie – the helmet of the Black scholar-activist.[1]

FIGURE 9.3 Cover of Claudia Rankine's *Citizen: An American Lyric*. © Graywolf Press.

NOTES

Introduction

1. For a thoughtful account of both the term 'classical' and the use of periodization itself in the study of ancient history, see Hallett (1993). On the term 'Classics' see Quinn (2018).
2. The ethnographic techniques of the Greek historian Herodotus have inspired especially rich analysis. See, for example, the groundbreaking study by Hartog (1988) and, more recently, Skinner (2012).
3. *Airs, Waters, Places*, part of the Hippocratic corpus of ancient medical writings, provides the lengthiest surviving account of this theory; see Kaufman in this volume.
4. This passage has elicited considerable debate; begin with Thomas (2001) and Munson (2014).
5. On the interpretation in later eras of Alexander's campaigns, which radically expanded both the geographic and demographic scope of the Greek world, see Parker in this volume. For an example of recent scholarship on Alexander's impact in the east, see Holt (2005), which draws explicit attention to the modern events that drive his interest in the topic (xi–xii).
6. A number of important studies have highlighted the complex ways Greek identity interacted with Roman identity in the eastern part of the Roman Empire, for example Woolf (1994), Goldhill (2001) and Whitmarsh (2010). More recently, Kaldellis (2019) has argued that Romanness played an important (and often underestimated) role in identity formation in the east during the later Byzantine period.
7. For a sense of the complex social interactions undertaken by Roman soldiers and army veterans, see Alston (1995).
8. For a detailed discussion of immigration to Rome, see Noy (2000: 53–84); for the different groups residing in Rome (205–84).
9. Given that the eastern part of the Roman Empire was built upon territories previously controlled by the Greek Hellenistic kingdoms, it was generally associated with Greek stereotypes in Roman thought; the term 'barbarian', on the other hand, was mostly applied to groups the Romans encountered in the west; see, for example, Woolf (2011).
10. Positive perceptions of Roman expansion were reinforced by the modern concept of 'Romanization', which emerged alongside the rise of Roman archaeology in the late nineteenth and early twentieth centuries. For a critical overview of 'Romanization' as a concept, including the assumptions about Roman power it has traditionally engendered, see Mattingly (2011: 38–41).
11. For one, the Romans on occasion expelled different groups or practices from the city of Rome; astrologers were a group often targeted, but there are also disputed references to the expulsion of Jews in both 139 BCE and 19 CE; see Rutgers (1994).
12. For more on the tax, see Goodman (1989). On Jewish – Roman relations more broadly, begin with Schäfer (1997); see also Buell in this volume.
13. The bibliography on Roman slavery is expansive; begin with Bradley (1994) and George (2013). On Greek slavery, see Skinner in this volume.

14 Ancient historians are increasingly exposing the varied ways identity was formed at local sites throughout the Roman world; for just one example, see Noy (2004). For a more comprehensive introduction, see Revell (2009).
15 Husband's analysis of Ligurian relied on six words cited by ancient authors, proper names that allegedly derived from Ligurian, and thirty-seven disputed inscriptions (1909: 72–5); from these, Husband concluded that Ligurian was primarily a Gallic language (81).
16 For an accessible account of the importance of Linear B and how it was decoded – one that brings to light the forgotten work of Alice Kober – see Fox (2014).
17 For a brief overview of the theory as it stood in the mid-twentieth century, see Daniel (1948).
18 For a helpful overview and evaluation of the many theories proposed to explain the Mycenaean 'collapse', see Dickinson (2006: 43–57).
19 The website *Pharos: Doing Justice to the Classics* (https://pharos.vassarspaces.net/) performs an invaluable service by tracking the ways various white supremacist and other hate groups employ classical history. For example, 'Site Blames "Decline" of Greece on Loss of Racial Purity' (*Pharos* 2018).
20 Many thanks to Naoíse Mac Sweeney and Dimitri Nakassis for help with this section. All errors are my own.
21 The relationship of *Black Athena* to Afrocentrism – including Bernal's reliance on the previous work of the Senegalese historian Cheikh Anta Diop – is complicated; for one perspective, see Carruthers (1992); also Early (1998).
22 Bernal himself acknowledged that his insistence on 'the diffusion of language and culture through conquest' went 'against the dominant trend in archaeology' which stressed 'indigenous development' (1987: 7). For more on the differences between diffusionism and isolationism, see Marchand and Grafton (1997). While outside the main period of his focus, Bernal also notably endorsed the historicity of both an Indo-European invasion in the fourth or third millennium and a Dorian invasion in the twelfth century BCE (1987: 20–1).
23 On craniometry in early anthropology, see Gould (1993). J. Lawrence Angel was one scholar who applied such methods specifically to the study of ancient Greece; in one article, Angel pointedly criticized 'the biometric school and other anthropologists' for eliding race and 'ethnic group', thus letting 'either racists or the general public continue to equate Nordics with Nazis, Mediterraneans with Italians, or Mediterraneans with Jews, no matter how scurrilous, unreal, or just plain inaccurate such equations are'; Angel urged instead that 'the physical anthropologist or human biologist must be most careful to recognize the dynamic genetic (racial) compositeness of any ethnic group' (1946: 3).
24 In the abstract for a 1930 talk entitled 'Modern Opinions about the Blond Type in Homeric and Classical Greece', Christopher George Brouzas provided an overview of scholarly interest in the 'physical type of the ancient Greeks' and noted that there was currently divided opinion about why the Greeks 'admired blond hair' – either they did so because they were blond themselves or because they were not; indicative of the subjective nature of such assessments, Brouzas favoured the former assumption, insisting that 'the principle that like attracts like must be accepted, at least for the Greeks of the earlier time' (1930: xxvi–xvii). More recently, Whitmarsh (2018) has discussed the difficulty of translating the term *xanthos* (often rendered as 'blonde') in relation to physical appearance in Homer.
25 Although a Roman emperor ceased to rule in the west in 476 CE, when and why the Roman period finally 'ended' remains hotly contested. For two very different recent approaches, see Heather (2010) and Harper (2017), the latter foregrounds climate and disease.
26 The research in this section was made possible by a National Endowment for the Humanities summer stipend.

27 The early American reception of classical antiquity has been much studied in recent decades; see, for example, Reinhold (1984), Richard (2008, 2009) and Malamud (2016).
28 Some sixty-five years later, Thompson (1981) was still addressing Frank's arguments; in his notes, Thompson cites a reprint of Frank's work in a 1963 collection entitled *The Fall of Rome*.
29 While the term 'aliens' has not been widely adopted by classical scholars in writing about identity and difference in the Roman world (perhaps for obvious reasons in an age of science fiction), it was the terminology employed by Balsdon in his important study (1979).
30 For example, Davis (1951) and Saddington (1975).
31 For treatment of the concept of 'racism' in classical scholarship, see Tuplin (1999, 2007a) and McCoskey (2006); see also Skinner in this volume.
32 On the 'cultural turn' and its impact on ancient historians more generally, see Martin (2005). Some examples of classical scholarship conducted under the umbrella of 'cultural identity' include: Laurence and Berry (1998), Goldhill (2001), Stephens (2008) and Gruen (2011b). In the field of archaeology more broadly, for example, Shennan (1994). There is also an important subset of classical scholarship that has tried to avoid the problem of modern terminology by echoing ancient terminology and using the concept of the 'barbarian'; see, for example, Coleman and Walz (1997), Harrison (2002), Bonfante (2011) and Vlassopoulos (2013a). Despite its usefulness, 'barbarian' obviously has some of its own modern connotations to contend with.
33 The claim that a refusal to use race was somehow more 'neutral' has been communicated to me many times over the years in personal conversations with other classical historians. Of course, neutrality is a complicated issue when it comes to race and racial justice, as was powerfully demonstrated when a prospective US juror was rejected for supporting Black Lives Matter in July 2020, a gesture that insinuated those who did not support BLM were innately 'neutral' and would be more 'objective' when hearing the case. See Vansickle (2020). This is not to say that adoption of the terminology of 'culture' for the sake of historical analysis is inherently apolitical; indeed, cultural studies itself has important roots in Marxism (Storey 1996); so, too, many classical scholars embraced 'culture' as a term that offered greater flexibility and range, for example Dougherty and Kurke (2003). Nonetheless, there has been such a palpable hostility towards the terminology of race in classical studies in recent decades, especially after the publication of *Black Athena*, that the motives behind these trends – whether conscious or not – demand careful unpacking in hindsight.
34 It is impossible not to think of George G. M. James's *Stolen Legacy* (1954) when reading Benn's phrasing, a text whose argument about the Egyptian origins of Greek philosophy was foundational to Afrocentrism; it (along with *Black Athena*) was one of the main targets of Mary Lefkowitz's polemic: *Not Out of Africa: How Afrocentrism Became an Excuse to Teach Myth as History* (1997).
35 On 'ethnicity' in classical studies, see McCoskey (2003). Examples of its adoption include: Mitchell and Greatrex (2000), Malkin (2001b), Kim (2009) and, most recently McInerney (2014b). In archaeology more broadly, for example, Jones (1997).

Chapter 1

1 Aracelis Girmay, excerpts from 'The Beauty of the World, Tenth Estrangement' from *The Black Maria*. Copyright © 2016 by Aracelis Girmay. Reprinted with the permission of The Permissions Company, LLC on behalf of BOA Editions, Ltd., boaeditions.org.
2 This upper-case 'B' is deliberate; I use 'Black people' to describe a contemporary, socially constructed, group and 'black people' to denote dark-skinned (ranging from chestnut to

jet-black) people in Greco-Roman antiquity. The use of 'black' as a visual marker inevitably lends comparison to current racial politics but is not a direct referent. In a similar vein, I use 'White' as a contemporary label and 'white' to describe an objective colour in Greco-Roman antiquity.

3. Another note on nomenclature: I define 'Greco-Roman antiquity'/'the ancient Greco-Roman world' as 'a historical period, from the eighth century BCE to the fourth century CE, during which Greece and Italy were the dominant powers in the Mediterranean region', and I denote 'Classics' as a study of Greco-Roman antiquity. My use of 'Greco-Roman antiquity'/'the ancient Greco-Roman world' aims to diminish the monopoly that classicists inadvertently reinforce when they treat the unmarked phrase 'antiquity' as a synonym for a specific geographic and temporal range. Rather than fossilize the use of 'Classics' as a fixed noun which marks other classical societies as secondary, I capitalize the word to mark the problematic ways that the discipline is propped up as an exemplar of the past (cf. Greenwood 2010: 12–13). Altogether, this orthographic practice aims to democratize the lower-cased 'Classics' and enable the broad term 'antiquity' to include societies beyond the Mediterranean Sea.

4. Snowden thoughtfully explains: '[some scholars] have regarded the black man of antiquity as a kind of Ralph Ellisonian "invisible man": they have refused to see him' (1988: 63–4).

5. I denote the ancient region in southern Egypt/northern Sudan (from the first to the sixth cataracts of the Nile) as 'Aithiopia' (transliterated from the ancient Greek word *Aithiopia*); this is distinct from the modern country of Ethiopia, which is located in the Horn of Africa.

6. Such as McCoskey (2003: 104–5; 2012: 27–34).

7. Thiong'o's literary fight against colonialism (and neocolonialism) spans many decades. For a comprehensive analysis of Thiong'o's career, see Gikandi (2000).

8. For those who think that the quest for a new definition of 'race' is a pedantic task, I concede that careful treatment of this vocabulary will cease to be important once our world is free from explosive acts of violence that are spurred by staunch identification with particular racial categories.

9. Scientists were also a part of this propaganda, such as Jean Riolan the Younger (*c*. 1618) who conducted experiments on Black people to identify on which layer of skin pigmentation was found. Also, in his essay '*de la dégéneration des animaux*' (1776), Georges Buffon asserted that hot climates caused people's skin colour to darken and concluded that a return to temperate climates would restore everyone's light skin colour (Curran 2011: 1–28).

10. Haunting can lead to 'that dense site where history and subjectivity make social life' (Gordon [1997] 2008: 8). See also Morrison (1993: 29–59, esp. 35), who examines the haunting of/in American literature.

11. Beardsley's and Snowden's scholarship were part of greater scholarly efforts to investigate black people in Greco-Roman antiquity, such as Jamaican pan-Africanist Marcus Garvey (1923, quoted in Jacques-Garvey [1925] 1967: 18–21); African American historian and journalist Drusilla Dunjee Houston ([1926] 1985); Senegalese anthropologist Cheikh Anta Diop ([1955] 1974); and Cameroonian Jesuit priest and art historian Engelbert Mveng (1972). In 1968/9, the rise of Afrocentrism, an academic movement that grew out of the African Heritage Studies Association (AHSA), also contributed to this investigation. For more on the history of the AHSA and its first president John Henrik Clarke, see Guedj (2016).

12. Through her examination of writers and plastic media (vases, drinking cups, pitchers), Beardsley conceded that depictions of Aithiopians were apotropaic and prophylactic. She concluded that depictions of Aithiopians in ancient Greece functioned solely as decorations.

13 See Snowden (1970) who used 'Negro' to describe black people in Greco-Roman antiquity. Snowden's nomenclature of black people in Greco-Roman antiquity was influenced by (then) contemporary anthropological categories. In his discussion of labels used to describe people of African descent ('colored', 'Negro', 'Afro American' and 'African American'), Robert B. Stepto envisions each designation as part of a metaphorical family tree that includes various time periods and circumstances. He reminds readers of the pitfalls that can occur with the alterations of terminology: 'each change that defines a generation may well cut that generation off from what has come before' ([1979] 1991: xiii). Beardsley and Snowden each focus on a particular branch of this 'history-laden narrative' (term from Stepto [1979] 1991: xii).

14 From critical race theory, the Black–White binary inaccurately simplifies the range of contemporary skin colour into two categories: 'Black' and 'White'. Even those who do not identify with either group are labelled as members of one. In this way, all 'non-White' experiences (already a nebulous category) are conflated into an amorphous minority perspective (Delgado and Stefancic 2012: 73–9).

15 Henderson and Jefferson-Jones (2020). For more on black people in classical Greek art, see Derbew (2018).

16 Dee (2003–4) challenges the importation of Whiteness into Greco-Roman antiquity. For more on the 'White race' in modernity, see Montagu (1997).

17 In a later publication, Thompson expresses an opposing view to Beardsley (1929). He elaborates: 'Beardsley told us far more about her own America of the 1920s than she did about Rome when she put forward the silly view that the Roman practice of decorating ordinary household objects and personal trinkets with depictions of blacks is clear evidence of a contemptuous attitude towards blacks as a "race"' (Thompson 1993: 21–2); later, 'Beardsley's pseudo-sociological forays … [are] hardly more than effusions (however unconscious) of the American racism of her own milieu' (25); and finally, 'many of her observations offer crude revelations of a mental and intellectual enslavement to the norms and assumptions of her own society' (25–6).

18 Discussions of ethnicity (e.g. Thomas 1998; McInerney 2014b) and identity (e.g. J. Hall 1997; Mattingly 2011) have also avoided direct engagement with skin colour. In McInerney (2014b), Smith discusses Nubian ethnicity and Shaw analyses African identity, but both steer away from an explicit discussion of skin colour.

19 Such as Haley (2009) and McCoskey (2003).

20 There is a voluminous literature about identity in the ancient Greco-Roman world. Focusing on Greek identity, Jonathan Hall (1997) treats it as oppositional and pairs it with ethnicity, Whitmarsh (2010) examines its local permutations, Hartog (1988) and Edith Hall (1989) assert that a binary model governs its construction. Scholars situate Roman identity in relation to its neighbours in the west (e.g. Revell 2016; Johnston 2017), east (e.g. Woolf 1994; Andrade 2013), north (e.g. Mullen 2013) and south (e.g. Mattingly 2011).

21 As opposed to the rigidity of Bernal's Aryan and Ancient models in volume 1 of *Black Athena* (1987). See also McCoskey in Mudimbe (1994: 95) and Edith Hall (2004) who cautions against substituting one faulty model (Aryan model) for another (Ancient model). Edith Hall instead focuses on the following questions: 'who on earth did Greeks *think* they were? Why did they think it? And what is it about the late twentieth century which renders the issue so important to *us*?' (2004: 149).

22 Beyond the academy, racecraft is seared into the public's consciousness, as is evidenced in national coverage discussing the criminalization of Blackness: 'Driving while Black' (LaFraniere and Lehren 2015), 'Napping while Black' (Caron 2018) and 'Jogging while Black' (Futterman and Minsberg 2020), all of which can be subsumed into the ontological category 'Living while Black' (Henderson and Jefferson-Jones 2020).

23 In Isaac's schema, proto-racism is the most extreme form of prejudice. He qualifies, 'the term proto-racism, then, may be used when Greek and Latin sources attribute to groups of people common characteristics considered to be unalterable because they are determined by external factors or heredity' (2004: 38).
24 Instead, a term like 'discrimination' usefully describes the violent opinions based on ancient notions of fundamental difference. This term punctures the denial of race's importance in Greco-Roman antiquity and acknowledges negative consequences to racial ideas in Greco-Roman antiquity.
25 Such as Egypt (Herodotus, *Histories* 2) and Scythia (Herodotus, *Histories* 4).
26 By highlighting their longevity, Herodotus draws an intertextual link with Homer's Aithiopians who cavort with Zeus, Poseidon and Iris (*Iliad* 1.423–4, 23.205–7; *Odyssey* 1.22–3). Another point of contact between the Homeric epics and Herodotus' *Histories* occurs when the Aithiopian king offers to reward any Persian who can easily string his bow with his kingdom (3.21, cf. *Odyssey* 21).
27 This edible bounty coincides with the rich sacrificial feasts that Homer's Aithiopians offered to the gods. Through this allusion, Herodotus emerges as an engaged reader and subversive narrator of Homer (Irwin 2014: 43, 68–9).
28 Later in the *Histories* (7.9), geography takes centre stage when Mardonius reminds Xerxes that Xerxes subdued the Aithiopians in order to extend the boundaries of the Persian Empire. The failure of Cambyses' invasion was well known (7.18); these conquered Aithiopians were probably northern Aithiopians who lived near the Egyptian border and fought on behalf of Persia against the Greeks (7.69).
29 It is important to note that with any translation of a language comes a subjective interpretation of culture as well. Therefore, the Fish-eaters' translation may include more than a mere report of what happened in Aithiopia. For more on language as a carrier of culture, see Thiong'o (1986).
30 In his Libyan ethnography (4.197), Herodotus explains that four groups inhabit this region of the world: two Indigenous groups (Libyans and Aithiopians) and two foreign groups (Phoenicians and Greeks).
31 Within the fourth layer, Egyptians also teach Aithiopians about Persians.
32 In this way, Herodotus implicitly protects himself from any blame. If the story turns out to be false, the distortion can be attributed to the various channels of transmission rather than solely to him.
33 Hartog (1988) recognizes Herodotus' inability to incorporate Greeks, Persians and Scythians into his model of foreigners.
34 Within his numerous mentions of Aithiopians in the *Histories* (2.29–30, 104, 110, 137–40, 162; 3.17–26, 94, 97; 4.183, 197–8; 7.90; 9.32), Herodotus discusses the Aithiopians' skin colour in three instances: he implies that their skin is black (2.104), he directly points out their black skin colour (3.101) and he emphasizes their artificial adoption of new colours (7.69).
35 The etymology of 'Aithiopia': *aithō* [I blaze] + *ops* [face].
36 Nonetheless, Greeks had access to iconographic representations of black people in the fifth century BCE. Snowden (1970) provides a comprehensive catalogue of fifth-century BCE depictions of black people in a variety of scenes. A few examples from ancient Greek pottery: a musician depicted on a shield painted on an *amphora*, attendants to Andromeda on a *hydria*, a pygmy fighting a crane on a *rhyton*, a crouching warrior on an *alabastron*, king Busiris on a *stamnos* (Snowden 1970: 51, 54, 98, 223, 232). See also Bindman and Gates (2010).
37 Morgan points out the similarities between Charicleia's father Hydaspes and the Aithiopian ruler Sabacos (Herodotus, *Histories* 2.139–40) who preferred to abdicate rather than rule

against the will of the gods (Morgan 2005: 310). Morgan also suggests a connection between Hydaspes and Herodotus' Aithiopian king (Herodotus, *Histories* 3.17–26, discussed in Morgan 1982: 237–8); Elmer takes this comparison further to propose that Heliodorus directly continues Herodotus' Aithiopian episode with Hydaspes playing the role of Herodotus' Aithiopian king who repudiates Cambyses' gifts (2008: 422–5).

38 There is uncertainty surrounding the date of Heliodorus' *Aithiopika*. Swain uses the potential comparison with Heliodorus the Arab and the historical decline of Emesa, Heliodorus' hometown, after *c.* 270 CE as evidence of a third-century date. He reads the similarity between the account of the siege of Syene (Heliodorus 9), a fictional battle, and Julian's account of the siege of Nisibis, a historical event, in 357 CE (Julian *Orations* 1, *Orations* 3) as evidence that Heliodorus was Julian's source and subsequently dates the *Aithiopika* to *c.* 230 CE (Swain 1996: 423–4). Conversely, Morgan ([1989] 2008) and Bowersock (1994) use the siege passages to argue for a fourth-century date. Bowersock draws parallels between the siege of Syene and the siege of Nisibis, the latter of which he dates to sometime after 350 CE (1994: 153–5). Bowersock further supports his claim by drawing parallels between *Aethiopika* 10 and the fourth-century CE *Historia Augusta* (156–60). Whitmarsh and Hägg agree with the fourth-century date (Whitmarsh 1999: 33–4n2; 2011: 5; Hägg 2000: 195). Also in agreement, Ross explains that Heliodorus' contemporary historiographers supply stylistic models for his descriptions of the siege; as he notes, 'participation in an event alone does not provide the literary ability to narrate it effectively' (2015: 22). Turning to the novel for additional evidence (in *Aethiopika* 9, the Axumites fight alongside the Meroites; in 10, the Axumites are the Meroites' distinguished guests), I concur with Morgan who explains that hints of Axum's later importance 'may be intended in the exceptional status of Axum among Hydaspes' allies' ([1989] 2008: 577n247). I read the non-tributary status of the Axumites as a way to allow readers to imagine a fictional past relationship with the Axumites that is vastly different from their historical context in the fourth century BCE, during which Axum contributes to Meroe's demise and potentially annexes Meroe to its empire.

39 The wandering of the Andromeda myth (from east to south) also bears similarities with Charicleia's travels. McGrath (1992) draws attention to the trope of black Andromeda that predates Heliodorus' lifetime, namely in Ovid's *Heroides* (15.36) and *Ars Amatoria* (1.53).

40 Reeve (1989) deems this chromatic transference 'the Andromeda effect'. Persinna entrusted Charicleia to Sisimithres after her birth; he raised her until she reached the age of seven, at which point he handed her over to the Greek priest Charicles.

41 Bradley points out a similar resonance within Latin literature; colour can signal one's origins and disposition yet blushing, tanning and/or intermarrying can enable people to alter their colour (2009: 145–60).

42 I borrow the language of a deterritorialized and diasporic discipline from DuBois (2010: 56).

Chapter 2

1 For related discussion of 'perceptual filters', see Sourvinou-Inwood (1991: 9–10).

2 Walsh (2018) argues that this amounts to a white racialization of the temperate climate: 'in Jones' translation the consistent choice of English words … cast the "heterogeneous" character in a positive light (e.g. "spirit" and "endurance" instead of "hot-temperedness" and "suffering") and the "homogeneous" character in a negative light (e.g. "slackness" instead of "ease")'. Given the competitive aspect of early enquiry, Walsh's argument that we risk 'foreclos[ing] the possibility that the text might be critiquing and/or reframing the

discourse about culture and environment' merits serious consideration. Jones's privileging of the 'heterogeneous' character does, however, tally with the sense we get from Herodotus, at least implicitly, that the Egyptians' reliance upon annual inundations of the Nile is less worthy than the Greeks' dependance upon Zeus for rain. See also Harrison (2003). For the impact of environment on human physiology, see Chiasson (2001).

3 See, for example, Gruen (2011a) and Moyer (2011). Recent calls to decolonize Classics include Ram-Prasad (2019).
4 These are invariably conceived in monolithic terms. See Moyer (2011) for the argument that focusing on Western imaginings leaves the Orient just as marginalized together with an attempt to address this via dialogic history. For the origins of this discourse, see Said (1978); also Vlassopoulos (2013b).
5 For the unfolding play of power and knowledge, Stuart Hall (1990).
6 Cf. McCoskey (2012: 24 and 25–6). For the workings of Greek identity, see Cartledge (2012).
7 See Harrison (2019), but also Vlassopoulos (2011).
8 For related discussion, see Isaac (2009) and Harrison (forthcoming).
9 Such comparisons underpin some of the most insightful work on this topic, for example Tuplin (1999), in which references to distinctions between Greeks and barbarians are assessed in order to distinguish whether they are couched in physical or genetic terms or whether the distinctions drawn are ethical or cultural in nature.
10 Although see the noticeably guarded comments in Edith Hall (1989: 75–6). For retrospective comment on the line adopted in this earlier (seminal) work, see Edith Hall (2006).
11 The idea that ethnography must necessarily take the form of *scientific* prose is itself a reflection of ideas which became entrenched from the Enlightenment era onwards.
12 This association has become the mainstay of work by scholars and activists seeking to address race and racism contemporary society.
13 Cf. McCoskey (2012: 24 and 25–6). For related discussion, see Cartledge (1993) and Harrison (2020).
14 Similar arguments are presented in summary form in Harrison (2020).
15 Although see repeated references to Frantz Fanon, including the memorable 'Shame. Shame and self-contempt. Nausea' (Fanon [1967] 1986: 116, quoted in Harrison 2020: 154).
16 For background and related discussion, see Braund (2011) and Lewis (2018).
17 See Schlaifer (1936) in reference to 'pan-Hellenic nationalism' (e.g. at 165); also Garlan (1987). For the status of helots as privately owned slaves, see Lewis (2018: 125–46).
18 The degree to which these communities relied upon servile labour varied considerably, as David Lewis has argued (2018). See Hesiod *Works and Days* (405–9) where it is anticipated that a farmer of even modest means should possess an ox and a female slave. Not being able to afford a slave to undertake craft production on your behalf was indicative of the meanest of livings (Lysias 24.6), although this does not discount domestic help. It is likewise implied that a citizen wife might expect a slave girl to assist her in household chores (Theophrastus, *Characters* 22.10). The number of slaves employed in Attica appears to have been quite considerable in the light of Thucydides' claim (7.27.5) that twenty thousand took advantage of the disruption caused by the Spartan occupation of Dekeleia to seek their freedom. Xenophon informs us that one of the wealthiest men of his day, Nicias, owned a thousand slaves who were leased for an obol a day to fellow Athenians (*Ways and Means* 4.14).
19 Even here, however, there was considerable scope for variation between the slave systems which operated in different regions of Greece as recent scholarship has shown. See Lewis (2018).

20 For discussion surrounding the origins of the term together with the argument that the Greeks' ethnographic thought and self-conception reflects Persian influence, see Kim (2013).
21 Indeed, it has recently been argued that a high proportion of popular ethnographic knowledge was related in some way to slave-ownership. See Harrison (2019); see also McCoskey in this volume for discussion of the emergence of the Greek/barbarian polarity as a result of external stimuli (the Persian Wars). For related discussion, see also E. Hall (2006), Vlassopoulos (2013a) and Harrison (2020: 154–5). Estimates vary as to the number of slaves who might have been employed in an Athenian household. For their likely origins and links between naming and origins, see Lewis (2018: 97).
22 See, for example, Aristotle, *Politics* 1254a14–18; 1254b27–33. See, however, Vlassopoulos (2011).
23 The same might reasonably be inferred from the rather more sustained musings of Aristotle himself.
24 In a similar vein, see Kennedy (2014) and Kasimis (2018).
25 For related discussion, see Hunt (2015) and Vlassopoulos (2010a).
26 For the Leoxos Stele, see *SEG* 49 619. Recovered during excavations of the necropolis at Olbia in 1895 the fragmentary stele is dedicated to a Leoxos, son of Molpagoras who died far from home (according to an accompanying epigram). Side A depicts the torso and upper thigh of a young nude male leaning on a spear. Side B consists of a figure in rider costume (long-sleeved jerkin over trousers with gorytus slung at the hip), facing left, examining an arrow for straightness. For the various ways in which the imagery has been interpreted, see Skinner (2012: 172–5). Invaluable discussion of both the stele and its wider funerary context are provided by Petersen (2010: 73–4). Cf. Vinogradov (1997). For 'Scythians' in Athens, see Miller (1991, 1997), Ivantchik (2005), Lissarrague (1990, 2002) and Bäbler (1998, 2005). For discussion of Dio's (somewhat fanciful) description of an encounter with an Olbiapolitan, see Bäbler (2007).
27 If the 'Old Oligarch' is to be believed there was scope for some confusion here as to who was who. For a markedly positive assessment of these 'free spaces', see Vlassopoulos (2007a).
28 Tuplin observes that 'there may be a sort of political correctness' in play 'which wishes to extend the stigma of "racism" to as many phenomena as possible' (1999: 47). For related discussion, see Harrison (2020). If allusions to Spartan xenophobia (Thucydides 2.39) are anything to go by then this is conceived as something referring to freeborn foreigners as opposed to slaves (cf. Herodotus 1.65).
29 See, for example, a forensic discussion as to whether ethical or physiognomical differences are being noted in Tuplin (1999: 53). For critique, see Isaac (2004: 69n54).
30 See, for example, Tuplin (1999) where he argues 'Racism flourishes best where clear physiological criteria define a single target' (53).
31 In other cases where the use of racism has been approved the effect is muted by subsequent use of less overtly charged terminology, for example Kim (2009: 10), followed by a switch to 'ethnocentrism'. Cf. Vlassopoulos: 'polarised representations of non-Greeks as an incarnation of everything that was different and opposed to the values and customs that the Greeks held dear … often reach the point of being xenophobic and jingoistic, and even similar, in some ways, to modern racism' (2013a: 35). Almost but not quite.
32 Harrison states: 'it seems possible at times that we are setting a threshold for ancient prejudice that would be difficult to meet in any environment – as if we were in a court process engineered for acquittal' (2020: 153).
33 Recognizing the structural inequalities which pervade modern society is key, DiAngelo (2018) argues, if we are to work towards a more just society. The impossibility of extricating

ourselves from our historical context means we can only ever be anti-racist as opposed to being free of racism entirely.

34 See, for example, the airline passenger who subjected their neighbour to an abusive tirade or the owners of Boone's Camp Event Hall in Booneville, Mississippi, who refused to rent their venue for weddings between mixed-race couples ('Ryanair Flight Rant Man Says He Is "not a racist"' 2018; 'Mississippi Wedding Venue Refuses Interracial Pair Over Owner's Christian Faith' 2019).

35 For discussion, see Harrison (2020: 152–3).

36 Against the backdrop of current moves to decolonize the curriculum or adopt an anti-racist position in an attempt to address white privilege it becomes reasonable to question if it is in anyone's interests for such distinctions to be upheld.

37 Depictions of boys/men being devoured by crocodiles include a rhyton by the Sotades Painter c. 460 BCE (Dresden 364; ARV² 764/11) whose main figure is characterized as a Pygmy by Lissarrague (2002: 106). Cf. an Apulian red-figured plastic rhyton from Capua, c. 340 BCE (British Museum GR 1873.8–20.268; Cat. Vases F 417). For discussion, see Lissarrague (2002: 101–10). Scholarly responses to the question of race/racism in antiquity bear comparison with tendencies linked to 'white fragility' by Robin DiAngelo: defensive posturing, the tendency to think about racism in the strictly binary terms of good/evil; see DiAngelo (2018: ch. 5). For Ethiopians in Greek art, discussed further below, see the seminal work by Frank Snowden (1970, 1983 and 1997), together with Wyk Smith (2009) and Bindman and Gates (2010).

38 The choice of ethnic may well have been significant insofar as Lydians were proverbially 'soft', so much so that Herodotus (1.155) had to adduce an anecdote in order to explain how the kingdom which once harried the Greek cities of Asia Minor subsequently became a vassal state. The latter relates a historically improbable intervention by the deposed monarch Croesus in an attempt to prevent the Lydians' annihilation following a revolt. The Lydians are banned from carrying weapons, encouraged to engage in retail and adopt new costumes. Elsewhere (1.93–4) it is related that they have resorted to prostituting their daughters.

39 For discussion, see Harris (2004). See, however, Harrison (2019) for the suggestion that individual slaves might have contributed to Greek constructions of the world (53). For arguments in a similar vein, although somewhat rose-tinted, see Mayor, Colarusso and Saunders (2014).

40 For related discussion, see Marshall (2013).

41 Hinted at perhaps in *Airs Waters Places* when discussing the fertility rates of Scythian women (21–2). See Harrison (2019: 42).

42 Wade argues: 'Racial discourses can and do create and impose fixity and a key element in this strategy is an appeal to the realm of nature. However, racial discourses make this appeal in subtle and changeable ways. We need to explore what is involved in an appeal to nature and to grasp the diversity of naturalising arguments' (2002: 15).

43 Study of the *Iliad* led Hilary Mackie to identify two opposing speech-cultures reflecting differences in genre, style, civic function and linguistic orientation; see Mackie (1996). Haubold has since critiqued this work on the grounds that 'the traits she [Mackie] uncovers are so subtle as to confirm my point, which is that though differences exist, they do not become overt markers of cultural identity' (2014: 21n13).

44 See Harrison (2019) for the suggestion that 'academic' ethnography sometimes found itself in dialogue with the 'popular' ethnographic knowledge of slavers/their clients (44). For the idea of a wider (i.e. popular) ethnographic discourse together with Herodoean engagement with contemporary audiences, see Skinner (2012, 2018).

45 Cf. a third-century account of Boeotia by Heracleides Kritikos in which blonde-haired and ruddy-faced people are attested at settlements such as Anthedon and Thebes (BNJ 369A F1. 19, 24).
46 This despite nuanced treatment of the iconography of Athenian vase painting. Such 'iconographic stereotypes' are juxtaposed with the experience of a high degree of physical diversity within modern populations.
47 Examples include the celebrated Aristonothos Krater, mid-seventh century BCE. Side A: Naval engagement involving two vessels of different design; Side B: Odysseus and his men blinding Polyphemus. Inv. Ca 172. Rome, Capitoline Museum. See also a Middle Protoattic neck amphora from Eleusis. H. 1.42 metres, c.650 BCE and a crater from Argos: Fr. Argos C149. H. 24.5, 675-650 BCE. Cf. Laconian cup by the Rider Painter. Paris, Cals. Med. 190. W. 21.4; (484) Pseudo Chalcidian neck amphora from Vulchi. Polyphemus group, London B154, H. 30. For further examples dating to the sixth to early fifth centuries BCE, see *LIMC* (s.v. 'Kyklops'). Also, Aristotle, *Politics* 1253a1–9.
48 The idea of Egyptians' reliance on the Nile waters to irrigate their crops appears to have made a great impression on Greeks accustomed to eking out a rather more precarious existence on the thin and stony soils of regions such as the Argolid or the islands. Reliance on Zeus, reported comments of priests (2.13), bountiful harvests, reliance on the river, and Egyptianness are inextricably linked as demonstrated by Herodotus' tale as to what happened when the citizens of Apis and Marea consulted the oracle of Ammon (2.18). For discussion, see Harrison (2003).
49 For polarity in the *Histories*, see Hartog (1988) together with Dewald (1990), a review of Hartog. For polarity in Greek thought in general, see Lloyd (1966).
50 For discussion and further references, see Harrison (2019: 53). For the bases upon which individuals might be identified, see Lee (2015).
51 It has become something of a rallying call among more progressive elements within classical scholarship for historical productions to be grounded in actual, lived experience, for example Vlassopoulos (2007b: 236).
52 Vessels 400 and 401 are listed by Robinson as coming from the same dwelling (Rooms e and b in House A vi 9). See Robinson (1933: 103–4). For the site in general, see Cahill (2002).
53 For the trefoil-spouted variant depicted in Figure 2.2 (vessel no. 408 in Robinson IV) cf. vessels 406–407 in Robinson IV; vessel 403 in Robinson VII; vessels 414 (in Room k of Villa of Good Fortune) and 415 in Robinson XIV. Vessels 400–401 in Robinson VII and vessels 413, 416 in Robinson XIV have likewise been linked to the same mould.
54 Eurybates, a companion of Odysseus, is described as black-skinned and woolly haired (Homer, *Odyssey* 19.246–7); see Murray in this volume on how translators work with this passage. The Hesiodic *Catalogue* also links Ethiopians to Africa as progenitor of the Libyans, Pygmies and 'Melanes' – again suggestive of negritude (Frag. 150, 17–19). Cf. Hesiod, *Theogony* 984–5 and Xenophanes (Frag. 16) on anthropomorphic conceptions of the divine.
55 Pseudo-Hesiod groups Ethiopians with Libyans and Scythians as men 'whose mind is superior to their tongue' (alongside 'black-skinned men', 'subterranean men' and 'the strengthless pygmies' (Hesiod, Frag. 97 14–15).
56 Memnon is the subject of a lost epic called the *Aithiopis* (a sequel to the *Iliad* in which Achilles avenges the former's killing of Antilochus, son of Nestor; cf. Homer, *Odyssey* 4.187–8).
57 For discussion including the verbal play of long-bowed/long-lived, see Irwin (2014).
58 Derbew cites the labelling of museum displays or print publications such as Lissarrague (2002: 109).

NOTES 183

59 Cf. Robinson: 'The Olynthian sat in his bath while his slave, perhaps a negro like those of whom we found in this house two terra-cotta representations, poured water over him in a kind of shower bath' (1930: 47).

Chapter 3

1 My deep thanks to Denise McCoskey, Toni Sacco and Phillip Webster.
2 Ancient religious practices also structured daily and local life in ways that could mark one by status (free or enslaved, citizen or not), sex (male or female) or relation to a household, profession or city.
3 Aryan/Semite plays a significant role within Orientalism (and its structuring binary of 'east' and 'west'; cf. Said 1978).
4 For example, during the Babylonian Empire and its immediate aftermath with the rise of the Persian Empire, sixth to fourth century BCE; during the Hellenistic period in the second half of the second century BCE; or during the fourth century CE.
5 Although legally permitted to follow Jewish law, some wrote Jewish marriage contracts that appeal instead to local customs. See Cotton (2013: 209–15).

Chapter 4

1 For discussion of the question, see Gruen (2011a), Isaac (2004) and McCoskey (2012).
2 Snowden (1970 and 1983) and Thompson (1989) are pathbreaking studies on the depiction of skin colour in Greek and Roman antiquity. For criticism of the common view that there was little skin-colour based prejudice in antiquity, see Goldenberg (2009).
3 For a recent survey of modern racial science, see Saini (2019).
4 For discussion of the intellectual context, see Müller (1972–80) and Thomas (2000: 75–101).
5 For a good introduction to the Hippocratic corpus, see Jouanna (1999) and Nutton (2004: 53–71).
6 For early Greek views of geography, see Romm (1992: 9–44); and focusing on the schema in *Airs, Waters, Places*, see Thomas (2000: 86–98).
7 I print the edition of the text by Jouanna (1996). Translations are by Chadwick and Mann (1983), with modifications.
8 For further discussion of the notion of environmental sympathy at play here, see Sassi (2001: 109–10).
9 For popular Greek stereotypes of non-Greeks in this period, see Hall (1989: esp. 79–84 and 102–13).
10 For a different line of interpretation that sees the polarity of Asia and Europe in the text as motivated by the author's aim of explaining the Greek victory in the Persian Wars on the basis of Greek superiority, see Backhaus (1976) and Jouanna (1996: 70–1). For critical discussion, see Gruen (2011a: 39n168) and, especially, Thomas (2000: 90–101).
11 For comparison of the division of the world in Aristotle and in *Airs, Waters, Places*, see Stazsak (1995).
12 For the idea that Greece and, more particularly yet, Athens has an exceptionally well-mixed climate, see Isocrates, *Areopagiticus* 74 and Plato, *Timaeus* 24c2–7.
13 For the significance of 'the mean' (τὸ μέσον) in Aristotelian ethics, see, for example, *Nicomachean Ethics* 2.2, 1104a11–26; 2.6, 1106a24–11067a7; *Eudemian Ethics* 2.3, 1220b1–35. For discussion of the Aristotleian notion of the mean in its intellectual context, see Tracy (1969).

14 For discussion of Aristotle's concept of natural slavery, see Schofield (1999) and Heath (2008).
15 For discussion of Aristotle's anti-slavery opponents, see Cambiano (1987).
16 For discussion of the role of Aristotle's biological works in underlying his ethnographic division of the world and his account of natural slavery, see especially the groundbreaking, recent work by Mariska Leunissen (2012, 2017).
17 For discussion of the reception of Aristotle in the Arabic tradition, see Alwishah and Hayes (2015) and Peters (1968). For analysis of the portrayal of Aristotle in the thirteenth-century Arabic illustrated text *Kitab Na't al-hayawan* (*Book of the Characteristics of Animals*), see Contadini (2012), who argues that the text depicts Aristotle with dark skin in order to highlight both his status as a non-Arab and as a wise man (75–7).
18 For a more detailed defense of this point, see Lloyd (1983: 22–3, 26–35, and esp. 32–3), Leunissen (2017: 26–31) and Sassi (2001: 117–18).
19 This comparison is developed in greater detail in Sassi (2001: 114–18) and Leunissen (2017: 45–8).
20 For discussion of the Pseudo-Aristotelian *Problems*, see Flashar (1983); for the ethnographic material in Book Fourteen, in particular, see Leunissen (2015).
21 For recent discussion of modern scientific racism, see Marks (2017), Saini (2019) and Sussman (2014). It is worth noting that Marks denies that there is any correlate to modern scientific racism in the ancient world on the grounds that they interpreted the variation between different groups of people 'in local, not continental, terms' (2017: 29). As we have seen, it is very difficult to maintain this thesis in light of the evidence from *Airs, Waters, Places* and Aristotle's ethnographic views.
22 For the influence of Aristotle's notion of natural slavery on defences of slavery after the discovery of the Americas, see Hanke (1959) and Lupher (2003). For the use of Aristotle's concept of 'natural slavery' in defense of slavery in the United States, see Campbell (1974) and Monoson (2011).
23 It is worth noting that while Aristotle did not focus much on appearance in his broad distinction between Greeks, Europeans and Asians, he does discuss the relationship of a person's appearance to their intellectual and ethical capacities elsewhere in his corpus; see, for instance, *History of Animals* 1.8, 491b11–14. For Aristotle's relationship to the post-classical physiognomic tradition, see Boys-Stones (2007) and Leunissen (2017: 66–77).
24 For a survey of the history and development of physiognomy, see Boys-Stones (2007) and Foerster (1893).
25 For discussion of Polemon's physiognomics and its intellectual context, see Barton (1994: 95–131) and Swain (2007a). References and translation of the Leiden Polemon are from the Arabic edition and English translation by Hoyland (2007).
26 For discussion of the authorship of the *Physigonomics*, see Vogt (1999) and Boys-Stones (2007).
27 For a good survey of the role of ethnicity in each of the extent physiognomic treatises, see Goldman (2016).
28 For physiognomic discussion of skin colour, see Leiden Polemon B33; Adamantius B31 and 33; Anon. Lat. 79; and Pseudo-Aristotle, *Physiognomics* 812a11–25.
29 For physiognomic discussion of hair type and hair colour, see Leiden Polemon B37; Adamantius B37; Anon. Lat. 14 and 73; and Pseudo-Aristotle, *Physiognomics* 806b6–18 and 812b30–1.
30 It is worth noting here that while, in the extant Arabic translation of his text, Polemon attributes reddish white skin and moderate red hair to the ideal Greek type, in the

parallel passages of Adamantius' Greek text, Adamantius uses the expressions 'rather pale' (ὑπόξανθος) (B33) and again 'gently rather pale' (πράως ὑπόξανθος) (B37) to describe the skin and hair colour, respectively, of the pure Greek. Given Adamantius's deep indebtedness to Polemon's *Physiognomy*, it thus seems not unlikely that in the Greek original of Polemon's text, Polemon, like Adamantius, described the pure Greek as having ὑπόξανθος as opposed to 'reddish' skin and hair. For the complicated connotations of 'reddish' skin in Republican and Imperial literature, see Bradley (2009: esp. 150–9). For discussion of Adamantius's *Physiognomy*, and its debt to Polemon's *Physiognomy*, see Foerster (1893: 1.c–cxxiii).

31 By contrast, Polemon argues that the red/white hair of Slavs and Turks indicates stupidity, while excessively red hair indicates a lack of modesty (B37).

32 The physiognomic handbooks include discussion of race both in chapters focused on racial difference – for instance, Polemon's *Physiognomy* includes distinct chapters on the people of the North, the South, and the East and West (B31), as well as on the Greeks (B32) – and in chapters focused on skin colour and hair colour and type.

33 I print the translation of Adamantius's *Physiognomy* by Repath (2007a).

34 For discussion, see Goldman (2016: 69–70).

35 The physiognomic handbooks were, to be sure, aware of this sort of difficulty and made some efforts to counter it by applying limitations to the use of physiognomy – see, for example, the discussion of Pseudo-Aristotle, *Physiognomics* 805a33–b10 on the difficulty of distinguishing between characteristic and merely temporary expressions of emotional dispositions. Nevertheless, short of providing a detailed causal account of the link between the features they identify and the traits they take them to express, their available responses to such an objection were quite limited.

36 For a good, recent biography of Galen that discusses his cultural, medical and philosophical context, see Mattern (2013).

37 For Galen's detailed and entertaining classification of eye type, see *Art of Medicine* 9, 1.329–32 Kühn.

38 For a good discussion of Galen's theory of mixtures, see van der Eijk (2015) and Singer and van der Eijk (2018).

39 Galen also discusses Polykleitos' canon in a number of other texts, each time appealing to the remarkable symmetry of its parts: see, for example, *On The Function of the Parts of the Body* 4.248, 4.352 Kühn; *Art of Medicine* 1.343 Kühn; *On the Doctrines of Hippocrates and Plato* 5.3.15–6 De Lacy. For discussion of his use of Polykleitos's Canon both in *Mixtures* and throughout his corpus, see van der Eijk (2014) and Pigeaud (1995). For a survey of the extensive interschool philosophical use of Polykleitos, see Boys-Stones (2009).

40 For the particular importance of touch, see *Mixtures* 1.9, 563–4 and 567–8 Kühn.

41 For instance, in *Capacities of the Soul*, Galen even argues that popular stereotypes about the environmentally determined differences between Northerners, Southerners, and 'well-mixed' (εὔκρατος) Greeks offer 'secure proofs' (βέβαιαι ἀποδέξεις) that the capacities of the soul depend on the particular mixture of the body: see *QAM* 4.805 Kühn.

42 For a good example of Galen's use of his theory of mixtures in his physiological accounts see the discussion in his *Art of Medicine* of the different mixtures of the heart and their quite detailed physiological and psychological implications, which catalogues all eight of the 'defective' mixtures described above: see *Art of Medicine* 10–11, 1.331–733 Kühn and, for discussion, von Staden (2012).

Chapter 7

1. One flaw of Aristotleian logic is that it relies on exclusive binary opposites for definition and catergorization. So, a woman is defined as not man; the enslaved are defined as not free. See Aristotle's *Politics* and his *Poetics*. Recent scholarship on artificial intelligence (AI) points to Aristotleian binary philosophies as the source of bias (implicit and overt) in AI.
2. For an example of the concept of 'creolization' applied in ancient studies, see Webster (2001).
3. I prefer this term to 'Greeks'. As Whitmarsh and Thomson state, 'Ancient Greece was not a nation state. Authoritative delineations of identity were impossible in an environment with no passports, where citizenship was tied to cities rather than countries' (2013: 5).
4. For a good discussion of these myths of racial origins, see J. Hall (1997: esp. ch. 3).
5. For more information on Aspasia, see Henry (1995); for metic women, see Kennedy (2014).
6. Much of this resonates with the treatment of enslaved Americans of African descent. Given the classical education of the men who constructed the parameters of slavery in the United States, this is hardly coincidental.
7. For more information on Helot women, see Ogden (1995).
8. This was the sexist role ascribed to Black women in the Black nationalist agenda of the 1960s and 1970s.
9. For further information on Spartan and Helot women, see Pomeroy (2002).
10. Cilicia was the south coastal region of Asia Minor and evidence of it as a political entity can be found as far back as the Hittite era (1600–717 BCE). It became a Roman province in 67 BCE and its capital city, Tarsus, remains famous for the meeting between Cleopatra VII and Marc Antony in 41 BCE.
11. In terms of recent popular culture and earlier reception studies, the moniker 'children of the sun' and its variants has long been associated with the peoples of Africa. In antiquity, Hellenic authors noted the special relationship between Ethiopia and the Hellenic gods. In the *Works and Days*, Hesiod remarks that, in the winter, Helios retreated to the 'peoples and homes of Black men' (line 527). Homer mentions Ethiopia twice in the *Iliad* and three times in the *Odyssey*. Interestingly, here, it is a favourite haunt of Poseidon and not Helios.
12. This is a common trope for Euripides. See Hippoltyus's diatribe against women in the *Hippolytus*, lines 616–67.
13. For the skin colour 'norm' for the Romans, see the introduction to the chapter.
14. For ancient sources on Cleopatra, see Jones (2006). For the condemnation of Cleopatra by Octavian, see the fabricated speech of Octavian from Cassius Dio in Jones (2006: 136–40).
15. Recall that bees figure prominently in characterizations of women and women's work in Semonides of Amorgos and Xenophon's *Oeconomicus*.
16. The Punic form of the name is *Saphanba'al*; the modern English form tends towards *Sophonisba*. The Roman tradition (as given by Livy) is *Sophoniba*, which will be used here. For more on Livy's portrayal, see also Haley (1989b, 1990).
17. For a discussion of the *Moretum* in scholarship, see Haley (2009: esp. 43–6).
18. The translation is mine. It is important to note that most translations of this piece have been done by men influenced by stereotypical descriptions of the physiognomy of African women. Consequently, I have deliberately made my rendering as Black feminist and empowering as the Latin will allow.
19. Most contemporary physical anthropologists reject both the ideology and determinants of 'scientific races'.

20 I have transcribed the graffito as it appears in *CIL*. The author seems to have known her/his Ovid; note these lines from Ovid:

> Luctantur pectusque leve in contraria tendunt
> Hac amor hac odium, sed puto, vincit amor.
> *Odero, si potero; si non, invitus amabo.*
>
> (*Amores* 3.11b. 33–5; my emphasis)

> Love and Hate struggle over my fickle heart and pull it
> Love in one direction Hate in the other – but Love, I think, is winning.
> *I would hate, if I could; if not, I will love unwilling.*

Chapter 8

1 For a collection of the racist objections to the series, see Ball et al. (2018a, b, c, d).
2 See Kaufman in this volume; see also Whitmarsh (2018).
3 Racecraft as a way of understanding the social construction of race is fully developed by Fields and Fields ([2012] 2014).
4 For scholars whose approaches to race take physical difference as the primary engine of racism and race construction, see Snowden (1970, 1983); Wiesen (1970); Watts (1976); Thompson (1989); and Goldenberg (2009). I reject this approach as a species of nineteenth century bio-racism, see Fields and Fields ([2012] 2014: 25–74).
5 I use the phrase Celluloid Classical World, which alludes to the 1995 documentary film *The Celluloid Closet: Homosexuality in the Movies* that examined the representation of the LGBTQ experience in film.
6 On *lieux de mémoire*, see Nora (1989); also relevant is Boym (2001).
7 For discussion of the film industry's history with race, see hooks (2009); for the representation of ancient slavery, see Hall, Alston and McConnell (2011).
8 The Jim Crow era began after the Civil War and ended in 1968 with civil rights legislation. 'The legal construct of separate-but-equal segregated government services – which would define the long era of Jim Crow in the twentieth century – had not yet been clearly established' (Blackmon 2009: 86).
9 On the transformation to colour-blind racism, see Bonilla-Silva (2001, 2006).
10 See Adler (2016) and Zuckerberg (2018); for recent discussions of the complicity of Classics as a discipline in maintaining a White supremacist vision of the ancient Greeks and Romans, see Dugan (2019, 2020) and Bostick (2020).
11 Fredrickson (2002); Painter (2010); Allen (2012); Battalora (2013); and Kendi (2016); on the role of Classics, see Richard (2009) and Barnard (2018).
12 For example Davis (1983); Bell (1992); Sidanius and Pratto (1999); Reed (2000); Bonilla-Silva (2001, 2006); Frederickson (2002); Isaac (2004); Haley (2009); Painter (2010); Allen (2012); Fields and Fields ([2012] 2014); McCoskey (2012); Battalora (2013); Taylor (2013) DiAngelo (2018); and Kendi (2019).
13 I develop the concepts of alienable and alienated humanity from human rights theory and philosophy: notably John Locke's theory of natural rights; for how it relates to race and slavery in colonial America, see Glausser (1990); Sanders and Adams (2004); and Farr (2008); on dehumanization, see Smith (2012).
14 Fields and Fields discuss sumptuary codes, kinship restrictions, centring and ritual deference ([2012] 2014: 25–74).
15 See Bradley (2000) and Joshel (2014); for a different view of monstrification, see Garland (2016). An example of monstrification is the association in the media of white skin with beauty and black skin with ugliness.

16 For example, Jim Crow laws that excluded Blacks from the more comfortable Whites-only car on a train, but allowed Whites to ride in the Black car.
17 Anti-miscegenation laws that prevent interracial marriage are obvious kinship restrictions.
18 For example, centring often occurs when social justice groups that are trying to help racialized communities fall into a White savior complex that takes the focus of attention away from the experience of the oppressed group and puts it squarely on the dominant group.
19 An example of ritual deference is the societal expectation in pre-independence Jamaica that Black adults address a White child as 'Miss' or 'Master', whereas they themselves would be addressed as 'boy' or 'girl'.
20 Still the best discussion of sexual asymmetry and race is Davis (1983). An example of sexual asymmetry would be slaves having no legal or moral recourse when raped by their master.
21 See Zuchtriegel (2018) on the archeological evidence for a subaltern group in most Greek colonies.
22 All translations are my own, unless otherwise indicated.
23 Dougherty (1999) offers an interesting reading of the Cyclops as a parody of Odyssean ethnography.
24 Cf. Samuels (2015) who suggests avoiding 'black skin' so as not to trigger modern racial associations. See also Haley (2009).

Chapter 9

1 Conversations with Princeton undergraduates in my Citizenships Ancient and Modern class first sparked in my mind the resemblance of the hoodie on the cover of Claudia Rankine's *Citizen* (2014) to a hoplite helmet; I have held on to that elective affinity ever since, in defiance of the neo-Nazi obsession with hoplite iconography (Mac Sweeney et al. 2019: 2–6). For their inspiration, I thank my students. For reading and commenting on this chapter, I thank Patrice Rankine and Mathura Umachandran; for affording me the space and the creative liberty to try out some of the ideas in this chapter, Shane Butler and the Department of Classics at Johns Hopkins University, and Caroline Stark and the Department of Classics at Howard University; for sending me a timely PDF, Sarah Derbew; and finally, for years of edifying conversation and collaboration, Sasha-Mae Eccleston.

BIBLIOGRAPHY

Adhikari, Mohamed (2005), *Not White Enough, Not Black Enough: Racial Identity in the South African Coloured Community*, Cape Town: Double Storey.
Adler, Eric (2016), *Classics, the Culture Wars, and Beyond*, Ann Arbor: University of Michigan Press.
Ahmed, Sara (2013), 'Making Feminist Points', *Feministkilljoys*, 11 September. Available online: https://feministkilljoys.com/2013/09/11/making-feminist-points/ (accessed 21 June 2019).
Ahmed, Sara (2017), *Living a Feminist Life*, Durham, NC: Duke University Press.
Ahmed, Siraj (2018), *Archaeology of Babel: The Colonial Foundation of the Humanities*, Stanford, CA: Stanford University Press.
Akrigg, Ben (2015), 'Metics in Athens', in Claire Taylor and Kostas Vlassopoulos (eds), *Communities and Networks in the Ancient Greek* World, 155–76, Oxford: Oxford University Press.
al-Azmeh, Aziz (2014), *The Emergence of Islam in Late Antiquity: Allāh and His People*, Cambridge: Cambridge University Press.
Alcoff, Linda Martín (2006), *Visible Identities: Race, Gender, and the Self*, Oxford: Oxford University Press.
Allen, Lindsay (2005), *The Persian Empire: A History*, London: The British Museum Press.
Allen, Theodore W. (2012), *The Invention of the White Race*, vol. 2, *The Origin of Racial Oppression in Anglo-America*, 2nd edn, Brooklyn, NY: Verso Books.
Alston, Richard (1995), *Soldier and Society in Roman Egypt: A Social History*, London: Routledge.
Alwishah, Ahmed, and Josh Hayes, eds (2015), *Aristotle and the Arabic Tradition*, Cambridge: Cambridge University Press.
Anderson, Carol (2016), *White Rage: The Unspoken Truth of Our Racial Divide*, New York: Bloomsbury Publishing.
Ando, Clifford (2000), *Imperial Ideology and Provincial Loyalty*, Berkeley: University of California Press.
Andrade, Nathanael J. (2013), *Syrian Identity in the Greco-Roman World*, Cambridge: Cambridge University Press.
Andre, Jacques, ed. (1981), *Traite de physiognomonie: Anonyme latin*, Paris: Les Belles Lettres.
Angel, J. Lawrence (1946), 'Race, Type, and Ethnic Group in Ancient Greece', *Human Biology*, 18 (1): 1–32.
Anidjar, Gil (2008), *Semites: Race, Religion, Literature*, Stanford, CA: Stanford University Press.
Armstrong, Caroline H. (2015), 'The Two Non-Blue Amuns of the Shrine of Taharqa at Kawa', *Journal of Egyptian Archaeology*, 101: 177–95.
Ashton, Sally-Ann (2008), *Cleopatra and Egypt*, Oxford: Wiley-Blackwell.
Bâ, Saër Maty (2011), 'Diegetic Masculinities: Reading the Black Body in Epic Cinema', in Robert Burgoyne (ed.), *The Epic Film in Worlds Culture*, 346–74, New York: Routledge.

Bäbler, Balbina (1998), *Fleissige Thrakerinnen und wehrhafte Skythen: Nichtgriechen im klassichen Athen und ihre archäologische Hinterlassenschaft*, Stuttgart: Teubner.

Bäbler, Balbina (2005), 'Bobbies or Boobies? The Scythian Police Force in Classical Athens', in David Braund (ed.), *Scythians and Greeks: Cultural Interactions in Scythia, Athens and the Early Roman Empire (Sixth Century BC–First Century AD)*, 122–44, Exeter: Exeter University Press.

Bäbler, Balbina (2007), 'Dio Chrysostom's Construction of Olbia', in David Braund and S. D. Kryzhitskiy (eds), *Classical Olbia and the Scythian World: From the Sixth Century BC to the Second Century AD*, Proceedings of the British Academy 142, 145–60, Oxford: Oxford University Press.

Backhaus, Wilhelm (1976), 'Der Hellenen-Barbaren-Gegensatz und die hippokratische Schrift περὶ ἀέρων ὑδάτων τόπων', *Historia*, 25: 170–85.

Badian, Ernst (1958), 'Alexander the Great and the Unity of Mankind', *Historia*, 7: 425–44.

Bahrani, Zainab (2006), 'Race and Ethnicity in Ancient Mesopotamia', *World Archaeology*, 38 (1): 48–59.

Baker, Cynthia M. (2017), *Jew*, New Brunswick, NJ: Rutgers University Press.

Baker, Cynthia M. (2009), '"From Every Nation Under Heaven": Jewish Ethnicities in the Roman World', in Laura Nasrallah and Elizabeth Schüssler Fiorenza (eds), *Prejudice and Christian Beginnings: Investigating Race, Gender and Ethnicity in Early Christian studies*, 79–99, Minneapolis, MN: Fortress Press.

Bal, Mieke (2018), 'Let's Abolish the Peer-Review System', *Media Theory*, 3 September. Available online: http://mediatheoryjournal.org/mieke-bal-lets-abolish-the-peer-review-system/ (accessed 19 June 2019).

Ball, Siobhan, et al. (2018a), 'Further Racist Backlash against "Black Achilles"', *Pharos: Doing Justice to the Classics*, 6 April. Available online: http://pages.vassar.edu/pharos/2018/04/06/further-racist-backlash-against-black-achilles/ (accessed 22 June 2020).

Ball, Siobhan, et al. (2018b), 'Scholars Respond to Racist Backlash against Black Achilles, Part 1: Ancient Greek Attitudes toward Africans', *Pharos: Doing Justice to the Classics*, 11 May. Available online: http://pages.vassar.edu/pharos/2018/05/11/scholars-respond-to-racist-backlash-against-black-achilles-part-1-ancient-greek-attitudes-toward-africans/ (accessed 22 June 2020).

Ball, Siobhan, et al. (2018c), 'Scholars Respond to Racist Backlash against Black Achilles, Part 2: What Did Achilles Look Like?', *Pharos: Doing Justice To The Classics*, 18 May. Available online: http://pages.vassar.edu/pharos/2018/05/18/scholars-respond-to-racist-backlash-against-black-achilles-part-2-what-did-achilles-look-like (accessed 22 June 2020).

Ball, Siobhan, et al. (2018d), 'Scholars Respond to Racist Backlash against Black Achilles, Part 3: What Makes a Homeric Hero a Hero?', *Pharos: Doing Justice To The Classics*, 25 May. Available online: http://pages.vassar.edu/pharos/2018/05/25/scholars-respond-to-racist-backlash-against-black-achilles-part-3-what-makes-a-homeric-hero-a-hero/ (accessed 22 June 2020).

Balsdon, J. P. V. D. (1979), *Romans and Aliens*, London: Duckworth.

Barnard, John Levi (2014), 'Ruins Amidst Ruins: Black Classicism and the Empire of Slavery', *American Literature*, 86 (2): 361–89.

Barnard, John Levi (2018), *Empire of Ruin*, New York: Oxford University Press.

Barton, Carlin A., and Daniel Boyarin (2016), *Imagine No Religion: How Modern Abstractions Hide Ancient Realities*, New York: Fordham University Press.

Barton, Tamsyn S. (1994), *Power and Knowledge: Astrology, Physiognomics, and Medicine under the Roman Empire*, Ann Arbor, MI: University of Michigan Press.

Bartsch, Shadi (1989), *Decoding the Greek Novel: The Reader and the Role of Description in Heliodorus and Achilles Tacitus*, Princeton, NJ: University of Princeton Press.

Battalora, Jacqueline (2013), *Birth of a White Nation: The Invention of White People and Its Relevance Today*, New York: Strategic Book Publishing and Rights Agency.

Beard, Mary (2007), *The Roman Triumph*, Cambridge, MA: Harvard University Press.

Beard, Mary (2019), 'What is Classics?', *Society of Classical Studies Sesquicentennial Public Lecture*, 5 January. Available online: https://classicalstudies.org/annual-meeting/2019/150/sesquicentennial-public-lecture-mary-beard (accessed 19 June 2019).

Beard, Mary, John North and Simon Price (1998a), *The Religions of Rome*, vol. 1, *A History*, Cambridge: Cambridge University Press.

Beard, Mary, John North and Simon Price (1998b), *The Religions of Rome*, vol. 2, *A Sourcebook*, Cambridge: Cambridge University Press.

Beardsley, Grace Hadley (1929), *The Negro in Greek and Roman Civilization: A Study of the Ethiopian Type*, Baltimore, MD: Johns Hopkins University Press.

Bedrick, Theodore (1949–50), 'The Race of Athletes: A Picture of the Past', *Classical Journal*, 45: 136–8.

Beliso-De Jesús, Aisha M., and Jemima Pierre (2019), 'Introduction. Special Section: Anthropology of White Supremacy', *American Anthropologist*, 30 December. https://doi.org/10.1111/aman.13351.

Bell, Derrick (1992), *Faces at the Bottom of the Well: The Permanence of Racism*, New York: Perseus Books.

Berkowitz, Beth (2013), 'The Afterlives of Torah's Ethnic Language: The Sifra and Clement on Leviticus 18.1–5', in Natalie B. Dorhmann and Annette Yoshiko Reed (eds), *Jews, Christians, and the Roman Empire*, 29–42, Philadelphia: University of Pennsylvania Press.

Bernal, Martin (1987), *Black Athena: The Afroasiatic Roots of Classical Civilization*, vol. 1, *The Fabrication of Ancient Greece, 1785–1985*, New Brunswick, NJ: Rutgers University Press.

Bernal, Martin (1989), 'Classics in Crisis: An Outsider's View In', in Phyllis Culham and Lowell Edmunds (eds), *Classics: A Discipline and Profession in Crisis?*, 67–74, Lanham, MD: University Press of America.

Bernstein, Adam (2007), 'Frank Snowden', *The Washington Post*, 22 February. Available online: https://www.washingtonpost.com/archive/local/2007/02/22/frank-snowden/d7ec2527-95b5-41ff-96e8-fde26c08b1de/?utm_term=.ee05536a5607 (accessed 20 June 2019).

Berzon, Todd S. (2016), *Classifying Christians: Ethnography, Heresiology, and the Limits of Knowledge in Late Antiquity*, Berkeley: University of California Press.

Bindman, David, and Henry Louis Gates, eds (2010), *The Image of the Black in Western Art*, vol. 1, New edn, Cambridge, MA: Belknap Press of Harvard University Press.

Bintliff, John (2012), 'Are There Alternatives to "Red-Figure Vase People"? Identity, Multi-Ethnicity and Migration in Ancient Greece', in Gabriele Cifani and Simon Stoddart (eds), *Landscape, Ethnicity and Identity in the Archaic Mediterranean Area*, 51–63, Oxford: Oxbow Books.

Black Classicists: A Selection of Portraits from the Late 1800s and Early 1900s (2018), Curated by M. V. Ronnick, organized by C. Stark. Center for Hellenic Studies, Washington.

Blackmon, Douglas A. (2009), *Slavery by Another Name: The Re-Enslavement of Black Americans from the Civil War to World War II*, New York: Knopf Doubleday Publishing Group.

Blanshard, Alastair J. L., and Kim Shahabudin (2011), *Classics on Screen: Ancient Greece and Rome on Film*, London: Bristol Classical Press.

Blok, Josine H. (2005), 'Becoming Citizens: Some Notes on the Semantics of "citizen" in Archaic Greece and Classical Athens', *Klio*, 87 (1): 7–40.

Blok, Josine H. (2009), 'Gentrifying Genealogy: On the Genesis of the Athenian Autochthony Myth', in Ueli Dill, Fritz Graf and Christine Walde (eds), *Antike Mythen: Medien, Transformationen Und Konstruktionen; [Fritz Graf Zum 65. Geburtstag]*, 251–75, Berlin: de Gruyter.

Boak, A. E. R. (1917), 'The Present Status of the Problem of Races in the Prehistoric Aegean Basin', *Classical Journal*, 13 (1): 25–36.

Bond, Sarah (2017), 'Why We Need to Start Seeing the Classical World in Color', *Hyperallergic*, 7 June. Available online: https://hyperallergic.com/383776/why-we-need-to-start-seeing-the-classical-world-in-color/ (accessed 19 June 2019).

Bonfante, Larissa, ed. (2011), *The Barbarians of Ancient Europe: Realities and Interactions*, Cambridge: Cambridge University Press.

Bonilla-Silva, Eduardo (2001), *White Supremacy & Racism in the Post-Civil Rights Era*, Boulder, CO: Lynne Rienner Publishers.

Bonilla-Silva, Eduardo (2006), *Racism Without Racists Color-Blind Racism and the Persistence of Racial Inequality in the United States*, 5th edn, Lanham, MD: Rowman & Littlefield Publishers.

Boris, Eileen, (2003), 'From Gender to Racialized Gender: Laboring Bodies That Matter', *International Labor and Working-Class History*, 63: 9–13.

Bostick, Dani (2020), 'Not For All: Nostalgic Distortions as a Weapon of Segregation in Secondary Classics', *American Journal of Philology*, 141 (2): 283–306.

Bowersock, G. W. (1994), *Fiction as History: Nero to Julian*, Berkeley: University of California Press.

Bowersock, G. W. (2017), *The Crucible of Islam*, Cambridge, MA: Harvard University Press.

Bowler, Peter J (1989), *The Invention of Progress: The Victorians and the Past*, Oxford: Blackwell.

Boym, Svetlana (2001), *The Future of Nostalgia*, New York: Basic Books. Kindle Edition.

Boys-Stones, George (2007), 'Physiognomy and Ancient Psychological Theory', in Simon Swain (ed.), *Seeing the Face, Seeing the Soul: Polemon's* Physiognomy *from Classical Antiquity to Medieval Islam*, 19–125, Oxford: Oxford University Press.

Boys-Stones, George (2009), 'Polyclitus Among the Philosophers: Canons of Classical Beauty', in Corinne Saunders, Ulrike Maude and Jane Macnaughton (eds), *The Body and the Arts*, 11–24, New York: Palgrave Macmillan.

Bradley, Keith R. (1994), *Slavery and Society at Rome*, Cambridge: Cambridge University Press.

Bradley, Keith R. (1998), *Slavery and Rebellion in the Roman World 140 B.C.–70 B.C.*, Bloomington: Indiana University Press.

Bradley, Keith R. (2000), 'Animalizing the Slave: The Truth of Fiction', *Journal of Roman Studies*, 90: 110–25.

Bradley, Mark (2009), *Colour and Meaning in Ancient Rome*, Cambridge: Cambridge University Press.

Braund, David (2011), 'The Slave Supply in Classical Greece', in Paul Cartledge and Keith Bradley (eds), *The Cambridge World History of Slavery*, vol. 1, *The Ancient Mediterranean World*, 112–33, Cambridge: Cambridge University Press.

Briant, Pierre (2002), *From Cyrus to Alexander: A History of the Persian Empire*, trans. Peter T. Daniels, Winona Lake, IN: Eisenbrauns.

Briggs, Ward W., Jr, ed. (1994), *Biographical Dictionary of North American Classicists*, Westport, CT: Greenwood Press.

Briggs, Ward W., and William M. Calder III, eds (1990), *Classical Scholarship: A Biographical Encyclopedia*, New York: Garland.

Brouzas, Christopher George (1930), 'Modern Opinions about the Blond Type in Homeric and Classical Greece', *Transactions of the American Philological Association*, 61: xxvi–xvii.

Buell, Denise Kimber (2005), *Why This New Race: Ethnic Reasoning in Early Christianity*, New York: Columbia University Press.

Buell, Denise Kimber (2009), 'God's Own People: Specters of Race, Ethnicity, and Gender in Early Christian Studies', in Laura Nasrallah and Elizabeth Schüssler Fiorenza (eds), *Prejudice and Christian Beginnings: Investigating Race, Gender and Ethnicity in Early Christian Studies*, 159–90, Minneapolis, MN: Fortress Press.

Burke, Meghan A. (2019), *Colorblind Racism*, Cambridge: Polity.

Burstein, Stanley M. (1993), 'The Hellenistic Fringe: the Case of Meroe', in Peter Green (ed.), *Hellenistic History and Culture*, 38–54, Berkeley: University of California Press.

Burstein, Stanley M., ed. (1998), *Ancient African Kingdoms: Kush and Axum*, Princeton, NJ: Marcus Wiener.

Byron, Gay L. (2002), *Symbolic Blackness and Ethnic Difference in Early Christian Literature*, London: Routledge.

Cahill, Nicholas (2002), *Household and City Organisation at Olynthus*, Newhaven, CT: Yale University Press.

Cambiano, Giuseppe (1987), 'Aristotle and Anonymous Opponents of Slavery', in Moses Finley (ed.), *Classical Slavery*, 21–41, London: Frank Cass.

Campbell, Mavis (1974), 'Aristotle and Black Slavery: A Study in Race Prejudice', *Race*, 15: 283–302.

Carbado, Devon W., Kimberlé Williams Crenshaw, Vickie M. Mays and Barbara Tomlinson (2013), 'Intersectionality: Mapping the Movements of a Theory', *Du Bois Review*, 10 (2): 303–12.

Caron, Christina (2018), 'A Black Yale Student Was Napping, and a White Student Called the Police', *The New York Times*, 9 May, sec. New York. Available online: https://www.nytimes.com/2018/05/09/nyregion/yale-black-student-nap.html (accessed June 1, 2020).

Carruthers, Jacob H. (1992), 'Outside Academia: Bernal's Critique of Black Champions of Ancient Egypt', *Journal of Black Studies*, 22 (4): 459–76.

Carter, J. Kameron (2008), *Race: A Theological Account*, Oxford: Oxford University Press.

Cartledge, Paul (1993), '"Like a Worm I' the Bud?" A Heterology of Classical Greek Slavery', *Greece and Rome*, 40: 163–80.

Cartledge, Paul (2012), *The Greeks: a Portrait of Self and Others*, 2nd edn, Oxford: Oxford University Press.

Chadwick, John, and William Mann, trans. (1983), *Airs, Waters, Places*, in G. E. R. Lloyd (ed.), *Hippocratic Writings*, London: Penguin.

Chae, Yung In (2018), 'White People Explain Classics to Us: Epistemic Injustice in the Everyday Experiences of Racial Minorities', *Eidolon*, 5 February. Available online: https://eidolon.pub/white-people-explain-classics-to-us-50ecaef5511 (accessed 17 June 2019).

Challis, Debbie (2010), '"The Ablest Race": The Ancient Greeks in Victorian Racial Theory', in Mark Bradley (ed.), *Classics and Imperialism in the British Empire*, 94–122, Oxford: Oxford University Press.

Challis, Debbie (2011), 'The Race for a Healthy Body: The Ancient Greek Physical Ideal in Victorian London', in Barbara Goff and Michael Simpson (eds), *Thinking the Olympics: The Classical Tradition and the Modern Games*, 141–55, London: Bristol Classical Press.

Chaniotis, Angelos, and Ulrich Thaler (2006), 'Altertumswissenschaften', in W. U. Eckart, V. Sellin and H. Wolgast (eds), *Die Universität Heidelberg im Nationalsozialismus*, 391–434, Heidelberg: Springer Medizin.

Cheng, Anne A. (2019), *Ornamentalism*, Oxford: Oxford University Press.

Chiasson, C. (2001), 'Scythian Androgyny and Environmental Determinism in Herodotus and the Hippocratic περὶ ἐρων ὑδάτων τόπων', *Syllecta Classica*, 12: 33–73.

Chidester, David (2014), *Empire of Religion: Imperialism and Comparative Religion*, Chicago: University of Chicago Press.

Chimko, Corey J. (2003), 'Foreign Pharaohs: Self-Legitimization and Indigenous Reaction in Art and Literature', *Journal for the Society for the Study of Egyptian Antiquities*, 30: 15–57.

Chitworth, Zachary (2015), 'The Scholiasts Speak: How Middle Byzantine Jurists Construed the Legal Status of Jews', in Robert Hoyland (ed.), *The Late Antique World of Early Islam: Muslims among Christians and Jews in the East Mediterranean*, 87–105, Princeton, NJ: Darwin.

Choi, Erica (2018), 'Capturing the Elusive Universality of Classics', *Cloelia*, 18 January. Available online: https://medium.com/cloelia-wcc/capturing-the-elusive-universality-of-classics-82ad46e77869 (accessed 20 June 2019).

Christensen, Joel (2019), '"Our Classics": Classics by Exclusion', *Sententiae Antiquae*, 4 June. Available online: https://sententiaeantiquae.com/2019/06/04/our-culture-classics-by-exclusion/ (accessed 26 June 2020).

Cioffi, Robert Louis (2013), 'Imaginary Lands: Ethnicity, Exoticism, and Narrative in the Ancient Novel', PhD diss., Harvard University, Cambridge, MA.

City of Boston (2019), 'Do You Support the Renaming of Dudley Square to Nubian Square?', 20 September. Available online: https://www.boston.gov/news/do-you-support-renaming-dudley-square-nubian-square (accessed 12 February 2021).

Cline, Eric H. (2014), *1177 B.C.: The Year Civilization Collapsed*, Princeton, NJ: Princeton University Press.

Coates, Ta-Nehisi (2013), 'What We Mean When We Say "Race is a Social Construct"', *The Atlantic*, 15 May. Available online: https://www.theatlantic.com/national/archive/2013/05/what-we-mean-when-we-say-race-is-a-social-construct/275872/ (accessed 16 July 2020)

Coates, Ta-Nehisi (2015), *Between the World and Me*, New York: Spiegel and Grau.

Cohen, Shaye J. D. (1999), *The Beginnings of Jewishness: Boundaries, Varieties, Uncertainties*, Berkeley and Los Angeles: University of California Press.

Coleman, John E., and Clark A. Walz, eds (1997), *Greeks and Barbarians: Essays on the Interactions Between Greeks and Non-Greeks in Antiquity and the Consequences for Eurocentrism*, Bethesda, MD: CDL Press.

Combahee River Collective Statement (1977), in Beverly Guy-Sheftall (ed.), *Words of Fire: An Anthology of African-American Feminist Thought*, 232–40, New York: The New Press.

Conkey, Margaret (2005), 'Dwelling at the Margins, Action at the Intersection? Feminist and Indigenous Archaeologies', *Archaeologies*, 1 (1): 9–59.

Contadini, Anna (2012), *A World of Beasts: A Thirteenth-Century Illustrated Arabic Book on Animals (the Kitāb Na't al-Ḥayawān) in the Ibn Bakhtīshū' Tradition*, Leiden: Brill.

Cook, William W., and James Tatum (2010), *African American Writers and Classical Tradition*, Chicago: University of Chicago Press.

Cotton, Hanna M. (2013), 'Change and Continuity in Late Legal Papyri from Palaestina Tertia: *Nomos Hellênikos* and *Ethos Rômaikon*', in Natalie B. Dorhmann and Annette Yoshiko Reed (eds), *Jews, Christians, and the Roman Empire*, 209–21, Philadelphia: University of Pennsylvania Press.

Crenshaw, Kimberlé (1989), 'Demarginalizing the Intersection of Race and Sex: A Black Feminist Critique of Antidiscrimination Doctrine, Feminist Theory and Antiracist Politics', *University of Chicago Legal Forum*, 1 (8): 139–67.
Crenshaw, Kimberlé (2017), 'Kimberlé Crenshaw on Intersectionality, More than Two Decades Later', Columbia Law School 'Stories and News', 8 June. Available online: law.columbia.edu/pt-br/news/2017/06/kimberle-crenshaw-intersectionality (accessed 1 May 2019).
Crenshaw, Kimberlé, Neil T. Gotanda, Gary Peller and Kendall Thomas, eds (1995), *Critical Race Theory: The Key Writings That Formed the Movement*, New York: New Press.
Curran, Andrew (2011), *The Anatomy of Blackness*, Baltimore, MD: Johns Hopkins University Press.
Daniel, John Franklin (1948), 'The Dorian Invasion: the Setting', *American Journal of Archaeology*, 52 (1): 107–10.
Davis, Angela Y. (1983), *Women, Race, & Class*, New York: Vintage.
Davis, Simon (1951), *Race-Relations in Ancient Egypt: Greek, Egyptian, Hebrew, Roman*, London: Methuen.
Dee, James H. (2003–4), 'Black Odysseus, White Caesar: When Did "White People" Become "White"?', *Classical Journal*, 99 (2): 157–67.
Delgado, Richard, and Jean Stefancic (2012), *Critical Race Theory: An Introduction*, 2nd edn, New York: New York University Press.
Dench, Emma (2017), 'Ethnicity, Identity and Culture', in Daniel S Richter and William A. Johnson (eds), *The Oxford Handbook of the Second Sophistic*, 99–114, Oxford: Oxford University Press.
Derbew, Sarah (2018), 'An Investigation of Black Figures in Classical Greek Art', *The Iris (Behind the Scenes at the Getty)*, 25 April. Available online: http://blogs.getty.edu/iris/an-investigation-of-black-figures-in-classical-greek-art/ (accessed 1 June 2020).
Derbew, Sarah, with Elena Giusti (2018), 'Decolonizing Blackness, Alongside the Classics Curriculum'. Available online: https://warwick.ac.uk/fac/arts/classics/students/modules/africa/interview/sarahderbew/ (accessed 20 June 2019).
Dewald, Carolyn (1990), 'Review of *The Mirror of Herodotus: The Representation of the Other in the Writing of History* by François Hartog', *Classical Philology*, 85 (3): 217–24.
DiAngelo, Robin J. (2018), *White Fragility*, Boston: Beacon Press.
Dickinson, Oliver (2006), *The Aegean From Bronze Age to Iron Age: Continuity and Change between the Twelfth and Eighth Centuries*, London: Routledge.
Diller, Aubrey (1937), 'Race Mixture Among the Greeks Before Alexander', *Illinois Studies in Language and Literature*, 20 (1–2): 9–187.
Diop, Cheikh Anta ([1955] 1974), *The African Origin of Civilization: Myth or Reality*, trans. Mercer Cook, Chicago: Lawrence Hill Books.
Dixon, Suzanne (2001), *Reading Roman Women*, London: Bloomsbury.
Dominik William J. (1997), 'Lloyd Arthur Thompson (1932–97): In Memoriam', *Scholia* (6): 2–10.
Donner, Fred (2010), *Muhammad and the Believers*, Cambridge, MA: Harvard University Press.
Doody, Margaret Anne (1997), *The True Story of the Novel*, Piscataway, NJ: Rutgers University Press.
Dougherty, Carol (1999), 'The Double Vision of Euripides' "Cyclops": An Ethnographic "Odyssey" on the Satyr Stage', *Comparative Drama*, 33 (3): 313–38.
Dougherty, Carol, and Leslie Kurke, eds (2003), *The Cultures within Ancient Greek Culture: Contact, Conflict, Collaboration*, Cambridge: Cambridge University Press.
Doxey, Denise M. (2018), *Arts of Ancient Nubia*, Boston: Museum of Fine Arts.

DuBois, Page (2010), *Out of Athens: The New Ancient Greeks*, Cambridge, MA: Harvard University Press.
Du Bois, W. E. B. (1940), *Dusk of Dawn*, Oxford: Oxford University Press.
Dubow, Saul (2008), 'Smuts, the United Nations and the Rhetoric of Race and Rights', *Journal of Contemporary History*, 43 (1): 45–74.
Dugan, Kelly P. (2019), 'The "happy slave" Narrative and Classics Pedagogy: A Verbal and Visual Analysis of Beginning Greek and Latin Textbooks', *New England Classical Journal*, 46 (1): 62–87.
Dugan, Kelly P. (2020), 'Antiracism and Restorative Justice in Classics Pedagogy: Race, Slavery, and the Function of Language in Beginning Greek and Latin Textbooks', Phd diss., University of Georgia, Athens, USA.
Early, Gerald (1998), 'Adventures in the Colored Museum: Afrocentrism, Memory, and the Construction of Race', *American Anthropologist*, 100 (3): 703–11.
Echeverría-Fenn, Stefani (2020), 'On Classics, Madness, and Losing Everything', *Sententiae Antiquae*, 4 January. Available online: https://sententiaeantiquae.com/2020/01/04/on-classics-madness-and-losing-everything/ (accessed 31 January 2020).
Elmer, David F. (2008), 'Heliodoros' "Sources": Intertextuality, Paternity, and the Nile River in the "Aithiopika"', *Transactions of the American Philological Association*, 138 (2): 411–50.
Engels, Johannes (2010), 'Macedonians and Greeks', in J. Roisman and Ian Worthington (eds), *A Companion to Ancient Macedonia*, 81–98, Oxford: Wiley Blackwell.
Eyre, Christopher (2013), *The Use of Documents in Pharaonic Egypt*, Oxford: Oxford University Press.
Fain, Kimberly (2015), *Black Hollywood: From Butlers to Superheroes, the Changing Role of African American Men in the Movies*, Santa Barbara, CA: Praeger.
Fanon, Frantz ([1952] 2008), *Black Skin, White Masks*, trans. Richard Philcox, New York: Grove Press.
Fanon, Frantz ([1967] 1986), *Black Skin, White Masks*, trans. Charles Lam Markmann, London: Pluto.
Farr, J. (2008), 'Locke, Natural Law, and New World Slavery', *Political Theory*, 36 (4): 495–522.
Felski, Rita (1995), *The Gender of Modernity*, Cambridge, MA: Harvard University Press.
Felski, Rita (2015), *The Limits of Critique*, Chicago: University of Chicago Press.
Fields, Karen E., and Barbara J. Fields ([2012] 2014), *Racecraft: The Soul of Inequality in American Life*, London: Verso Books.
Finley, Moses I. (1959), 'Was Greek Civilisation Based on Slave Labour?', *Historia*, 8: 145–64.
Finley, Moses I., ed. (1981), *The Legacy of Greece: A New Appraisal*, Oxford: Oxford University Press.
Fischer-Bovet, Christelle (2018), 'Official Identity and Ethnicity: Comparing Ptolemaic and Early Roman Egypt', *Journal of Egyptian History*, 11: 208–42.
Flashar, Hellmut (1983), *Aristoteles: Problemata Physica*, 3rd edn, Berlin: Akademie-Verlag.
Foerster, Richardus, ed. (1893), *Scriptores Physiognomonici Graeci et Latini*, 2 vols, Leipzig: Teubner.
Foucault, Michel ([1978] 2013), 'Right of Death and Power Over Life', in Timothy Campbell and Adam Sitze (eds), *Biopolitics: A Reader*, 41–60, Durham, NC: Duke University Press.
Fowler, Robert L. (1999), 'Genealogical Thinking, Hesiod's Catalogue, and the Creation of the Hellenes', *Cambridge Classical Journal*, 44: 1–19. https://doi.org/10.1017/S0068673500002200.

Fox, Margalit (2007), 'Frank M. Snowden Jr., 95, Historian of Blacks in Antiquity, Dies', *The New York Times*, 28 February. Available online: https://www.nytimes.com/2007/02/28/obituaries/28snowden.html (accessed 20 June 2019).

Fox, Margalit (2014), *Riddle of the Labyrinth: The Quest to Crack an Ancient Code*, New York: Ecco.

Frank, Tenney (1916), 'Race Mixture in the Roman Empire', *American Historical Review*, 21 (4): 689–708.

Frank, Tenney (1932), *Aspects of Social Behavior in Ancient Rome*, Martin Classical Lectures, vol. 2, Cambridge, MA: Harvard University Press.

Frankenberg, Ruth, ed. (1997), *Displacing Whiteness: Essays in Social and Cultural Criticism*, Durham, NC: Duke University Press.

Fredrickson, George M. (2002), *Racism: A Short History*, Princeton, NJ: Princeton University Press.

Fricker, Miranda (2007), *Epistemic Injustice: Power and the Ethics of Knowing*, Oxford: Oxford University Press.

Fuentes, Agustín, and Carolyn Rouse (2016), 'New Articulations of Biological Difference in the 21st Century: A Conversation', *Anthropology Now*, 8 (3): 1–12.

Futterman, Matthew, and Talya Minsberg (2020), 'After a Killing, "Running While Black" Stirs Even More Anxiety', *The New York Times*, 8 May, sec. Sports. Available online: https://www.nytimes.com/2020/05/08/sports/Ahmaud-Arbery-running.html (accessed 1 June 2020).

Garlan, Y. (1987), 'War, Piracy and Slavery in the Greek World', in M. I. Finley (ed.), *Classical Slavery*, 7–21, London: F. Cass.

Garland, Robert (2016), 'The Invention and Application of Racial Deformity', in Rebecca Futo Kennedy and Molly Jones-Lewis (eds), *The Routledge Handbook of Identity and the Environment in the Classical and Medieval Worlds*, 45–61, New York: Taylor and Francis.

Gates-Foster, Jennifer E. (2014), 'Achaemenids, Royal Power, and Persian Ethnicity', in Jeremy McInerney (ed.), *A Companion to Ethnicity in the Ancient Mediterranean*, 175–93, Chichester, UK: John Wiley and Sons.

Gehrke, Hans-Joachim (2014), *Geschichte als Element antiker Kultur. Die Griechen und ihre Geschichte(n)*, Berlin: De Gruyter.

George, Michele, ed. (2013), *Roman Slavery and Roman Material Culture*, Toronto: University of Toronto Press.

Gikandi, Simon E. (2000), *Ngugi wa Thiong'o*, Cambridge: Cambridge University Press.

Girmay, Aracelis (2016), *The Black Maria*, Rochester, NY: BOA Editions.

Gladwell, Malcolm (2019), *Talking to Strangers: What We Should Know about the People We Don't Know*, Ashland, OR: Blackstone.

Glausser, Wayne (1990), 'Three Approaches to Locke and the Slave Trade', *Journal of the History of Ideas*, 51 (2): 199–216.

Goldenberg, David M. (2009), 'Racism, Color Symbolism, and Color Prejudice', in Miriam Eliav-Feldon, Benjamin Isaac and Joseph Ziegler (eds), *The Origins of Racism in the West*, 88–108, Cambridge: Cambridge University Press.

Goldhill, Simon, ed. (2001), *Being Greek Under Rome: Cultural Identity, the Second Sophistic and the Development of Empire*, Cambridge: Cambridge University Press.

Goldman, Max (2016), 'Ethnic Bodies: Physiognomy, Identity, and the Environment', in Rebecca Futo Kennedy and Molly Jones-Lewis (eds), *The Routledge Handbook of Identity and the Environment in the Classical and Medieval Worlds*, 62–73, London: Routledge.

Goodman, Martin (1989), 'Nerva, the *Fiscus Judaicus* and Jewish Identity', *Journal of Roman Studies*, 79: 40–4.

Goodman, Martin (2004), 'Trajan and the Origins of Roman Hostility to the Jews', *Past & Present*, 182: 3–29.

Gordon, Avery ([1997] 2008), *Ghostly Matters: Haunting and the Sociological Imagination*, Minneapolis: University of Minnesota Press.

Gould, Stephen Jay (1993), 'American Polygeny and Craniometry before Darwin: Blacks and Indians as Separate, Inferior Species', in Sandra Harding (ed.), *The 'Racial' Economy of Science: Toward a Democratic Future*, 84–115, Bloomington: Indiana University Press.

Gozzoli, Roberto B. (2009), 'Kawa V and Tarharqo's BYΣWT: Aspects of Nubian Royal Ideology', *Journal of Egyptian Archaeology*, 95: 235–48.

Grafton, Anthony, Glenn W. Most and Salvatore Settis, eds (2010), *The Classical Tradition*, Cambridge, MA: Harvard University Press.

Graham, Shawn (2018), 'Editorial Note: Citation as an Act of Enchantment', *EPOIESEN: A Journal for Creative Engagement in History and Archaeology*, 2: 1–7. http://doi.org/10.22215/epoiesen/2018.10.

Grant, Madison (1916), *The Passing of the Great Race or the Racial Bias of European History*, New York: Charles Scribner's Sons.

Graziosi, Barbara (2005), 'Review of *Futuro del Classico* by Salvatore Settis', *Journal of Hellenic Studies*, 125: 206–8.

Greenwood, Emily (2009), 'Re-rooting the Classical Tradition: New Directions in Black Classicism', *Classical Receptions Journal*, 1 (1): 87–103.

Greenwood, Emily (2010), *Afro-Greeks: Dialogues between Anglophone Caribbean Literature and Classics in the Twentieth Century*, Oxford: Oxford University Press.

Griffin, M. T. (1982), 'The Lyons Tablet and Tacitean Hindsight', *Classical Quarterly*, 32 (2): 404–18.

Gruen, Erich S. (2011a), *Rethinking the Other in Antiquity*, Princeton, NJ: Princeton University Press.

Gruen, Erich S., ed. (2011b), *Cultural Identity in the Ancient Mediterranean*, Los Angeles: Getty Publications.

Guedj, Pauline (2016), 'Pan-Africanism in the Academia: John Henrik Clarke and the African Heritage Studies Association', *Nuevo mundo mundos nuevos*, October: 1–17.

Haarhoff, T. J. (1931), *Vergil in the Experience of South Africa*, Oxford: Blackwell.

Haarhoff, T. J. (1948), *The Stranger at the Gate: Aspects of Exclusivism and Co-operation in Ancient Greece and Rome, with Some Reference to Modern Times*, Oxford: Blackwell.

Haarhoff, T. J. (1949), *Vergil the Universal*, Oxford: Blackwell.

Hadas, Moses (1943), 'From Nationalism to Cosmopolitanism in the Greco-Roman World', *Journal of the History of Ideas*, 4 (1): 105–11.

Hägg, T. (2000), 'The Black Land of the Sun: Meroe in Heliodoros' Romantic Fiction', *Graeco-Arabica*, 7–8: 195–220.

Haley, Shelley P. (1989a), 'Classics and Minorities', in Phyllis Culham and Lowell Edmunds (eds), *Classics: A Discipline and Profession in Crisis?*, 333–8, Lanham, MD: University Press of America.

Haley, Shelley P. (1989b), 'Livy's Sophoniba', *Classica et Mediaevalia*, 40: 171–81.

Haley, Shelley P. (1990), 'Livy, Passion and Cultural Stereotypes', *Historia*, 39 (3): 375–81.

Haley, Shelley P. (1993), 'Black Feminist Thought and Classics: Re-membering, Re-claiming, Re-empowering', in Nancy S. Rabinowitz and Amy Richlin (eds), *Feminist Theory and the Classics*, 23–43, New York: Routledge.

Haley, Shelley P. (2009), 'Be Not Afraid of the Dark: Critical Race Theory and Classical Studies', in Laura Nasrallah and Elizabeth Schüssler Fiorenza (eds), *Prejudice and Christian*

Beginnings: Investigating Race, Gender and Ethnicity in Early Christian studies, 27–49/50, Minneapolis, MN: Fortress Press.

Hall, Budd L., and Rajesh Tandon (2017), 'Decolonization of Knowledge, Epistemicide, Participatory Research and Higher Education', *Research for All*, 1 (1): 6–19.

Hall, Edith (1989), *Inventing the Barbarian: Greek Self-Definition Through Tragedy*, Oxford: Clarendon Press.

Hall, Edith (2004), 'When Is a Myth not a Myth? Bernal's "Ancient Model"', repr. in Thomas Harrison (ed.), *Greeks and Barbarians*, 133–52, Edinburgh: Edinburgh University Press.

Hall, Edith (2006), *The Theatrical Cast of Athens: Interactions between Ancient Greek Drama and Society*, Oxford: Oxford University Press.

Hall, Edith, Richard Alston and Justine McConnell, eds (2011), *Ancient Slavery and Abolition: From Hobbes to Hollywood*, Oxford: Oxford University Press.

Hall, Jonathan M. (1997), *Ethnic Identity in Greek Antiquity*, Cambridge: Cambridge University Press.

Hall, Jonathan M. (2002), *Hellenicity: Between Ethnicity and Culture*, Chicago: University of Chicago Press.

Hall, Kim F. (1995), *Things of Darkness: Economies of Race and Gender in Early Modern England*, Ithaca, NY: Cornell University Press.

Hall, Stuart (1990), 'Cultural Identity and Diaspora', in Jonathan Rutherford (ed.), *Identity: Community, Culture Difference*, 222–37, London: Lawrence and Wishart.

Hallett, Judith P. (1993), 'Feminist Theory, Historical Periods, Literary Canons, and the Study of Greco-Roman Antiquity', in Nancy Sorkin Rabinowitz and Amy Richlin (eds), *Feminist Theory and the Classics*, 44–72, New York: Routledge.

Hallett, Judith P., and Thomas Van Nortwick, eds (1997), *Compromising Traditions: The Personal Voice in Classical Scholarship*, London: Routledge.

Hamilakis, Yannis (2018), 'Decolonial Archaeology as Social Justice', *Antiquity*, 92 (362): 518–20.

Hanink, Johanna (2017), 'It's Time to Embrace Critical Classical Reception', *Eidolon*, 1 May. Available online: https://eidolon.pub/its-time-to-embrace-critical-classical-reception-d3491a40eec3 (accessed 14 June 2019).

Hanke, Lewis (1959), *Aristotle and the American Indians: A Study of Race Prejudice in the Modern World*, London: Hollis and Carter.

Haraway, Donna J. (1994), 'A Game of Cat's Cradle: Science Studies, Feminist Theory, Cultural Studies', *Configurations*, 2 (1): 59–71.

Harman, Rosie (2013), 'Looking at the Other: Visual Mediation and Greek Identity in Xenophon's *Anabasis*', in Eran Almagor and Joseph Skinner (eds), *Ancient Ethnography: New Approaches*, 79–96, London: Bloomsbury.

Harper, Kyle (2017), *The Fate of Rome: Climate, Disease, and the End of an Empire*, Princeton, NJ: Princeton University Press.

Harris, Edward M. (2004), 'Notes on a Lead Letter from the Athenian Agora', *Harvard Studies in Classical Philology*, 102: 157–70.

Harris, W. V. (1999), 'Demography, Geography and the Sources of Roman Slaves', *Journal of Roman Studies*, 89: 62–75.

Harrison, Thomas (2003), 'Upside Down and Back to Front: Herodotus and the Greek Encounter with Egypt', in Roger Matthews and Cornelia Römer (eds), *Ancient Perspectives on Egypt*, 145–55, London: UCL Press.

Harrison, Thomas (2019), 'Classical Greek Ethnography and the Slave Trade', *Classical Antiquity*, 38 (1): 36–57.

Harrison, Thomas (2020), 'Reinventing the Barbarian', *Classical Philology*, 115: 139–63.
Harrison, Thomas (forthcoming), 'Classical Greek Racism', in Vicky Manolopoulou, Joseph Skinner and Christina Tsouparapoulou (eds), *Identities in Antiquity*, London: Routledge.
Harrison, Thomas, ed. (2002), *Greeks and Barbarians*, New York: Routledge.
Hartog, François (1988), *The Mirror of Herodotus: The Representation of the Other in the Writing of History*, trans. Janet Lloyd, Berkeley: University of California Press.
Haubold, Johannes (2014), 'Ethnography in the *Iliad*', in Marios Skempis and Ioannis Ziogas (eds), *Geography, Topography, Landscape: Configurations of Space in Greek and Roman Epic*, 19–36, Berlin: DeGruyter.
Haverfield, F. J. (1906), *The Romanization of Roman Britain*, London: British Academy.
Heath, Malcolm (2008), 'Aristotle on Natural Slavery', *Phronesis*, 53 (3): 243–70.
Heather, Peter (2010), *Empires and Barbarians: The Fall of Rome and the Birth of Europe*, New York: Oxford University Press.
Hemker, Julie (1985), 'Rape and the Founding of Rome', *Helios*, 12: 41–7.
Henderson, Taja-Nia Y., and Jamila Jefferson-Jones (2020), '#LivingWhileBlack: Blackness as Nuisance', *American University Law Review*, 69 (3): 863–914.
Heng, Geraldine (2018), *The Invention of Race in the European Middle Ages*, Cambridge: Cambridge University Press.
Henry, Madeleine (1995), *Prisoner of History: Aspasia of Miletus and her Biographical Tradition*, Oxford: Oxford University Press.
Heschel, Susannah (1998), *Abraham Geiger and the Jewish Jesus*, Chicago: University of Chicago Press.
Heschel, Susannah (2008), *The Aryan Jesus: Christian Theologians and the Bible in Nazi Germany*, Princeton, NJ: Princeton University Press.
Hickman, Jared (2010), 'Globalization and the Gods, or the Political Theology of "Race"', *Early American Literature*, 45 (1): 145–82.
Highet, Gilbert (1942), 'Review of *La letteratura di Roma repubblicana ed Augustea* by Augusto Rostagni', *American Journal of Philology*, 63: 92–104.
Hobsbawm, Eric, and Terence Ranger, eds (1983), *The Invention of Tradition*, Cambridge: Cambridge University Press.
Holt, Frank L. (2005), *Into the Land of Bones: Alexander the Great in Afghanistan*, Berkeley: University of California Press.
Honigman, Sylvie (2013), '"Jews as The Best of All Greeks": Cultural Competition in the Literary Works of Alexandria Judaeans of the Hellenistic Period', in Eftychia Stavrianopoulou (ed.), *Shifting Social Imaginaries in the Hellenistic Period: Narrations, Practices, and Images*, 207–32, Leiden: Brill.
Hooker, Juliet (2017), *Theorizing Race in the Americas: Douglass, Sarmiento, Du Bois, and Vasconcelos*, Oxford: Oxford University Press.
hooks, bell (2009), *Reel to Real: Race, Sex and Class at the Movies*, New York: Taylor and Francis.
Hopkins, Keith (1978), *Conquerors and Slaves: Sociological Studies in Roman History*, vol. 1, Cambridge: Cambridge University Press.
Houston, Drusilla Dunjee ([1926] 1985), *Wonderful Ethiopians of the Ancient Cushite Empire*, vol. 1, Baltimore, MD: Black Classic Press.
Hoyland, Robert, trans. (2007), 'A New Edition and Translation of the Leiden Polemon', in Simon Swain (ed.), *Seeing the Face, Seeing the Soul: Polemon's Physiognomy from Classical Antiquity to Medieval Islam*, 329–464, Oxford: Oxford University Press.

Hui, Andrew (2017), 'The Many Returns of Philology: A State of the Field Report', *Journal of the History of Ideas*, 78 (1): 137–56.
Hunt, Peter (2015), 'Trojan Slaves in Classical Athens. Ethnic Identity among Athenian Slaves', in Claire Taylor and Kostas Vlassopoulos (eds), *Communities and Networks in the Ancient Greek World*, 129–54, Oxford: Oxford University Press.
Husband, Richard Wellington (1909), 'Race Mixture in Early Rome', *Transactions and Proceedings of the American Philological Association*, 40: 63–81.
Irwin, E. (2014), 'Ethnography and Empire: Homer and the Hippocratics in Herodotus' Ethiopian logos, 3.17-26', *Histos*, 8: 25–75.
Isaac, Benjamin (2004), *The Invention of Racism in Classical Antiquity*, Princeton, NJ: Princeton University Press.
Isaac, Benjamin (2006), 'Proto-racism in Graeco-Roman Antiquity', *World Archaeology*, 38 (1): 32–48.
Isaac, Benjamin (2009), 'Racism: A Rationalization of Prejudice', in Miriam Eliav-Feldon, Benjamin Isaac and Joseph Ziegler (eds), *The Origins of Racism in the West*, 32–56, Cambridge: Cambridge University Press.
Ivantchik, A. I. (2005), 'Who Were the "Scythian" Archers on Archaic Attic Vases?', in David Braund (ed.), *Scythians and Greeks: Cultural Interactions in Scythian, Athens, and the Early Roman Empire (Sixth Century BC–First Century AD)*, 100–14, Exeter: University of Exeter Press.
Jacques-Garvey, Amy, ed. ([1925] 1967), *Philosophy and Opinions of Marcus Garvey*, vol. 2, 2nd edn, New York: Augustus M. Kelley. ('Who and What is a Negro?' was written on 16 January 1923.)
James, George G. M. (1954), *Stolen Legacy*, Nashville, TN: James C. Winston Publishing Company.
Jansen, Jonathan, and Cyrill Walters, eds (2020), *Fault Lines: A Primer on Race, Science and Society*, Stellenbosch: African Sun Media.
Jenkyns, Richard, ed. (1992), *The Legacy of Rome: A New Appraisal*, Oxford: Oxford University Press.
Jhally, Sut (1997), 'Race, the Floating Signifier, Featuring Stuart Hall', Media Education Foundation, Northampton, MA.
Johnson, Sylvester A. (2004), *The Myth of Ham in Nineteenth-Century American Christianity: Race, Heathens, and the People of God*, New York: Palgrave Macmillan.
Johnson-Hodge, Caroline (2007), *If Sons, Then Heirs*, Oxford: Oxford University Press.
Johnston, Andrew C. (2017), *The Sons of Remus: Identity in Roman Gaul and Spain*, Cambridge, MA: Harvard University Press.
Jones, Prudence (2006), *Cleopatra: A Sourcebook*, Norman: Oklahoma University Press.
Jones, Siân (1997), *The Archaeology of Ethnicity: Constructing Identities in the Past and Present*, London: Routledge.
Joshel, Sandra R. (2014), *The Material Life of Roman Slaves*, New York: Cambridge University Press.
Jouanna, Jacques (1999), *Hippocrates*, trans. M. B. DeBevoise, Baltimore, MD: Johns Hopkins University Press.
Jouanna, Jacques, ed. (1996), *Hippocrate, Airs, Eaux, Lieux*, Paris: Les Belles Lettres.
Jowett, Benjamin, trans. (1984), *Aristotle: Politics*, in Jonathan Barnes (ed.), *The Complete Works of Aristotle*, 2.1986–2129, Princeton, NJ: Princeton University Press.
Kahlos, Maijastina (2011), 'Who is a Good Roman? Setting and Resetting Boundaries for Romans, Christians, Pagans, and Barbarians in the Late Roman Empire', in Maijastina

Kahlos (ed.), *The Faces of the Other: Religious Rivalry and Ethnic Encounters in the Later Roman World*, 259–74, Turnhout: Brepols.

Kaldellis, Anthony (2019), *Romanland: Ethnicity and Empire in Byzantium*, Cambridge, MA: Harvard University Press.

Kapparis, Konstantinos A. (2018), *Athenian Law and Society*, London: Routledge.

Kasimis, Demetra (2018), *The Perpetual Immigrant and the Limits of Athenian Democracy*, Cambridge: Cambridge University Press.

Kaylan, Melik (2019), 'The Glory That Was Nubia', *Wall Street Journal*, 19 November. Available online: https://www.wsj.com/articles/the-glory-that-was-nubia-11574202653 (accessed 29 July 2020).

Keita, Maghan (2000), *Race and the Writing of History: Riddling the Sphinx*, Oxford: Oxford University Press.

Kelley, Shawn (2002), *Racializing Jesus: Race, Ideology, and the Formation of Modern Biblical Scholarship*, London: Routledge.

Kendi, Ibram X. (2016), *Stamped from the Beginning: The Definitive History of Racist Ideas in America*, New York: Nation Books.

Kendi, Ibram X. (2019), *How to Be an Antiracist*, New York: One World.

Kennedy, Rebecca Futo (2014), *Immigrant Women in Athens: Gender, Ethnicity, and Citizenship in the Classical City*, New York: Routledge.

Kennedy, Rebecca Futo (2017), 'We Condone It By Our Silence: Confronting The Classics' Complicity in White Supremacy', *Eidolon*, 11 May. Available online: https://eidolon.pub/we-condone-it-by-our-silence-bea76fb59b21 (accessed 20 June 2019).

Kennedy, Rebecca Futo (2019), 'Is There a "Race" or "Ethnicity" in Greco-Roman Antiquity?', *Classics at the Intersections*, April. Available online: https://rfkclassics.blogspot.com/2019/04/is-there-race-or-ethnicity-in-greco.html (accessed 17 June 2019).

Kennedy, Rebecca Futo, C. Sydnor Roy and Max L. Goldman, eds (2013), *Race and Ethnicity in the Classical World: An Anthology of Primary Sources in Translation*, Indianapolis, IN: Hackett Publishing.

Kidd, Colin (2006), *The Forging of Races: Race and Scripture in the Protestant Atlantic World 1600–2000*, Cambridge: Cambridge University Press.

Kies, B. M. (1953), 'The Contribution of the Non-European Peoples to World Civilisation', A. J. Abrahamse Memorial Lecture: Teachers' League of South Africa.

Kim, Eunsong, and Maya I. Mackrandilal (2014), 'The Whitney Biennial for Angry Women', *The New Inquiry*, 4 April. Available online: https://thenewinquiry.com/the-whitney-biennial-for-angry-women/ (accessed 14 June 2019).

Kim, Hyun Jin (2009), *Ethnicity and Foreigners in Ancient Greece and China*, London: Duckworth.

Kim, Hyun Jin (2013), 'The Invention of the "Barbarian" in Late Sixth-Century Ionia', in Eran Almagor and Joseph Skinner (eds), *Ancient Ethnography: New Approaches*, 25–48, London: Bloomsbury.

Kitchen, K. A. (1986), *The Third Intermediate Period in Egypt, 1100–650 B.C.*, 2nd edn, Warminster: Aris & Phillips.

Kosmin, Paul J. (2014), *The Land of the Elephant Kings: Space, Territory, and Ideology in the Seleucid Empire*, Cambridge, MA: Harvard University Press.

Krebs, Christopher B. (2011), *A Most Dangerous Book: Tacitus' Germania from the Roman Empire to the Third Reich*, New York: Norton.

LaFraniere, Sharon, and Andrew W. Lehren (2015), 'The Disproportionate Risks of Driving While Black', *The New York Times*, 24 October, sec. US. Available online: https://www.

nytimes.com/2015/10/25/us/racial-disparity-traffic-stops-driving-black.html (accessed 1 June 2020).
Lake, Marilyn, and Henry Reynolds (2008), *Drawing the Global Colour Line: White Men's Countries and the International Challenge of Racial Equality*, Cambridge: Cambridge University Press.
Lambert, Michael (2011), *The Classics and South African Identities*, London: Bristol Classical Press.
Lape, Susan. (2010), *Race and Citizen Identity in the Classical Athenian Democracy*, Cambridge: Cambridge University Press.
Laurence, Ray, and Joanne Berry, eds (1998), *Cultural Identity in the Roman Empire*, London: Routledge.
Lee, Mireille (2015), *Body, Dress and Identity in Ancient Greece*, Cambridge: Cambridge University Press.
Lefkowitz, Mary (1997), *Not Out of Africa: How Afrocentrism Became an Excuse to Teach Myth as History*, New York: Basic Books.
Leunissen, Mariska (2012), 'Aristotle on Natural Character and Its Implications for Moral Development', *Journal of the History of Philosophy*, 50 (4): 507–30.
Leunissen, Mariska (2015), 'The Ethnography of *Problemata* 14 in its (Mostly Aristotelian) Context', in Robert Mayhew (ed.), *The Aristotelian Problemata Physica: Philosophical and Scientific Investigations*, 190–213, Leiden: Brill.
Leunissen, Mariska (2017), *From Natural Character to Moral Virtue in Aristotle*, Oxford: Oxford University Press.
Lewis, David M. (2018), *Greek Slave Systems in their Eastern Mediterranean* Context, *c. 800–146 BC*, Oxford: Oxford University Press.
Lewis, Naphtali (1999), *Life in Egypt Under Roman Rule*, Atlanta: Scholars Press.
Lieu, Judith M. (2004), *Christian Identity in the Jewish and Graeco-Roman World*, Oxford: Oxford University Press.
Liew, Tat-Siong Benny (2017), 'Black Scholarship Matters', *Journal of Biblical Literature*, 136 (1): 237–44.
Lin, Yii-Jan (2016), *The Erotic Life of Manuscripts: New Testament Criticism and the Biological Sciences*, Oxford: Oxford University Press.
Linderski, Jerzy (1999), 'Tenney Frank', *American National Biography*, 8: 367–8. (Republished in Jerzy Linderski (2007), *Roman Questions II*, 578–80, Stuttgart: Franz Steiner Verlag.)
Lissarrague, François (1990), *L'autre guerrier: Archers, peltastes, cavaliers dans l'imagerie attique*, Paris: Ecole française de Rome.
Lissarrague, François (2002), 'The Athenian Image of the Foreigner', trans. Antonia Nevill, in Thomas Harrison (ed.), *Greeks and Barbarians*, 101–27, New York: Routledge.
Lloyd, Geoffrey E. R. (1966), *Polarity and Analogy: Two Types of Argument in Early Greek Thought*, Cambridge: Cambridge University Press.
Lloyd, Geoffrey E. R. (1983), *Science, Folklore, and Ideology: Studies in the Life Sciences in Ancient Greece*, Cambridge: Cambridge University Press.
Lloyd-Jones, Hugh (1982), *Blood for the Ghosts: Classical Influences in the Nineteenth and Twentieth Centuries*, London: Duckworth.
Lohsemann, Volker (1977), *Nationalsozialismus und Antike: Studien zur Entwicklung des Faches Alte Geschichte 1933–1945* (= *Reihe historische Perspektiven*. Band 7), Hamburg: Hoffmann und Campe.

Lohwasser, Angelika (2001), 'Queenship in Kush: Status, Role and Ideology of Royal Women', *Journal of the American Research Center in Egypt*, 38: 61–76.

Loraux, Nicole (2000), *Born of the Earth: Myth and Politics in Athens*, trans. Selina Steward, Ithaca, NY: Cornell University Press.

Low, Polly, ed. (2008), *The Athenian Empire*, Edinburgh: Edinburgh University Press.

Lucy, Sam (2005), 'Ethnic and Cultural Identities', in Margarita Díaz-Andreu García, Sam Lucy, Babić Staša and David N. Edwards (eds), *The Archaeology of Identity: Approaches to Gender, Age, Status, Ethnicity and Religion*, 86–109, London: Routledge.

Lupher, David (2003), *Romans in a New World*, Ann Arbor, MI: University of Michigan Press.

Lupher, David, and Elizabeth Vandiver (2011), 'Yankee She-Men and Octoroon Electra: Basil Lanneau Gildersleeve on Slavery, Race, and Abolition', in Richard Alston, Edith Hall and Justine McConnell (eds), *Ancient Slavery and Abolition: From Hobbes to Hollywood*, 319–46, Oxford: Oxford University Press.

Luraghi, Nino (2014), 'The Study of Greek Ethnic Identities', in Jeremy McInerney (ed.), *A Companion to Ethnicity in the Ancient Mediterranean*, 213–27, Chichester, UK: John Wiley and Sons.

Lye, Suzanne (2016), 'Gender and Ethnicity in Heliodorus' *Aithiopika*', *Classical World*, 109 (2): 235–62.

Maas, Michael (2000), *Readings in Late Antiquity: A Sourcebook*, London: Routledge.

Macadam, Miles Frederick Laming (1955), *The Temples of Kawa: Oxford University Excavations in Nubia II*, Oxford: Ashmolean Museum.

Mackie, Hilary (1996), *Talking Trojan: Speech and Community in the Iliad*, London: Rowman & Littlefield.

Mac Sweeney, Naoíse (2017), 'Separating Fact from Fiction in the Ionian Migration', *Hesperia*, 86: 379–421.

Mac Sweeney, Naoíse, et al. (2019), 'Claiming the Classical: The Greco-Roman World in Contemporary Political Discourse', *Council of University Classical Departments Bulletin*, 48. Available online: https://cucd.blogs.sas.ac.uk/files/2019/02/MAC-SWEENEY-ET-AL-Claiming-the-Classical.pdf (accessed 19 June 2019).

Mairs, Rachel (2014), *The Hellenistic Far East: Archaeology, Language and Identity in Greek Central Asia*, Berkeley: University of California Press.

Malamud, Margaret (2016), *African Americans and the Classics: Antiquity, Abolition and Activism*, London: I.B. Tauris.

Malkin, Irad (2001a), 'Introduction', in Irad Malkin (ed.), *Ancient Perceptions of Greek Ethnicity*, 1–28, Cambridge, MA: Harvard University Press; Washington, DC: Center for Hellenic Studies.

Malkin, Irad, ed. (2001b), *Ancient Perceptions of Greek Ethnicity*, Cambridge, MA: Harvard University Press; Washington, DC: Center for Hellenic Studies.

Mallory, J. P. (1989), *In Search of the Indo-Europeans: Language, Archaeology, and Myth*, London: Thames and Hudson.

Mansukhani, Kiran, and Nicole Nowbahar (2019), '"γυμνοὺς κριτέον ἁπάντων τούτων": A Recap of The Sportula's *Naked Soul Conference* 2019', Paper delivered at the 15th Congress of the Fédération international des associations d'études classiques and the Classical Association Annual Conference, London.

Marchand, Suzanne L. (1996), *Down from Olympus: Archaeology and Philhellenism in Germany, 1750–1970*, Princeton, NJ: Princeton University Press.

Marchand, Suzanne L. (2009), *German Orientalism in the Age of Empire: Religion, Race, and Scholarship*, Cambridge: Cambridge University Press.

Marchand, Suzanne L., and Anthony Grafton (1997), 'Martin Bernal and His Critics', *Arion*, 5 (2): 1–35.
Maré, Gerhard (2015), *Moving Beyond the Dead-End of Race in South Africa*, Johannesburg: Jacana.
Marks, Jonathan (2017), *Is Science Racist? Debating Race*, Malden, MA: Polity.
Marshall, C. W. (2013), 'Sex Slaves in New Comedy', in Ben Akrigg and Rob Tordoff (eds), *Slaves and Slavery in Ancient Greek Comic Drama*, 173–96, Cambridge: Cambridge University Press.
Martin, Dale B. (2005), 'Introduction', in Dale B. Martin and Patricia Cox Miller (eds), *The Cultural Turn in Late Ancient Studies: Gender, Asceticism, and Historiography*, 1–21, Durham, NC: Duke University Press.
Mattern, Susan (2013), *The Prince of Medicine: Galen in the Roman Empire*, Oxford: Oxford University Press.
Mattingly, David J. (2011), *Imperialism, Power and Identity: Experiencing the Roman Empire*, Princeton, NJ: Princeton University Press.
Matzner, Sebastian, and Stephen Harrison, eds (2019), *Complex Inferiorities: The Poetics of the Weaker Voice in Latin Literature*, Oxford: Oxford University Press.
Mayor, Adrienne, John Colarusso and David Saunders (2014), 'Making Sense of Nonsense Inscriptions Associated with Amazons and Scythians on Athenian Vases', *Hesperia*, 83: 447–93.
Mbembe, Achille (2019), *Necropolitics*, Durham, NC: Duke University Press.
McCoskey, Denise Eileen (2002), 'Race Before "Whiteness": Studying Identity in Ptolemaic Egypt', *Critical Sociology*, 28: 13–39.
McCoskey, Denise Eileen (2003), 'By Any Other Name? Ethnicity and the Study of Ancient Identity', *Classical Bulletin*, 79 (1): 93–109.
McCoskey, Denise Eileen (2006), 'Naming the Fault in Question: Theorizing Racism among the Greeks and Romans', *International Journal of the Classical Tradition*, 13 (2): 243–67
McCoskey, Denise Eileen (2012), *Race: Antiquity and its Legacy*, Oxford: Oxford University Press.
McCoskey, Denise Eileen (2018a), 'Bad to the Bone: The Racist Application of DNA Science to Classical Antiquity', *Eidolon*, 18 June. Available online: https://eidolon.pub/bad-to-the-bone-617ca3e37347 (accessed 10 September 2019).
McCoskey, Denise Eileen (2018b), 'Black Athena, White Power: Are We Paying The Price for Classics' Response to Bernal?', *Eidolon*, 15 November. Available online: https://eidolon.pub/black-athena-white-power-6bd1899a46f2 (accessed 19 June 2019).
McGrath, Elizabeth (1992), 'The Black Andromeda', *Journal of the Warburg and Courtauld Institutes*, 55: 1–18.
McInerney, Jeremy (2014a), 'Ethnicity: An Introduction', in Jeremy McInerney (ed.), *A Companion to Ethnicity in the Ancient Mediterranean*, 1–16, Chichester, UK: John Wiley and Sons.
McInerney, Jeremy, ed. (2014b), *A Companion to Ethnicity in the Ancient Mediterranean*, Chichester, UK: John Wiley and Sons.
Meier, Harry O. (2011), 'Dominion from Sea to Sea: Eusebius of Caesarea, Constantine the Great, and the Exegesis of Empire', in Mark Vessey, Sharon Betcher, Robert A. Daum and Harry O. Maier (eds), *The Calling of the Nations: Exegesis, Ethnography, and Empire in a Biblical-Historic Present*, 149–75, Toronto: University of Toronto Press.
Michaels, Walter Benn (1995), 'Race into Culture: A Critical Genealogy of Cultural Identity', repr. in Kwame Anthony Appiah and Henry Louis Gates Jr (eds), *Identities*, 32–62, Chicago: University of Chicago Press.

Mignolo, Walter (2005), 'Imperial/Colonial Metamorphosis: From the Ottoman and Spanish Empires to the US and the European Union', in Candido Mendes (ed.), *Islam, Latinité, Transmodernité*, 91–145, Rio de Janeiro: Académie de la Latinité.

Miller, Margaret C. (1991), 'Foreigners at the Greek Symposium?', in William J. Slater (ed.), *Dining in a Classical Context*, 59–83, Ann Arbor, MI: University of Michigan Press.

Miller, Margaret C. (1997), *Athens and Persia in the Fifth Century* BC: *A Study in Cultural Receptivity*, Cambridge: Cambridge University Press.

Mills, Charles (2015), 'Decolonizing Western Political Philosophy', *New Political Science*, 37 (1): 1–24.

'Mississippi Wedding Venue Refuses Interracial Pair Over Owner's Christian Faith' (2019), *BBC News*, 3 September. Available online: https://www.bbc.com/news/world-us-canada-49571207 (accessed 29 July 2020).

Mitchell, L. B. (1922), 'Background of the Roman Revolution', *Classical Journal*, 17 (6): 316–23.

Mitchell, Stephen (1993), *Anatolia: Land, Men, and Gods in Asia Minor*, Oxford: Clarendon Press.

Mitchell, Stephen, and Geoffrey Greatrex, eds (2000), *Ethnicity and Culture in Late Antiquity*, London: Duckworth and the Classical Press of Wales.

Monoson, Sara (2011), 'Recollecting Aristotle: Pro-Slavery Thought in Antebellum America and the Argument of *Politics* Book I', in Edith Hall, Richard Alston and Justine McConnell (eds), *Ancient Slavery and Abolition: From Hobbes to Hollywood*, 247–78, Oxford: Oxford University Press.

Montagu, Ashley (1997), *Man's Most Dangerous Myth: The Fallacy of Race*, 6th edn, Walnut Creek, CA: AltaMira Press.

Morgan, J. R. (1982), 'History, Romance, and Realism in the *Aithiopika* of Heliodorus', *Classical Antiquity*, 1 (2): 221–65.

Morgan, J. R. (2005), 'Le Blanc et le Noir: Perspectives Païennes et Chrétiennes sur l'Éthiopie d'Héliodore', in Bernard Pouderon (ed.), *Lieux, décors et paysages de l'ancien roman des origines à Byzance*, Collection de la Maison de l'Orient et de la Méditeraneé 34, 309–18, Tours: L'Université François-Rabelais de Tours.

Morgan, J. R., trans. ([1989] 2008), 'Heliodorus: An Ethiopian Story', in B. P. Reardon (ed.), *Collected Ancient Greek Novels*, with a new foreword by J.R. Morgan, 349–588, Berkeley: University of California Press.

Morrison, Toni (1993), *Playing in the Dark: Whiteness and the Literary Imagination*, New York: Vintage.

Moten, Fred (2003), *In The Break: The Aesthetics of the Black Radical Tradition*, Minneapolis: University of Minnesota Press.

Moxnes, Halvor (2012), *Jesus and the Rise of Nationalism: A New Quest for the Nineteenth-Century Historical Jesus*, London: I.B. Taurus.

Moya, Paula M. L., and Hazel Rose Markus (2010), 'Introduction: Doing Race', in Hazel Rose Markus and Paul M. L. Moya (eds), *Doing Race: 21 Essays for the 21st Century*, 1–102, New York: Norton.

Moyer, Ian S. (2011), *Egypt and the Limits of Hellenism*, Cambridge: Cambridge University Press.

Moyer, Ian, Adam Lecznar and Heidi Morse, eds (2020), *Classicisms in the Black Atlantic*, Oxford: Oxford University Press.

Mudimbe, V. Y. (1994), *The Idea of Africa*, Bloomington: Indiana University Press.

Mullen, Alex (2013), *Southern Gaul and the Mediterranean: Multilingualism and Multiple Identities in the Iron Age and Roman Periods*, Cambridge: Cambridge University Press.

Mullen, Alex, and Patrick James, eds (2012), *Multilingualism in the Graeco-Roman Worlds*, Cambridge: Cambridge University Press.

Müller, Klaus E. (1972–80), *Geschichte der antiken Ethnographie und ethnographischen Theoriebildung*, 2 vols, Wiesbaden: F. Steiner.

Munson, Rosaria Vignolo (2014), 'Herodotus and Ethnicity', in Jeremy McInerney (ed.), *A Companion to Ethnicity in the Ancient Mediterranean*, 341–55, Chichester, UK: John Wiley and Sons.

Mveng, Engelbert (1972), *Les sources grecques de l'histoire négro-africaine depuis Homère jusqu'à Strabon*, Paris: Présence Africaine.

Myśliwiec, K. (1988), *Royal Portraiture of the Dynasties XXI–XXX*, Mainz: Verlag Philipp von Zabern.

Narain, A. K. (1957), *The Indo-Greeks*, Oxford: Clarendon Press.

Narayan, Yasmeen (2019), 'Intersectionality, Nationalisms, Biocolonality', *Ethnic and Racial Studies*, 42 (8): 1225–44.

Nongbri, Brent (2015), *Before Religion: A History of a Modern Concept*, New Haven, CT: Yale University Press.

Nora, P. (1989), 'Between Memory and History: *Les Lieux de Mémoire*', *Representations*, 26: 7–24.

Norton, Charles Eliot (1900), 'The Work of the Archaeological Institute of America: An Address', *American Journal of Archaeology*, 4 (1): 1–16.

Nott, Josiah Clark, and George Robins Gliddon (1854), *Types of Mankind; or, Ethnological Researches, Based upon the Ancient Monuments, Paintings, Sculptures, and Crania of Races, and upon their Natural, Geographical, Philological, and Biblical History*, Philadelphia: Lippincott, Grambo.

Novick, Peter (1988), *That Noble Dream: the 'objectivity question' and the American Historical Profession*, Cambridge: Cambridge University Press.

Noy, David (2000), *Foreigners at Rome: Citizens and Strangers*, London: Duckworth.

Noy, David (2004), 'Being an Egyptian in Rome: Strategies of Identity Formation', in Jürgen Zangenberg and Michael Labahn (eds), *Christians as a Religious Minority in a Multicultural City: Modes of Interaction and Identity Formation in Early Imperial Rome*, Journal for the Study of the New Testament Supplement Series 243, 47–54, London: T & T Clark International.

Nutton, Vivian (2004), *Ancient Medicine*, London: Routledge.

Ogden, Daniel (1995), 'Women and Bastardy in Ancient Greece and the Hellenistic World', in Anton Powell (ed.), *The Greek World*, 219–44, London: Routledge.

Olender, Maurice (1992), *The Languages of Paradise: Race, Religion, and Philology in the Nineteenth Century*, trans. Arthur Goldhammer, Cambridge, MA: Harvard University Press.

Omi, Michael, and Howard Winant ([1986] 2015), *Racial Formation in the United States*, 3rd edn, New York: Routledge.

Orrells, Daniel, Gurminder K. Bhambra and Tessa Roynon, eds (2011), *African Athena: New Agendas*, Oxford: Oxford University Press.

Oxford English Dictionary (1989), s.v. 'valet', 2nd edn, Oxford: Oxford University Press.

Padilla Peralta, Dan-el (2015a), 'From Damocles to Socrates: The Classics in/of Hip-Hop', *Eidolon*, 8 June. Available online: https://eidolon.pub/from-damocles-to-socrates-fbda6e685c26 (accessed 10 September 2019).

Padilla Peralta, Dan-el (2015b), *Undocumented: A Dominican Boy's Odyssey from a Homeless Shelter to the Ivy League*, New York: Penguin Press.

Padilla Peralta, Dan-el (2017a), 'Classics Beyond the Pale', *Eidolon*, 20 February. Available online: https://eidolon.pub/classics-beyond-the-pale-534bdbb3601b (accessed 20 June 2019).

Padilla Peralta, Dan-el (2017b), 'The Colorblind Bard: Letter to the Editors', *The New Criterion*, 31 August. Available online: https://www.newcriterion.com/blogs/dispatch/colorblind-bard-exchange (accessed 19 June 2019).

Padilla Peralta, Dan-el (2019a), 'Racial Equity and the Production of Knowledge', Paper delivered at the 150th SCS and AIA Joint Annual Meeting, San Diego, California. Available online: https://www.dropbox.com/s/0gfxoljbi9nsr8r/Padilla%20Peralta%20SCS%20 2019%20Future%20of%20Classics%20Equity%20and%20the%20Production%20of%20 Knowledge%20ed%20w%20tables.pdf?dl=0 (accessed 19 June 2019).

Padilla Peralta, Dan-el (2019b), 'Some Thoughts on AIA-SCS 2019', *Medium*, 7 January. Available online: https://medium.com/@danelpadillaperalta/some-thoughts-on-aia-scs-2019-d6a480a1812a (accessed 19 June 2019).

Painter, Nell I. (2010), *The History of White People*, New York: W. W. Norton.

Papadopoulou, Chrysanthi (2017), 'The Living and Their Dead in Classical Athens: New Evidence from Acharnai, Halai Aixonidai & Phaleron', *Archaeological Reports*, 63: 151–66.

Parker, Grant (2001), *The Agony of Asar: A Treatise on Slavery by the Former Slave, Jacobus Elisa Johannes Capitein, 1717–1747*, Princeton, NJ: Markus Wiener Publishers.

Parker, Grant (2007), 'Hellenism in an Afghan Context', in Himanshu Prabha Ray and Daniel T. Potts (eds), *Memory as History: The Legacy of Alexander in Asia*, 170–91, New Delhi: Aryan Books International.

Parker, Grant (2010), 'Heraclitus on the Highveld: The Universalism (Ancient and Modern) of T.J. Haarhoff', in Susan A. Stephens and Phiroze Vasunia (eds), *Classics and National Cultures*, 217–34, Oxford: Oxford University Press.

Parker, Grant (2017a), 'The Azanian Man: Classicism in Unexpected Places', in Grant Parker (ed.), *South Africa, Greece, Rome: Classical Confrontations*, 3–52, Cambridge: Cambridge University Press.

Parker, Grant, ed. (2017b), *South Africa, Greece, Rome: Classical Confrontations*, Cambridge: Cambridge University Press.

Parmenter, Christopher S. (2021), '"A Happy Coincidence": Race, the Cold War, and Frank M. Snowden, Jr's *Blacks in Antiquity*', *Classical Receptions Journal*. https://doi.org/10.1093/crj/clab001.

Penn, Michael Philip (2015), *Envisioning Islam: Syriac Christians and the Early Muslim World*, Philadelphia: University of Pennsylvania Press.

Perkinson, James W. (2004), *White Theology: Outing Supremacy in Modernity*, New York: Palgrave Macmillan.

Pesditschek, Martina (2005), 'Die Karriere des Althistorikers Fritz Schachermeyr im Dritten Reich und in der Zweiten Republik', *Mensch, Wissenschaft, Magie. Mitteilungen der österreichischen Gesellschaft für Wissenschaftsgeschichte*, 25: 41–71.

Peters, Francis E. (1968), *Aristoteles Arabus*, Leiden: Brill.

Petersen, Jane H. (2010), *Cultural Interactions and Social Strategies on the Pontic Shores. Burial Customs in the Northern Black Sea Area C. 550–270 BC*, Aarhus: Aarhus University Press.

Pharos (2018), 'Site Blames "Decline" of Greece on Loss of Racial Purity', *Pharos: Doing Justice to the Classics*, 29 June. Available online: https://pages.vassar.edu/pharos/2018/06/29/site-blames-decline-of-greece-on-loss-of-racial-purity/ (accessed 18 July 2020).

Pharos (2020), 'Report: White Supremacy and the Past and Future of Classics Roundtable', *Pharos: Doing Justice to the Classics*, 24 January. Available online: http://pages.vassar.edu/pharos/2020/01/24/report-white-supremacy-and-the-past-and-future-of-classics-roundtable/ (accessed 24 January 2020).

Pigeaud, Jackie (1995), *L'art et le Vivant*, Paris: Gallimard.

Pollmann, Karla (2011), 'Unending Sway: The Ideology of Empire in Early Christian Latin Thought', in Mark Vessey, Sharon Betcher, Robert A. Daum and Harry O. Maier (eds), *The Calling of the Nations: Exegesis, Ethnography, and Empire in a Biblical-Historic Present*, 176–99, Toronto: University of Toronto Press.

Pomeroy, Sarah B. (2002), *Spartan Women*, Oxford: Oxford University Press.

Porter, James I., ed. (2006), *Classical Pasts: The Classical Traditions of Greece and Rome*, Princeton, NJ: Princeton University Press.

Quinn, Josephine Crawley (2017), *In Search of the Phoenicians*, Princeton, NJ: Princeton University Press.

Quinn, Josephine Crawley (2018), 'Time to Move On: Arguing against Traditional Definitions of the "Classics"', *TLS*, 21 September. Available online: https://www.the-tls.co.uk/articles/time-to-move-on/ (accessed 16 July 2020).

Quinn, Josephine Crawley (2019), 'After San Diego: Reflections on Racism in Classics', *Council of University Classical Departments Bulletin*, 48. Available online: https://cucd.blogs.sas.ac.uk/files/2019/01/Quinn-AFTER-SAN-DIEGO.pdf (accessed 19 June 2019).

Ram-Prasad, Krishnan (2019), 'Reclaiming the Ancient World: Towards a Decolonized Classics', *Eidolon*, 3 July. Available online: https://eidolon.pub/reclaiming-the-ancient-world-c481fc19c0e3 (accessed 20 September 2019).

Rankine, Claudia (2014), *Citizen: An American Lyric*, Minneapolis, MN: Greywolf Press.

Rankine, Patrice D. (2006), *Ulysses in Black: Ralph Ellison, Classicism, and African American Literature*, Madison: University of Wisconsin Press.

Rankine, Patrice D. (2019), 'The Classics, Race, and Community-Engaged or Public Scholarship', *American Journal of Philology*, 140 (2): 345–59.

Raven, Susan (1993), *Rome in Africa*, 3rd edn, London: Routledge.

Ray, Victor (2018), 'The Racial Politics of Citation', *Inside Higher Ed*, 27 April. Available online: https://www.insidehighered.com/advice/2018/04/27/racial-exclusions-scholarly-citations-opinion (accessed 20 June 2019).

Rebeggiani, Stefano (2018), 'Buried Treasures, Hidden Verses: (Re)Appropriating the Gauls of Pergmon in Flavian Rome', in Matthew P. Loar, Carolyn Macdonald and Dan-el Padilla Peralta (eds), *Rome, Empire of Plunder: The Dynamics of Cultural Appropriation*, 69–81, Cambridge: Cambridge University Press.

Redfield, James (1985), 'Herodotus the Tourist', *Classical Philology*, 80: 97–118.

Reed, Adolph, Jr (2000), 'Skin Deep', in *Class Notes: Posing as Politics and Other Thoughts on the American Scene*, 139–43, New York: The New Press.

Reeve, Michael (1989), 'Conceptions', *Proceedings of the Cambridge Philological Society*, 215: 81–112.

Reinhold, Meyer (1984), *Classica Americana: The Greek and Roman Heritage in the United States*, Detroit, MI: Wayne State University Press.

Repath, Ian, trans. (2007a), 'Anonymus Latinus, *Book of Physiognomy*', in Simon Swain (ed.), *Seeing the Face, Seeing the Soul: Polemon's* Physiognomy *from Classical Antiquity to Medieval Islam*, 549–636, Oxford: Oxford University Press.

Repath, Ian, trans. (2007b), 'The *Physiognomy of Adamantius the Sophist*', in Simon Swain (ed.), *Seeing the Face, Seeing the Soul: Polemon's* Physiognomy *from Classical Antiquity to Medieval Islam*, 487–548, Oxford: Oxford University Press.

Reuben, Gabriel H., and Sheila Schwartz (1974), *How People Lived in Ancient Greece and Rome*, Chicago: Benefic Press.
Revell, Louise (2009), *Roman Imperialism and Local Identities*, Cambridge: Cambridge University Press.
Revell, Louise (2016), *Ways of Being Roman: Discourses of Identity in the Roman West*, Oxford: Oxbow Books.
Richard, Carl J. (2008), *Greeks and Romans Bearing Gifts: How the Ancients Inspired the Founding Fathers*, Lanham, MD: Rowman & Littlefield.
Richard, Carl J. (2009), *The Golden Age of the Classics in America*, New York: Harvard University Press.
Richardson, Edmund, ed. (2019), *Classics in Extremis: The Edges of Classical Reception*, London: Bloomsbury.
Richardson, Luke (2017), 'Teaching the Classical Reception "Revolution"', *Council of University Classical Departments Bulletin*, 46. Available online: https://cucd.blogs.sas.ac.uk/files/2015/01/RICHARDSON-Revolutions-Reception-Revolution.pdf (accessed 20 June 2019).
Ridgeway, William (1896), 'What People Produced the Objects Called Mycenaean?', *Journal of Hellenic Studies*, 16: 77–119.
Rives, James B. (1999), 'The Decree of Decius and the Religion of the Empire', *Journal of Roman Studies*, 89: 135–54.
Robinson, C. A., Jr (1939), 'Review of *Race Mixture among the Greeks before Alexander* by Aubrey Diller', *Classical Philology*, 34 (2): 184–6.
Robinson, David M. (1930), *Excavations at Olynthus, Part 2. Architecture and Sculpture: Houses and Other Buildings*, John Hopkins University Studies in Archaeology 9, Baltimore, MD: Johns Hopkins University Press.
Robinson, David M. (1931), *Excavations at Olynthus, Part 4. The Terracottas of Olynthus Found in 1928*, John Hopkins University Studies in Archaeology 12, Baltimore, MD: Johns Hopkins University Press.
Robinson, David M. (1933), *Excavations at Olynthus, Part 7. The Terracottas of Olynthus Found in 1931*, John Hopkins University Studies in Archaeology 20, Baltimore, MD: Johns Hopkins University Press.
Robinson, David M. (1952), *Excavations at Olynthus, Part 14. Terracottas, Lamps and Coins Found in 1934 and 1938*, John Hopkins University Studies in Archaeology 39, Baltimore, MD: Johns Hopkins University Press.
Roche, Helen, and Kyriakos Demetriou, eds (2018), *Brill's Companion to the Classics, Fascist Italy and Nazi Germany*, Leiden: Brill.
Romm, James (1992), *The Edges of the Earth in Ancient Thought*, Princeton, NJ: Princeton University Press.
Ronnick, Michele Valerie (2004), 'Twelve Black Classicists', *Arion*, 11 (3): 85–102.
Ronnick, Michele Valerie, ed. (2005), *The Works of William Sanders Scarborough: Black Classicist and Race Leader*, Oxford: Oxford University Press.
Root, Margaret Cool (1979), *The King and Kingship in Achaemenid Art: Essays on the Creation of an Iconography of Empire*, Leiden: Brill.
Rosivach, Vincent J. (1987), 'Autochthony and the Athenians', *Classical Quarterly*, 32: 294–306.
Rosivach, Vincent J. (1999), 'Enslaving *Barbaroi* and the Athenian Ideology of Slavery', *Historia*, 48: 129–57.
Ross, Alan (2015), 'Syene as Face of Battle: Heliodorus and Late Antique Historiography', *Ancient Narrative*, 12: 1–26.

Rostovtzeff, M. (1929), 'Roman Exploitation of Egypt in the First Century A.D.', *Journal of Economic and Business History*, 1 (3): 337–64.

Roy, James (2014), 'Autochthony in Ancient Greece', in Jeremy McInerney (ed.), *A Companion to Ethnicity in the Ancient Mediterranean*, 241–55, Chichester, UK: John Wiley and Sons.

Roymans, Nico, and Ton Derks, eds (2009), *Ethnic Constructs in Antiquity: The Role of Power and Tradition*, Amsterdam: Amsterdam University Press.

Ruggini, Lellia Cracco (1987), 'Intolerance: Equal, and Less Equal in the Roman World', *Classical Philology*, 82 (3): 187–205.

Rutgers, Leonard Victor (1994), 'Roman Policy towards the Jews: Expulsions from the City of Rome during the First Century CE', *Classical Antiquity*, 13 (1): 56–74.

'Ryanair Flight Rant Man Says He Is "not a racist"' (2018), *BBC News*, 26 October. Available online: https://www.bbc.com/news/uk-england-essex-45988890 (accessed 29 July 2020).

Saddington, D. B. (1975), 'Race Relations in the Early Roman Empire', *Aufstieg und Niedergang der Römischen Welt*, 2 (3): 112–37.

Said, Edward (1978), *Orientalism*, New York: Vintage.

Saini, Angela (2019), *Superior: The Return of Race Science*, Boston: Beacon Press.

Samuels, Tristan (2015), 'Herodotus and the Black Body: A Critical Race Theory Analysis', *Journal of Black Studies*, 46 (7): 723–41.

Sanders, Barry, and Francis Adams (2004), *Alienable Rights*, New York: Harper Collins.

Sassi, Maria M. (2001), *The Science of Man in Ancient Greece*, trans. Paul Tucker, Chicago: University of Chicago Press.

Schachermeyr, Fritz (1939a), 'Der Begriff des Arteigenen im frühzeitlichen Kunstgewerbe', *Klio* 14: 339–57.

Schachermeyr, Fritz (1939b), *Zur Rasse und Kultur im minoischen Kreta*, Heidelberg: Winter.

Schachermeyr, Fritz (1940). *Lebensgesetzlichkeit in der Geschichte. Versuch einer Einführung in das geschichtsbiologische Denken*, Frankfurt: Klostermann.

Schachermeyr, Fritz (1944), *Indogermanen und Orient*, Stuttgart: Kohlhammer.

Schachermeyr, Fritz (1960), *Griechische Geschichte: Mit besonderer Berücksichtigung der geistesgeschichtlichen und kulturmorphologischen Zusammenhänge*, Stuttgart: Kohlhammer.

Schachermeyr, Fritz (1969), *Perikles*, Stuttgart: Kohlhammer.

Schachermeyr, Fritz (1973), *Alexander der Grosse: Das Problem seiner Persönlichkeit und seines Wirkens*, Vienna: Österreichische Akademie.

Schachermeyr, Fritz (1981), *Die Tragik der Voll-Endung*, Vienna: Koska.

Schäfer, Peter (1997), *Judeophobia: Attitudes toward the Jews in the Ancient World*, Cambridge, MA: Harvard University Press.

Scheerlinck, Eline, Danny Praet, and Sarah Rey (2016), 'Race and Religious Transformations in Rome', *Historia*, 65 (2): 220–43.

Schlaifer, R. (1936), 'Greek Theories of Slavery from Homer to Aristotle', *Harvard Studies in Classical Philology*, 47: 165–204.

Schmitt, R. (2000), *The Old Persian Inscriptions of Naqsh-I Rustam and Persepolis*, London: SOAS.

Schneider, Rolf Michael (2012), 'The Making of Oriental Rome: Shaping the Trojan Legend', in Peter Fibiger Bang and Dariusz Kolodziejczyk (eds), *Universal Empire*, 76–129, Cambridge: Cambridge University Press.

Schofield, Malcolm (1999), 'Ideology and Philosophy in Aristotle's Theory of Slavery', in Malcolm Schofield (ed.), *Saving the City: Philosopher Kings and Other Classical Paradigms*, 115–40, Cambridge: Cambridge University Press.

Schuller, Kyla (2018), *The Biopolitics of Feeling: Race, Sex, and Science in the Nineteenth Century*, Durham, NC: Duke University Press.

Schwartz, Seth (2001), *Imperialism and Jewish Society, 200 B.C.E. to 640 C.E.*, Princeton, NJ: Princeton University Press.

Seaford, Richard (1982), 'The Date of Euripides' Cyclops', *Journal of Hellenic Studies*, 102: 161–72.

Sen, Sharmila (2018), *Not Quite Not White: Losing and Finding Race in America*, New York: Penguin.

Settis, Salvatore (2006), *The Future of the Classical*, trans. Alan Cameron, Cambridge: Polity.

Sharpe, Christina (2016), *In the Wake: On Blackness and Being*, Durham, NC: Duke University Press.

Shaw, Brent D. (2014), 'Who Are You? Africa and Africans', in Jeremy McInerney (ed.), *A Companion to Ethnicity in the Ancient Mediterranean*, 527–40, Chichester, UK: John Wiley and Sons.

Shaw, Brent D, ed. (2001), *Spartacus and the Slave Wars: A Brief History with Documents*, Boston: Bedford/St. Martin's.

Shennan, Stephen, ed. (1994), *Archaeological Approaches to Cultural Identity*, London: Routledge.

Sherwin-White, Adrian N. (1967), *Racial Prejudice in Imperial Rome*, Cambridge: Cambridge University Press.

Sherwin-White, Adrian N. (1973), *The Roman Citizenship*, 2nd edn, Oxford: Clarendon Press.

Shipley, Frederick W. (1922), 'Race Mixture and Literary Genius in the Roman Provinces', *Washington University Studies*, 9 (2): 99–118.

Shipley, Graham (2000), *The Greek World After Alexander, 323–30 B.C.*, London: Routledge.

Sidanius, Jim, and Felicia Pratto (1999), *Social Dominance: An Intergroup Theory of Social Hierarchy and Oppression*, New York: Cambridge University Press.

Singer, Peter N., and Philip van der Eijk, eds and trans. (2018), *Galen: Works on Human Nature*, vol. 1, Cambridge: Cambridge University Press.

Skinner, Joseph E. (2010), 'Fish Heads and Mussel-Shells: Visualizing Greek Identity', in Lin Foxhall, Hans-Joachim Gehrke and Nino Luraghi (eds), *Intentional History: Spinning Time in Ancient Greece*, 137–60, Stuttgart: Franz Steiner Verlag.

Skinner, Joseph E. (2012), *The Invention of Greek Ethnography: From Homer to Herodotus*, Oxford: Oxford University Press.

Skinner Joseph E. (2018), 'Herodotus and His World', in Thomas Harrison and Elizabeth Irwin (eds), *Interpreting Herodotus*, 187–222, Oxford: Oxford University Press.

Smedley, Audrey, and Brian D. Smedley (2012), *Race in North America: Origin and Evolution of a Worldview*, 4th edn, Boulder, CO: Westview Press.

Smith, David Livingstone (2012), *Less Than Human: Why We Demean, Enslave, And Exterminate Others*, New York: St. Martin's Press.

Smith, Kirby Flower (1910), 'Review of *A Literary History of Rome from the Origins to the Close of the Augustan Age* by J. Wight Duff', *American Journal of Philology*, 31 (2): 222–6.

Smith, Stuart Tyson (2014), 'Nubian and Egyptian Ethnicity', in Jeremy McInerney (ed.), *A Companion to Ethnicity in the Ancient Mediterranean*, 194–212, Chichester, UK: John Wiley and Sons.

Smith-Christopher, Daniel ([1996] 2002), 'Between Ezra and Isaiah: Exclusion, Transformation and Inclusion of the "Foreigner" in Post-exilic Biblical Theology', in Mark G. Brett (ed.), *Ethnicity and the Bible*, 117–42, Leiden: Brill.

Smuts, J. C. (1926), *Holism and Evolution*, New York: Macmillan.

Snowden, Frank M. Jr (1947), 'The Negro in Classical Italy', *American Journal of Philology*, 68 (3): 266–92.

Snowden, Frank M., Jr (1948), 'The Negro in Ancient Greece', *American Anthropologist*, 50 (1): 31–44.

Snowden, Frank M., Jr (1970), *Blacks in Antiquity: Ethiopians in the Greco-Roman Experience*, Cambridge, MA: Harvard University Press.

Snowden, Frank M., Jr (1983), *Before Color Prejudice: The Ancient View of Blacks*, Cambridge, MA: Harvard University Press.

Snowden, Frank M., Jr (1988), 'Μέλας-λευκός and Niger-candidus Contrasts in Classical Literature', *Ancient History Bulletin*, 2 (2): 60–4.

Snowden, Frank M., Jr (1997), 'Greeks and Ethiopians', in John E. Coleman and Clark A. Walz (eds), *Greeks and Barbarians: Essays on the Interactions Between Greeks and Non-Greeks in Antiquity and the Consequences for Eurocentrism*, 103–26, Bethesda, MD: CDL Press.

Snowden, Frank M., Jr (2002), 'A Lifetime of Inquiry', in Benjamin P. Bowser and Louis Kushnick (eds), *Against the Odds: Scholars Who Challenged Racism in the Twentieth Century*, 41–62, Amherst: University of Massachusetts Press.

Sollors, Werner (1996), 'Foreword: Theories of American Ethnicity', in Werner Sollors (ed.), *Theories of Ethnicity: A Classical Reader*, x–xliv, New York: New York University Press.

Sommer, Michael (2010), 'Shaping Mediterranean Economy and Trade: Phoenician Cultural Identities in the Iron Age', in Shelley Hales and Tamar Hodos (eds), *Material Culture and Social Identities in the Ancient World*, 114–37, Cambridge: Cambridge University Press.

Soudien, Crain (2019), *The Cape Radicals: Intellectual and Political Thought of the New Era Fellowship, 1930s–1960s*, Johannesburg: Wits University Press.

Sourvinou-Inwood, Christiane (1991), *'Reading' Greek Culture: Texts and Images, Rituals and Myths*, Oxford: Clarendon Press.

Sousa Santos, Boaventura de (2014), *Epistemologies of the South: Justice Against Epistemicide*, Boulder, CO: Paradigm Press.

Spillers, Hortense J. (2003), 'Mama's Baby, Papa's Maybe: An American Grammar Book', in Hortense J. Spillers, *Black, White and in Color: Essays on American Literature and Culture*, 203–29, Chicago: University of Chicago Press. (First published in 1987 in *Diacritics*, 17 (2): 64–81.)

Stazsak, Jean-François (1995), *La géographie d'avant la géographie: le climat chez Aristote et Hippocrate*, Paris: Editions L'Harmattan.

Stepan, Nancy (1982), *The Idea of Race in Science: Great Britain 1800–1960*, London: Archon Books.

Stephens, Susan (2008), 'Cultural Identity', in Tim Whitmarsh (ed.), *The Cambridge Companion to the Greek and Roman Novel*, 56–71, Cambridge: Cambridge University Press.

Stepto, Robert B. ([1979] 1991), *From Behind the Veil: A Study of Afro-American Narrative*, 2nd edn, Urbana: University of Illinois Press.

Stevens, Kathryn (2019), *Between Greece and Babylonia: Hellenistic Intellectual History in Cross-Cultural Perspective*, Cambridge: Cambridge University Press.

Stewart, Roberta, and Dominic Machado (2019), 'Progress and Precarity: 150 Years of *TAPA*', *Transactions of the American Philological Association*, 149 (2) (suppl.): 39–60.

Stoler, Ann Laura (1997), 'Racial Histories and Their Regimes of Truth', *Political Power and Social Theory*, 11: 183–206.

Storey, John, ed. (1996), *What is Cultural Studies? A Reader*, London: Arnold.

Sussman, Robert W. (2014), *The Myth of Race: The Troubling Persistence of an Unscientific Idea*, Cambridge, MA: Harvard University Press.

Swain, Simon (1996), *Hellenism and Empire: Language, Classicism, and Power in the Greek World AD 50–250*, Oxford: Oxford University Press.

Swain, Simon (2007a), 'Polemon's *Physiognomy*', in Simon Swain (ed.), *Seeing the Face, Seeing the Soul: Polemon's* Physiognomy *from Classical Antiquity to Medieval Islam*, 125–203, Oxford: Oxford University Press.

Swain, Simon, ed. (2007b), *Seeing the Face, Seeing the Soul: Polemon's* Physiognomy *from Classical Antiquity to Medieval Islam*, Oxford: Oxford University Press.

Tanner, Benjamin Tucker (1902), *The Negro in Holy Writ*, Philadelphia: Pine Street.

Taylor, Paul C. (2004), *Race: A Philosophical Introduction*, Cambridge: Polity.

Taylor, Paul C. (2013), *Race*, Malden, MA: Wiley.

Thalmann, William G. (1998), 'Female Slaves in the *Odyssey*', in Sandra R. Joshel and Sheila Murnaghan (eds), *Women and Slaves in Greco-Roman Culture: Differential Equations*, 22–34, London: Routledge.

Thiong'o, Ngugi wa (1986), *Decolonising the Mind: The Politics of Language in African Literature*, Portsmouth, NH: Heinemann Press.

Thomas, Bridget M. (1998), 'Negotiable Identities: The Interpretation of Color, Gender, and Ethnicity in Aeschylus' *Suppliants*', PhD diss., Ohio State University, USA.

Thomas, Rosalind (2000), *Herodotus in Context: Ethnography, Science, and the Art of Persuasion*, Cambridge: Cambridge University Press.

Thomas, Rosalind (2001), 'Ethnicity, Genealogy, and Hellenism in Herodotus', in Irad Malkin (ed.), *Ancient Perceptions of Greek Ethnicity*, 213–33, Cambridge, MA: Harvard University Press; Washington, DC: Center for Hellenic Studies.

Thompson, Dorothy, J. (1997), 'The Infrastructure of Splendour: Census and Taxes in Ptolemaic Egypt', in Paul Cartledge, Peter Garnsey and Erich S. Gruen (eds), *Hellenistic Constructs: Essays in Culture, History, and Historiography*, 242–58, Berkeley: University of California Press.

Thompson, Lloyd A. (1981), 'The Concept of Purity of Blood in Suetonius' *Life of Augustus*', *Museum Africum*, 7: 35–46.

Thompson, Lloyd A. (1989), *Romans and Blacks*, Norman: University of Oklahoma Press.

Thompson, Lloyd A. (1993), 'Roman Perceptions of Blacks', *Scholia: Studies in Classical Antiquity*, 2 (1): 17–30.

Thonemann, Peter (2019), 'Gender, Subject Preference, and Editorial Bias in Classical Studies, 2001–2009', *Council of University Classical Departments Bulletin*, 48: 1–24. Available online: https://cucd.blogs.sas.ac.uk/files/2019/09/THONEMANN-Gender-subject-preference-editorial-bias.pdf (accessed 30 July 2020).

Todd, O. J. (1925), 'The Authorship of the *Moretum*', *Classical Philology*, 20 (4): 336–40.

Todd, Robert B., gen. ed. (2004), *The Dictionary of British Classicists*, 3 vols, Bristol: Thoemmes Continuum.

Todorov, Tzvetan (1993), *On Human Diversity: Nationalism, Racism and Exoticism in French Thought*, trans. Catherine Porter, Cambridge, MA: Harvard University Press.

Tracy, H. L. (1944), 'Review of *The Challenge of the Greek and Other Essays* by T. R. Glover', *Classical Journal*, 40 (3): 178–80.

Tracy, Theodore (1969), *Physiological Theory and the Doctrine of the Mean in Plato and Aristotle*, Chicago: Loyola University Press.

Tsigarida, Bettina (2017), 'Figurines of Ancient Olynthos', in Polyxeni Adam-Veleni, Angeliki Koukouvou, Ourania Palli, Evangelia Stefani and Elektra Zografou (eds), *Figurines: A Microcosmos of Clay*, 80–2, Archaeological Museum of Thessaloniki, Exhibition catalogue.

Tuplin, C. J. (1999), '"Greek Racism?" Observations on the Character and Limits of Greek Ethnic Prejudice', in G. R. Tsetskhladze (ed.), *Ancient Greeks West & East*, 47–77, Leiden: Brill.

Tuplin, C. J. (2007a), 'Racism in Classical Antiquity? Three Opinions', *Ancient West and East*, 6: 327–38.

Tuplin, C. J., ed. (2007b), *Persian Responses: Political and Cultural Interaction with(in) the Achaemenid Empire*, Oxford: Oxbow.

Umachandran, Mathura (2019), 'More Than a Common Tongue: Dividing Race and Classics Across the Atlantic', *Eidolon*, 11 June. Available online: https://eidolon.pub/more-than-a-common-tongue-cfd7edeb6368 (accessed 14 June 2019).

Ureña, Carolyn (2019), 'Decolonial Embodiment: Fanon, the Clinical Encounter, and the Colonial Wound', *Disability and the Global South*, 6 (1): 1640–58.

Van de Mieroop, Marc (2011), *A History of Ancient Egypt*, Malden, MA: Wiley-Blackwell.

van der Eijk, Philip (2014), 'Galen on the Nature of Human Beings', in Peter Adamson, Rotraud Hansberger and James Wilberding (eds), *Philosophical Themes in Galen*, 89–134, London: University of London Press.

van der Eijk, Philip (2015), 'Galen on the Assessment of Bodily Mixtures', in Brooke Holmes and Klaus-Dietrich Fischer (eds), *The Frontiers of Ancient Science: Essays in Honor of Heinrich von Staden*, 675–98, Berlin: De Gruyter.

Vansickle, Abbie (2020), 'You Can Get Kicked out of a Jury Pool for Supporting Black Lives Matter', *The Marshall Project*, 7 July. Available online: https://www.themarshallproject.org/2020/07/07/you-can-get-kicked-out-of-a-jury-pool-for-supporting-black-lives-matter (accessed 18 July 2020).

Varto, Emily (2015), 'Stories Told in Lists: Formulaic Genealogies as Intentional Histories', *Journal of Ancient History*, 3: 118–49.

Vasunia, Phiroze (2003), 'Hellenism and Empire: Reading Edward Said', *Parallax*, 9 (4): 88–97.

Vinogradov, J. G. (1997), 'Die Stele des Leoxos, Molpagores' Sohn, aus Olbia und die Skythisch-Griechischen Beziehungen im frühen 5. Jh. v.Chr.', in J. G. Vinogradov and H. Heinen (eds), *Pontische Studien. Kleine Schriften zur Geschichte und Epigraphik des Schwarzmeerraumes*, 230–41, Mainz: Philipp von Zabern.

Vitello, Paul (2013), 'Martin Bernal, "Black Athena" Scholar, Dies at 76', *The New York Times*, 22 June. Available online: https://www.nytimes.com/2013/06/23/arts/martin-bernal-black-athena-scholar-dies-at-76.html (accessed 18 July 2020).

Vlassopoulos, Kostas (2007a), 'Free Spaces: Identity, Experience and Democracy in Classical Athens', *Classical Quarterly*, 57 (1): 33–52.

Vlassopoulos, Kostas (2007b), *Unthinking the Greek Polis: Ancient History beyond Eurocentrism*, Cambridge: Cambridge University Press.

Vlassopoulos, Kostas (2010a), 'Athenian Slave Names and Athenian Social History', *ZPE*, 175: 113–44.

Vlassopoulos, Kostas (2010b), 'Constructing Antiquity and Modernity in the Eighteenth Century: Distantiation, Alterity, Proximity, Immanency', in Lin Foxhall, Hans-Joachim Gehrke and Nino Luraghi (eds), *Intentional History: Spinning Time in Ancient Greece*, 343–62, Stuttgart: F. Steiner.

Vlassopoulos, Kostas (2011), 'Greek Slavery: From Domination to Property and Back Again', *Journal of Hellenic Studies*, 131: 115–30.

Vlassopoulos, Kostas (2013a), *Greeks and Barbarians*, Cambridge: Cambridge University Press.

Vlassopoulos, Kostas (2013b), 'The Stories of the Others: Storytelling and Intercultural Communication in the Herodotean Mediterranean', in Eran Almagor and Joseph Skinner (eds), *Ancient Ethnography: New Approaches*, 49–76, London: Bloomsbury.

Vogt, Sabine, ed. and comm. (1999), *Aristoteles: Physiognomonica*, Berlin: Akademie Verlag.

von Staden, Heinrich (2012), 'The Phyisology and Therapy of Anger: Galen on Medicine, the Soul, and Nature', in Felicitas Opwis and David Reisman (eds), *Islamic Philosophy, Science, Culture, and Religion*, 63–87, Leiden: Brill.

Wade, Peter (2002), *Race, Nature and Culture: An Anthropological Perspective*, London: Pluto Press.

Wallinger, Hanna (2005), *Pauline E. Hopkins, A Literary Biography*, Athens: University of Georgia Press.

Walsh, Lisl (2018), 'What a Difference an ἤ Makes: Hippocrates, Racism, and the Translation of Greco-Roman Thought', *Society for Classical Studies Blog*, 1 November. Available online: https://classicalstudies.org/scs-blog/lisl-walsh/blog-what-difference-%E1%BC%A4-makes-hippocrates-racism-and-translation-greco-roman (accessed 29 July 2020).

Wasserman, Mira Beth (2017), *Jews, Gentiles, and Other Animals: The Talmud After the Humanities*, Philadelphia: University of Pennsylvania Press.

Watts, W. J. (1976), 'Race Prejudice in the Satires of Juvenal', *Acta Classica*, 19: 83–104.

Webster, Jane (2001), 'Creolizing the Roman Provinces', *American Journal of Archaeology*, 105 (2): 209–25.

Weiss, Roberto (1988), *The Renaissance Discovery of Classical Antiquity*, Oxford: Blackwell.

Welsby, Derek A. (1998), *The Kingdom of Kush: The Napatan and Meroitic Empires*, Princeton, NJ: Marcus Wiener.

Wenger, Ayelet (2017), '"Our" "Classics": Problems of Difference in Western Civilization', *Eidolon*, 28 August. Available online: https://eidolon.pub/our-classics-93292adafbb2 (accessed 20 June 2019).

Whitmarsh, Tim (1999), 'The Writes of Passage: Cultural Initiation in Heliodorus' *Aethiopica*', in Richard Miles (ed.), *Constructing Identities in Late Antiquity*, 16–40, London: Routledge Press.

Whitmarsh, Tim, ed. (2008), *The Cambridge Companion to the Greek and Roman Novel*, Cambridge: Cambridge University Press.

Whitmarsh, Tim (2009), *The Second Sophistic*, Cambridge: Cambridge University Press.

Whitmarsh, Tim, ed. (2010), *Local Knowledge and Microidentities in the Imperial Greek World*, Cambridge: Cambridge University Press.

Whitmarsh, Tim (2011), *Narrative and Identity in the Ancient Greek Novel: Returning Romance*, Cambridge: Cambridge University Press.

Whitmarsh, Tim (2018), 'When Homer Envisioned Achilles, Did He See A Black Man?', *Aeon*, 9 May. Available online: https://aeon.co/essays/when-homer-envisioned-achilles-did-he-see-a-black-man (accessed 19 June 2019).

Whitmarsh Tim, and Stuart Thomson (2013), *The Romance between Greece and the East*, Cambridge: Cambridge University Press.

Wiegman, Robyn (1999), 'Whiteness Studies and the Paradox of Particularity', *boundary 2*, 26 (3): 115–49.

Wiesen, David S. (1970), 'Juvenal and the Blacks', *Classica et mediaevalia*, 31 (1–2): 132–50.

Wimbush, Vincent L. (2012), *White Men's Magic: Scripturalization as Slavery*, Oxford: Oxford University Press.

Wimbush, Vincent L. (2017), *Scripturalectics: The Management of Meaning*, Oxford: Oxford University Press.

Wing, Adrien Katherine (2003), *Critical Race Feminism: A Reader*, New York: New York University Press.

Wilson, Emily, trans. (2018), *Homer: The Odyssey*, New York: W. W. Norton & Company.

Wong, Helen (2018), 'Classics Makes Me Happy; Is That Enough? An Undergraduate Student of Color Examines Feelings of Guilt', *Eidolon*, 23 July. Available online: https://eidolon.pub/classics-makes-me-happy-is-that-enough-a5a9f19a63af (accessed 20 September 2019).

Wong, Stephanie (2019), 'The Life of the Oriental Mind: Introducing the Asian and Asian American Classical Caucus', *Eidolon*, 8 April. Available online: https://eidolon.pub/the-life-of-the-oriental-mind-609e3d2dde7 (accessed 19 September 2019).

Woolf, Greg (1994), 'Becoming Roman, Staying Greek: Culture, Identity, and the Civilizing Process in the Roman East', *Proceedings of the Cambridge Philological Society*, 2nd series, 40: 116–43.

Woolf, Greg (1998), *Becoming Roman: the Origins of Provincial Civilization in Gaul*, Cambridge: Cambridge University Press.

Woolf, Greg (2011), *Tales of the Barbarians: Ethnography and Empire in the Roman West*, Chichester, UK: Wiley-Blackwell.

Wrenhaven, Kelly (2013), 'Barbarians at the Gate: Foreign Slaves in Greek City-States', *Electryone*, 1: 1–17.

Wyk Smith, M. (2009), *The First Ethiopians: The Image of Africa and Africans in the Early Mediterranean World*, Johannesburg: Wits University Press.

Zuchtriegel, Gabriel (2018), *Colonization and Subalternity in Classical Greece*, New York: Cambridge University Press.

Zuckerberg, Donna (2018), *Not All Dead White Men: Classics and Misogyny in the Digital Age*, Cambridge, MA: Harvard University Press.

CONTRIBUTORS

Denise Kimber Buell is Cluett Professor of Religion at Williams College, USA. Her area of specialty is early Christian history and its interpretation. Her research asks how contemporary and ancient concerns affect the interpretation and reconstruction of early Christian history and texts, with particular attention to race, ethnicity, gender, and the relations between humans and non-humans. Her work has appeared in multiple articles as well as in *Making Christians: Clement of Alexandria and the Rhetoric of Legitimacy* (1999) and *Why This New Race: Ethnic Reasoning in Early Christianity* (2005).

Sarah Derbew is Assistant Professor of Classics in collaboration with the Center for Comparative Studies in Race and Ethnicity at Stanford University, USA. Previously, she was a Junior Fellow at the Harvard Society of Fellows. Her forthcoming monograph, *Untangling Blackness in Greek Antiquity*, examines representations of Black people in ancient Greek literature (tragedy, historiography, satire and the novel) and art. Her interests extend to the twenty-first century; she has written about the reception of Greco-Roman antiquity in Africa and the African diaspora.

Shelley P. Haley is the Edward North Chair of Classics and Professor of Africana Studies at Hamilton College in Clinton, New York, USA. Her publications include 'Be Not Afraid of the Dark: Critical Race Theory and Classical Studies' (2009) and '"When I Enter": Black Women and Disruption of the White, Heteronormative Narrative of Librarianship' (2018). She is completing two print monographs: *Signifying Dido: Constructs of Race and Gender in Augustan Rome* and *'To Educate My People': Nineteenth Century Black Feminists and Classics*. In 2021, she is the President of the Society of Classical Studies and is the first Black woman to be elected to that position in the organization's 152-year history.

David Kaufman is Associate Professor of Classics and Philosophy at Transylvania University (Lexington, KY), USA. His research focuses on Greek and Roman philosophy and medicine. His recent publications include articles on Greek tragedy, Roman epic, Stoicism and Galen. He is currently working on a book on the Stoic theory of emotions and a critical edition of Book One of Chrysippus's *On Providence*.

Naoíse Mac Sweeney is Professor of Classical Archaeology at the University of Vienna, Austria. She has previously held positions at the University of Leicester (UK), the University of Cambridge (UK) and Harvard's Center for Hellenic Studies (USA). Her books include *Troy: Myth, City, Icon* (2018), *Foundation Myths and Politics in Ancient Ionia* (2013) and *Community Identity and Archaeology* (2011). She is currently the Principal Investigator of the ERC project, *Migration and the Making of the Ancient Greek World*.

Denise Eileen McCoskey is Professor of Classics and an affiliate of Black World Studies at Miami University (Ohio), USA. She is a past recipient of the John J. Winkler Memorial Prize and was awarded the American Philological Association Award for Excellence in Teaching at the College Level in 2009. Her primary research interests include the role of race in the ancient Greek and Roman worlds, as well as the reception and distortion of ancient ideas about race in more modern eras. She is the author of *Race: Antiquity & Its Legacy* (2012) and, with Zara Torlone, *Latin Love Poetry* (2013); she is currently working on a project examining the role of eugenics in early twentieth-century American classical scholarship.

Jackie Murray is Associate Professor of Classics and African American and Africana Studies at the University of Kentucky, USA. She has held fellowships at the Center for Hellenic Studies (2020), University of Cincinnati (Margo Tytus, 2019) and the American Academy in Rome (2012). Her primary research area is Hellenistic poetry, its reception of Archaic Greek poetry and its influence on Latin and Imperial Greek literature. Her secondary area is race and the classics, especially the reception of classics in African American and Afro-Caribbean literature. She has published widely on various aspects of Hellenistic poetry and is currently finishing a monograph on Νεῖκος: *Apollonius' Argonautica and the Poetics of Controversy*.

Dan-el Padilla Peralta is Associate Professor of Classics at Princeton University, USA, with affiliations to the Programs in Latino Studies and Latin American Studies and the University Center for Human Values. He is the author of *Undocumented: A Dominican Boy's Odyssey from a Homeless Shelter to the Ivy League* (2015) and *Divine Institutions: Religions and Community in the Middle Roman Republic* (2020); and co-editor of *Rome, Empire of Plunder: The Dynamics of Cultural Appropriation* (2017). His current projects include a co-authored study of 338 BCE and the origins of Roman imperialism, an edited volume on Rome in the long fourth century BCE and a co-authored book-length essay on race and racism in the disciplinary matrix of Classics.

Grant Parker studied at the University of Cape Town, South Africa, and Princeton University, USA, held a postdoctoral fellowship at the University of Michigan, USA, and taught at Duke University, USA, and (since 2006) at Stanford University, USA. His publications include *South Africa, Greece, Rome: Classical Confrontations* (2017), as editor. His current research is on monumentality and collective memory.

Joseph Skinner is Lecturer in Ancient Greek History at Newcastle University, UK. His research interests encompass both the history of early ethnographic thought and related concepts such as ancient concepts of race, ethnicity and culture. His publications include *The Invention of Greek Ethnography: From Homer to Herodotus* (2012); *Ancient Ethnography: New Approaches* (2013, co-edited with Eran Almagor) and *Herodotus in the Long Nineteenth Century* (2020, co-edited with Thomas Harrison). He is currently working on his next monograph, *Neglected Ethnographies: the Visual and Material* (as co-editor) and a Routledge Companion to *Identities in Antiquity*.

INDEX

Achaemenid Empire 108, 114, 118
Achilles 139
Actium, battle of 125
Adamantius 78
the *Aeneid* 91, 121, 125–9
Aeolian peoples 5, 122
Aeschylus 26, 35, 43
Aesop 41
the *Aethiopica* 117, 121, 133
Afghanistan 89
African Americans 50–1, 98, 101, 125, 161
African National Congress 93
Airs, Waters, Places (guide) 33–4, 68, 70, 73, 82, 113
Aithiopia 27–31
the *Aithiopika* 29–30
albus descriptor 121
Alcoff, Linda Martin 160, 170
Alexander the Great 5–6, 54, 74, 89–90, 97, 114
Alexandria 8
alienation 143–6, 151
Allen, Theodore 143
American classicists 13, 16
Amun-Re of Kawa 106–8
Amun-Re of Thebes 107
ancestry, fixity of 114
'ancient environmental theory' of race 4
Andromeda 117, 133
Anidjar, Gil 53
animals
    blood of 74–5
    features of 77
    humans as 74–5, 80
anthropology, philosophical 101
antiquity, meaning of 1–2
anti-racism 93, 157
Antony, Mark 125, 127
apartheid 93, 101, 122

Apollonides 40
apostates 62
Arabic language 60
Arch of Titus, Rome 63–4
archaeology 10, 97
Aristides, Aelius 91
Aristophanes 86
Aristotle 5, 34, 37, 43, 77–82, 86–7, 120
    on ethnography, natural slavery and environmental determinism 71–6
Aryans 9, 51–2, 110–11
Asian characteristics 72, 75
Asian classicists 169
Asian climate 68
Aspasia 122
assimilation 100
Athens 5, 36–7, 113, 115
Augustus, emperor *see* Octavian/Augustus
autocratic style 90

Badian, Ernst 89–90
Baker, Cynthia M. 57
'barbarians' 5, 7, 34–5, 38–40, 43, 46, 53, 63–4, 67, 113–14, 125, 163
    'visible' 64
Bashir, Lana 100
Beard, Mary 52, 55
Beardsley, Grace Hadley 23
Beauvoir, Simone de 167
Bedrick, Theodore 12
Bernal, Martin 2, 11, 19, 105, 158, 161, 166–7
Biographical Dictionary of American Classicists 166
biological determinism 51
biological race and biological racism 3–4, 160, 163–4
black actors 137, 146
black classicists 165–9
Black Lives Matter movement 39

blackness 23, 100, 167–8
Boak, A.E.R. 10
body, human 66
Boris, Eileen 120–1
Boston Museum of Fine Arts (MFA) 97–101
brownness 121
Buddhism 49
Buell, Denise Kimber 218; *author of Chapter 3*
bulls 74–5

Caesarea 58–9
Calder, William M. 166
Callimachus 114–15
Cambyses II, king 27–9
Capitein, Jacobus Elisa Johannes 87–8
Caracalla, emperor 8, 54, 83
Carbado, Devon W. 119
Carthage 96, 127, 130
Cassius 83
The Catalogue of Women (poem) 112
Celluloid Classical World 141, 145
 exclusion of black people from 141
centring (of the dominant group's perspective) 144, 148–9
Chamberlain, Houston Stewart 14, 97
Chariclea 117
chattel slavery 5
Cheng, Anne 169
Christianity 49–59, 63–4
 break from Judaism 51
Cicero 49, 54, 126
Circe 123
circumcision 61, 63, 124
citizen communities 36
citizenship 7, 54, 122, 125–6, 130–1
civil rights movement 141
civilizing mission 51, 64
classical antiquity 2–3, 9, 16, 93, 100
Classics as an academic discipline 2, 9–13, 16, 19–21, 24, 101–2, 142, 158, 165, 169–70
Claudius, emperor 7, 83
Clement of Alexandria 58
Cleopatra 6, 114
climate 68, 75
Cline, Eric 10

Coates, Ta-Nehisi 120–1
Codex Theodosianus 63
cold regions 75–6
collective identity 50, 60–1, 66
colonization 86, 122
'coloured' people, use of the term 93; *see also* skin colour
conceptual maps 42–3
concubinage 122
Conkey, Margaret 119
conquered peoples, representations of 63
Constantine, emperor 55, 59, 63
conversion, religious 51, 61–3
corruption 94
cosmopolitanism 11, 16, 90, 92, 97
Crenshaw, Kimberlé 4, 119
creolization 120
critical race feminism (CRF) 119
critical race theory 4, 18, 25–6, 119, 159, 169–71
cross-cultural interaction 84
cultural history 3, 5, 157
 of race 19–20
cultural identity 18, 91
culture
 alignment of 41
 changeability of 113–14
 definition of 33
 as distinct from ethnicity and race 104
Cyclopes 145–6, 151
Cyclops (play) 138–9, 151–4
Cyprus 43, 57
Cyrene 86
Cyrus Cylinder 100

Darius I, king 108–10
Decimus Brutus 83
Decius, emperor 54
decolonization 169–70
deer 74–5
Delian League 113
Della Porta, Giovanni Battista 77
Derbew, Sarah 46, 120, 162, 218; *author of Chapter 1*
diaita 41
Dictionary of British Classicists 166
Diller, Aubrey 1–3, 6, 11

Diodorus Siculus 101, 115
Dionysius of Halicarnassus 62
discrimination 36
    racial 27, 141
Dixon, Suzanne 127
Diyarbarkir 59
Dorian peoples 5, 10, 122
double standards 144–7, 151–2, 157
Doxey, Denise 97
dress 147
Du Bois, W.E.B. 144
Dudley, Thomas 98
Dumézil, Georges 10

Economic Freedom Fighters (EFF) party 94–5
Egypt and Egyptians 2, 6, 8, 11, 54, 61, 91, 98, 106–7
environmental determinism 68, 71, 82
epic poetry 123, 146
'epistemological apartheid' 160
Erechtheus, Temple of 112
Erechtheus (play) 111
Ethiopian characteristics 56–7
ethnicity 51, 121, 143
    concept of 19
    definition of 85, 103
    as distinct from race 103–18
ethnography 35, 71–3, 76, 82
Euboea 86
eugenics 14, 120–3
Eumaeus 146–50
Euripides 111–14, 125, 138–9, 151
Eurocentrism 120
European characteristics 72, 75
European climate 68
Eurybates 154–5
Eusebius of Caesarea 63–4
exceptionalism 76, 82, 112–13
exoticism 45
Ezra 57, 62

Fanon, Frantz 158, 167–9
feminism and feminist scholarship 119–20, 127, 154, 164
Fields, Karen E. and Barbara J. 26, 157–8
film-making 137–41
fiscus Iudaicus 8

fish-eaters 27–9
Foucault, Michel 158
Frank, Tenney 16
Frazier, Demita 119
Freedom Charter memorial, Soweto 95
Frick, Wilhelm 95

Galen of Pergamon 79–82
Gauls 83, 85, 114–18
    physical features 115
gender and race 119–36
genealogical exceptionalism 112
genealogy, dynastic 107–8
genetics 103–4
Germans and Germanic features 13, 77, 116, 118
Gibbon, Edward 13
Gildersleeve, Basil Lanneau 166
Girmay, Aracelis 21, 31
Giusti, Elena 162
Gliddon, G.R. 11–12
globalization 11
Gnomon of the Idios Logos 6
Gobineau, Joseph Arthur de 1, 52, 61
Goodman, Martin 8
graffiti 136
Grant, Madison 13–15
Graziosi, Barbara 166
Great Zimbabwe 98
Greece, geographical position of 72
Greek civilization 2–3
    origins of 10–11
    race in 5–9, 27–30
Greek language 7, 170
Greek people 96
    as ideal types 78, 80
    natural superiority of 73–6
Greekness 5, 36, 112–13, 118
    features of 53–4
Gruen, Erich 18, 158, 162–3
Günther, Hans F.K. 96–7
Gyasi, David 137–8, 155

Haarhoff, T.J. 83–5, 89–97
Hadas, Moses 16
Hagar 60
Hagerty, James 162
hair colour and type 77–8, 82, 115

Haley, Shelley P. 159, 218; *author of Chapter 7*
Hall, Jonathan 4–5, 10, 16, 19, 121
Hall, Stuart 19, 35, 46
Hanink, Johanna 158
Haraway, Donna 136
Harrison, Thomas 36, 39
head-vases 44, 46
Heath, Malcolm 73
hegemony 113, 161
Helen of Troy 152
Heliodorus 22, 27–31, 117–18, 121, 133–4
Hellenes ad Hellenic peoples 5–6, 75–90, 120–5
Hellenocentrism 82
Helots 122
Heng, Geraldine 53
herders 145, 149–53
heretics 62
heritable characteristics 51
Herodotus 5, 22, 26–31, 34, 41–4, 53, 62, 101, 123, 125
Higher, Gilbert 12
Hippocrates 34, 79
Hippocratic Corpus 67
Hitler, Adolf 14, 97
the Holocaust 16
Homer 12, 35, 41–6, 85–6, 118, 137–8
humanistic discourse 170
Husband, Richard Wellington 9
hybridity and hybridization 1, 120

identity 5–6, 26
    cultural 18, 91
    racial 18, 36, 85
    social performance of 104 *see also* collective identity
ideology, racial 3, 144–5
the *Iliad* 85, 123, 154, 156
imperialism, Roman 91
inbreeding 116
inequality, social 44
intermarriage 116
intersectionality 119, 136, 166
the *Ion* (play) 113–14
Ionian peoples 5, 122
Isaac, Benjamin 23–7, 39, 164

Ishmael 60
Isis 61
Islam 49, 60
Isocrates 5, 89, 113
isomorphism 68
Italian migrants 15

Jainism 49
Jerusalem, the Temple in 63
Jhally, Sut 35
Jones, W.H.S. 33
Judaism and Jewishness 49, 57–8, 92
    recognition and exclusion of 63
Judith 57, 61
Julius Caesar 83
    Gallic Wars 7
Justinian, emperor 55, 64–5
Juvenal 7, 92

Kahlos, Maijastine 62
Kapparis, Konstantinos 122
Kaufman, David 218; *author of Chapter 4*
Khepri 50
Kies, Benjamin 84, 93, 95
kinship restrictions 144, 147

Lady Sennuwy statue 98–100
Laestrygonians 145–6, 151
landscape 68
Latin language 170
League of Nations 92
legal codes 62–3
Liew, Tat-Siong Benny 159
'Linear B' 10
links between groups 62
Linz 95
literary creativity 16
Livy 91, 121, 125–33
Lloyd-Jones, Sir Hugh 165–6
Loving, Mildred and Richard 17
Lumumba, Patrice 21, 31
Lye, Suzanne 133–4

McCoskey, Denise Eileen 33, 219; *editor and author of Introduction*
McInerney, Jeremy 19–20
Macrobioi 46
Mac Sweeney, Naoíse 218; *author of*

Chapter 6
Malan, D.F. 93
Malema, Julius 94
Mallory, J.P. 9
Mandela, Nelson 93–4
Mani 55
Manicheism 49, 55, 62
manifest destiny 7
manumission 16
Marcus Brutus 83
marginalization 63, 93
Markus, Hazel Rose 85
marriage, legitimacy of 122
marriageability 151
Marxism 120
masculinity 129–30, 133
Masinissa 129–32
Mbeki, Thabo 94
meaning-making 46, 52, 142
Medea 125–6
Meister, Karl 97
Melanthius 149–50, 153
'melting pot' terminology 13, 16
Memnon 46, 124
menstruation 123
Meroitic language 99–100
Michaels, Walter Benn 18–19
Mignolo, Walter 170
migration 1, 6
Miletus 42, 122
military honor 90
Miller, Margaret C. 89
Minoan civilization 10
Mitchell, L.B. 13
mixing
 of human qualities 80
 of racial groups 16, 78
monstrification 144–6, 151–4
Moors 60
the *Moretum* 134–6
Morrison, Toni 159
Moses 61
Moya, Paula M. 85, 89
Muhammad the Prophet 59
multiculturalism 163
Murray, Gilbert 92–3
Murray, Jackie 219; *author of Chapter 8*
Muslim communities 59–60

Mycenaean civilization 10
'mythistory' 86, 91

Narain, A.K. 90
Narayan, Yasmeen 120–1
nationalism 94, 97, 101, 141
naturalistic theories 67–8
Nazi regime 10, 12, 95–7, 101
Negroes 23
Nehemiah 57, 62
New York Times 161
Newsweek 11
Nineveh 105–6
nomos 41–2
Nordic countries and Nordic race 10–16, 96–7
North, John 52, 55
Norton, Charles Eliot 2
Nott, J.C. 11
Nubia 84, 97–101, 106–7, 118

Octavian/Augustus 90, 125–6
the *Odyssey* 86, 123, 138–9, 142–5, 149–56
Old Testament 58
Olympian Games 86
Olympic movement, modern 12
Olynthus and Olynthians 44–6
Omi, Michael 85
oriental migrants 50
oriental religions 51–2
Orientalism 163
ornamentalism 169
Orpheus 71
'othering' and 'otherness' 36, 143, 146
Ottoman Empire 54
'outsider' status 37
Oxford English Dictionary 155

Padilla Peralta, Dan-el 20, 219; *author of Chapter 9*
Painter, Nell Irvin 9
pale skin 80, 115, 117, 137–8
Parker, Grant 219; *author of Chapter 5*
patricians 9
patriotism 91
Paul, St 61
peer review 159

Penthesilea 139
Pentheus 61
performativity 66
Pericles 96, 112, 122
Persian characteristics 55–6
Persian Empire 5; *see also* Achaemenid Empire
Persian Wars (491–479 BCE) 87–9
Phaeticians 145
Pharos: Doing Justice to Classics 137
Philip II of Macedon 74
philology 9, 165
Phoenicians 11, 148
physiognomy 82, 104, 117–18
  handbooks of 76–80
Pindar 35
Pitt, Brad 155–6
plebeians 9, 15–16
Plutarch 42, 123, 131
Poe, Edgar Allan 100
Polemon of Laodicea 42, 76–9
political correctness 39
politics 63, 74, 76
  and race 83–102
Pollman, Karla 61
Polybius 130
Polykleitos Standard 80–1
Polyphemus 151–3
population groups 11
positivism 119, 163
Praet, Danny 52
Praxithea, queen 111
prejudice 36
  racial 16–18, 23, 67, 160
  social 7
Price, Simon 52, 55
Procopius 64
proto-racism 26, 39
Prudentius 61, 63
public sphere 26
'pure' races 1

Quintilian 7
the Qu'ran 59

race
  ancient and modern views of 4, 23–4
  avoidance of the term 18, 20
  concept of 51, 94, 141–2
  and culture 96
  definition of 22–7, 103, 139
  and ethnicity 103–18
  as found in antiquity 3–16, 34–41
  and gender 119–36
  as the main engine of human society 3
  as a marker of class difference 95
  and politics 83–102
  relational nature of 143
  and religion 49–66
  representations and interpretations of 21–2
  and science 67–82
  and sexuality 137–56
  social construction of 4, 51, 85, 119, 141–4
  theories of 2–4, 19
  transhistorical description of 142–5
  use of the term in different senses 51, 85
race relations 18
racecraft 142–6, 151–9, 164–5, 169–71
racial biographies 2
racial boundaries 4, 6
racial categories 53, 142
  changeability of 51
racial stereotypes 77–8
racial thinking 34, 47, 163–4
racialized gender 120–5, 129–31, 134–6
racism 18, 35–9, 42, 44, 90, 94, 96, 101, 137–8, 141–3, 146, 154, 157–8, 161, 166–7, 170
  concept of 27
  definition of 35
  root of modern form of 26
  see also anti-racism
rape culture 151–2
rape of the Sabine women 125
reception studies, classical 158, 167, 169
'red-figure vase people' 42
Reed, Adolph 143
Reisner, George 97–100
religion
  ancient mapping of 53–6
  framework for study of 49–51
  and power 62–5
  and race 49–66

Roman 52
'universal' 51
uses of 61–2
religious festivals 86
Renaissance thinking 2
reparative justice 157
Reuben, Gabriel, H. 164
revolts 8
Rey, Sarah 52
rhetoric 91
Rhodes, Cecil John 93
ritual deference 144, 149–50
Robinson, C.A. Jr 10
Robinson, David M. 44, 46
Roman civilization 3, 6–8, 54–5
  state's tolerance of variety 8
Roman Empire
  Christianization of 64
  Constitution of (212 CE) 83
  decline of 50
'Romanization' 91
Rome, city of 2, 7, 91–2, 125–6
Romulus and Remus 125
Root, Michael 159
Rostovtzeff, Michael Ivanovich 8
Ruggini, Lellia Cracco 7

Said, Edward 163
Sartre, Jean-Paul 167
satyrs 151–3
Scarborough, William Sanders 166
Schachermeyr, Fritz 84, 90, 95–7
scholarship 49, 53
  classical 9, 16–19, 22, 26
  histories of 158, 165–6
Schwartz, Sheila 164
science and race 67–82
scientific racism 1, 4, 76, 82
Scybale 134
Second Sophistic 118
Second World War 3, 16
secularism 52
segregation, racial 93
self, sense of 4
self-reflection 22
Semitic peoples 51–2, 96
senate of Rome 83
Seneca the Younger 7
Sennacherib, king 105

Sepúlved de Ginés, Juan 86
sexual asymmetry 144, 150–2
sexual relationships 150
sexuality and race 137–56
Sharpe, Christina 25
Sherwin-White, Adrian N. 18, 160
Shipley, Frederick 15–16
Sicily 151
Silenius 153
skin colour 4, 18–19, 22–4, 27–30, 44, 56, 67, 77–8, 82, 107, 118, 120–1, 133, 137–43, 154; *see also* pale skin
Skinner, Joseph 219; *author of Chapter 2*
slavery 8, 16, 22, 36–7, 44, 72, 86–7, 148
  natural 37, 73–6, 86, 142
  in the Roman Empire 161
Smedley, Audrey and Brian 3
Smith, Barbara 119
Smith, Beverly 119
Smith, Kirby Flower 13
Smuts, J.C. 92–3
Snowden, Frank M. Jr 16–19, 23, 134, 158–63, 167
social construction 119–22, 139–44, 151
social contamination 52
soft power 91, 141
Solon 26, 122
Sophoniba 129–34
sources of information on the ancient world 54, 60
South Africa 92–7
Spartacus 8
species differences 75
Spengler, Oswald 96
spiritedness 73
state capture 94
stereotyping 22–3, 34, 36, 42, 71, 74, 76, 141
  racial 77–82
Stoicism 89
storytelling 138, 141–2, 154
Strabo 26
subaltern groups 34, 143–6, 149
Suetonius 83
sumptuary codes 144–7
Sussman, Robert Wald 3
Syriac Christianity 60

Table of the Sun 27
Tacitus 7–8, 83, 96–7, 105–8, 116
Tanyidamani, kIng, stele of 98–100
Tarn, W.W. 89–90
taxation 8
Telemachus 147
terror 146
Theodosius, emperor 54, 86
Thesprotians 147–8
Thiong'o, Ngũgĩ wa 22
Thirty Years' War 97
Thompson, Dorothy 6, 19
Thompson, Lloyd 1, 17, 23–4, 121, 160
Thucydides 85–7, 151
Toynbee, Arnold 96
Tracy, H.L. 19
transhistorical description of race 142–5
translation 139–41
triumphs 83
Troy: The Fall of a City 137, 141–2, 146, 155
Troy and the Trojan War 85–6, 91, 127, 129
Tuplin, Christopher 43
'turns' in the study of antiquity 66
Tutu, Desmond 94

Umachandran, M. 160
Umayyid Caliphate 60
United Kingdom 166
United Nations 92
    Economic, Scientific and Cultural Organization (UNESCO) 92
United States 97, 101–2, 166
    Emergency Quota Act (1921) 13–14
    Supreme Court 17

Valladolid Controversy 86
Vergil *see* Virgil
Villa of Good Fortune 45
Virgil 31, 91–2, 115, 121, 126–9, 134

'Waldheim phenomenon' 96
Wall Street Journal 100
Walsh, Lisl 33
Washington Post 161
well-being (physical and mental) 80
Welsh people 104
Western civilization, origins of 100, 164–5
white supremacy 139–42, 146, 154–6, 160, 166, 169–71
whiteness 4, 23, 26, 93, 104, 158, 164, 171
Whitmarsh, Tim 120, 137, 143
Wilson, Emily 154–5
Winant, Howard 85
Wing, Adrien Katherine 119
women
    African 134
    bias in 125
    of colour 119
    sexual symmetry with 151
Woolf, Greg 4
worship 54, 61

Xenophon 38, 40

Yiddish language 9

Zoroastrianism 49, 55, 108
Zuma, Jacob 94